Writing Without Taboos

Writing Without Taboos
The New East German Literature

J.H. REID

OSWALD WOLFF BOOKS
BERG
New York / Oxford / Munich
Distributed exclusively in the US and Canada by
St. Martin's Press, New York

First published in 1990 by
Berg Publishers Limited
Editorial Offices:
165 Taber Avenue, Providence RI 02906, USA
150 Cowley Road, Oxford OX4 1JJ, UK
Westermühlstraße 26, 8000 München 5, FRG

© Berg Publishers Limited 1990

All rights reserved.
No part of this publication may be reproduced
in any form or by any means
without the written permission
of Berg Publishers.

Library of Congress Cataloging-in-Publication Data
Reid, J.H.
  Writing without taboos: the new East German literature / by J.H. Reid.
    p. cm.
  Includes bibliographical references.
  ISBN 0–85496–020–1 : $34.50 (est.)
  1. German literature—Germany (East)—History and criticism.
  2. German literature—20th century—History and criticism.
  I. Title.
  PT3705.R45 1990
  830.9'9431—dc20   89–37552
                                                                  CIP

British Library Cataloguing in Publication Data
Reid, J.H., 1938–
  Writing without taboos : the new East German
  literature.
  1. Fiction in German. East German writers, 1945–
  Critical studies
  I. Title
  833'.914'099431
  ISBN 0–85496–020–1

Printed and bound in Great Britain by
Short Run Press Ltd, Exeter

For Ingrid, Christopher and Martin

Contents

Preface ix

1. Congruence and Divergence 1

2. Writers, Politicians and Taboos 29

3. Beyond Formalism 61

4. Difficulties Crossing the Plain 94

5. How Did We Become As We Are? 128

6. Stalinism Past and Present 151

7. Prussians, Saxons and Others 174

8. En Route to Utopia 198

Bibliography 227

Index 247

Preface

When Erich Honecker assumed the leadership of the East German communist party in 1971 one of his first announcements was to proclaim the relaxation of the hitherto strict cultural policies prevailing in the GDR: with certain provisos there were to be 'no taboos'. Since the advent of Mikhail Gorbachev in the Soviet Union, however, the East German authorities have found themselves increasingly out of step with their comrades in Eastern Europe with regard to the democratic freedoms of information and discussion. Whereas a traditional slogan was 'To learn from the Soviet Union is to learn to win', Honecker now found it necessary to ban, for example, an issue of the Soviet journal *Sputnik*, which suggested that Stalin had committed worse crimes than Hitler. Matters came to a head in the summer of 1989. Dissatisfaction with the regime's record on democracy and its paternalistic information policies led to mass emigration to West Germany through Hungary and Poland, and resulted in October in the replacement of Honecker by Egon Krenz, who himself resigned on 6 December. At the time of writing the pace of change in East Germany is breathtaking. As the scale of establishment corruption becomes known, angry crowds are taking to the streets and besieging army barracks and the headquarters of the secret police. The country is in turmoil.

Where it will end is impossible to predict. Some tentative prognostications made in the study which follows, written prior to the summer of 1989, may have to be regarded as historical. What has been reinforced, however, is the relative coherence of the period it covers, which now turns out to be the 'Honecker era'. It is an examination of the literature produced in the GDR during the past two decades relating it both to the GDR's cultural tradition and to the circumstances under which it was written, and attempting to determine to what extent it differs from the literature which has been appearing simultaneously in West Germany and Austria. Concentrating on fiction rather than poetry or drama, although examples from both of these genres are taken into account where appropriate, I have traced the roots of the GDR's 'new' literature in develop-

Preface

ments which were already taking place in the latter half of the 1960s. The individual chapters are to a large extent autonomous, viewing the GDR's literature from eight different angles. The first examines the question of the extent to which the GDR has evolved a literary identity different from that of West Germany. The second reviews the vicissitudes of cultural policies. The third examines some of the developments in literary forms, in particular the way in which literature itself becomes a theme of literature. The other five chapters take up the three modes of time: a chapter on contemporary topics is followed by three on the stages of history treated by the GDR's authors, and a final chapter investigates the dimension of the future.

Some of the material has been adapted from my contributions to *Renaissance and Modern Studies*, *Honecker's Germany* (edited by David Childs), *The GDR approaches the 1990s* (edited by Mike Dennis) and *Literature on the Threshold*, details of which can be found in the bibliography. I am grateful to the editors and publishers of these volumes for permission to include this material.

The translations are my own, although I have consulted Christopher Middleton's translation of Wolf's *The Quest for Christa T.* (New York: Farrar, Straus and Giroux, Inc. 1970) and Hannah and Stanley Mitchell's translation of Lukács's *The Historical Novel* (London: Merlin Press 1962).

I should like to express my thanks to the many people who have stimulated my ideas, in particular Karin Baier, Hans Joachim Bernhard, Elizabeth Boa, Greg Bond, Steve Giles, Walfried Hartinger, Frank Hörnigk, Elisabeth Kaufmann, Paul O'Doherty, Karin McPherson, Theo Mechtenberg, Monika Melchert, Joseph Pischel, Ingrid Reid, Hans Richter, Klaus Schuhmann, Gisela Shaw, Dennis Tate, Ian Wallace and Martin Watson. Any errors are entirely my responsibility.

J.H. Reid
University of Nottingham
December 1989

–1–

Congruence and Divergence

> Were it a whole, I should still be divided;
> the half
> Is but a quarter for me, I'm in agreement
> with you.[1]
> (Volker Braun, 'Berlinische Epigramme': *Langsamer knirschender Morgen*)

In 1984 Dieter Schlenstedt, one of the GDR's most respected literary scholars, claimed: 'There are GDR authors whose international reception proves them to be – modestly speaking – writers whose European stature radiates into the entire world. There are not many of them. But for a relatively small country two are a lot – I'm thinking of Christa Wolf and Heiner Müller. Four or five further authors I would certainly consider of European significance'[2] (Haase et al 1984, p. 1611). Literature, of course, should not be placed in the same category as sport, a domain in which the German Democratic Republic has produced rather more 'world-class' competitors. There is, moreover, a certain irony in Schlenstedt's choice of examples. Wolf and Müller have had more than their fair share of difficulties with the authorities of their country. Müller was expelled from the Writers' Union in 1965 and readmitted only in 1987. His plays have been more frequently performed in the Federal Republic than in the GDR, where some have not yet been performed at all. Wolf had to suffer some biting public criticism in 1969 over her novel *Nachdenken über Christa T.* and was effectively silenced for a number of years thereafter. More recently the 'home' edition of her *Kassandra* appeared almost a year after the West German one, and then only in a sanitised version. Nevertheless, it must be true that the achievements of these two writers more than any others have helped to awaken awareness internationally that there is 'another' German literature besides that of Günter Grass and Heinrich Böll.

Over the past two decades East German studies in Western Europe and the United States have greatly expanded. Since the relative normalisation of relations between the two German states in 1972 West German publishers have been keen to exploit their readers' interest in East German literature, and East German writers have become a prominent feature of their publishing programmes. Academic studies have also flourished: Fritz J. Raddatz's 1972 survey *Traditionen und Tendenzen* led the way, and a yearbook on GDR literature has been appearing since 1980. In other Western countries interest has been almost as strong. In the United States there has been a regular conference on GDR affairs since 1973. In the United Kingdom, meanwhile, biennial conferences on the GDR have been organised by Ian Wallace, editor of the periodical *GDR Monitor*, established in 1979. There is scarcely an academic institution in the UK in which GDR studies do not figure in some form or other: Ulrich Plenzdorf's *Die neuen Leiden des jungen W.* is a popular school text, while in higher education there has been a steady stream of dissertations on the GDR, its writers and its institutions.

One reason for this upsurge of interest is the improvement in East–West relations which took place at the beginning of the 1970s. Prior to that Cold War attitudes on both sides combined to produce an implacable hostility on the part of the West Germans to their Eastern neighbour and a corresponding entrenchment of doctrinaire attitudes in East Germany. In 1969 West German Chancellor Kiesinger described the GDR simply as 'a phenomenon' (cit. Sontheimer and Bleek 1972, p. 11). Official West German pronouncements referred to the GDR as 'the so-called GDR', the 'Soviet Zone' or, at best, with ironic punctuation, 'the "GDR"', as the right-wing West German Springer Press continued to do until July 1989. Since 1972 official terminology at least has been more neutral.

The thaw in the political climate has had its effect on literary relations too. No longer would it be possible for a West German foreign minister to place the late lyric poems of Bertolt Brecht, who had settled in the GDR on his return from exile in America, in the same category as the Nazi propaganda of a Horst Wessel, as Heinrich von Brentano did in 1957. In fact Brecht's *Buckower Elegien* express considerable reservations about the direction socialist society was moving in; propaganda they are not. Brecht was in any case an exception: his major plays were performed in West Germany throughout the 1950s, some of them even before the GDR adopted them, but they had all been written before the division of Germany. Where the significance of contemporary socialism was too overt, as in the first scene of *Der kaukasische Kreidekreis*, it could easily be excised; Harry Buckwitz's West German première in Frankfurt in 1955 simply omitted the scene. Prior to the mid-1960s it was hard to find anyone in the Federal Republic who would admit that there was literature of any value to be found in the GDR. It is no doubt true that the 'reconstruction literature' of an Eduard Claudius would have been exotic for West German readers, although hardly more exotic than many of the American novels which poured into West Germany from 1945 onwards. The portrayal of the division of Germany by GDR authors in such a way as to suggest that the war-mongering villains resided in the West while the hard-working, peace-loving Germans were in the East would have been hard to take. But the failure to appreciate such notable accounts of fascism and its effects as Anna Seghers's *Die Toten bleiben jung*, Franz Fühmann's *Kameraden* and Bruno Apitz's *Nackt unter Wölfen* can only have had grounds of political opportunism related to the Cold War. Thus a West German literary history for schools, published in 1955, found room for Gottfried Benn but not Bertolt Brecht, Ina Seidel but not Anna Seghers, Ernst Jünger but not Arnold Zweig (Seufert 1955).

However, there were also more specifically literary reasons for the reluctance to accept the validity of the other German literature. West German literary theory in the 1950s and into the 1960s was dominated by theories of modernism, hermeticism and abstract lyricism. Hugo Friedrich's influential book on lyric poetry, *Die Struktur der modernen Lyrik,* first published in 1956, operates with these categories. Elsewhere Wolfgang Kayser and Emil Staiger set the tone with their versions of Anglo-American 'New Criticism', purporting to interpret literature entirely according to concepts derived from the text itself. Neither Kayser nor Staiger was particularly interested in contemporary literature in any case. But for Theodor W. Adorno, who was developing his critical theory in Frankfurt, modernism and the avant-garde were the keys to an understanding not only of literary processes but of society itself. The literary text was an autonomous entity, whose relevance to contemporary reality lay precisely in its refusal to have any truck with society or to possess any 'relevance' in the cruder sense. In East Germany the opposite point of view prevailed. Literature was expected to be both overtly partisan and comprehensible to all. There was little room in this view for the avant-garde. Consequently Adorno (1961) dismissed East German writing as 'boy meets tractor literature' and was sceptical even of Brecht, although his friend Walter Benjamin had been one of Brecht's early proponents.

From the early to mid-1960s onwards, as Helmut Kreuzer (1975) has pointed out, radical changes were taking place in the attitudes of West German writers and critics towards literature. The 'Gruppe 61' was founded in Dortmund in 1961 to propagate a literature of the working classes more akin to that which was being written on the other side of the inner-German border. 'Documentary literature' became fashionable, especially in the theatre, and was diametrically opposed to the esoteric, symbolist literature demanded in the 1950s. 'Literature', it was even briefly claimed, was 'dead', at least inasmuch as it had been elitist. At best it had to be placed in the service of propaganda and agitation (Michel 1968; Enzensberger 1968). Academic studies turned to the sociology of literature. So-called 'trivial literature', popular literature, what the masses actually read rather than what an educated minority was expected to read, became an important subject for research. In the second half of the 1960s the movement associated with student unrest in the universities rediscovered Marx and Marxist theorists such as Georg Lukács and Herbert Marcuse, who were more concerned with the relation between literature and praxis than Adorno had been. Lukács, in particular, was an interesting discovery, since he had dominated literary theories in the GDR from its inception. It became easier to see positive qualities in the literature of the GDR once a certain congruence between literary theory and practice in the two German states had been established. Paradoxically, however, just as West German writers were beginning to move in the direction of a more reader-oriented literature, East German writers, as we shall see, were moving in the opposite direction, towards a literature which was more adventurous in its techniques and more demanding of its readership. This too facilitated the reception of East German literature in the West.

These developments, however, also raise the question of the extent to which East German literature should be treated in isolation. Are there two German literatures or merely one? This question is intimately related to the 'German question' itself. How permanent is the postwar division of Germany? To what extent have the two German states developed distinct identities through their fundamentally differing social, political and economic structures?

Official West German pronouncements on the 'German question' have remained consistent since 1949 independently of the party in power: the division of Germany is a temporary one; the aim of West German politics must be to overcome it; consequently all 'ethnic Germans', whether they live in the GDR or in the diaspora of the Soviet Union or Eastern Europe, have an automatic right to German, i.e. West German, citizenship. What has varied over the years has been the degree of vigour with which this policy has been pursued. In the early years the opposition Social Democrats accused the ruling Christian Democrats of placing the Western Alliance before German unity. During the 1950s and 1960s the Federal government refused to recognise the existence of a separate East German state and threatened to break off diplomatic relations with any country which did so. The international isolation of what was presented as a wholly artificial political entity would, it was believed, lead to that entity's collapse and eventual merger with the 'natural' Germany represented by the Federal Republic.

The effects of this policy on East German citizens are the subject of one of the episodes of Hermann Kant's novel *Das Impressum,* in which David Groth describes his own development and that of the GDR from the standpoint of 1967. In 1959 he and a colleague are delegated to attend an exhibition in London, board the wrong aircraft and arrive in Lisbon instead. Their visas from the Allied Travel Bureau in West Berlin bear the grotesque legend 'Presumed German' and the Portuguese official refuses to admit them: 'It says here, it is presumed, it is thought possible, it may be the case that you are Germans, but we are not obliged to accept this assumption. For us you are an undesirable foreigner of unknown nationality'[3] (p. 268). In the end they reach London via Puerto Rico and New York.

With the new policies of rapprochement with Eastern Europe, pursued by Willy Brandt's social–liberal coalition from 1969 onwards, the reunification of Germany was regarded as something which would be realised eventually as the two German states came to understand one another better. Rapprochement would itself bring about the democratisation of the GDR in the Western sense and thereby facilitate reunification. The Basic Treaty signed between the two German states in 1972 accepted the territorial rights of each within its own borders, although the West German government insisted at the same time that for historical reasons neither could be 'foreign territory' for the other. Since 1982 the conservative government of Helmut Kohl has been pursuing the goal of reunification with rather more vigour, insisting on the continued existence of 'Germany' within the frontiers of 1937, and that, for example, more time should be devoted to discussing the 'German question' in schools. Almost simultaneously, however, the West German left, especially the Greens and the peace movement, has taken up the issue. A reunified but demilitarised and neutral Germany would, it is claimed, help to defuse the tensions in Europe (Sandford 1985). The paradox is compounded by the recent emergence of the extreme right-wing Republican Party, which likewise demands the reinstatement of the frontiers of 1937.

Writers have played a prominent role in the controversies. The new mood was captured by the West German Martin Walser in 1977:

Germany cannot be expunged from my historical awareness.... I refuse to take part in the liquidation of history. In me a different Germany still has its chance. It would be one which does not have its socialism imposed on it by a victor power but is allowed to develop it completely by itself; and it would be one which does not have to stumble along the path of its development towards democracy in the rhythm of the crises of capitalism. This other Germany, I believe, might be useful today. The world would not have to shudder at such a Germany. And yet at the moment it is purely a utopia.... Trembling at my own boldness, I tell myself we should no more recognise the FRG than the GDR. We must keep open the wound called Germany.[4] (1979, p. 100)

A few years later the East German writer Stefan Heym was making similar points in an address in Munich. For Heym, too, the division of Germany was an 'open wound', but it was inconceivable that a future united Germany would be formed after the model of either the FRG or the GDR. Already Heym saw the two countries gradually 'converging' for purely pragmatic reasons, chronic unemployment in the West caused by increased automation, in the East the need to compete economically with the West. This process must be accelerated by the simple need to survive:

These two Germanys, which have at least this one common interest in survival, these two Germanys are situated precisely in the centre of the Theatre of War, that is to say that stage on which, in the minds of certain army people, nuclear war is to take place. These two Germanys, divided and yet united in one concern, could they not, should they not even, each in the bloc to which it belongs, work towards the goal of becoming free of nuclear weapons?

Two nuclear-free Germanys – that would be a beginning for many things.[5] (1983, p. 72)

In the GDR itself the view of the German question taken by the ruling communist party, the Socialist Unity Party (SED), has changed considerably over the years. The 1949 constitution insisted that Germany was 'an indivisible democratic republic' with 'only one German citizenship'. For most of the 1950s, this conception of the temporary nature of the division of Germany found its parallel in the cultural domain. Whereas the West Germans, both in practice and in official pronouncements, were implying the existence of two German cultures, one of which they regarded as worthless, the East Germans continued to uphold the cultural unity of the nation. In 1955, for example, the editors of the journal *Neue deutsche Literatur*, the official organ of the East German Writers' Union, complained that many more West German authors were being published in the

Congruence and Divergence

GDR than East German authors in the Federal Republic (anon 1955, p. 3). The unity of German culture was being endangered on the one hand by American cosmopolitanism and on the other by Cold War attitudes on the part of the West German authorities. As the 1950s progressed, however, it became increasingly difficult to sustain this view. Lenin's doctrine of the 'two cultures' was adopted: in every national culture there existed side by side a dominant, bourgeois culture and elements of a democratic, socialist culture, to the latter of which, as far as Germany was concerned, the GDR was heir. By 1961 the division of German culture into a 'progressive' one East of the border and a 'reactionary' one in the West had been sealed. While the new constitution of 1968 continued to uphold the notional unity of the German nation it declared that this nation lived in two separate states, the GDR being a 'socialist state of the German nation'. In 1974 yet another constitution was proclaimed: now the GDR had become 'a socialist state of workers and peasants' and all references to Germany and Germans were excised. Only the names of the ruling party, its daily newspaper *Neues Deutschland* and its satellite political groupings were left as a reminder of the *status quo ante bellum*. Although in an interview of 1981 Erich Honecker, First Secretary of the SED and effectively Head of State, allowed for some future reunification once the Federal Republic had become socialist (Volkmer 1984, p. 16), the official view is that there are two German states each with its own identity.

It is one of many paradoxes that at the very moment that the GDR's culture was growing closer to that of its Western neighbour its self-definition politically was moving in the opposite direction. This in turn made it necessary to stress the cultural differences. At the Eighth Congress of the Writers' Union in 1978 Stephan Hermlin described himself as a 'German writer . . . , connected to everything, whether positive or negative, that has been and is being written in the German language'.[6] Although he also insisted that he was 'a writer of the GDR' and that it was self-evident that such a person must have a different relationship to the literature of the German past than one who lived in the Federal Republic, in Austria or in Switzerland, he was attacked by Jurij Brězan, Klaus Höpcke and Erik Neutsch among others, for failing to stress sufficiently the autonomy of the socialist literature of the GDR (Fischbeck, ed., 1979, pp. 134–8).

The question of the cultural identity of Germany cannot ignore the related question of Austrian and Swiss culture. A large part of the difficulty resides in the fact that the name for the language in which not only West and East Germans, but also Austrians and many Swiss, write is the same, 'deutsch', even although the borders of the country which takes its name from the language have never coincided with those of the language itself. The West German Peter Schneider has pointed out that the present situation represents a return to the origins of German history. Uniquely among the nations of Europe, 'deutsch' did not denote a specific tribe but meant simply 'demotic', pertaining to the people, as distinct from the Latin of church and administration (1984, pp. 108–9). The unity of Germany was based originally on a common language, not on common political structures. Not until 1871 was there a united German state, and even then Austria and Switzerland were excluded. Hitler partly made good the deficiency with the annexation of Austria in 1938. The closest approximation between linguistic and political frontiers thus lasted only seven years, from 1938 to 1945. Any discussion of reunification must bear this in mind: exactly what territory is to be reunified? When in 1988 Martin Walser reiterated his reluctance to accept the division of Germany he provocatively also mentioned Königsberg, historically a German town, birthplace of the philosopher Kant, but now in the postwar dispensation part of the Soviet Union. The response of Jurek Becker (1988), an East German writer living in West Berlin, was a furious one. Becker's memories of a united Germany were not those of Walser. As a Jew he had spent his childhood first in a ghetto, then in concentration camps. He could see no purpose in such speculations, which could only lead to conflict.

If the territorial unity of Germany is so extraordinarily problematical what about its cultural unity? Walter Hinck points out that in the nineteenth and early twentieth centuries Austrian citizens such as Grillparzer and Hofmannsthal, and Swiss citizens such as Gottfried Keller, regarded themselves none the less as 'German writers' (1981, pp. 21–2). There is a long-standing tradition according to which the national unity of Germany is constituted not by political institutions but by culture. Joseph Rovan has shown how it was the German intellectuals who kept alive the notion of a national identity between the Reformation and Bismarck. Thereafter they found themselves either drafted into supporting the state or turned into opponents of the very state they had been advocating, ending in emigration or in concentration camps. Since 1945 and the dissolution of Germany into three parts, the Federal Republic, the Democratic Republic and Austria, the intellectuals have found themselves back in their ancient position, defending the unity of a divided nation (Weidenfeld, ed., 1983, p. 235). Günter Grass is one of the most prominent of these intellectuals. Unlike Walser he regards the political division of Germany as a fact which has to be accepted. Postwar German literature, however, is the one pan-German feature remaining: 'Now as ever, in spite of frontier, in spite of Wall, in spite of ideological and other demarcations, in spite of dependence on the one or the other block system, in spite of all these pressures and constraints, German culture as it emerged historically, as it has developed, as it is at the present time, has not been divisible'[7] (1980, p. 10). Grass, however, ducks the question of the status of Swiss and Austrian authors such as Max Frisch and Peter Handke, preferring, as he puts it, Bismarck's solution, the exclusion of Switzerland and Austria (p. 13).

For an outsider a degree of cultural imperialism may be detected in West German attitudes to the GDR's literature, and it is one which is extended to the literatures of the other German-speaking countries, Austria and Switzerland. While the Austrian Institute would not dream of organising a symposium on contemporary literature other than that which has been written by Austrians, the West German cultural institutions have no such inhibitions. At a symposium held in West Berlin for West German, British and Irish Germanists under the auspices of the West German Academic Exchange Service (DAAD) in 1982 a sizable proportion of the writers discussed were Austrian (Thomas Bernhard, Peter Handke) or East German (Volker Braun, Christa Wolf) (Bullivant and Althof, eds., 1987). One is reminded of the attitude taken only a decade or so ago by some of the more conservative academics in English departments in the United Kingdom towards the literature of the United States, denying either that it had any value or that it was at all autonomous. In Scotland, Ireland or Australia there are few inhibitions about studying indigenous literature as something which is different and independent of 'main-stream' English literature. It is particularly paradoxical that assertions of the unity of German culture should be increasing precisely at a time when throughout Europe minority cultures such as Catalan, Basque, Breton or Welsh are clamouring for autonomy.

Within the Federal Republic itself a feature of the past twenty years has been the interest in literatures which can be identified with a particular landscape or dialect. Partly it is a question of scale. It is much more difficult to pinpoint the specific qualities of the literature of West Germany, a state of over sixty million people, than those of Austrian, Swiss, Bavarian or East German literature. Clearly there is a difference in nature between the GDR, primarily a political unit created only forty years ago, and Austria, whose origins go back to the Middle Ages, or Swabia, a much more compact geographical concept. Nevertheless, it would be surprising if the political and social structures created in the GDR over the past forty years had not led to a specific East German cultural identity.

Even the linguistic unity of the 'German-speaking' area may be called in question. Some linguisticians – and not only East Germans – claim that the GDR has developed a language which is appreciably different from that of the Federal Republic, just as Australian and American English are different from that of the United Kingdom (Lerchner 1974; Winter 1974; Good 1974). That the GDR is for a West German or an Austrian reader almost as exotic a state as Japan or Indonesia is implicitly conceded by the West German publishers of East German novels when they furnish a glossary of terms which are common currency in the East but unknown in the West. West German readers of Rolf Schneider's *Die Reise nach Jarosław* have to be informed, as their East German counterparts do not, that, among other things, an 'E-O-Es' is an 'Erweiterte Oberschule', a term which itself needs further explanation, and that *Wochenpost* is the GDR's largest Sunday newspaper. A West German edition of Volker Braun's poems explains that a 'Jugendobjekt' is a place of production or building site run by young people, and that of Erich Loest's *Es geht seinen Gang* spells out in full the abbreviations 'AWG', 'EOS', 'BGL', 'GST', 'ABF', 'DSF' and 'WPO', without, however, defining the institutions referred to. West German readers of East German books and audiences for East German plays face a basic difficulty of interpretation when they encounter such references: is membership of the 'GST', even when this organisation is explained as the 'Society for Sport and Technology', a good thing or a bad thing, does it denote conformism to the system or is it merely a harmless hobby like breeding rabbits (Roßmann 1986)? Linguistic usage is revealing in other ways. Visitors to the Olympic Stadium in Munich will note that in the table of medal-winners West German athletes are allotted to the state 'Deutschland', their East German counterparts to the 'DDR'. Popular usage in the West tends generally to confirm that, unconsciously at least, people assume that there are two Germanys (Berschin 1980). As Hermann Rudolph has pointed out, when journalists and politicians refer to those East German writers such as Günter Kunert and Wolf Biermann who now live in West Germany as being in 'exile', by implying the parallel with the situation of writers such as Thomas Mann and Bertolt Brecht who spent the Nazi years in America they are, possibly unintentionally but certainly in a revealing way, admitting the existence of two Germanys (Weidenfeld, ed., 1983, p. 196).

Congruence and Divergence

The case for the separate identity of the GDR's literature has been put by the East German academic Horst Haase (1986). Admitting that linguistic differences are merely 'nuances', he insists on the determining factors of social and historical circumstances on the development of literature and on the expectations which its readers hold. Those who claim that there is no difference between East and West German literature invariably restricted themselves to a few exemplary authors, usually those who were critical of certain features of GDR society. A national literature, however, had to be viewed as a whole, including its literature for children and its science fiction, where the GDR has, as even West Germans admit, developed a tradition which has both quality and uniqueness. Even if one restricted one's view to works which have achieved an international reputation such as Christa Wolf's *Kassandra*, here too, the specific East German qualities could not be ignored. *Kassandra*, according to Haase, draws on East German traditions in a number of respects: the use of myth had been a characteristic of GDR literature since the 1960s; the concern for international peace and understanding had dominated GDR literature since its earliest beginnings; Christa Wolf, like her great model Anna Seghers, was committed to enlightenment; and the central role she ascribes to women had been a commonplace in the literature of her country. But still more crucial for Haase is the fact that *Kassandra* is fundamentally a debate between its author and her own society. Not everyone was in agreement with the conclusions drawn by Wolf, but nobody could deny the high moral fervour with which the debate had been pursued. Finally Haase draws parallels between *Kassandra* and the work of the Soviet writer Chingiz Aitmatov, suggesting that if one were to look for congruence it might well be found elsewhere. Haase is not the only GDR critic to draw parallels between developments in the literature of the GDR and those in the Soviet Union: Klaus Schuhmann finds in both an increasing insistence on the moral self-determination of the individual (1980, pp. 16–17), while Hans Kaufmann stresses, for example, the theme of interpersonal relationships, not least those between the sexes, which has taken on central importance in both socialist countries since the mid-1960s (1981, pp. 38–9). Western critics tend to ignore these literary links.

Some at least of Haase's theses have considerable weight. Few West German commentators would wish to argue that conformist authors such as Erik Neutsch or Helmut Sakowski were part of a pan-German cultural heritage. But the notion that 'top-class' authors such as Christa Wolf, Volker Braun and Heiner Müller are 'Germans', while only the 'inferior' ones are 'East Germans' is cultural imperialism at its worst. Reader-response theory lays great weight on concepts such as the reader's 'horizon of expectation', which in the case of an East German must be different from that of a West German. For this reason Norbert Mecklenburg (Pestalozzi, ed., 1986, pp. 3–15) is more ready to admit the autonomy of the GDR's literature than of Austria's. Austrian society being similar to that of West Germany, Austrian readers hold similar expectations from literature; East German readers, however, will read texts differently from their West German counterparts. Peter Hacks's play *Adam und Eva*, widely performed in both West and East Germany, may serve as an example. The final scene, after Adam and Eve have eaten of the forbidden fruit, contains a debate about God's 'plan' and the role of freedom within God's will – somewhat recondite issues, one might think, in an atheist society. References to the failure of the 'plan', however, provoked much merriment from East German audiences, all too aware of the problems of the GDR's own planned economy. Less trivially, any debate on freedom in an authoritarian East German context must have a different resonance from that in the more liberal West. This is true of many other aspects of contemporary culture. Some of the West German literary fashions of the 1970s appear to have been repeated in the GDR: a turning away from political commitment towards subjectivity, an apocalyptic air of pessimism in view of the seemingly insuperable problems of ecological destruction and the threat posed by nuclear weapons. But in context these attitudes take on unique features. In a society which insists on the political significance of everything, an overt rejection of politics is itself a political act; in a society which officially believes that the future is a bright-eyed socialist one, any expression of pessimism is more than despair.

Haase was reacting in part to a shift in West German views of the cultural unity of Germany. In the first half of the 1970s it was commonly agreed in West and East that the literature of the GDR was distinct from that of the Federal Republic. The opening sentence of Fritz J. Raddatz's seminal book *Traditionen und Tendenzen* (1972) was unambiguous: 'There are two German literatures.'[8] But in 1978 Raddatz executed a spectacular volte-face on the question. Referring to his earlier thesis he declared: 'Today this statement is false'[9] (1979, p. 28). A few months later Raddatz explained that Germany's contemporary 'national literature' was a literature of angst; extracts from texts by the West German Nicolas Born and the East German Karl Mickel would be indistinguishable, if one did not know their author (1980b, p. 52). While this may well be true, it is a test which would have a similar outcome if applied, for example, to

Congruence and Divergence

translations of selected works of Latin American literature, widely read in both East and West Germany but hardly 'German' in Raddatz's sense. His implied critical methodology is revealing. It represents a regression to the positions of New Criticism, regarding the Work as a verbal icon complete in itself, and ignoring the conditions under which literature is produced and consumed.

It is no coincidence that the occasion of Raddatz's recantation was a meeting in Berlin of the newly constituted 'cultural circle' of that old warhorse of the Cold War, the 'Undivided Germany Committee' ('Kuratorium Unteilbares Deutschland'). The political climate itself had changed. By 1978 the relaxed atmosphere of the early 1970s had given way to increased tension and distrust between the two Germanys. Brandt, the architect of détente, had been forced out of office by the discovery that an East German spy had been active in his immediate entourage. Suspicions in the West were growing as to how genuinely peaceful Soviet intentions were, the invasion of Afghanistan and the revival of the arms race were just round the corner.

Walter Hinck's approach is a more measured one than that of Raddatz. Hinck is careful to avoid all statements which might imply 'cultural colonialism'. Pointing out some of the specific qualities associated with Austrian literature, he admits that literature in the GDR has taken a different path from that in the West, so that it might be possible to speak of 'two camps' within contemporary German literature, that of the GDR on the one hand and that of the Federal Republic, Austria and Switzerland on the other. In contradiction of Raddatz he asserts that it is seldom difficult to tell from the first few sentences of a text whether it was written in the East or in the West. Comparing novels by the East German Hermann Kant and the West German socialist author August Kühn, he concludes that where the former insists on leading his readers in the correct direction, the latter allows them to draw their own conclusions, treating them as emancipated beings (1981, pp. 28–31). Ultimately, however, Hinck is more inclined to stress community than difference. He rejects the notion of a 'socialist national literature'; the concept of a national literature has always included that of all classes. As we have seen, however, this is not the case, otherwise Brecht and Seghers would not have been rejected as unliterary in the 1950s. Hinck's attempt to depoliticise what must be a political issue is belied by the actual behaviour of politicians and critics over the years.

Hinck stresses the literary heritage that is common to both parts of Germany: 'The common historical heritage, not least everything that is bound up with the concept of literary, classical Weimar, cannot be divided, continuity cannot be interrupted or broken off by the decisions of a Party'[10] (p. 32). By contrast, Werner Ross, another West German who has addressed himself to the issue, sees precisely this aspect as one which separates the two literatures. Taught by Bertolt Brecht and Peter Huchel the East Germans have developed a relation to the classical past both in themes and in style which is lacking in the Federal Republic. This is a topic which we shall investigate in greater detail elsewhere. For Ross East German literature, compared with its Western counterpart, has 'the greater seriousness and the more decided ethos'[11] (1982, p. 74), partly because it is taken seriously by its own state. This is a view which is not universally shared. Helga Schubert, for example, herself an East German writer, considers literature to be 'incredibly overvalued' by the powers that be (Barthélémy-Toraille 1987, p. 13). That literature attracts the state's interest is a mixed blessing. It gives writers an influence and a function which they lack in the West. The view of Wolfgang Hildesheimer, who lives in Switzerland, that in the face of current global problems literature is an unforgivable luxury, would be unlikely in the GDR. The price to be paid for public status, however, is the loss of artistic freedom. Conversely, those East German writers who have emigrated to the West quickly realise that the price of artistic freedom may be a lack of social resonance. How the state has exercised its control over writers is the subject of a subsequent chapter. But in case one imagines that state interference is peculiar to the Eastern bloc it is worth remembering that where it counts, where there is a genuine mass audience, as for television, Western governments, too, take a lively interest in what their subjects are allowed to watch. This, too, may be a boon or a bane. At the 1988 International Television Festival in Edinburgh Christine Ockrent, who had until recently been deputy director general of France's TFI, unconsciously echoed Ross's sentiments when she told her British audience: 'You are very lucky to have a prime minister so passionately involved in the media' (cit. Twisk 1988).

The question of how meaningful it is to speak of a specifically East German identity is not one which can be dealt with in detail here. Against Walser's assertion of the common identity of the inhabitants of Stuttgart and Dresden may be set statements such as those of Franz Xaver Kroetz, another West German socialist writer: 'To me the GDR is as alien as Mongolia'[12] (cit. Walser 1988, p. 66). It is partly a question of generations. Walser, Heym and Hermlin are all old enough to remember a unified Germany, whereas Kroetz was born in 1946. For Christoph Hein, born two years earlier, West

Germans of his generation such as Kroetz, Botho Strauß and Lothar Baier, have an entirely different personal history and the literature they write is quite distinct from his and that of his GDR contemporaries. He, too, sees greater similarities between West German and Austrian literature than between West and East German literature (Jachimczak 1988, pp. 358–9). Hermann Rudolph points out that even where the East German population as a whole refuses to identify with the monolithic official definition of the GDR the very fact that there is such a definition which is constantly being thrust at them is a determining factor. Moreover, the GDR's identity is created not only in relation to its Western neighbour but also to its position in the Eastern bloc (Weidenfeld, ed., 1983, pp. 193–209). Since the early 1960s this position has been one of economic superiority, resulting in national pride and occasionally in condescension towards Poles and Czechs. In this context the presentation of the historic guilt of the Germans towards the Poles, for example, which we shall encounter elsewhere, has again its specifically East German aspects.

Günter Gaus has described the GDR as a 'society of niches' ('Nischengesellschaft'): because of pressures from the West and the Party, because of the much slower pace of industrialisation and modernisation, East German society has an old-fashioned, prewar air about it when compared to the West, and cultivates 'niches' such as family life, privacy – and culture (1981, pp. 27ff). Officials like to boast that the GDR is 'a country of readers', and it is indeed the case both that the GDR publishes proportionately more books than almost any country in the world and that substantially more books are owned and borrowed per household than in the Federal Republic. One reason is that reading is a private activity out of reach of the all-embracing attentions of the Party. Another, however, is that literature is allotted additional functions to those which it has in the West. It has become a commonplace in recent years, even in the GDR, to lament the inadequacy of the East German press, radio and television. Christoph Hein, for example, explains the popularity of literature by the reading public's expectation that books will fill the gap left by the media; whereas his friends in the West may spend five or six days reading newspapers, his readers in the GDR spend at most five minutes a day on the press and have the rest of their time for literature (Barthélémy-Toraille 1987, p. 14). The distinguished economist Jürgen Kuczynski has expressed his belief that future historians will find more relevant material in the fiction of the age than in its sociological studies and its newspapers, which report only the successes (1980, pp. 158–9). This in turn makes the study of the GDR's contemporary literature particularly interesting for outsiders.

In one sense, however, it might be meaningful to deny the autonomy of East German literature. That would be if one were to hold the view that there is only 'good' literature and 'bad' literature, that there is only one kind of literature worth discussing. It is the view, for example, of Reiner Kunze, one of the GDR's émigrés: 'What nonsense to speak of two German literatures because the one has a different social background from the other! Every German book is German literature and, if it is literature, LITERATURE'[13] (cit. Pestalozzi, ed., 1986, p. 95). Walter Hinck, too, considers that the time has come to dispense with the notion of autonomous national literatures and to speak with Goethe of 'world literature' ('Weltliteratur') (1981, p. 33). Literature should be a means by which countries come closer to one another, and whether it is written in France, England, Japan, the Soviet Union or Zimbabwe is immaterial. That is a view which can be respected, although it is a particularly lofty one. According to it all literature has the function of widening the reader's consciousness of himself as a human being, not, that is to say, primarily as a Frenchman, Russian, Englishman, Zimbabwean, Japanese or indeed West or East German. Undoubtedly that is indeed a fundamental function of literature. The problem it entails, however, is that it seems to assume there is a general *condition humaine*, one which all citizens of humanity share, transcending both geographical and historical frontiers. That a Zimbabwean peasant, for example, has much in common with a present-day Japanese industrialist, however, must be regarded as questionable.

One of the features of recent GDR literature has been precisely a tendency to see people as individual human beings rather than as what Marx called the 'ensemble of social connections'. There is a strong existentialist current in the novels of Christa Wolf, Ulrich Plenzdorf, Klaus Schlesinger and others, and by concentrating on 'eternal' human characteristics – mortality, identity, suffering, love – East German writers have indeed been producing literature which more closely approximates to West European expectations. Nevertheless, even these 'eternal' characteristics have their peculiarly East German context. For in a state which asserts that socialism has given human relationships a new quality, even to imply that it has not done so after all is to make a point which would be meaningless in a West European context.

One practical problem remains. What is 'GDR literature'? The answer might be: GDR literature is literature written by East German writers. A work such as Günter Grass's play *Die Plebejer proben den Aufstand,* which is set in East Berlin in 1953, would thus quite reasonably be excluded. But who is an East German writer? This question is more difficult to answer. Manfred Bieler *was* an East German writer; *Der Mädchenkrieg* was published in the GDR before its author emigrated to the West in 1968. His 1983 novel *Der Bär* is even set in part in East Germany, but it would surely not be reasonable to include it here as an 'East German novel'. Since 1976 and the expatriation of the chansonnier Wolf Biermann a large number of writers have followed Bieler to the West, leading Fritz Raddatz (1988a) to contradict himself yet again, when he speaks of a 'third German literature', the distinctive contribution of the writers from the GDR who now live in the West.

In this book I intend to restrict myself almost entirely to works which were written by writers living in the GDR and which have been published there. At times this may appear an arbitrary decision. It is partly intended to reduce the potential material to more manageable proportions. But it must in any case be of interest and significance to consider only those works which have been able to appear in the GDR under the relatively tightly controlled conditions imposed by the censorship in that country. The novel *Gertrud* by Einar Schleef, for example, draws wholly on its author's recent experiences of the GDR, as does Stefan Schütz's *Medusa,* a massive allegorical novel about the GDR written by one who had only just turned his back on that country. Neither Schütz nor Schleef was a GDR citizen, however, when their novels appeared. *Medusa* is so obscenely hostile to the GDR that it could never have appeared there in any case, and in that sense it is not a 'GDR novel'. It was not written under the peculiar circumstances of the GDR's cultural and political climate. However, there are other, related, problematical cases. Where does one place works which, while written in the GDR by authors who were and still are living there, have, because of the vagaries of East German censorship, appeared only in the West? Stefan Heym's *5 Tage im Juni,* his *Collin* and his *Schwarzenberg* are all intimately concerned with the GDR, its history and its development. None has been published in the country where their author lives and *Collin,* in particular, seems unlikely ever to be so. Heym must have been aware of this. Written 'for the West', it might be argued, these are 'German' texts but not 'East German' texts. Heiner Müller moves freely between East and West and has spent some time in the United States. Although the position is currently being rectified, not all his plays have been performed or even published in the GDR, and they have tended to be premiered at Bochum in West Germany. The theme of pan-German history which he uses in a number of works in the 1970s has earned him the soubriquet 'Müller-Deutschland' and amusingly the West German documentation of the 1982 peace discussions of writers from East and West allots him on separate occasions to the GDR and to the FRG (Akademie der Künste, ed., 1982, pp. 5, 175). Perhaps more complicated still are the cases of Jurek Becker and Klaus Schlesinger. Both have been living in the West since the end of the 1970s, but have retained their East German passports with long-term exit visas. Schlesinger's *Matulla und Busch* is set wholly in West Germany, where it originally appeared, but it has also been published in the GDR. Becker's *Aller Welt Freund* is notable mainly for its geographical anonymity. It, too, was written in the West but has, after some delay, appeared in the East. The same author's *Bronsteins Kinder* is set in the GDR and has appeared there, but it was written in West Berlin. In a few years' time it may be impossible to make such distinctions. At the time of writing the GDR's cultural policies are in a state of flux; Heym's *Ahasver* has at last appeared and the chances of publication for his *5 Tage im Juni* are relatively hopeful. In this sense the period covered by this study, the two decades between 1968 and 1988, may in retrospect turn out to have been more homogeneous than what follows them.

One literary feature of the relationship between East and West Germany has been the willingness of writers to treat the division of Germany as a theme. In an exhaustive investigation of early East German literature Peter Hutchinson found that it was arguably 'the most common specific theme in East German writing up to 1970' (1977, p. 9). Major authors such as Anna Seghers (*Die Entscheidung*), Franz Fühmann (*Böhmen am Meer*), Christa Wolf (*Der geteilte Himmel*) and Hermann Kant (*Die Aula*) treated the topic in some depth and with more or less sophistication, showing the contrast between capitalist exploitation and socialist equality, between the GDR's determination to wipe out the remnants of fascism and the West's continuing flirtation with the old Nazis, between the poor but honest workers of the GDR and the wealthy but unscrupulous capitalists of the FRG. These works were partly a contribution to the GDR's search for a separate identity. In West Germany in these years by contrast the theme was of little importance. The most significant exception was Uwe Johnson (*Mutmaßungen über Jakob*, *Zwei Ansichten*), but Johnson himself had emigrated from the GDR in 1959. Since 1970 the picture has changed East German writers have been much more concerned with topics such as self-fulfilment within a socialist society or the GDR's own relation to the Nazi past or the Prussian heritage, than with its Western neighbour. In West Germany, on the other hand, the 1980s have seen a veritable upsurge of literary interest in the topic. Peter Schneider's *Der Mauerspringer* is a mixture of reflections and anecdotes set in divided Berlin. Dieter Lattmann's substantial novel *Die Brüder* traces the history of the division of Germany by means of the fictional biography of two octogenarian brothers, both former officers in Hitler's army, of whom the one now lives in East, the other in West Germany. In Martin Walser's novella *Dorle und Wolf* the eponymous couple are spying for the GDR in Bonn. Wolf is an accomplished pianist who now plays only with his left hand in tribute to the fragmentary state of Germany.

This is not to say that the theme of divided Germany is absent from recent East German literature. Hermann Kant's *Das Impressum* has already been mentioned. It contrasts, for example, the fates of two representative individuals, both called Hermann A. The one, a communist, was imprisoned in the Third Reich and became editor-in-chief of *Neues Deutschland* in the 1950s. The other, a banker, was imprisoned by the Allies after the war for helping the Nazis but today he is a banker once more in the Federal Republic. Heiner Müller treats the topic in terms of two warring brothers in his plays *Die Schlacht* and *Germania Tod in Berlin*. Erik Neutsch's vast history of the postwar development of Germany, *Der Friede im Osten*, presents the division of Germany in much the same aggressively anti-Western manner as did earlier novels. In the lower reaches of the GDR's literature the topic persists, just as it does in Western Europe for the writers of popular thrillers such as Len Deighton and John Le Carré. Harry Thürk's *Der Gaukler* treats the Solzhenitsyn affair as a spy-story, allotting the role ascribed to the KGB in Western versions of the genre to the CIA. Jochen Hauser's chronicle of working-class Berlin life *Familie Rechlin* includes an entertaining account of a family divided by the Berlin Wall. Initially hostile to the authorities for separating them from their daughter in the West, the Rechlins learn to appreciate the security afforded them by socialism in contrast to the rat-race of capitalism with its single-minded pursuit of materialist goals.

Beside this mainly conventional literature there is another which treats the question less in political than in existential terms, seeing it more as a cause for grief, for wry amusement or as a symbol of man's divided nature. Sarah Kirsch's poem 'Datum' describes the meeting of two lovers from the two halves of Berlin. The poet asks:

> Darling shall we be Juliet and Romeo?
> Circumstances

> Are favourable, we live
> In the same town to be sure, but the states
> Our registered states are fussing, mine
> Holds me and holds me tight it is so attached to me we
> Could be very unhappy ...[14]
>
> *(Katzenkopfpflaster*, p. 96)

Who now remembers the cause of the quarrel between the Montagus and the Capulets? The division of Berlin is for the speaker no more than that. By contrast the lovers in Christa Wolf's *Der geteilte Himmel* were separated by two political and social systems, one wealthy but cold and ultimately without any sense of direction and meaning, the other poor but concerned with human dignity and solidarity.

The narrator of Helga Schubert's 'Das verbotene Zimmer' was born in 1940 in what is now West Berlin; in 1978 she is a writer living in the eastern half of the city, and for the first time since the building of the Wall in 1961 is given the opportunity to revisit her birthplace and report on her experiences there. The motif of 'the traveller' was, as Hutchinson has shown, a traditional way of contrasting the two German states. (1977, pp. 29–65). Schubert's piece, however, is prefaced with a quotation from Kafka's 'The building of the Wall of China': 'I had the good fortune that when at the age of twenty I had sat the highest examination of the lowest school the building of the wall was just beginning'[15] (*Blickwinkel*, p. 126). Although at no point does the narrator return to Kafka's fragment, the implications are striking, for the narrator herself was twenty when a rather different wall was built. Kafka's wall may be seen as a symbol of the vanity of human aspirations, like the tower of Babel. Its immediate purpose remains unclear, for the marauding northern tribes against which it ostensibly gives protection have never actually been seen; but in any case nobody should try too hard to understand the commands of the leaders. All these parallels with the Berlin Wall imply its absurdity rather than its political meaningfulness. The story itself confirms this diagnosis. The divided city *is* absurd. Subterranean tunnels cross East Berlin conveying West Berliners from North to South on the underground railway. Occasionally the sound of trains which 'don't belong' can be heard by East Berliners. By implication West Berlin is part of the reality of East Berlin in spite of the authorities' efforts to exclude it. The man who used to live in East Berlin working as a driver on the metropolitan railway continues to do so even after he has been allowed to settle in West Berlin, for the 'S-Bahn' is controlled by the GDR in both halves of Berlin and in that way he can preserve his pension rights.

The title is from the world of the folk tale. In 'Bluebeard', for example, there is one room which the queen is forbidden to enter. Her curiosity, however, is too great. In the King's absence she unlocks the door and finds behind it the corpses of his former wives. She, too, is thereupon condemned to die. West Berlin is for the narrator just such a 'forbidden room'. So great is the power of political propaganda that when the narrator does cross the frontier she is constantly on edge, waiting for something to happen, feeling she is being watched. Like most visitors from the East she is struck by the prosperity of West Berlin, the flowers and the colourful journals, the smells of the cars and the people. She has to force herself to remember the underlying negative features, such as the expensive advertising which is attempting to restrict women to their traditional roles. She notes the elegant ladies buying dresses in C & A but hiding them in more expensive-looking carrier bags, the shoplifter whom she does not report to the police although at home she would have done so. She visits a feminist bookshop where she sees contact numbers for victims of rapes or beatings and has a brief argument over the rights and wrongs of excluding men. The caretaker of the house where she was born makes her a present of an astrological journal. All these features could be seen as negative. There is nothing strident about the story, however, no overt commitment to socialism as there was in *Der geteilte Himmel* or *Die Aula*. Contrary to her folk-tale expectations, the narrator returns safely to East Berlin, only to find that she had visited the wrong house.

Schubert's story is more an appeal for the relaxation of travel restrictions. The folk-tale allusion suggests that it is precisely the prohibition of travel to the West that makes the desire to do so overwhelming. This is a recurrent motif in recent East German literature. In Ulrich Plenzdorf's *Die neuen Leiden des jungen W.* the teenage hero reflects wistfully at one point that everyone would like to see the world. In the same author's *Legende vom Glück ohne Ende* there is a fantastic episode in which Paul, who is a paraplegic, crosses the border into West Berlin on his wheelchair, waved on by the guards and without having to show any papers. He rides around for a few hours before returning, when he has the same cordial reception. This is fantastic, as everyone knows reality is not like that. On the other hand it would be 'fantastic' in the more popular sense of the word if it were. The state's lack of trust in its citizens is the central theme of Volker Braun's *Unvollendete Geschichte*. Frank is falsely suspected of intending to defect to the West; his girlfriend Karin is warned to have nothing more to do with him, but nobody will tell her or Frank why. In the course of the story Frank attempts to commit suicide, Karin falls out with her parents and loses her job. At one point in the story one of the officials reflects that it is the GDR's constant compulsion to compete with its Western neighbour that causes the pollution of the rivers. The story, however, is more concerned with the pollution of human relationships through the state's authoritarian behaviour. When in Klaus Schlesinger's *Alte Filme* the protagonist Kotte encounters the Wall in the course of his peregrinations it represents not the temptations of an alternative political system as might have been the case in earlier fiction, but more the existential barriers between individuals in any society. Margret Eifler (1988) suggests that the setting of divided Berlin in Irmtraud Morgner's *Amanda* echoes the division which patriarchy has created in individuals between their emotional and their rational lives.

Helga Schütz's *Julia oder Erziehung zum Chorgesang* may be read as a counterstatement to Hermann Kant's immensely popular *Die Aula*. Both works deal in part with the lives of students at a Workers' and Peasants' Faculty in the 1950s, an institution set up in the early years of the GDR to enable students from the appropriate social and political background to acquire the necessary qualifications to attend university. In Kant's novel the ideological commitment of the students is unquestioned. Their difficulties are rather with the interpretation of ideology in the Stalinist era. The principal protagonists are males, whose relations to the female students are shy. In Schütz's work, by contrast, the perspective is that of a woman, Julia, who is studying music in Potsdam. Much of her emotional energies are devoted to men, especially Pagel, one of her teachers. She is ideologically unsound: when the students unmask a shopkeeper who has been illegally hoarding provisions she feels only sorrow for the object of their triumph, and she is fascinated by the philosophy of Schopenhauer rather than by dialectical materialism. It is only when Ulrich comes on the scene that she is properly 'converted', becomes a member of the socialist collective and learns, as the subtitle puts it, to 'sing in chorus'. But we do not learn this until the end of the novel, which is told largely in flashback. At its opening Julia is leaving Ulrich, having discovered his infidelity after eighteen years together, and has also left the choir to become a hospital auxiliary. The novel's subtitle is thus ironic, Julia's education into conformism having failed to last.

In this context the theme of the division of Germany has its role to play. In *Die Aula*, too, it was important, Kant balancing out his criticism of Stalinist attitudes in the GDR with an uncompromising presentation of corruption in West German society. This remains a common device: the negation of Western life-styles implies support for the GDR, however critical the author may be of the details. Thus Christa Wolf's *Nachdenken über Christa T.* includes a visit to a cold and thoughtless West Berlin and Christoph Hein's *Der fremde Freund* features a West German intellectual whose chattering on every subject unmasks his basic emptiness.

In *Julia* the division between West and East is far less between black and white than it was in *Die Aula*. As a student in the 1950s Julia would visit West Berlin from time to time, not, however, in order to distribute leaflets extolling the benefits of socialism, as orthodoxy would expect, but in order to buy articles unobtainable in the East such as a seductive petticoat. Encounters with fellow-students on similar errands were a source of some embarrassment. Living in Potsdam, to the West of West Berlin, she had difficulty in explaining to her son Robert that the sun rose in the East over the skyline of 'the West'. In the novel's present, the late 1970s, she obtains permission to attend the wedding of relatives in West Germany along with her current boyfriend Gabriel Tischer, who is making a documentary film on 'the generations and the two German states' (p. 62) and is looking for representative material on both sides. They curtail their visit to the relatives, however, choosing instead to seize the opportunity and go on a trip to the Rhine. When they run out of money Julia sells her long hair to a wigmaker, only to realise afterwards that this is going to cause problems for the film.

Although, as in conventional East German accounts, West Germany is on the whole a place of prosperity and materialism, this is no monolithic caricature, as the idealistic opponents of nuclear power are also encountered and the activities of the Baader-Meinhof terrorists are a major topic of people's conversation. Indeed the GDR itself is portrayed as a place of thoughtless consumption of material goods: Nicole, Robert's girlfriend, visits restaurants and eats the leftovers from the diners' plates in protest against waste in a world where others are starving. Julia's grandfather appears to speak for the novel when he remarks: 'Two states, two sets of politics, and everywhere you have to work'[16] (p. 22), and 'There's just a lot of propaganda about, over here and over there'[17] (p. 94). *Julia* makes no attempt to defend the division of Germany on ideological grounds; for the most part it is a plausible account of the unpolitical way in which the majority of Germans behave and think. The border between the two states is an irritating barrier, but one which perhaps reflects the barriers between people in general. If the theme of the division of Germany is to be integrated into the novel as a whole it must be seen as relating to the separation of Julia from

Ulrich and of Julia's eighteen-year-old son Robert's from his mother as he leaves to set up an independent existence.

Only at a couple of points does the theme take on more sinister overtones, and in both cases it is wholly at the expense of the GDR. The border separating the two states is mined on the East German side and the neighbour's dog is killed when it strays into the minefield. More importantly, Robert is now eligible for national service. His school is visited by an officer of the People's Army, who asks him if he is prepared to serve on border duty. Robert replies in the negative, explaining that he could not shoot at anybody trying to get out. As a consequence his headmaster and form teacher are reprimanded for failing to educate him into a reliable citizen and Robert's application for a university place in medicine is rejected. The novel refuses to take the side of the state in this, something which one of the reviewers found most provocative (Berger 1981). The official line is that the frontier needs to be protected against enemies from without and that any unauthorised attempt to cross it is a crime which must be prevented by force if necessary. Schütz, like Julia, refuses to 'sing in chorus'.

A further recent East German novel which deals with the division of Germany is Eberhard Hilscher's *Die Weltzeituhr*. On one level it is the picaresque biography of Guido Möglich. Guido is born in 1928 and through the eccentric but liberal upbringing of his parents develops into a handsome, intelligent and charming young man. His wits prevent him from being too heavily involved with the Nazis; the closest to active service he experiences is a posting to Copenhagen. After the war he settles with his mother in the Soviet sector of Berlin and opens a second-hand bookshop. Up until the building of the Wall in 1961 he is able, like all Berliners, to move freely between East and West. Two amorous attachments are of special importance, one with Annette, the daughter of former Jewish neighbours who had emigrated in the 1930s, the other with Sigune, a watchmaker; both live in West Berlin. The affair with Annette ends when she will no longer accept his domineering arrogance and goes off to the United States to join a medical research team. That with Sigune is terminated by external events, the building of the Wall. Here the specifically East German literary echoes become most insistent. In Christa Wolf's *Der geteilte Himmel* the love affair between Rita and Manfred ends with the defection of the latter and Rita's refusal to follow him. The sealing of the border in August 1961 seals their separation and leads to a mental breakdown in Rita from which she only slowly recovers. Rita is the young idealistic socialist, Manfred the rather older man whose ideals have been successively so frustrated by fascism and Stalinism that he has developed a carapace of cynicism. In *Die Weltzeituhr* these roles are to some extent reversed. Although Guido is a merciless womaniser, he also has his postwar ideals of international cooperation and understanding, ideals which the Cold War and the rearming of the two German states are set to thwart. He becomes apathetic, takes to drink, and only the relationship with the naive Sigune gives his life any meaning. The closing of the border brings that relationship to an end, he is eventually placed in a psychiatric institution, from which he disappears without trace. In the earlier novel Rita recovers with the aid of sympathetic colleagues and representatives of the Party; Guido has no such good fortune.

But *Die Weltzeituhr* is not only a biographical novel. Guido Möglich's name ('möglich' = possible) implies that the principal character has representative significance. He was born in a place called 'Paradies' (paradise). Germany's fall from grace through National Socialism is embodied in a character who started out with every possibility, who might even have become 'guide' (rather than 'Führer'), but whose development was stunted by historical events. His biography is embedded in two further narrative sequences, set off from each other typographically. The first is a year-by-year account of historical events between Guido's birth-year 1928, and 1962, the year in which he disappears. The second is a series of anecdotes, episodes from the development of modern science and modern culture, scenes from the lives of Albert Einstein, Auguste Piccard, Gerhard Domagk, Pablo Picasso, Otto Hahn, Albert Schweitzer, Konrad Zuse, Norbert Wiener, Thomas Mann, Bertolt Brecht, Jurij Gagarin and Neil Armstrong. In the chronological survey the interpretation of history given largely conforms to that current in East German orthodoxy. The division of Germany was caused by Western policies. The currency reform carried out in the three Western zones in June 1948 forced the Soviet government to impose a blockade on West Berlin in order to prevent the undermining of the Eastern zone's economy by a flood of now valueless marks from the West. The founding of the GDR in October 1949 was a response to the founding of the FRG one month previously. Rational and genuine proposals for negotiations between the two German states were invariably rejected by Adenauer and the Western allies.

On the other hand the tone is witty and ironic. Hitler, for example, is called 'Ahi', and the Nazis 'Schowis' (a linguistic anachronism, for 'Schowis' is contemporary feminist slang for 'male chauvinists', such as Guido himself), while Walter Ulbricht is referred to as 'Comrade W'. The outbreak of the Korean war is reported twice, as it appeared in the West German and East German press: 'Two reports, two worlds, two interpretations, two truths!'[18] (p. 239); 'Since then Guido Möglich dimly realised that in history and politics there were no neutral views, only evaluations which depended on one's personal standpoint and system of references. Everyone had to make up his own mind'[19] (p. 240).

Although this analysis is completely in keeping with Marxism-Leninism, the expected comment on which decision would be the historically correct one is lacking, thus a certain degree of relativism enters the novel. This in turn is linked to the novel's title, a reference to the 'world clock' on East Berlin's Alexanderplatz which displays the time in various cities around the world. The simultaneity of disparate events, world views and political systems likewise relativises each possible interpretation. Hence the importance of Einstein in the novel. Twentieth-century science has been two-sided. On the one hand there have been the remarkable advances in medicine and the understanding of the universe. On the other hand there has been the apparently inexorable advance in man's ability to destroy himself. Einstein's theories led to the splitting of the atom, but the splitting of the atom is the symptom of a much wider issue: the fragmentation of the world into conflicting systems and the possibility of a literal and permanent fragmentation of the earth itself. At the end of the novel Guido asks angrily: 'Why do people not understand one another? Why do the rulers not understand one another? Why do the nations not understand one another? Brothers are quarrelling and tearing us apart, you understand? The star is dividing into two parts and atomising'[20] (p. 392).

It is not then just the division of Germany that Guido is angry about, but the division of the planet. In this respect *Die Weltzeituhr* is not untypical of literary developments in these years. The question whether East or West Germany is in the right becomes less important in the face of the threat to the very existence of humanity posed by the arms race in the 1980s. These are issues which will occupy us in subsequent chapters. First, however, we must look at the development of the GDR's cultural policies in more detail.

Congruence and Divergence

Notes

1. Wär sie ein Ganzes, ich wäre doch gespalten; die halbe / Ist ein Viertel für mich, da bin ich einig mit dir.
2. Es gibt DDR-Autoren, deren internationale Rezeption sie – bescheiden ausgedrückt – als Schriftsteller europäischen Ranges mit Strahlungen in die Welt ausweist. Das sind nicht sehr viele. Für ein relativ kleines Land sind aber zwei schon viel – ich denke an Christa Wolf und Heiner Müller. Europäische Bedeutung würde ich sicher vier bis fünf weiteren Autoren zurechnen.
3. Hier steht, man nimmt an, man hält es für möglich, es könnte sein, daß Sie Deutsche sind, aber wir sind zu so einer Annahme nicht verpflichtet. Für uns sind Sie unerwünschter Ausländer unbekannter Nationalität.
4. Aus meinem historischen Bewußtsein ist Deutschland nicht zu tilgen ... Ich weigere mich, an der Liquidierung der Geschichte teilzunehmen. In mir hat ein anderes Deutschland immer noch seine Chance. Eines nämlich, das seinen Sozialismus nicht von einer Siegermacht draufgestülpt bekommt, sondern ihn ganz und gar selber entwickeln darf; und eines, das seine Entwicklung zur Demokratie nicht ausschließlich nach dem kapitalistischen Krisenrhythmus stolpern muß. Dieses andere Deutschland könnte man, glaube ich, heute brauchen. Die Welt müßte vor einem solchen Deutschland nicht mehr zusammenzucken. Und doch ist es im Augenblick reine Utopie.... Wir dürften, sage ich mir vor Kühnheit zitternd, die BRD so wenig anerkennen wie die DDR. Wir müssen die Wunde namens Deutschland offenthalten.
5. Diese beiden Deutschland, die wenigstens dieses eine gemeinsame Interesse haben: zu überleben – diese beiden Deutschland liegen genau in der Mitte des Theatre of War, jener Bühne also, auf der, nach der Vorstellung gewisser Militärs, der Atomkrieg stattfinden soll. Diese beiden Deutschland, getrennt und doch vereint in dem einen Interesse, könnten sie, ja müßten sie nicht, ein jedes in dem Block, dem es zugehörig ist, darauf hinwirken, daß sie frei werden von Atomwaffen? Zwei atomwaffenfreie Deutschland – das wäre ein Anfang für vieles.
6. ... ein deutscher Schriftsteller ..., verbunden mit allem, im Positiven wie im Negativen, was deutsch geschrieben wurde und deutsch geschrieben wird.
7. Die deutsche Kultur ist nach wie vor, trotz Grenze, trotz Mauer, trotz ideologischer, trotz sonstiger Abgrenzung, trotz Abhängigkeit im einen und anderen Blocksystem, trotz all dieser Belastungen und Bedingungen, wie sie historisch entstanden ist, wie sie sich entwickelt hat, wie sie gegenwärtig da ist, nicht teilbar gewesen.
8. Es gibt zwei deutsche Literaturen.
9. Dieser Satz ist heute falsch.
10. Das gemeinsame historische Erbe, nicht zuletzt alles, was mit dem Begriff des literarischen, des klassischen Weimar verknüpft ist, kann nicht geteilt, eine Kontinuität durch Parteibeschlüsse nicht unter-oder abgebrochen werden.
11. den größeren Ernst und das entschiedenere Ethos.
12. Mir ist die DDR so fremd wie die Mongolei.
13. Was für ein Widersinn, von zwei deutschen Literaturen zu sprechen, weil bei der einen ein anderer gesellschaftlicher Hintergrund gegeben ist als bei der anderen! Jedes deutsche Buch ist deutsche Literatur und, wenn es Literatur ist, LITERATUR.
14. Herzschöner wollen wir Julia und Romeo sein?/ Der Umstand/ Ist günstig, wir wohnen/ Wohl in der gleichen Stadt, aber die Staaten/ Unsere eingetragenen Staaten gebärden sich, meiner/ Hält mich und hält mich er hängt so an mir wir/ Könnten sehr unglücklich sein ...
15. Ich hatte das Glück, daß, als ich mit zwanzig Jahren die oberste Prüfung der untersten Schule abgelegt hatte, der Bau der Mauer gerade begann.
16. Zwei Staaten, zwei Richtungen, und überall muß gearbeitet werden.
17. Es wird eben viel Propaganda gemacht, hüben und drüben.

-27-

18. Zwei Meldungen, zwei Welten, zwei Deutungen, zwei Wahrheiten!
19. Seitdem ahnte Guido Möglich, daß es in Geschichte und Politik keine unparteiischen Ansichten gab, sondern nur Bewertungen, die vom persönlichen Standort und Bezugssystem abhingen. Jedermann mußte sich entscheiden.
20. Warum verstehen sich die Menschen nicht? Warum verstehen sich Regenten nicht? Warum verstehen sich Völker nicht? Der Bruderzwist zerreißt uns, verstehen Sie? Der Stern zerfällt in zwei Teile und atomisiert sich.

–2–

Writers, Politicians and Taboos

> Turned down! – What? You don't say? – Not
> we . . . – Who then? – Quiet, no-one.
> But circumstances . . . – Ah. Now they're
> working all on their own.[1]
> (Volker Braun, 'Berlinische Epigramme': *Langsamer knirschender Morgen*)

In 1955, in the course of a conversation with Stefan Heym, Bertolt Brecht is reported to have said that the Soviet Union could claim to possess a literature only when it was possible to publish a novel there which began with the words: 'Minsk is one of the most boring cities in the world'[2] (Schubbe, ed., 1972, p. 1057). In 1972 Volker Braun's play *Die Kipper* was published and performed in the GDR. It centres on a group of contemporary building workers, one of whom in the course of the play declares: 'This is the most boring country in the world'[3] (*Stücke*, p. 18). Braun must have been aware of Brecht's words. He had begun to write his play ten years earlier, revising it in 1965 to take account of Party criticism. Only in 1972 could it be performed, although the phrase quoted was one to which Erich Honecker publicly took exception (Rüß, ed., 1976, p. 777). Might it be that the GDR now, in 1972, could in Brecht's terms be said to possess a literature?

In East German cultural politics 1971 was a significant caesura, and for all the upheavals which have taken place subsequently its legacy is still in many ways valid. In that year Honecker replaced Walter Ulbricht, who as First Secretary of the SED had dominated the political scene in the GDR since its inception. The change coincided with the Party's quinquennial Congress, the eighth of these occasions, which are used by the leadership to take stock of the past five years' successes and to point the way ahead. As is customary, Honecker's address to the assembled delegates did not confine itself to economic or political matters, but included a review of cultural affairs. Praising the artists and writers of the GDR for their recent achievements, he went on to admit that superficiality and tedium were not absent from some of their products and promised the full cooperation of the Party in the quest for improvements. Three passages from his speech appeared especially significant. One was the encouragement of a 'frank, objective, creative debate' on literary matters. The second was a broadening of the topics available to writers and artists to include 'not only the correct themes, those which are of use to our socialist society . . . but also the whole breadth and variety of the latest expressions of life'. Thirdly he promised full support for writers and artists in their 'creative search for new forms'[4] (Rüß, ed., 1976, pp. 180–1). In other words, the old dogma of socialist realism appeared to have been abandoned. A few months later Honecker was even more precise: 'If the starting-off point is the firm position of socialism, then in my opinion there can be no taboos in the area of art and literature. This applies both to questions of the presentation of content and to style . . .'[5] (ibid., p. 287).

Admittedly there was an important proviso at the beginning of the statement, one which would enable the cultural bureaucracy to continue to determine what might or might not be published. Nevertheless, writers were, at least initially, euphoric at what they regarded as their new freedoms. The atmosphere was vividly described by Klaus Schlesinger in 1980 in an interview with a West German journalist. It was

> a time of strong democratic tendencies, of a growing critical awareness, a time in which we had all invested great expectations. I can say that I could not have felt so free in any other country as in these early seventies, meaning by the writer's freedom his freedom with regard to his themes, his subject-matter – and of course with the possibility of publishing his books. I believe I am not wrong to say that these expectations at that time dominated practically the *whole* of society, that's the bottom as well as the top . . .[6] (Raddatz 1980a, p. 33).

In order fully to understand the significance of Honecker's words and the particular qualities of the literature which was published thereafter, it is necessary to look back at developments on the East German cultural scene from 1945 onwards. One general point must be made from the outset: cultural politics in the GDR (or anywhere), as the term implies, do not take place in a political vacuum. Culture is not an autonomous human activity which can be divorced from other human activities and the various vicissitudes of East German cultural politics can invariably be traced to developments in the world outside, especially those affecting relations between East and West.

Initially, as we have seen, the continued unity of German culture was stressed. The Soviet zone of occupation was to be shown to be the true heir to the cultural heritage which the Nazis had debased and despoiled. The numerous writers who had emigrated from Germany in protest against or in fear of fascism were encouraged to return to the Eastern zone rather than the Western ones; in this way a progressive culture could be established, bringing together the values of the past and the socialism of the present. When the Red Army swept through Silesia in 1945 they had strict instructions to respect and protect the octogenarian Gerhart Hauptmann, one of the few writers of stature to remain in Germany in the Third Reich but whose early work *Die Weber* was regarded as a revolutionary socialist drama. When the Germans were forcibly evacuated from Silesia, now part of Poland, he was invited to settle in the Soviet zone and assist in the work of socialist reconstruction. Hauptmann died before he could make the move. Heinrich Mann, too, died shortly before he was due to leave California for the new socialist Germany. Others were more fortunate. The novelists Anna Seghers and Arnold Zweig, the dramatists Friedrich Wolf and Bertolt Brecht and the poet Johannes R. Becher were among the most prominent writers to prefer the Soviet zone of occupation to any of the Western ones. Brecht was the most celebrated of the returning exiles. Although his relations with the authorities were never straightforward, his theatre, the Berliner Ensemble, was to become in the 1950s the most important German-language theatre anywhere, much to the chagrin of the West Germans. Anna Seghers, too, was internationally known, largely because of her novel *Das siebte Kreuz*, which was first published in English in 1941 and later filmed. Her *Die Toten bleiben jung*, begun in exile, appeared in 1949 and remains one of the most impressive attempts to present the various strands of interwar German society and the roles they played in the rise and fall of National Socialism. In the area of the cinema, too, helped by the fact that the DEFA studios were in the Soviet zone of occupation, films such as Wolfgang Staudte's *Die Mörder sind unter uns* of 1946 were initially more impressive than the products of the Western zones.

By contrast those former exiles who chose the West, Leonhard Frank and Alfred Döblin, for example, frequently encountered aloofness and even hostility (Mertz 1985). As they had not shared the sufferings of the wartime German population, they were regarded as alien, unable to understand the situation and having no right to intervene. Döblin eventually departed for France in despair.

In the Eastern zone, where social policies attempted to unite the population in the name of a denazification programme which, by distinguishing between the criminals and the fellow-travellers, was more successful than the comprehensive measures taken in the Western zones, cultural policies in these early years were relatively liberal. The Cold War brought this liberalism to an end. The German Democratic Republic was founded on 9 October 1949 from the Soviet Zone of Occupation, in response to the creation of the West German Federal Republic a month earlier out of the three Western Zones of Occupation. A full-blooded programme of socialism was set in motion, so that by the beginning of the 1960s East Germany's industry had been largely nationalised and its agriculture collectivised. At the same time the SED, formed out of the old Social Democratic and Communist Parties, began a Zhdanovite campaign against Western, decadent, 'formalist' trends in the arts. In a quite naive way it was believed that there was a direct correlation between literature and material circumstances, between what one read and the way one behaved, to the extent that literature might even be used to increase economic productivity. If the economy could be planned, so too could literature, and this in turn would affect the economy. If today this strikes one as comic, and not just in the West, it is also an indication of the high regard in which literature was held. Thus although the GDR was making great strides socially and economically as compared to the FRG – an assertion which was itself dubious – it was said to be lagging in the cultural sphere because its writers were being seduced by Western decadence. Works which placed form above content were 'formalist'; abstractionism, subjectivism, perspectivism were by their nature anti-humanist and anti-democratic (Schubbe, ed., 1972, pp. 178–86). But the literature of despair, of the absurd, the nihilism of so much of Western culture in the 1950s was similarly classed as formalist. While European modernists such as Marcel Proust, James Joyce, Virginia Woolf, André Gide and Franz Kafka were proscribed at a time when they were being avidly read and imitated in West Germany, 'realists' such as Hemingway, Steinbeck and Graham Greene were likewise rejected.

For the 'realism' of these writers was not 'socialist'. 'Socialist realism' had been adopted as official literary policy at the First Pan-Soviet Writers' Congress in 1934 and was declared binding on all East German writers from the beginning of the 1950s. To this day the statutes of the East German Writers' Union include a commitment to the method of socialist realism, which all members are officially expected to observe. 'Socialist realism is the truthful, historically concrete representation of reality in its revolutionary development'[7] (Schmitt and Schramm, eds., 1974, p. 390). This deceptively simple definition, incorporated first into the statutes of the Soviet Writers' Union, begs many questions. What is truth and what is reality? For the medieval philosopher realism was the belief that universals were real and the particular manifestations of these universals merely secondary; 'nominalists' by contrast considered universals to be no more than names. The history of European realism is the history of the reversal of this standpoint: for the realist writers of the nineteenth century it was the particular, individual, material objects that counted, not any idea of them (Watt 1957, pp. 11–12). Socialist realism, however, might be regarded as a reversion to the original medieval standpoint. Realism is a representation of the 'truth', not of the ostensible, superficial appearance of things. And this truth is the Marxist-Leninist interpretation of history.

In the 1950s socialist realism tabooed both religious and sexual themes. If religion was incompatible with a materialist ideology, it was prudishness in the Stalinist era that dismissed as pornographic explicit representations of sexuality. For Wilhelm Girnus pornography was often an essential component of formalist works (Schubbe, ed., 1972, p. 172). Literature had to be essentially optimistic. If reality was moving inexorably in the direction of communism, then there could be no tragedies. Fascism and imperialism would be overcome, the enemies of the revolution would be unmasked and liquidated, the economy would progress from strength to strength. At a time when Western literature was fascinated with the concept of the anti-hero, socialist literature was to propagate the 'positive hero', someone who was wholly committed to socialism and who would stride triumphantly onwards as a model to readers. But above all socialist realist literature was both popular ('volksverbunden') and partisan ('parteilich'). It was popular in the sense that it was accessible to all, as formalist literature was not. As early as 1948 Anton Ackermann had attacked the elitist nature of high culture and demanded that the division between the popular and the so-called serious arts should be overcome (Schubbe, ed., 1972, pp. 86–7). One of the ideals of Johannes R. Becher, the GDR's first Minister of Culture, was a 'literature society', a community of readers which embraced the whole population united in their appreciation of Goethe and the other German classics (Becher 1972, pp. 344–9; first published 1952). It was even more important that literature should be partisan. In Marxist terms all literature takes sides, overtly or covertly: that which purports to be neutral is simply upholding the political system under which it is written (Pracht, ed., 1975, pp. 335–41). In the 1950s socialist realist literature was expected to be overtly partisan, both in the general sense that it supported the oppressed and exploited and showed history to be moving in the direction of communism, and in the special sense that the political *party* which represents these interests, namely the Communist Party, was incorporated in the text. Thus the hero would always be able to find guidance and advice from his friendly local Party secretary, and in many cases his development was one from a position of noncommitted sympathy with the Party's aims to membership itself.

The peculiarly German dimension in this lay in the role played by the German classical heritage, especially by the later Goethe. The classics have always played an important role in German Marxist thinking from Marx and Engels themselves down to Adorno and Lukács. In the 1930s there were heated debates between the exiled left-wing German writers on the relation between Marxism and modernism. To what extent should the new socialist writers model themselves on their bourgeois contemporaries? Was there a proletarian aesthetic? Did the modernist techniques of a Joyce and a Proust represent merely the crisis of late-capitalist society or did the new realities demand new forms? Prominent among the contributors to the debate were Anna Seghers, Bertolt Brecht and Ernst Bloch, all of whom were to settle in the GDR after the war and who were all, at least to some extent, on the side of modernism.

Their main opponent was Georg Lukács, however, and he was to dominate GDR aesthetics during the 1950s. For Lukács the 'subjectivism' of a Joyce and a Dos Passos represented a 'capitulation' to the inhumanity of late capitalism (1971, pp. 230–2). Lukács believed in the importance of plot, of well-defined characters who developed organically, and of the omniscient narrator who guided readers in their understanding of events. These conditions were fulfilled by the traditional German 'novel of education' (*Entwicklungsroman*), most notably by Goethe's *Wilhelm Meisters Lehrjahre* and Gottfried Keller's *Der grüne Heinrich*, in which, with the aid of a succession of mentors, a representative protagonist develops into a fully integrated member of society. Although Lukács himself was much too sensitive a critic to do so, it was not difficult to make the parallel between, for example, Goethe's 'Society of the Tower', which keeps a watchful eye over Wilhelm Meister and prevents him from making irrevocable errors, and the Communist Party in the literature of socialist realism. Accordingly the novel of education was to be a dominant mode in the 1950s. Lukács's proclivity for Weimar classicism was complemented by his rejection of the German Romantics and of those other traditions in German culture which contradicted Goethe's harmonising outlook.

Although Lukács was disgraced by his involvement with the Nagy government in Hungary in 1956, his influence remained strong through the 1960s. Günter de Bruyn, for example, looking back a decade after the publication of his first novel, *Der Hohlweg*, in 1963, wrote that he had chosen Wilhelm Meister as the model for his hero rather than Hamlet, Josef K. or Schwejk: 'For I had allowed myself to be persuaded that a novel had to be a novel of education, to have a positive ending and to present totality'[8] (*Im Querschnitt*, p. 327). Today de Bruyn has nothing but scorn for *Der Hohlweg*. His second novel, *Buridans Esel*, published in 1968, far from adopting the Goethean model, begins with a Kafka allusion.

Since the end of the 1960s there is scarcely an aspect of cultural policies as outlined above which has not been modified or called in question. It is no longer Goethe but his antagonists such as Kleist and Lenz, and the Romantic writers such as Hoffmann and Jean Paul who have become the cultural heritage for many GDR authors. Helga Schütz's *Julia*, as we have seen, reverses the pattern of the novel of education which it implies in its subtitle. The Communist Party is no longer such an overt presence. Formalist experiment has made much recent literature anything but accessible to all. Those who attempt to reconcile these developments with a continued adherence to socialist realism are forced to take refuge in claims that the population at large is better educated than in the 1950s or in a reduction of the concept of partisanship to a sense of responsibility to society and mankind (Pracht, ed., 1975, pp. 358, 341).

Before turning to the 1970s, however, we must briefly look at some of the significant events which preceded them and which provide a context within which more recent GDR literature must be judged. One of these was the Bitterfeld Conference of Writers and Politicians in 1959, possibly the most ambitious attempt of the ruling party to 'administer' literature and to overcome the division between culture and society. Production workers were encouraged to become writers, describing their own experiences in factories and agricultural combines; writers were exhorted to become workers, joining factories and portraying at first hand conditions there. Today one detects a degree of embarrassment among East German cultural functionaries when they are asked about this episode. It was, however, important for a number of reasons. It represented a turning away from the bourgeois conception of culture associated with Lukács, predating similar developments in West Germany, where the 'Gruppe 61' and later the 'Werkkreis Literatur der Arbeitswelt' likewise encouraged workers to articulate their problems. Moreover it produced at least two substantial works by new writers, *Der geteilte Himmel* by Christa

Wolf and *Spur der Steine* by Erik Neutsch. A second Bitterfeld Conference in 1964, however, replaced the emphasis on the role of the production worker with one on the importance of planners and managers, society's 'pacemakers' – as we shall see in a later chapter, echoes of this controversial revision of Marxist doctrine continue to reverberate to this day.

The building of the Berlin Wall in 1961 stemmed the outflow of labour to the West and helped to stabilise the East German economy. It also enabled a degree of relaxation in cultural policies. Both Wolf and Neutsch levelled a degree of criticism at dogmatism and Stalinism, as did Hermann Kant in *Die Aula*. In December 1965, however, alarmed by developments in Czechoslovakia which were to lead to the Prague Spring, a plenary session of the Central Committee of the SED called a halt to this liberalisation. A number of writers were attacked for their heretical presentation of the GDR's past, their criticism of present policies, or their capitulation to what was regarded as the sex-and-violence fashion of the West. The most important figures were Wolf Biermann, who together with the physicist Robert Havemann was propagating a socialism different from the 'actually existing socialism' of the GDR, Stefan Heym, whose unpublished novel *Der Tag X* criticised the role of the Party in the 1953 unrest, Peter Hacks, whose play *Moritz Tassow* exposed the Party's vacillations during the agricultural reforms of the postwar period, and Heiner Müller, whose play *Der Bau*, based on Neutsch's *Spur der Steine*, was accused of representing the Party as cold and alien. In the following years two other prominent writers were singled out for criticism, the poet Reiner Kunze, who protested against the GDR's part in the invasion of Czechoslovakia by the armies of the Warsaw Pact countries in 1968, and Christa Wolf, whose novel *Nachdenken über Christa T.* was massively attacked at the Writers' Congress of 1969 for its subjectivism. It is against this background that the liberal words of Erich Honecker in 1971 had their impact.

At the beginning of that year Walter Ulbricht and the Central Committee of the SED had already been lobbied by some forty of the GDR's most prominent writers with the request for greater artistic freedom. Clearly it was easier for a new leader to begin a new chapter in relations between writers and politicians. But there were other, more complex reasons for the liberalisation which eventually took place. In 1969 Willi Brandt had become Chancellor in West Germany and was actively pursuing detente with the Federal Republic's Eastern neighbours. The most important, and most difficult, of these neighbours was the GDR. If the GDR presented a more liberal image to the West German diplomatic recognition by the Bonn government would be facilitated. In due course the Basic Treaty was signed, the GDR obtained the international status it had been seeking for over twenty years, and in 1973, along with the Federal Republic, it entered the United Nations. That was one consideration. Another was more for internal consumption. It was becoming clear that Ulbricht's promise that the GDR would outstrip West Germany economically was unlikely to be fulfilled in the foreseeable future. It was easier to claim cultural superiority, a vaguer concept, and a claim which might be strengthened by a liberalisation of cultural policies. Moreover freedom in the cultural sphere gives the illusion of political freedom, the cultural revolution can be a surrogate for true socialism. In turn social conflicts can be absorbed by cultural conflicts, whether these are debates about literature and the arts or tensions within the literary work itself (Weisbrod 1980, pp. 242–3). In fact the cultural liberalism of Honecker's keynote address to the Party Congress in 1971, admitting a degree of autonomy to literature, was balanced elsewhere by a renewed stress on the primacy of politics over the technology and economics which Ulbricht had favoured in the last few years of his stewardship.

The 'creative debate' which Honecker encouraged came to centre on three main areas: lyric poetry, the cultural heritage and the text *Die neuen Leiden des jungen W.* by Ulrich Plenzdorf. The debate on poetry was the first to take shape, partly because it had been simmering under the surface for a number of years, partly because poetry is the genre of literature least amenable to being administered from above. As early as 1962 Stephan Hermlin had incurred the wrath of the authorities when he allowed a number of new poets, including Volker Braun, Sarah Kirsch and Wolf Biermann, to read from their works at the Academy of Arts and subsequently to discuss their problems frankly and publicly. In 1966 Adolf Endler and Karl Mickel's anthology of East German poetry *In diesem besseren Land* provoked a debate in the magazine *Forum* until it became too lively and was broken off. Honecker's words were evidently taken by Endler as a signal to return to the attack, for at the end of 1971 he published a furious polemic in the journal *Sinn und Form*, using a review of a collection of essays on lyric poetry by Hans Richter to claim, for example, that the GDR's literary scholars were totally incompetent, having lost the ability to be the least moved by a literary artefact (1971, p. 1364). The debate that followed comprised some twenty contributions in *Sinn und Form* and *Weimarer Beiträge* during 1972, and it flared up again briefly in 1974 and 1975. It covered two major areas: the nature of lyric poetry itself and the cultural policies which allowed it to thrive. Should poetry be political and immediate, or might it also be individualistic and esoteric? Endler complained that too many of the younger poets were unable to publish their poems at all because of prevailing restrictive cultural policies. His complaint was supported by the poet Heinz Czechowski (1972). Günter Kunert was another writer to intervene: literature was dynamic, theory static; the act of writing was an act of 'self-liberation . . ., self-understanding, self-realisation, one of the only possible form of individuation, namely the successful finding of one's identity'[9] (1972, p. 1102). This insistence on the individual and on the importance of self-realisation was to be central to developments in the GDR's literature in the 1970s and beyond.

A second area of debate was the role of the literary heritage. The insistence that culture should no longer be the preserve of one class had as its corollary the demand that the revolutionary proletariat 'appropriate' to itself the cultural heritage of the past. Lukács had stressed the primacy of the Goethean model. From 1970 onwards this normative view of past literary works and forms was being called in question. Dramatists such as Peter Hacks and Heiner Müller and poets such as Volker Braun were appropriating the literary past in a more dynamic way, revising, reinterpreting the classics, using them to shed light on contemporary reality. In the wake of the iconoclastic student movement of the late 1960s West German scholars, too, were attacking the reverential approach to Goethe. At the beginning of 1973 *Sinn und Form* published three substantial contributions to the debate. Werner Mittenzwei discussed approvingly Brecht's far from reverential treatment of the classics, implying a model for East German writers. Helmut Holtzhauer took the opposite standpoint, triumphantly claiming that in view of the West German dismissal of the classics the GDR was more than ever the true heir to the German past. Wolfgang Harich, meanwhile, launched an extraordinarily virulent and witty diatribe against Heiner Müller's 1972 adaptation of Shakespeare's *Macbeth*, accusing Müller of succumbing to Western-style pornography, violence and historical pessimism. A more measured approach was adopted elsewhere by Hans Kaufmann (1973), who, quoting the *Communist Manifesto*, warned against allowing the past to dominate the present, while at the same time insisting on the intrinsic achievements of the German classics. In the event it was the conservatives Holtzhauer and Harich who were defeated.

Related to this debate, which was on the whole restricted to writers and academics, was a much more public discussion of a text which appeared in *Sinn und Form* in 1972, Ulrich Plenzdorf's *Die neuen Leiden des jungen W*. For this text, as its title makes explicit, was a less than orthodox 'appropriation' of a work by Goethe, *Die Leiden des jungen Werthers*. It also indirectly related to the polemic against the academic scholars initiated by Endler. Edgar Wibeau, a gifted teenager, runs away from home, where he has a socially successful but domineering mother, and his workplace with its insensitive training programme. He lives in a summerhouse in Berlin, falls in love, tries to construct a new kind of paintspray on his own but blows himself up in the process. There are parallels between the story of Edgar Wibeau and that of his eighteenth-century predecessor; but the author also includes overt references to and quotations from Goethe's work. By his own account Plenzdorf was reacting against the way in which the classics were taught (Girnus, ed., 1973, p. 243). In his text the young hero finds a copy of Goethe's work in the toilet and uses the cover and the pages with the editor's introduction for his immediate needs. He goes on to read the text uninfluenced by any academic guidance. Wibeau uses Goethe, without knowing it is Goethe, in order to understand himself better. To keep others at bay he baffles them, to the reader's hilarity, by firing off quotations from *Werther* at them. In other words Plenzdorf's work upholds the value of the cultural heritage while at the same time disputing the official views of that same heritage. Part of the problem for the authorities lay, however, in the fact that *Werther* is usually interpreted by GDR scholars as a work in which the potentially revolutionary intellectual is shipwrecked on the rock of feudal social relationships (Müller 1969). The parallel therefore implies that contemporary GDR society resembles politically backward Germany in the eighteenth century.

Die neuen Leiden was first published as a piece of narrative fiction, but a dramatised version was staged in Halle in May of the same year which, after some initial hesitancy, was to become an unparalleled success, especially with teenage audiences, who regarded it as documenting their own frustrations with a monolithic, authoritarian society. The response of one teenager in particular indicates the reasons and also the change in cultural policies as they were perceived at the time:

> It's the first time they've looked under the table-cloth! Normally everything looks so nicely smooth and so nicely white from above! They've looked underneath for once and they've brought all that to the surface, turned it over if you like.... He [Edgar] just doesn't want to do everything according to plan. With us everything is too organised in advance, education, your whole career.[10] (Klein et al. 1973, p. 140)

−39−

Because of this popularity *Die neuen Leiden* was potentially more subversive than the other objects of debate. A month after the play's premiere a forthright condemnation of the text came from the lawyer and broadcaster F. K. Kaul, who wrote to the editor of *Sinn und Form*, Wilhelm Girnus, protesting against its publication in the very periodical which had been founded by Johannes R. Becher as the representative literary journal of the GDR. Kaul claimed that the text abused the cultural heritage through its insolent confrontation of Goethe's Werther and a contemporary dropout, one, moreover, who speaks mainly in teenage slang, and regarded it as an infringement of socialist realism inasmuch as it centred on a character whom he regarded as a social deviant rather than a 'typical' East German teenager and failed to balance this figure with a positive alternative.

Girnus published extracts from Kaul's letter early in 1973, inviting responses and specifying issues which he thought should be covered. They included central tenets of socialist realism: should literature present only 'representative', i.e. model characters? Must there be a positive counter-balance to a negative hero? Meanwhile, however, there had already taken place a symposium on the work at the Academy of Arts in Berlin, at which Robert Weimann had delivered a paper on the relation between *Die neuen Leiden* and Goethe's *Werther*, followed by a discussion in which among others Wieland Herzfelde, Stephan Hermlin, Ernst Schumacher, the play's director Horst Schönemann and the author himself took part. The response to Girnus's invitation was most lively: *Sinn und Form* devoted over one hundred mainly densely-set pages to a debate on Plenzdorf's text in 1973, and even if the insights gained were not in proportion to the size of the coverage the contributors were evidently seizing the opportunity to use the new freedom of discussion. Other journals debated the text, including *Neue deutsche Literatur* and especially *Forum*, the journal of the Free German Youth and therefore officially the closest to Wibeau and his generation, which found in a questionnaire that Wibeau's views were shared by substantial numbers of its members. Warnings came from the political sector. At a meeting of the SED's Central Committee in May 1973 Erich Honecker and Kurt Hager, while naming no names, respectively accused certain writers of 'imposing their own sufferings on others' and of idealising the bourgeois notion of the autonomous individual embodied in *Robinson Crusoe*, one of the books admired by Plenzdorf's hero (Rüß, ed., 1976, pp. 777, 781). Generally, however, these voices were ignored. *Die neuen Leiden des jungen W.* has been reprinted again and again. For Hans Kaufmann it is one of the successful contemporary appropriations of the classical heritage (1980, p. 11).

This was one text which was able to appear only after the Eighth Party Congress. During the debate at the Academy of Arts Plenzdorf revealed that he had tried to realise the project earlier but had been repeatedly rebuffed (Girnus, ed., 1973, p. 243). This original version was published in the GDR in 1986, having already appeared in West Germany four years earlier. Plenzdorf was, and remains, a scriptwriter for the DEFA film studio and his text was intended for a film. That the project was not realised is attributed revealingly in a postscript by Dieter Wolf to the 'difficulty of assessing public opinion and the mass effectiveness of the cinema'[11] (*Filme*, p. 360). This must be taken into account when assessing the significance of the work's eventual publication in 1972. The private nature of the act of reading makes novels and poems less subversive than plays and films.

A comparison of the original with the later versions of the *Die neuen Leiden* reveals the extent and the limitations of the new liberalism of the Honecker era. Apart from the ending the story has remained basically the same. To that extent the liberalisation is genuine. Originally Wibeau attempted to commit suicide when his invention failed, but the rope he was to hang himself with breaks and the gun he was to shoot himself with goes off in the wrong direction, his workmates find him in the ruins of his summerhouse and realise that he was working on the right lines. In due course he is feted as a great inventor. In the final version Wibeau dies and there is no suggestion that he would ever have succeeded. One effect of this, as Gerd Labroisse points out (1975), is to play down the social benefits of Wibeau's invention, or, as Andy Hollis suggests in his detailed and perceptive comparison of all the extant versions, to insist that society must take account of the needs of all individuals, not just of the gifted ones (Bartram and Waine, eds., 1984, pp. 59–70). The development of the text is in the direction of an increased stress on individuality. It is not, however, the case, as Hollis believes, that the final text is therefore the most radical one. The 'happy ending' of the original is so obviously ironic that it cannot be regarded as softening the social criticism. On the contrary, the social criticism is given much more weight in the film script, where in three successive scenes the tensions between apprentices and management are played out. In one of them Edgar actually broadcasts a recorded extract from a trades-union meeting over the works intercom, in which the resolutions of the People's Chamber on the improvement of training for apprentices are quoted. This is a direct, political provocation which has no parallel in subsequent versions.

The first, unrealised version of *Die neuen Leiden* is in many ways reminiscent of Gerd Bieker's novel *Sternschnuppenwünsche* of 1965, in which a group of teenagers invent a device to clean the printing presses, find no cooperation or interest from trades union or management, go it alone, and are eventually hailed as innovators. Bieker's presentation of the deficiencies of the Establishment was regarded at the time as so subversive that he had substantially to rewrite his novel (Reid 1983/84). In general one may say that pre-1970s literature was more directly concerned with political structures and therefore frequently came in conflict with the administration. Since 1971 writers have tended to concern themselves more with private, individual issues. In a heavily politicised society this has its political implication, but it is an indirect one.

There were other works which were released for publication under the new, more liberal regime. Christa Wolf published a collection of essays, *Lesen und Schreiben*, in 1971, her first book since the disastrous reception of *Nachdenken über Christa T.* Its title piece, a lucid and penetrating account of her view of literature as a contribution to human emancipation and a clear statement against socialist realism, had been written in 1968 and was to be one of the primary works of literary theory of the 1970s. Hermann Kant's *Das Impressum*, parts of which had been serialised in the late 1960s, appeared at last in its entirety in 1972. Volker Braun's *Die Kipper* was performed in the same year, while his *Das ungezwungene Leben Kasts*, an episode of which describes the consternation which met the news of the invasion of Czechoslovakia, had appeared a year previously. Stefan Heym, one of the victims of the 1965 upheavals, was rehabilitated. His novel *Der König David Bericht*, a satire on GDR bureaucracy and opportunistic historiography disguised under the mantle of similar phenomena under King Solomon of Israel, appeared in 1973, as did a volume of poems by Reiner Kunze, *Brief mit blauem Siegel*, and a second edition of Wolf's *Nachdenken über Christa T.* Irmtraud Morgner's novel *Leben und Abenteuer der Trobadora Beatriz* was published in 1974. It included extracts from a previous work by the author, *Rumba auf einen Herbst*, which had been written in 1964 but suppressed, probably for its presentation of Stalinism, but also because the relations between the communist Pakulat and his teenage son Benno, a jazz trumpeter, imply a conflict of generations, which was a major taboo area in the 1960s (Reid 1983/84; Watson 1987). Finally, Braun's *Unvollendete Geschichte* was published by *Sinn und Form* in 1975. It is a text which goes much further than Plenzdorf's *Die neuen Leiden* in directly confronting the *political* issues of press censorship and state authoritarianism. Indeed one might say that the publication of this text was a genuine test of the Party's nerves. If *Unvollendete Geschichte* was acceptable, then the euphoria described by Klaus Schlesinger was justified. Unfortunately it was not to be; orders went out to withdraw all unsold copies of that issue of *Sinn und Form*, and subsequent bibliographies of Braun's works listed only the West German edition, which appeared in 1977 (Watson 1987, pp. 169–70). There was no 'creative debate' on this text.

In any case there were clear indications that there remained limitations on writers' freedom to publish. Stefan Heym's *Der Tag X* was published in West Germany in 1974 under the title *5 Tage im Juni*, but not in the GDR. Reiner Kunze and his family were still being subjected to pressure and discrimination from the security forces. In 1976 he published *Die wunderbaren Jahre* in the Federal Republic, a series of vignettes satirising everyday life under 'actually existing socialism' in which the most trivial signs of youthful nonconformism led to repression from the authorities, beside which Plenzdorf's Wibeau appeared almost mollycoddled. The indoctrination of schoolchildren with militaristic attitudes was attacked, as were the shooting of would-be defectors at the border and, with especial bitterness, the invasion of Czechoslovakia in 1968. Kunze was expelled from the Writers' Union at the beginning of November 1976.

Neither Robert Havemann nor Wolf Biermann had been rehabilitated and it was over the latter, shortly after Kunze's expulsion, that the most serious crisis since 1965 came. Biermann had been living in a kind of internal exile in Berlin, financing himself with the royalties which he received from West German publishers of his texts and his recordings and continuing to maintain that the best hope for socialism lay in the GDR but that it must be of a different kind from that administered by the SED. In the summer of 1976 there were signs that he, too, might be becoming acceptable when he was allowed to give a private concert in a church, his first for over a decade. In November of that year he was invited by the West German Metal Workers' Union to perform in Cologne, and obtained an exit visa from the East German authorities, who assured him that he would be allowed to return to the GDR afterwards. The concert was broadcast by West German television. Four days later the GDR authorities claimed that because Biermann had defamed his country at the concert his passport had been withdrawn and he was no longer a citizen of the GDR. Just two years after the Soviet Union had rid itself of Alexander Solzhenitsyn, the GDR was shot of its most troublesome dissident.

Why the authorities chose to act as they did is not entirely clear.

Derek Fogg lists three possible motives. Soviet pressure on Honecker to harden his policies may have been a factor, although I should argue that the degree of interest taken by the Soviet administration in East Germany's cultural affairs is generally overestimated. The huge increase in oil prices sparked off by the Yom Kippur War brought an abrupt end to the steady economic progress registered by the GDR over the previous few years and may have led to the urge to neutralise internal political criticism at all cost. Thirdly the international conference of communist parties which took place at the end of June 1976 in East Berlin gave prominence to the eurocommunism of the West, which was close to Biermann's views, and may, as Biermann himself believed, have acted as a catalyst (Wallace, ed., 1984a, pp. 137–8). Melvyn Dorman points out that at his concert Biermann had gone out of his way to express his support for Reiner Kunze (1979, p. 39). It may simply have been a miscalculation, a rash decision to seize the opportunity to rid the authorities of a thorn in their side. As always the international climate must be taken into account. Brandt's *Ostpolitik* was intended to bring the two Germanys closer together; the agreements facilitated travel between the two countries, and a flood of West Germans seized the opportunity, bringing with them direct evidence of Western prosperity and potentially subversive ideas. In October 1973 Honecker had declared that peaceful coexistence made it more than ever necessary to continue the ideological struggle (Weber, ed., 1986, pp. 337–8), and the new constitution of 1974 consolidated the division of Germany. In 1975 the Conference on European Security and Cooperation had ended in Helsinki with a Final Act which appeared to signal the end of the Cold War in Europe. But while the East European countries emphasised the clauses on economic cooperation and the acceptance of existing frontiers, those in the West tended to stress those on human rights, and this awakened demands in the GDR for greater personal freedoms than the regime was willing to grant (Weber 1985, p. 434). The Biermann affair must also be seen in this light. The concert was given enormous publicity in the West, which made ideological capital out of Biermann's criticisms of the GDR, often ignoring his fundamentally socialist stance.

Whatever the reasons, the storm of protest which the measure unleashed was unparalleled in East Germany's cultural history, and the GDR's literature has not properly recovered from the affair to this day. A letter was sent to the SED protesting against the expatriation and requesting it to reconsider its decision. Biermann was described as 'difficult', but a socialist society, in which, as Marx had put it, the revolution was constantly criticising itself, ought to be able to live with such a person. While the signatories did not agree with everything Biermann had said and done, and wished to have nothing to do with attempts to use him against the GDR, they believed he had left no doubt on whose side he stood. The letter was signed by Sarah Kirsch, Christa Wolf, Volker Braun, Franz Fühmann, Stephan Hermlin, Stefan Heym, Günter Kunert, Heiner Müller, Rolf Schneider, Gerhard Wolf, Jurek Becker and Erich Arendt, and they demanded that the letter be published in *Neues Deutschland* without delay. When this did not happen it was passed to Agence France Presse and quickly publicised in the West. Within a few days a hundred more writers, artists, actors and musicians had added their names to the original letter. They included Ulrich Plenzdorf, Klaus Schlesinger, Günter de Bruyn, Karl-Heinz Jakobs and Helga Schütz.

From the point at which the letter was in the hands of the Western media the rupture between the signatories and the administration was complete. The SED had been left no escape route, they could not be seen to back down in the face of Western pressure; this may have been a tactical error by the instigators of the petition. *Neues Deutschland* never did publish the letter; instead it published numerous letters supporting the decision to expatriate Biermann, from, among others, Hermann Kant, Erik Neutsch and Dieter Noll. The signatories were placed under great pressure to recant. Volker Braun criticised the publication of the protest in the West, but not its content. Some, including Gerhard Wolf, Jurek Becker and Sarah Kirsch, were expelled from the SED. Others lost their posts in the Writers' Union. Christa Wolf suffered a heart attack. Initially she insisted on being treated like her husband Gerhard and being expelled from the Party, but she was persuaded by Hermann Kant not to go so far. Anna Seghers disapproved of the way in which the affair had been treated both by the signatories and by the authorities and is reported to have been alone in defending the former at a meeting of the Writers' Union. Robert Havemann, who had protested independently, was placed under house arrest. Younger, less prominent writers suffered the greatest hardships. Some, including Jürgen Fuchs and Frank Schoene, were arrested and given prison sentences for 'activities hostile to the state'.

The Biermann affair was a catalyst which destroyed the illusions some writers had held about their intellectual freedoms. The atmosphere of the following three years was exceedingly unpleasant. Works were published in the West which could not appear in the East, writers emigrated, temporarily or permanently, personal hostilities broke out, and insults were exchanged among colleagues. Some were given more favourable treatment than others. Christa Wolf's novel *Kindheitsmuster* had been published just before the news of Biermann's expatriation broke. In spite of her role in the subsequent affair it received respectful, even enthusiastic, reviews. Another text by her, *Kein Ort. Nirgends*, appeared in 1979, as did Stephan Hermlin's *Abendlicht*, Günter de Bruyn's *Märkische Forschungen* and Ulrich Plenzdorf's *Die Legende vom Glück ohne Ende*. Works by the other signatories did not at once disappear from bookshops or public libraries. Gradually, however, the pressures intensified. Although Sarah Kirsch's *Zaubersprüche* had been reprinted in 1977, the refusal to reprint a book or grant a travel visa was a sanction applied increasingly frequently. At the Eighth Writers' Congress in May 1978, Hermann Kant was elected president in succession to the 77-year-old Anna Seghers; his address was, by his own account, an attempt at conciliation. But the congress met without Franz Fühmann, Stefan Heym, Günter Kunert, Ulrich Plenzdorf, Klaus Schlesinger, Rolf Schneider and Gerhard and Christa Wolf, none of whom had been selected by their local group to attend. Stephan Hermlin, who did attend, was attacked by a number of his colleagues when he pointed out that writers were individuals, not sheep, and that it was the prerogative of the poet 'to dream without reason' (Fischbeck, ed., 1979, p. 136).

It is an exaggeration to claim that the history of East German literature in the years 1977 to 1979 is the history of works which could not be published there, but the list is substantial: Hans Joachim Schädlich's *Versuchte Nähe*, Jurek Becker's *Schlaflose Tage*, Klaus Poche's *Atemnot*, Karl-Heinz Jakobs's *Wilhelmsburg*, Stefan Heym's *Collin*, Rolf Schneider's *November*. There were other scandals. In 1978 Rudi Strahl's television play *Die Flüsterparty* was cancelled. It satirised the state-sponsored system of 'Intershops', which allow the privileged citizen with Western currency to buy goods which are otherwise unobtainable. The question is whether the events of November 1976 marked a change in the SED's cultural policies, whether these works might have been published in the GDR before 1976. In view of the fate of *Unvollendete Geschichte* the answer must probably be no. In June 1979 Honecker quoted his own statement of 1971 that provided the starting-off point was the 'fixed positions of socialism' there could be 'no taboos' in art and literature, and emphasised that this was more than ever the case (cit. Kleinschmid 1979c, p. 900). But the proviso had also remained the same. Socialism was defined by the SED and any work which called in question the role of the SED was per se anti-socialist. As Reinhard

Michalke put it when *Die Flüsterparty* was banned: 'For there is one taboo for certain: the question of power and the leading role of the Party'[12] (cit. Kleinschmid 1978, p. 1246). This is most obvious with a work such as Heym's *Collin*, which explicitly criticises the behaviour of the German communist party from its collaboration with the National Socialists to destroy Weimar democracy, its support of Stalinism both in the 1930s and in the 1950s, down to its present-day bureaucracy. Schneider's *November* is a fictionalised account of the Biermann affair, querying again a decision of the Party. Schädlich's *Versuchte Nähe* includes a piece on the remoteness of the Party leader from the population at large. In Becker's *Schlaflose Tage* it is the role of the People's Army which is called in question when a teacher loses his job for encouraging one of his pupils to ask what are seen as provocative questions about the soldier's freedom to discuss commands. This is perhaps the least controversial of these texts. Helga Schütz's *Julia*, published just two years later, introduces the even thornier question of the policy of shooting at would-be defectors at the frontier. In Becker's case the banning may have been more a punishment for the author's actions than for the content of his work.

The fact that all these works were published in the West is one indication of the interest taken in the GDR's affairs by West Germans. The new policies of détente had led to the presence of a substantial number of West German journalists in the GDR. The Biermann petition was known to East Germans through West German radio and television, readily received in most parts of the GDR. From 1977 to 1979 East German writers consciously used the Western media to pursue controversies which they could not pursue in their own country, and it is possible to view the works mentioned as an aspect of this process. In some cases at least they cannot have expected the GDR authorities to publish them. This was especially true of one non-literary work, Rudolf Bahro's *Die Alternative* published in 1977 in West Germany, a plea for socialism, but again one different from that operated by the SED, which Bahro accused of exploiting the people of the GDR. Bahro was arrested and sentenced to eight years' imprisonment as a 'Western agent'. He was freed and allowed to settle in the West in 1979. In that same year the SED decided to call a halt to the use of Western media by GDR writers. It had always been illegal to publish in the West without permission, but in view of the hard currency which thereby accrued to the GDR, the authorities had usually been willing to overlook it or to fine offenders a mere 300 marks – what Stefan Heym described as a 'tax'. Now unauthorised publication could incur a much heavier fine, even imprisonment; at the same time much more restrictive press laws were enacted, prohibiting unauthorised interviews with Western journalists.

The immediate victims of the new laws were Havemann and Heym, who were both indicted for possible infringements of the currency laws. Heym gave an unauthorised interview with a West German journalist, who was promptly expelled from the GDR. In a private letter eight writers appealed to Honecker on behalf of Heym: Jurek Becker, Klaus Poche, Klaus Schlesinger, Erich Loest, Kurt Bartsch, Adolf Endler, Dieter Schubert and Martin Stade. Trying to avoid the errors committed over the Biermann letter, they waited a week; when there was no reply they revealed the existence of the letter, not its content, to a Western press agency, whereupon Hermann Kant claimed that the West knew of the letter before its recipient. Dieter Noll publicly described Heym and Schneider as 'washed-out' and quite unrepresentative of writers in the GDR (Kleinschmid 1979b, p. 677). Heym was fined a punitive 9,000 marks for publishing *Collin* in the West, Havemann 10,000 marks for a similar offence. At a meeting of the Berlin branch of the Writers' Union at the end of May Bartsch, Endler, Heym, Jakobs, Poche, Schlesinger, Schneider, Schubert and Joachim Seyppel were expelled.

Two controversial novels which did appear in these years, both published by the Mitteldeutscher Verlag, were Werner Heiduczek's *Tod am Meer* and Erich Loest's *Es geht seinen Gang*. Neither author had signed the Biermann petition. Heiduczek's novel, an account of opportunism in the founding years of the GDR, in which among other things it is related how the narrator was paid 100 marks to join the Party, sold out at once and has never been reprinted. The difficulties faced by Loest have been described in detail by the author in *Der vierte Zensor*, a kind of 'novel of the novel', a revealing account of the mechanisms of censorship in the GDR published in West Germany after he had settled there in 1981. Loest began writing *Es geht seinen Gang* in the relaxed climate of 1974 and signed a preliminary contract with his publishers for it at the end of that year. Honecker's words had impressed him and one impulse behind the novel was to test the 'taboo' placed on the way in which the behaviour of the authorities had alienated citizens in the past. As all writers in the GDR are aware of the conventions governing publication, self-censorship is a powerful influence. This 'first censor', the author himself, determined nevertheless to proceed. The narrator and protagonist of *Es geht seinen Gang* is as old as the GDR itself. The repressive behaviour of the state in 1965 has caused him to remain largely aloof. Not unexpectedly this was a topic which caused grave misgivings with the 'second censor', the publisher; there were discussions with the publisher's readers in which he was urged to relativise the standpoint of his protagonist. The months went by; the economic climate worsened, as did the political climate, and a fifth version of the novel was written. The Biermann affair intervened, not unfavourably for Loest, who had not been involved. In April 1977 the publisher's reader discussed the manuscript of the novel with him on twenty-six points of detail. At the end of it he felt like a boxer after a hard-fought bout; but they had reached agreement on the version which was to be passed to the 'third censor', the department responsible for publications in the Ministry of Culture, which made no further demands. The notorious paper shortage prevented publication for a further twelve months, during which the author gave frequent public readings from his work, which came out at last early in 1978 and was an instant success. A second printing, to appear in the same year, was promised. Then a few weeks later came the bombshell: further editions of both *Tod am Meer* and *Es geht seinen Gang* had been prohibited. Loest set everything in motion to have the ban overturned: contacts with influential authors, the Writers' Union, threats of legal action. At every turn he came across a mysterious wall, a 'fourth censor'. Public readings were cancelled or sabotaged. Reviews were hostile and readers' letters protesting against them were not published. His perseverance led in the end to an agreement that the novel would be reprinted once, but in a limited edition and with a different, more obscure publisher (this edition, too, sold out at once). Most extraordinarily, he was paid by the Mitteldeutscher Verlag for the second edition it had promised but which had not materialised. At the end of 1979 he resigned from the Writers' Union, and in 1981 he left the GDR.

What was the 'fourth censor'? Loest speculates that it must have been someone in the Politbüro itself. In one scene of the novel the protagonist imagines Erich Honecker coming to Leipzig and lamenting his economic problems. Possibly someone had reported this to Honecker and implied that it was a joke at his expense (which it was not), after which he may have had the novel banned.

The 1970s, which had begun so optimistically, ended sourly. Internationally things were no better: in the autumn of 1979 the Soviet Union invaded Afghanistan, whereupon, prompted by West German chancellor Helmut Schmidt, NATO agreed to modernise its nuclear weapons and the arms race began afresh. The Biermann and Heym affairs were bad publicity for the GDR. Relations between a substantial number of the GDR's writers and the state had been shattered. The most disastrous and lasting effect, however, was the wave of emigration which took place. In 1972 Peter Huchel had been allowed to move to the West. Since after his dismissal as editor of *Sinn und Form* at the end of 1962 he had been unable to publish anything in the GDR, his move may be regarded as a humanitarian act. Not so the emigrations from 1977 onwards. Judging, probably correctly, that dissident writers were of interest to the Western media only as long as they were living in the GDR, the SED was exceptionally generous in allowing writers to obtain the exit visas which were withheld from ordinary citizens. Bernd Jentzsch was in Switzerland at the time of the Biermann affair, protested independently and did not return. Reiner Kunze, Thomas Brasch, Sarah Kirsch, Jürgen Fuchs, Hans-Joachim Schädlich and Jurek Becker departed in 1977, followed in 1979 by Joachim Seyppel, Günter Kunert and Klaus Poche, then in 1980 by Klaus Schlesinger and Kurt Bartsch, and in 1981 by Erich Loest, Karl-Heinz Jakobs and Stefan Schütz. Some received favourable treatment: Jurek Becker was granted a ten-year exit visa. Others were on a somewhat shorter leash, and many, among them Loest, made it clear that they had no intention of returning. On 2 February 1981 Christa Wolf noted in her diary the growing 'list of those who are leaving' and her accompanying feelings of paralysis (*Kassandra*, p. 124). Elsewhere it is perfectly normal for writers to live abroad: many established English writers have settled in countries with a more pleasant climate; of those associated with West Germany and Austria Peter Weiss lived in Sweden, Erich Fried and Uwe Johnson in England and Peter Handke spent a number of years in Paris. For the GDR with its official insistence on the intimate connection between literature and the political and social structures under which it is composed this cannot be so. At the 1987 Writers' Congress Hermann Kant spoke conciliatory words in the direction of the exiles, encouraging at least some of them to return. Whether they will do so remains to be seen. It is a measure of the country's reserves of talent that in spite of the losses there remained the formidable figures of Christa Wolf, Volker Braun and Heiner Müller, all of whom produced substantial and controversial works in the 1980s; Günter de Bruyn, Irmtraud Morgner and Helga Schütz have continued to write, and at least one new author, Christoph Hein, has emerged to take on international significance.

Apart from their turbulent ending the 1980s were relatively unproblematical, perhaps even dull. There have been occasional scandals. Günter de Bruyn's *Neue Herrlichkeit* is an ironic account of the privileges which top party officials and their offspring enjoy and includes a horrifying portrayal of a home for old people, whose desolation and squalor matches anything to be found in the West. An extract had appeared in *Sinn und Form* in 1982. Due to appear simultaneously in East and West in 1984, it was printed and advertised in the GDR, but at the last moment the entire print run was shredded and it was published only in the West. A year later there was a change of heart and it came out at last. Helga Schubert's *Blickwinkel* appeared in West Germany in 1982 under the title *Das verbotene Zimmer*. When the East German edition eventually appeared in 1984 it lacked three of the original pieces, one of which is a straightfaced account of what the Party has meant to the narrator, inscrutable, paternalistic, always right – even when it was admitting its mistakes. Gabriele Eckart's collection of interviews *Mein Werderbuch*, some of which had already been published in *Sinn und Form*, was due to appear in 1984, but cancelled for political reasons – some of the speakers were too forthright in their statements. It was published in West Germany as *So sehe ick die Sache*. Indeed 1984 was something of a crisis year. A fresh wave of emigrations took place, this time of younger writers who were less well-known: Katja Lange-Müller, Christa Moog, Michael Bozenhard, Karsten Behlert, Volker Palma, Michael Rom and Cornelia Schleime. Gabriele Eckart joined their ranks in 1987, while Monika Maron left the following year.

Most embarrassing was the fate of Christa Wolf's *Kassandra*, due to be published in East and West Germany simultaneously in 1983. In the event it initially appeared only in the West, and although the East German edition is dated 1983 it was not distributed until February 1984. It consists of four lectures given by Wolf in West Germany at the University of Frankfurt in 1982 and the story 'Kassandra', to which the lectures relate, a retelling of the fate of the prophetess daughter of Priam of Troy. The reason for the delay was immediately and embarrassingly obvious: the third lecture, extracts from a working diary kept between May 1980 and August 1981, was labelled 'abridged version', and suspension points drew attention to the omission of eight passages. In these the author implies that both East and West are to blame for the arms race, appeals to the East to make the gesture of unilateral disarmament, refers to censorship and self-censorship on the part of East German writers, and to the rulers who cultivate hatred and self-hatred for their own ends and who are so shielded from reality that they are ignorant of what ordinary people feel. These, it seems, remain taboo areas. In a conversation of 1979 Klaus Wagenbach and Stephan Hermlin spoke of the symmetry of the rearmament of East and West Germany; Hermlin described the respective armies as preparing for civil war. The East

German version of the conversation omits this passage (Wagenbach 1979b, p. 55; Hermlin 1983, p. 408). The day the censored version of *Kassandra* appeared, RIAS in West Berlin broadcast the offending passages for East Germans to record and study at their leisure (Graves 1986).

Two lessons emerge. One is the relative impotence of the authorities to suppress uncomfortable works. The other is the changing status of literature *qua* literature in the GDR. One may safely assume that Christa Wolf would have had no difficulty over the publication of the *story*. Literature which uses a mythological or historical or fantastic mode is assimilable and not perceived as a threat, and it is no coincidence that many writers have been turning to these modes in recent years. By contrast, direct statement, journalism or documentation are more problematic, regarded as more potentially subversive. Another important development of the past decade has been the emergence of a 'documentary literature' which has not infrequently incurred official disapproval.

The debates which Honecker encouraged at the beginning of the 1970s have not on the whole been repeated. *Kassandra* provoked some shadow-boxing in *Sinn und Form*, when one of Wolf's lectures was published there before the book as a whole was available, and was subjected to a virulent attack by Wilhelm Girnus (1983a). Wolf defended herself two issues later, only to be again attacked by Girnus. But she was also defended by three indignant readers, who accused her opponent of intolerance and lack of taste. Girnus had claimed that Wolf was playing into the hands of the West by espousing the peace issue on what he regarded as their terms. This puzzled one of Wolf's supporters, as the published extract had almost nothing to say on this topic, but of course Girnus, unlike the majority of East Germans, had had access to the other lectures. Otherwise, however, the element of debate has been mainly confined to the series 'Für und wider' in *Weimarer Beiträge*, in which academics and literary journalists give their sometimes conflicting opinions on a topical text.

Kassandra, as has been indicated, relates to the peace issue which has been a dominant theme of the decade, and although some of Wolf's thoughts on the topic were censored, the authorities have been more conciliatory than might have been expected. In December 1981 Stephan Hermlin was permitted to organise a conference of writers from East and West in Berlin to discuss ways of 'furthering peace'. This meeting brought together such disparate figures as Günter Grass and Hermann Kant, Bernd Engelmann and Erik Neutsch, Stefan Heym and Dieter Noll. It was attended by Christa

Wolf, Volker Braun and Heiner Müller as well as by Helmut Sakowski and Max Walter Schulz and even two of those who had turned their backs on the GDR a few years previously, Thomas Brasch and Jurek Becker. A follow-up meeting took place in The Hague a few months later, dominated again by East and West Germans, and there was a second Berlin meeting, this time in the West of the city, in 1983. Although the proceedings of these encounters were not published in their entirety in the GDR the political counter-offensive on behalf of the official view that peace could only be guaranteed by armed strength had only a limited scope: anthologies of 'writings for peace' were brought out, for some months *Neue deutsche Literatur* included a regular section devoted to the peace issue, and writers were encouraged to go into factories to put the official line in debates with workers and apprentices. Much of the time, however, it was the second and third elevens which were being fielded.

In 1984 the GDR celebrated the thirty-fifth anniversary of its founding. While it was an occasion for a certain degree of nostalgia, a contribution in June by Klaus Höpcke, Deputy Minister of Culture with special responsibilities for literature, voiced a more alarming allusion to the past when he attacked those who believed that literature should have the function of 'criticising' society and went on to demand more works which presented 'the typical' and the 'positive hero' (1984c; see Jäger 1984). Such concepts, the standard armoury of the 1950s, had been thought long since dead. His words were echoed by Erich Honecker in September (Kleinschmid 1985a, p. 118) and by Kurt Hager in his review of cultural policies before the SED's Eleventh Congress in 1986. In the event, however, Höpcke, Honecker and Hager have been almost totally ignored. A feature of the 1980s is the gap which has grown between cultural politicians and writers. The former may admonish and exhort, they may prevent works from being published in the GDR, but they have only limited powers to mobilise writers on behalf of policies and ideas and practically none at all to influence the way they write (Tate, in Wallace, ed., 1984b, pp. 15–30; Grunenberg 1986).

In any case the cultural politicians themselves have not always been consistent. In a discussion with colleagues in 1984 Dieter Schlenstedt proposed that in order to take account of current developments in the GDR's literature the term 'socialist critical realism' might be coined, an interesting concept which combines the 'critical realism' associated with progressive writers in the West and 'socialist realism' with its positive answers to the problems presented. Writers today, Schlenstedt argued, while indubitably socialist in standpoint, were unhappy with the facilely optimistic solutions of the past (Haase et al. 1984, p. 1605). In 1986, demanding from East German writers a greater awareness of the positive qualities exhibited by the working classes in the GDR, Kurt Hager repudiated Schlenstedt's proposal (1986, p. 22), but a few months earlier he himself (1985) had been widening the concept of the 'cultural heritage' to embrace the avant-garde of the twentieth century, precisely those elements which since the GDR's beginnings had been condemned as 'decadent' or 'formalistic'. In practice this reappraisal of an alternative cultural tradition to the socialist one has been more fruitful than the appeals for socialist realism. In the last decade East German publishers have produced a succession of editions of works by the bourgeois avant-garde: James Joyce's *Ulysses* and Robert Musil's *Der Mann ohne Eigenschaften* appeared in 1980, Marcel Proust's *Der Gleichgültige* in 1981. Franz Kafka is an especially striking case. Already in 1979 Hermann Kant had reflected ruefully on the 'bizarre catastrophes' which used to threaten if Proust or Broch or Kafka were printed (1981, p. 246). Not only were a two-volume edition of Kafka's narrative works and a handsome edition of the *Amtliche Schriften* printed in 1983 and 1984 respectively, but the centenary of his birth was marked on 28 June 1983 by a one-day conference organised by the Central Institute for the History of Literature at the Academy of Sciences in Berlin and the following year the June issue of *Weimarer Beiträge* with a photograph of the writer as its frontispiece published three of the papers from the conference (Reid 1985a). The appearance of Peter Weiss's novel *Die Ästhetik des Widerstands* in the GDR in 1983 was an important impulse, inasmuch as the novel itself takes issue with the official socialist rejection of the cultural avant-garde in the 1930s, and attempts a synthesis of political and cultural revolutions (see Krenzlin 1984). In the summer of 1986 *Krapp's Last Tape* was performed at the Theater im Palast in Berlin, the first play by Samuel Beckett to be staged in the GDR, and the following year *Waiting for Godot* was produced in Dresden, thirty years after its Paris premiere. One outstanding name is still missing, that of Gottfried Benn, the guru of West German lyric poetry in the 1950s. Benn's nihilistic elitism and his temporary support of the National Socialists make him a peculiarly difficult case, and although the publishers Volk und Welt had planned an edition of his work they later abandoned the project.

The new cultural agreement between East and West Germany signed in 1985 has helped to facilitate the exchange of literature between the two states and an unprecedented number of editions of works by West German and Austrian authors were published. As a corollary to the new acceptability of elitist avant-garde literature the old concept of the unity of socialist literature has been implicitly abandoned. Whereas in the past the notion of the 'popularity' of literature had denied that there could be any difference in a socialist society between literature for an elite and literature for the masses such as existed under capitalism, now conferences are held and papers written on such forms of popular literature as the detective story, science fiction and the novelette (Bloss 1986; Simon and Spittel 1982).

In other ways, too, there has been a more conciliatory approach by the authorities. A number of works which were banned during the clamp-down at the end of 1965 have been revived. Peter Hacks's *Moritz Tassow* is now regularly in the repertoire of the GDR's theatres. Heiner Müller's *Philoktet*, first published in 1965, was premiered in 1977, *Der Bau*, which had specifically incurred the wrath of the Party, followed in 1980, an event which inspired Martin Linzer to comment ironically on the tactics of 'testing plays for their classical qualities by careful storage'[13] (1980, p. 9). *Sinn und Form* marked the death of its one-time editor Peter Huchel with the publication of four of his poems in 1982, the first to be published in twenty years by the man who was arguably the GDR's greatest poet. In the same year Hanns Eisler's *Johann Faustus* was performed for the first time, thirty years after it had aroused the hostility of the cultural establishment for its unorthodox presentation of a national hero. Even Volker Braun's *Unvollendete Geschichte* has been republished. The wooing of the émigrés has already been touched on. Both Jurek Becker and Klaus Schlesinger have had recent works published in the GDR, although they are living elsewhere. The play *Mercedes* by Thomas Brasch has been performed in Schwerin, and the author interviewed for *Sinn und Form*. The first poems by Günter Kunert to be published in the GDR since his departure in 1979 were printed by the same journal in 1987 and a collection of his recent poems appeared in 1989.

The 'taboos' have certainly become fewer. The prudishness of early GDR literature has gone; sensuality, the erotic are accepted features of human life and although pornography, however one defines it, is absent from the GDR's bookstalls, nude scenes in films had become by 1981 so prevalent that protests were registered (Kersten 1981, p. 232). The publication of Günter Grass's *Die Blechtrommel*, a novel which in its time perturbed West German cultural bureaucrats sufficiently for them to retract the prize they had awarded its author, suggests that attitudes have considerably relaxed. Homosexuality and lesbianism are topics which can openly be discussed. What remains problematical is anything which touches on political topics and can in any way be regarded as calling in question the role of the ruling SED.

As we saw in the case of *Die neuen Leiden des jungen W.*, it is sometimes possible to follow the vagaries of cultural policies by comparing the first version of a text with subsequent versions. In 1965 in *Neue deutsche Literatur* under the title 'Rummelplatz' Werner Bräunig published a chapter from a long novel he was working on. Set in the early years of the GDR, part of it portrayed a drunken orgy at a fairground in which workers at the Wismut uranium mines in the south of the GDR were involved. This extract was attacked by Erich Honecker at the SED's December meeting in the same year for its alleged obscenities and for giving a distorted picture of the early years of the GDR. Bräunig never fully recovered from the attacks. He, after all, had coined the slogan 'Greif zur Feder, Kumpel' ('Reach for your pen, mate!') for the Bitterfeld conference of 1959 and he regarded himself as a loyal socialist. He died in 1976.

Five years later an anthology of his writings was brought out, containing substantial passages from the incomplete novel and including a revised version of the 'Rummelplatz' chapter. Two changes are particularly interesting, one comic, the other less so. The original did indeed contain an obscene anecdote, the one which Honecker found objectionable. The men are discussing how to avoid contracting VD; one of them declares: 'That's quite easy. First I always go for it with my tobacco finger. If she winces there the frigate's leaking'[14] ('Rummelplatz', p. 9). In the revised version the passage has become 'an obscenity, completely beyond the pale, you can't tell it in front of grown-up women and daughters for example, so we'll leave it out'[15] (*Ein Kranich am Himmel*, p. 60). The 'grown-up women and daughters' were, of course, in reality the men of the Politbüro; this was Bräunig's revenge. Today such an alteration would almost certainly not be required. The other major change, however, relates to the presentation of the Soviet Union. All pejorative references to Russian soldiers have been excised, but in particular the sentence: 'The Wismut is a state within the state and vodka is its national beverage'[16] ('Rummelplatz', p. 8). The GDR is notoriously short of raw materials; its one major asset is uranium; but the entire uranium output, mined by East German workers for the Wismut company, has gone to the Soviet Union (Zimmermann, ed., 1985, pp. 1399–400). Bräunig's ironic reference to the Soviet Union as controlling a 'state within the state' was thus provocative and had to be removed.

It is appropriate to conclude this chapter with an examination of relations between the GDR and the Soviet Union, which have in general been surrounded by taboos. The SED has traditionally been most wary of offending its 'big brother' in Moscow, the first socialist state, a model for the GDR to copy in all areas, and the guarantor of the GDR's own socialism with a large military presence and a willingness to intervene, as demonstrated in 1956 in Hungary and 1968 in Czechoslovakia. To what extent the Soviet authorities take an interest in East German cultural policies is unclear. The East Germans may well be unnecessarily timid. At any rate the taboos are being gradually dismantled. The 1961 play *Die Physiker* by the Swiss dramatist Friedrich Dürrenmatt confronts a Soviet agent and an American agent, both of whom are endeavouring to uncover the secrets of the nuclear physicist Möbius. The play was evidently considered harmless enough by the Soviet authorities to be performed in Moscow as early as 1964. In the GDR, however, although most of Dürrenmatt's other plays had been produced, it was not staged until 1977 (see Reid 1984a).

For many years the Soviet armies which invaded Germany in 1945 were portrayed as liberators, heroes, chivalrous and helpful. While there can be no question that they did indeed liberate Germany from fascism, it is now possible to point out that, as Jürgen Kuczynski puts it, they were also 'human beings' with human weaknesses (1980, p. 157). In Hermann Kant's *Das Impressum*, for example, we read of Gerhard Rikow, a prisoner of the Russians at the end of the war, who scribbles a note to his parents on a scrap of cardboard, and to the protracted merriment of his cynical fellow-prisoners gives it to one of the guards; but the message does arrive. In Eberhard Panitz's 1974 novel *Die unheilige Sophia* incidents of Soviet atrocities at the end of the war are discovered to have been perpetrated by Germans in disguise. But Christa Wolf's *Kindheitsmuster* (1976) shows German women nightly terrorised by drunken Soviet soldiers, the narrator of Werner Heiduczek's *Tod am Meer* (1979) cannot forget the rapings, and in the third volume of Erwin Strittmater's *Der Wundertäter* (1980) a young German girl is raped to death by three young soldiers. These works are in no sense anti-Soviet propaganda. On the contrary, Strittmatter emphasises the even more barbaric behaviour of the Germans in the Soviet Union, and Heiduczek uses the incident to condemn war in general through the words of a Soviet writer: 'Greeks or Romans, Osmans or Chinese, Americans or Russians, British, French or Germans, send them to war and there will be murder, robbery, looting and rape. I find it stupid to place a man in the position of an animal and then meditate on his immorality'[17] (p. 77).

Initially Kurt Hager dismissed Mikhail Gorbachev's new policies by saying that when one's neighbour redecorated his living-room, one did not have to follow suit (1987, p. 656). The statement itself indicated a degree of self-assurance with regard to the Soviet Union. Even before the autumn of 1989, however, *glasnost* was breaking out in the literary if not in the political sphere. The title of Volker Braun's play *Die Übergangsgesellschaft* seemed symptomatic: a society in transition. Loest's 'third censor' has officially been abolished. The Tenth Congress of the Writers' Union, held in November 1987, was a much more open and conciliatory affair than its two predecessors had been. A paper by Christoph Hein on the absurdities of censorship provoked a lively discussion. And although while the Congress was in session the offices of part of the unofficial peace movement were raided and some representatives of the movement expelled to the West, all the speeches and contributions made at the meeting have been published. In an article on his early work as editor of *Neue deutsche Literatur*, Günther Deicke has referred frankly and openly to the mistakes of the past in the area of cultural policies; the special issue on the death of Stalin made 'embarrassing reading', especially in view of the 'corrections of contemporary historiography being undertaken in Gorbachev's programme of glasnost' (1988, p. 338); and 'it was precisely those writers who suffered the most violent official attacks (Kunert, Kirsch, Bieler, Biermann, Christa Wolf, Heiner Müller) who avoided the latent danger of provincialism and created works that aroused attention on the international stage'[18] (p. 341). That even Wolf Biermann thus appears to be on the road to rehabilitation is not the least of the current uncertainties. There have been false dawns in the past and it would be unwise to speculate on the future. Three points may perhaps be made. Firstly, however independent of Moscow the GDR's writers and politicians may pretend to be, the fate of the GDR's literature will depend in large measure on the success or otherwise of Gorbachev's reforms. Secondly, freedom in the cultural sphere is not necessarily linked to democratic freedoms in general. Still one of the most orthodoxly authoritarian states of Eastern Europe, the GDR's rulers are clearly apprehensive about developments in Hungary and Poland, which are viewed as a threat not only to socialism but to the very existence of the GDR itself, which, unlike these other countries, could easily be swallowed up by its Western neighbour. The recent cultural liberalisation may well be an attempt to stave off political dissent. And finally, *pace* Höpcke, it seems most unlikely that there will ever be a return to the dogmatic days of socialist realism and the 'struggle

Writers, Politicians and Taboos

against formalism'. Just how far the GDR's writers have moved in the aesthetic sphere away from these early positions, is the subject of the chapter which follows.

Notes

1. Abgelehnt! – Wie? Ihr sagt? – Wir nicht... – Wer denn? – Still doch, niemand. / Doch die Verhältnisse... – Ach. Arbeiten sie schon allein.
2. Minsk ist eine der langweiligsten Städte der Welt.
3. Das ist das langweiligste Land der Erde.
4. offenherzigen, sachlichen, schöpferischen Meinungsstreit / nicht nur die richtigen, unserer sozialistischen Gesellschaft nützlichen Themen..., sondern auch die ganze Breite und Vielfalt der neuen Lebensäußerungen / schöpferische Suche nach neuen Formen.
5. Wenn man von der festen Position des Sozialismus ausgeht, kann es meines Erachtens auf dem Gebiet von Kunst und Literatur keine Tabus geben. Das betrifft sowohl die Fragen der inhaltlichen Gestaltung als auch des Stils...
6. eine Zeit mit starken demokratischen Tendenzen, mit wachsendem kritischem Bewußtsein, in die wir alle große Erwartungen gesetzt hatten. Ich kann sagen, daß ich mich in keinem anderen Land so frei hätte fühlen können wie in diesen frühen siebziger Jahren, wenn ich unter der Freiheit eines Schriftstellers die Freiheit gegenüber seinen Stoffen, seinen Gegenständen verstehe – und natürlich mit der Möglichkeit, seine Bücher zu publizieren. Ich glaube, ich irre mich nicht, wenn ich sage, die Erwartungen beherrschten seinerzeit beinahe die *ganze* Gesellschaft, also unten wie oben...
7. Der sozialistische Realismus ist die wahrheitsgetreue, historisch-konkrete Darstellung der Wirklichkeit in ihrer revolutionären Entwicklung.
8. Denn ich hatte mir einreden lassen, daß ein Roman Entwicklungsroman sein, positiv enden und Totalität geben müsse.
9. einer der Selbstbefreiung..., des Selbstverständnisses, der Selbstverwirklichung, einer der einzig möglichen Individuation, nämlich der geglückten Identitätsfindung.
10. Zum erstenmal haben die unter die Tischdecke geguckt! Sonst sieht alles immer von oben so schön glatt aus und so schön weiß! Die haben mal drunter geguckt und haben das mal nach oben geholt, sozusagen umgedreht.... Er [Edgar] will eben nicht immer alles nach Plan machen. Bei uns ist alles zu sehr im voraus organisiert, die Ausbildung, der ganze Lebensweg.
11. schwer berechenbare öffentliche Meinung und die Massenwirksamkeit im Kino.
12. Denn ein Tabu gibt es gewiß: die Frage der Macht und der führenden Rolle der Partei.
13. Stücke durch sorgfältiges Ablagern auf ihre Klassizität zu überprüfen.
14. Das ist ganz einfach. Zuerst gehe ich immer mit dem Tabakfinger ran. Wenn sie da zuckt, ist die Fregatte leck.
15. eine Zote..., die war jenseits aller Kritik, die kann nicht zugemutet werden erwachsenen Frauen und Töchtern etwa, die lassen wir also aus.
16. Die Wismut ist ein Staat im Staate, und der Wodka ist ihr Nationalgetränk.
17. Ob Griechen oder Römer, Osmanen oder Chinesen, Amerikaner oder Russen, Engländer, Franzosen oder Deutsche, schick sie in den Krieg, und es wird Mord

geben, Raub, Plünderung und Vergewaltigung. Ich finde es dumm, den Menschen in den Zustand des Tieres zu versetzen und dann über seine Unmoral zu meditieren.

18. Korrekturen der gegenwärtigen Geschichtsschreibung unter Gorbatschows Programm von Glasnost. . . . Es waren gerade die am heftigsten unter offizielle Kritik geratenen Schriftsteller (Kunert, Kirsch, Bieler, Biermann, Christa Wolf, Heiner Müller), die so der latenten Gefahr des Provinzialismus entschlüpften und Werke schufen, die auf der internationalen Szene Aufsehen erregten.

−3−

Beyond Formalism

> A story? Something solid, tangible, like a jug with two handles, to be grasped and drunk out of?
> A vision perhaps, if you understand what I mean.[1]
> (Christa Wolf, 'Juninachmittag')

The most systematic account of the changes which took place in the GDR's fiction in the course of the 1970s is by Peter Weisbrod (1980). His findings may be summed up as follows. Where earlier writers, after Lukács, attempted to create totality by means of the 'typical', in the 1970s the unique individual becomes the focus of interest. Instead of social conflicts, in whose resolution the individual becomes integrated with society, private topics, those of love, personal identity, alienation, come to the fore. Political and social issues such as responsibility for the catastrophes of the Third Reich or for the construction of socialism in the new German state are treated in terms of the way they impinge on the individual. Social institutions are criticised, implicitly or explicitly, in terms of the extent to which they stifle the development of the individual personality. Fantasy is given a fresh role in literature, and literature itself becomes a theme. New social groupings are the subject of attention: instead of the male working-class heroes of the past, increasing attention is devoted to women, artists, teenagers, even children. The individual is no longer defined by class, whether positively or negatively. Conflicts tend to be individual, rather than class-based, and are frequently left unresolved. The traditional 'omniscient' narrator loses his/her dominant status and is replaced by a necessarily unreliable personal narrator or by a network of varying viewpoints. The through-going story-line is dissolved in favour of montage; episodic narration, in turn, is often associated with essayistic reflection. Finally, the conventional literary language of the past is frequently abandoned in favour of dialect, slang or irony. These findings are confirmed by most of the GDR's own scholars (Schlenstedt 1979; Schuhmann 1980; Kaufmann 1981).

It is not the intention here to go over the same ground as Weisbrod has done. What will be stressed is the high degree of aesthetic self-consciousness which is illustrated in the GDR's fiction of the past twenty years. Prior to the late 1960s literature was regarded largely as a means to an end, the end being the increasing of productivity or the creation of a socialist national identity. Formalism, in the words of the SED's declaration of 1951, was the denial that the decisive meaning of art lay in its content; the preoccupation with form at the expense of content was viewed as anti-humanist and anti-democratic (Schubbe, ed., 1972, p. 179). Since the later 1960s, however, literature has been increasingly concerned with itself, questioning its own premises, methods, even authors. When in 1971 Honecker encouraged writers to experiment with new techniques, he was giving official sanction to what had been already happening for some time. Writing is itself the theme. This, however, is not merely navel-gazing, a concern with art for art's sake. Rather, it is a sign of the continued high status held by art in the GDR and of new, more personal functions allotted to it. However, it also has social, even political connotations which ensure that the interaction of art and society remains one of the distinctive aspects of the GDR's literature.

This can be illustrated by Christa Wolf's short story 'Juninachmittag', which was first published in 1967, and whose opening programmatic words form the epigraph to this chapter. 'Tell me a story' is the plea of a child to its parent, and the narrator of 'Juninachmittag' is a mother, sitting in her suburban garden on a Sunday afternoon, trying to read but being constantly interrupted by her two children, her husband, aircraft overhead and passing neighbours. The request for a 'story' here, however, comes from an adult stranger, as the formal mode of address makes clear. This person wishes literature to be no more than a vessel out of which a useful, tangible message may be taken. It was Brecht who described the bourgeois theatre of the interwar years as 'culinary theatre', where the spectator ingested passively; epic theatre, by contrast, was to 'activate' the audience's energies. Christa Wolf is subtly allying herself with the socialist writer Brecht against the cultural establishment's demand for socialist realism. The narrator is not prepared to fulfil this demand. Instead she is offering a 'vision', tentatively at first, for she is not sure that the reader will understand her.

At once a relationship is established between two persons, a speaker and a listener. What is the nature of this relationship? The 'vision' which follows is one which introduces numerous patterns of authority. The narrator's husband is pinching out the sideshoots on his tomato plants, the neighbour is engaged in a fruitless battle against the dandelion seeds invading his tidy, weedless plot. Civilisation is being imposed on nature. The frontier between East and West, near which the narrator's garden is situated, is a political assertion of authority. During the afternoon the family play a word game; they each have to say the first compound noun that comes into their heads and then experiment by combining the elements of these words into absurd and entertaining neologisms. Another neighbour joins in, an engineer, the embodiment of technological, rational man. But he cannot switch off his consciousness and the game is spoiled. Rationality insists on imposing its authority on spontaneity. At the centre, there is the relationship between the mother and her daughters, one in which the adult is anxious for the wellbeing of her children but at the same time wishes them to grow naturally and spontaneously. This mother is not authoritarian; indeed she is not even an authority on the plants growing in her own garden or on the creatures which live there, about which the younger child seems to know far more. And it is this relationship between mother and child which is mirrored in the relationship between narrator and narratee. Here is no authoritarian, omniscient guide and mentor, to whom the reader merely has to listen and all will be revealed. A key feature of Wolf's style from 'Juninachmittag' onwards is to be the use of unanswered questions rather than authoritative statements, demanding the reader's cooperation in the creative act. Our active participation is required in other respects too. The stream of consciousness technique employed by Christa Wolf requires us to distinguish between the statements made to us and those made to the narrator's family, to work out the context of the abrupt breaks in the narrative for ourselves.

'Juninachmittag' is one of the texts adduced by Wolfgang Emmerich in support of his argument that since the late 1960s the GDR's fiction has, with modifications, undergone a process similar to that which West European fiction underwent between 1910 and 1930 and which is usually termed 'modernism' (Hohendahl and Herminghouse, eds., 1983, pp. 153–92). Its development is characterised, Emmerich claims, by the rejection of a through-going story-line, the subjectivisation of time, scepticism with regard to traditional views of the individual personality, and a radical change in the narrator's relation to his or her audience. Writing some years earlier, the GDR critic Kurt Batt had contrasted East and West German fiction: the latter had 'executed' the narrator (1974) and was monological; in a representative East German story such as Anna Seghers's *Überfahrt*, however, narration appeared 'not as a speaking-to-oneself, bordering on silence, but as communication requiring a partner'[2] (1980, p. 322). Since the early 1970s, according to Emmerich, this assertion can no longer be upheld. The narrators to be found in the GDR's recent fiction are no longer able to present model experiences for their readers to learn from. They have abandoned 'dialogical, communicative narration' and reached the position of their West German counterparts, correctly diagnosed by Batt as one of monologising quasi-silence. In a review article of 1986 the GDR critic Rüdiger Bernhardt took issue with Emmerich's thesis. Admitting that it was an accurate description of a number of works written by authors of the younger generation, he denied that it could be generalised in this way. On the contrary Bernhardt claimed to find in the 1980s evidence of an increasing tendency towards 'authorial' narration in the GDR's fiction, where the 1970s had been dominated by personalised narrative techniques. Furthermore, inasmuch as he treated the reader as a 'partner', the authorial narrator had a social function, implying that the dialogical nature of the GDR's fiction was very much alive.

Bernhardt's postulation of a 'partnership' between reader and narrator is misleading. The narrators he quotes are 'authorities'; the reader is more of a pupil than a partner. This would, if it were true, represent a regression behind the position diagnosed by Dieter Schlenstedt a few years earlier: whereas in the GDR's earlier fiction the writer was 'the embodiment of history', today his text is an 'offer, whose value is decided only through the participation of the readers'[3] (1979, pp. 40–1). But Emmerich's argument is equally difficult to follow. In 'Juninachmittag', for example, it is true that, as we have seen, the narrator is no reliable guide for the reader, but to suggest that this makes it an example of 'monological' writing is perverse. Wolf's writing always implies an addressee, sometimes personalised, as with the brother in *Störfall*, more usually an implied reader who is invited to engage in 'dialogue', to seek answers to the questions posed by a narrator. The story *Kassandra* is her most monological text, but even then it is embedded in a series of essays with explicit addressees. When, using the analogy of Volker Braun's *Unvollendete Geschichte*, Emmerich proceeds to characterise many of the stories written in the 1970s as 'unfinished', he is implicitly admitting the appeal to the reader to find an ending, just as Brecht's theatre, itself produced by the same 'modernist' years of the first half of the twentieth century, encourages its audience in the words of the epilogue to *Der gute Mensch von Sezuan* to 'find an ending for itself' (vol. 4, p. 1607). Contrary to Emmerich's thesis, a distinctive feature of the GDR's literature remains its continued belief that literature is relevant and important and that it can activate the reader in a meaningful way.

That reading is important is already mirrored in 'Juninachmittag'. The narrator is reading a book, and it is striking, as Martin Watson has shown, how many figures in the GDR's fiction are characterised by their reading habits (1987, pp. 321–95). Wolf's essay 'Lesen und Schreiben', its title giving equal weight to reading and writing, was written a year after the story. In one passage of the essay Wolf tries to imagine a world without books: no folk-tales, no Homeric epics, no *Werther*, no *Madame Bovary*, no *Anna Karenina*. She remembers the National Socialist attempt to isolate the German people from the literature of the outside world and the resulting stunting of the Germans' sensibility. A world without books would be a world of increasing barbarity. More than this, without the books she has read, she would not be what she is; in a sense it is reading that constitutes the personality, reading that enables one to understand oneself, to sharpen one's moral sensitivity, to train one's psychic apparatus.

But, the essay asks, has fiction not lost its place in a world in which the writer's traditional functions have been taken over by professionals: journalists, historians, scientists, technologists, filmmakers? The answer is that it *would* be superfluous if it were to continue to be written in the old-fashioned style of a Balzac. Plot, character, linear time, always conventions but useful in their time, have become clichés. Reality itself is no longer the surface reality of the nineteenth century – science has seen to that. Realism cannot therefore content itself with reproducing the surfaces of things. To the three dimensions of surface reality the writer of prose fiction can add a fourth, the 'coordinate of depth', the 'dimension of the author'. Wolf appears to makes no distinction between author and narrator. In her own practice, especially in *Nachdenken über Christa T.* and *Kindheitsmuster*, the blurring of the distinction is an essential part of her technique. But in any case she is not referring to the 'omniscient' narrator of conventional fiction, who for Lukács was essential to guide the reader. For Wolf it is only when reality can no longer be taken for granted that one begins to write. Prose fiction, she claims, should try to become unfilmable. This is an interesting assertion in view of the success of the film of her first novel, *Der geteilte Himmel*, and one which implies a rejection of the early work. Writing is inextricably bound up with the individual's imagination, the individual's subjective vision of reality, which has to be conveyed with the greatest exactitude. Imaginative literature is a 'playing with open possibilities'[4] (1987, p. 478), in that sense it is therefore experimental. The phrase which Wolf later coined for this form of writing is 'subjective authenticity'[5] (1987, p. 781).

Wolf is fighting on two fronts. In the first place, although she does not use the term, she is rejecting socialist realism. Balzac was one of Lukács's chief witnesses; he is now out of date. When she suggests that one should leave it to mirrors to 'reflect', as they cannot do anything else, she is clearly dismissing Lukács's demand that literature 'reflect' reality. Indeed the opening words of the essay echo some of the arguments put forward by Seghers and Brecht in their debates with Lukács in the 1930s: 'The need to write in a new way follows, albeit later, a new way of being in the world'[6] (1987, p. 463). 'Lesen und Schreiben' belongs in many ways to the main stream of European modernism. One is reminded in particular of Virginia Woolf's early essay 'Modern Fiction', which repudiates the realism of Arnold Bennett and H.G. Wells in the name of the way in which the mind actually works. But Wolf also explicitly rejects the *nouveau roman* of Alain Robbe-Grillet and therefore some of the more extreme manifestations of the West European avant-garde.

Robbe-Grillet, disagreeing with Sartre, declared that literature could not influence life, that the writer's *engagement* was a nonsense. This, for Wolf, is capitulation. His attempt to excise the narrator from his fiction is 'inhuman'. Western scepticism denies the importance of the individual, indeed in some cases denies the existence of the individual, and thus, Wolf asserts, is related to fascism. 'Lesen und Schreiben' was written in 1968, the year in which in West Germany Hans Magnus Enzensberger's *Kursbuch* spectacularly proclaimed that imaginative literature was dead because it was irrelevant to the class struggle. Writers should engage rather in documentation, he claimed, precisely one of the activities Wolf dismisses. Wolf's poetics are more akin to those of Heinrich Böll, who in 1960 had likewise attacked the *nouveau roman* (1979, pp. 355–7) and who sought to combine realism with fantasy, or even with those of the young Peter Handke, who in an essay of 1968 spoke of literature as 'a means whereby one's consciousness does not become *wider* but *more exact*, a means to make one more sensitive, to irritate, to activate, a means to come into the world'[7] (1969, p. 306). What gives Wolf's essay its East German dimension is her insistence that not only does her view of literature not contradict the premises of socialism, but that it is only in a socialist society that they can be properly fulfilled, since it is only such a society which enables individuals to unfold their personality. Socialism is a stage in which humanity reaches maturity. It is the function of literature to support this process, to enable individual citizens to become autonomous beings, to help them to find self-realisation. The reader, too, is an adult. Conventional literature merely confirms what one already knows, enabling one to live 'as a quotation' (1987, p. 483). By writing in accordance with her personal experiences, the author is giving her readers the self-confidence to come to terms with theirs.

'Lesen und Schreiben' was not published until 1971. But the novel *Nachdenken über Christa T.*, of which the essay was a justification, was published in 1968, although, as we have seen, its reception was generally hostile. In the essay Wolf distanced herself from the notion that the writer is writing 'for all' (p. 499). Her novel is a complex biographical essay which presupposes a sophisticated reader able to find a path through a maze of analepses and prolepses, to distinguish between various focalisers who at times merge into one another, to pick out a host of allusions to other works of literature, and all without the crutch of a conventional plot. Self-realisation is its central topic, as the motto, a quotation from Johannes R. Becher, the GDR's first Minister of Culture makes clear: 'What is it, this coming-to-oneself?'[8] When Christa T. first encounters the new socialist pamphlets by Gorky and Makarenko and others she is convinced that 'this is the road to the self'[9] (p. 33); and that socialism is the prerequisite for self-realisation is made equally clear by the novel's final words, 'When if not now?',[10] taking up the question posed by Christa T. in June 1953 when she began to have doubts about the way in which socialism was developing. When *will* the individual find fulfilment if not today under socialism?

Nachdenken über Christa T. was problematical because of the often negative references to the GDR's development and its failure to provide a positive alternative to a non-conforming protagonist whose last years are overshadowed by the struggle against leukaemia. The optimists, the 'shining heroes' of the newpapers, are shown to be made of cardboard, the healthy successes are opportunists. Disease and death are central motifs of Romantic and post-Romantic literature down to Thomas Mann (Weigand 1933, pp. 39–58); Goethe had declared that Romanticism represented that which was unhealthy, classicism that which was healthy, and Weimar classicism was still the official model in the GDR. Death by leukaemia was a decadent, morbid, unsuitable topic for socialist literature, even if one rejects the notion expressed by the West German reviewer Reich-Ranicki that leukaemia is a metaphor for actually existing socialism (1979, p. 208). Reich-Ranicki and Wolf's GDR critics overlooked the comment that Christa T. was 'born too soon' and that 'before long people won't still be dying of this disease'[11] (p. 177). It is a comment which undermines a further criticism of the novel, that it is hostile to science (Haase 1969, p. 182). Science is still imperfect, but it is progressing. The GDR is a

–67–

society in transition, but it will, it must move on to a stage in which individual and collective interests can be harmonised.

Nachdenken über Christa T. is also a novel about the writing of a novel. How does one present individuality in words, since words themselves by generalising deny individuality? The relation between the individual and the collective, the central theme of so much socialist fiction, is reflected on the aesthetic level too. One way of dealing with the problem is to thematise it, raising the readers' consciousness so that they may make the necessary allowances. In her preamble the narrator registers her alarm at the way she is able to 'dispose' of her dead friend, to fix her into a static image. Later she makes a connection between 'dichten', meaning to write fiction, and 'dicht machen', meaning to make watertight (pp. 20, 23). This 'fixing' process is identical with death (p. 171). Instead she wishes the readers to continue her friend's life, allowing her to grow old as she could not in reality. Hence the avoidance of the mechanisms of the traditional novel, what in her essay Wolf called 'divine mechanisms', an association with the *deus ex machina* of ancient tragedy. Here is no omniscient narrator; on the contrary we are assured again and again that there are blank spaces in the life of Christa T. How much easier it would be, the narrator reflects, if her subject-matter were pure fiction and therefore unambiguous (p. 45). There is no plot, no love-triangle other than a highly self-conscious, literary affair with a young forester. The narrator is remembering her friend, asking what can be learned from her life for the future, reminding readers of human potential. To write is 'to furnish examples' (p. 45). Christa T. was an example without being exemplary; she is no heroine, no model to be imitated (p. 46). Memory links past, present and future almost randomly. Time therefore is treated in a non-linear fashion with constant switches between these temporal modes. The episodic narrative is held together by the personality of the narrator, but also by the use of leitmotivs: a red and white ball running along the beach, gestures which have lodged in the narrator's memory, and above all the negative experiences of a false collective embodied in the recollections of a cat being killed, a magpie's nest being destroyed and a toad having its head bitten off. There is also a highly individualistic questioning of language itself. The well-adjusted conformists have no scruples about such words as 'completely' (p. 40) or 'adapting' (p. 109). Political slogans, not false in themselves, become a substitute for reality (pp. 56–7). The narrator tests the secret implications of words (and the skills of the translator!) when, like the family of 'Juninachmittag', she explores the potential of German compound nouns and verbs. Her opening sentence, 'Nachdenken, ihr nach-denken', means something like 'Reflect on her, follow her in her thought processes'. Christa T. herself is 'afraid of imprecise, inept words' (p. 166), and this hampers her in her writing.

For there are two writers in the novel, the narrator and the subject of the narrative. Writing was for Christa T. an entirely private affair. We are given samples of her writing from time to time: poems, diaries, letters, stories, descriptions. They do not appear to have been intended for publication, rather they were a means whereby their author could articulate herself and find a relationship with the world around her. 'To think that I can only cope with things by writing!'[12] she self-reproachfully confides to her diary (p. 36). Writing as pure self-expression without thought of a reader is a wholly individualistic attitude to art, one respected, if not shared, by the narrator.

In a preview of the novel Wolf described how in the course of writing the relation between narrator and protagonist became central to the work (1987, p. 32). *Nachdenken über Christa T.* belongs to a German literary tradition of the biographical novel, in which a conventional, even philistine narrator tells the life story of a much more gifted but unconventional nonconformist. The best known example is Thomas Mann's *Doktor Faustus*, but earlier examples include novels by the nineteenth-century writer Wilhelm Raabe. Therese Hörnigk suggests that the narrator is not well defined (in Münz-Koenen, ed., 1987, pp. 182–3); but reading between the lines we discover a number of implications, most of them negative. The narrator's life and that of her friend run parallel: school, university, marriage, children. She was an unthinking admirer of her Nazi teacher until the newcomer Christa T. opened her eyes. In the new socialist society she was part of the collective: 'For we were fully occupied with making ourselves unassailable ... Not only to admit into our minds nothing alien – and all sorts of things we considered alien! – also to let nothing alien emerge inside ourselves, and if it did – a doubt, a suspicion, observations, questions – then not to let is show'[13] (p. 52).

Christa T., while wishing the same, was more sceptical. The narrator's marriage is a conventional one, as far as we know, and if the key to health is to conform (p. 72), the healthy narrator is a conformist. But the narrator is also a writer and, unlike her friend, a successful one. The evidence is the book itself. Her writing is not merely self-expression, rather it is an attempt to communicate the essence of one human being, Christa T., to another, the reader. And she, the narrator, mediator between reader and Christa T., the one who is 'reflecting' on Christa T., has been influenced by her protagonist. She 'needs' her, and by the end of the novel she can use her friend's words as if they were her own: 'When, if not now?'

If *Nachdenken über Christa T.* is itself about writing, then it belongs in the context of twentieth-century modernist literature. One tendency of this feature is to stress literature's autonomy. The novel becomes self-reflecting, complete in itself, 'different' from 'real life', and for radical modernist theories of modernity it is this 'difference' which gives literature its value. Nothing could be further removed from socialist realism. Clearly Wolf's novel is not an example of literature of either kind. For it is also about reading. Like the act of writing, the act of reading is thematised throughout in the numerous allusions to other works of literature, which assume that the reader is acquainted with such diverse texts as Sophie La Roche's *Das Fräulein von Sternheim*, Gustave Flaubert's *Madame Bovary* and Thomas Mann's *Tonio Kröger*. The students discussing *Kabale und Liebe* suddenly find their own love lives contradicting the officially sanctioned interpretation of Schiller's play, while Christa T.'s dissertation on Theodor Storm finds contemporary relevance in a minor nineteenth-century author. In the world of this novel reading is at least as important an aspect of human life as any other, something which only the worst examples of philistine conformism deny. The narrator is not the author. The former insists throughout that Christa T. was a historical personage. The *author*, signing herself 'C.W.', assures us in her preface that 'Christa T. is a fictional character'. To the narrator of the novel there corresponds a narratee, just as to the author there corresponds an implied reader. Although they are not identical – the reader, unlike the narratee, must assume the fictionality of Christa T. – it is probably not very useful to separate them. Who is the implied reader of *Christa T.*? To whom are the numerous questions of the novel addressed? When the narrator, referring to her friend, declares 'we need her' (p. 8) she implies a collective readership, one in which the values of the narrator are shared by her readers. The implied reader is clearly a socialist, sympathetic to the ideal if not the reality of the GDR state. In this sense, too, *Nachdenken über Christa T.* is a GDR novel.

An implied collective readership is one of the most distinctive features of GDR fiction. It is to be found again, for example, in Plenzdorf's *Die neuen Leiden des jungen W.*, whose youthful protagonist and part-narrator is constantly addressing his readers, anxious that they should not misunderstand what is going on. Most commonly, however, it is implied in the use of present-tense narrative. The present tense is very common in East German fiction which it might almost be taken to characterise in general. Examples taken almost at random include Klaus Schlesinger's *Alte Filme*, Jurek Becker's *Irreführung der Behörden*, Erich Köhler's *Der Krott*, Wolf's *Kein Ort. Nirgends*, Manfred Pieske's *Schnauzer*, Uwe Saeger's *Nöhr* and *Warten auf Schnee*, Andreas Montag's *Karl der Große* and numerous shorter narratives by many other writers. This is not a new development in the GDR's writing; it is the tense, for example, of Johannes Bobrowski's *Levins Mühle* and before that of large sections of Wolf's *Der geteilte Himmel* and Erwin Strittmatter's *Ole Bienkopp*. The historic present, which has been condemned as artificial if used at length (Hamburger 1951, p. 6), is traditionally associated with the attempt to convey immediacy. In the GDR's literature, however, its function is more to create a feeling of intimacy between author and reader, narrator and narratee. The present tense is the most important colloquial tense, the tense used when one person is speaking to another, frequently even when speaking of past events. In it the populist orientation of traditional socialist realism lives on.

In this context therefore Christoph Hein's novella *Der fremde Freund* appears radically different. Six months after the funeral of her 'stranger friend' Henry, Claudia, the narrator, is recounting the events of the year of their liaison. But there is nowhere any evidence for the presence of a recipient of her story. Rather it seems to be directed entirely to herself, just as the photographs she takes in her spare time are not for publication and are put away in a drawer after they have been developed and printed. *Der fremde Freund* is almost unique in East German fiction in its portrayal of a complete lack of human solidarity and community. Its narrative stance underlines this lack. Here, if anywhere, the 'monological' literature of which Emmerich speaks is to be found. Hein has described the 'omniscient' narrator of the GDR's early novels as a 'signpost' indicating the direction to be followed. He, by contrast, could not point the way ahead, which he knew no more than his reader. And yet he believes in what he calls 'the dialogical principle in literature', his reader being a 'partner' who would continue where the writer left off (Jachimczak 1988, pp. 347–9). 'Dialogue' here is one between equals.

The influence of *Nachdenken über Christa T.* can scarcely be overstated. The conservative riposte to Wolf's novel, *Auf der Suche nach Gatt* by Erik Neutsch, appeared in 1973. Neutsch's work bears many of the hallmarks of traditional socialist realism. Gatt is a convinced socialist but one given to outbursts of impetuosity which cause him to transgress party discipline. His wife leaves him when his dogmatism prevents him from giving her the trust and support she needs, he loses his posts as a journalist and party secretary because of his inability to keep up with the times; finally he wins back both his wife and his job by dint of his unstinting socialist commitment. Gatt is 'exemplary' as Christa T. could never be. He, too, is sickly, but his illness is the after-effects of bullet-wounds he suffered in a heroic attempt to arrest the murderers of a policeman during what is presented as the attempted putsch on 17 June 1953. Christa T., by contrast, was filled with doubts around the same time. Near the beginning of the novel there is a direct allusion to Wolf's work. Wolf's narrator had defended the naive idealism of the early years with the words: 'Once in one's life, at the right time, one ought to have believed in the impossible'[14] (p. 53). Neutsch's narrator has 'recently read' a statement to that effect, but he asks: 'Why only once? Our generation is distinguished by its impatience. We want more, we want more and more again'[15] (pp. 34–5). The title of his novel is a further allusion to *Nachdenken über Christa T.*, but again one which underlines the difference between the two works. Wolf's title suggests passivity, inwardness, subjectivity; Neutsch's suggests dynamism and the concrete social life. Narration is thematised: the narrator is determined to find out the truth about Gatt and travels to find him and interview him on a number of occasions; his narrative includes internal narratives, by Gatt himself and later his wife. The omniscient narrator of earlier GDR fiction apparently has been abandoned. But only apparently. For although he periodically reminds himself that he wishes to tell the story in Gatt's words, Neutsch's narrator has no compunction about telling the reader what was going on in the minds of the protagonists. He is seeking the 'truth' about Gatt; but this truth is akin to the contents of the 'jug with two handles' which Christa Wolf had rejected. He reflects from time to time on the question 'What is a human being?' His answer comes in terms of social action. *Auf der Suche nach Gatt* bears a greater resemblance to nineteenth-century models such as Franz Grillparzer's *Der arme Spielmann*. In the GDR's earlier literature Franz Fühmann's *Böhmen am Meer* had used similar narrative patterns.

There are other works with a greater similarity to Wolf's, however. In Ulrich Plenzdorf's *Die neuen Leiden des jungen W.* Edgar Wibeau, like Christa T., is seeking self-realisation. His individualism is expressed in the immature terms of a teenager determined to have no other models than himself. His search, too, ends in death. Again it is a text which embodies the 'quest' for an individual, as Edgar's father, by interviewing those who knew him, tries to find out how his son came to meet his death. In Jurek Becker's *Der Boxer* the narrator has spent two years interviewing Aron Blank, a survivor of the Holocaust whose experiences have scarred him to the extent that he is suspicious of everyone and everything he meets. The narrator is trying to find out what 'makes him tick' but in the end has to confess himself baffled. Waldtraut Lewin's historical novel *Federico* is a further work in which the subject of a search, Emperor Frederick II, proves elusive and, unlike Gatt, ultimately refuses to give up his secret. Lewin models herself explicitly on Dante, appropriately in view of his proximity to Frederick's times. Her narrator, Truda, descends to the underworld in search of her subject and is guided there by various Virgils. She discovers a man full of contradictions, capable of both extreme tenderness and barbaric cruelty, a scholar and a sportsman, a man of vision and a man of war. At the end of her quest she has a mystical encounter with Frederick. She still does not know what to make of him, monster or saint. Perhaps, she suggests to him, his essence was a kind of Faustian striving, and he does not disagree. 'Prefer the movement to the goal',[16] was one of Christa T.'s mottoes (*Nachdenken*, p. 43). The striving was more important than the achievement; so, too, the search is more important than the finding.

The thematisation of the act of writing is related to the distrust of the 'omniscient' narrator expressed by Hein. In *Die neuen Leiden* the constant interruptions by Edgar himself with his sardonic comments and corrections from beyond the grave are partly comic. They also imply the impossibility of literary 'omniscience' – only the dead know all. Telling a story from the perspective of an external, anonymous, all-knowing narrator was in the eighteenth and nineteenth centuries an indication of confidence in the ultimate meaningfulness of the world. The narrator embodied in large measure the values of the text. In early socialist realist literature this was, naturally enough, the standpoint of the Party: reality was knowable, values were clear and embodied in the collective wisdom of the proletariat. The avoidance of this standpoint by large numbers of contemporary GDR authors is not therefore merely an indication that the GDR's literature is catching up with 'modernist' literary fashions; it also suggests that the optimism of early socialism has given way to scepticism. At the very least it implies that authors no longer believe that the Party, like God, is always right. Exceptions prove the rule. Orthodox writers such as Erik Neutsch continue to use the older style. Erwin Strittmatter does so, too, but with much irony and humour. Günter de Bruyn, whose literary model is the early nineteenth-century writer Jean Paul, employs an ironic narrator who leaves the reader in some considerable doubt as to where he is supposed to stand and whose values cannot at all be identified with the supporters of actually existing socialism encountered in the texts.

The clearest association between 'omniscient' narration and the dictates of the Party is to be found in Volker Braun's *Hinze-Kunze-Roman*, and it is a highly ironic one. For here the anonymous narrator has taken great pains to ensure that his text conforms to the values and norms of the Party. *Hinze-Kunze-Roman* is a novel about the writing of a novel, under the peculiar circumstances of the GDR's cultural policies. The narrator has discussed his project with the 'central administration' (p. 14). He repeatedly stresses the importance of reconciling 'personal' and 'social interests' (pp. 9 et passim). He alludes to Erich Honecker's statement of 1971, 'From certain fixed positions there are no taboos'[17] (p. 8). But because his readers are 'numerous, uncontrolled and not altogether responsible'[18] he leaves them in the canteen while Kunze, one of the GDR's top officials, attends an important meeting (p. 40). In places words are omitted – as happened to the real Christa Wolf's *Kassandra*; elsewhere the conclusion of a story is suppressed. The narrative is subject to constant revisions. When Kunze visits Lise one evening in the data processing department where she works, his suggestion that she should try to improve her qualifications is ridiculed. Women, she says, always play a subordinate role and their only means of promotion are sexual. At once the narrator breaks off, withdraws this version of events and gives the conventional socialist realist account, in which Lise gratefully accepts Kunze's suggestion. But even here 'reality', rather than its socialist realist version, intervenes, as Lise's boss brushes against her breasts and electromagnetic waves put the computers out of action. The narrator of *Hinze-Kunze-Roman* is never fully in control. His 'omniscience' does not mean that he understands everything that is going on. People do not always behave in the manner predicted by orthodox socialism. Hinze, the novel's representative of the proletariat, fails to oppose the high-handed behaviour of his master Kunze. Had he shown more resistance a 'conflict' would have developed, and the novel would have become 'easily comprehensible' (p. 34). In this way the conventional narrative standpoint of socialist realism is undermined.

Instead of extradiegetic narration, first-person narratives are common. They are an obvious way of conveying subjective authenticity and are appropriate for a confessional kind of literature centred on the individual rather than on society. Novels such as Gerti Tetzner's *Karen W.*, Erich Loest's *Es geht seinen Gang* and Uwe Saeger's *Nöhr* are all stories of an individual breaking out of a conformist existence and are related by the chief protagonist in retrospect. Werner Heiduczek's *Tod am Meer* emphasises the claim to authenticity in the time-honoured way by including an introduction by an 'editor' and contradictory comments from three people who had known the narrator. The most extreme form of first-person narration is the stream of consciousness narrative associated with early twentieth-century modernism and tabooed by the GDR's literary arbiters of taste in the 1950s. While it cannot be said that this form of narration is widespread (any more than elsewhere in the German-speaking world), examples are numerous enough to show that here, too, a convention has been destroyed. Ulrich Plenzdorf's 'kein runter kein fern', which is the inner monologue of a mentally retarded teenager excited at the prospect of hearing the Rolling Stones perform on the other side of the Wall, won him the Ingeborg-Bachmann-Prize in Klagenfurt in 1978. It has not yet been published in the GDR, presumably because it juxtaposes the teenager's thoughts with the official running commentary on a military parade. But the more complex mental processes of the teenager of Bernd Ulbrich's 'Fang die Sonne auf' *have* been published, a story which mingles masturbatory fantasies with fragments from newspapers, classroom exercises and tales for children. Among its many types of narration Karl-Heinz Jakobs's *Die Interviewer* includes a brief passage in stream of consciousness technique. Again it is to Christa Wolf that we must look for the most sophisticated example. Her *Kein Ort. Nirgends* covers the events of a single day; its extensive use of flashback and memory creates an atmosphere of timelessness and its inner monologues and narratorial voices merge so imperceptibly with one another that on occasion one cannot be sure who is speaking, who is thinking. 'Who is speaking?', indeed, is the question addressed to the reader at the beginning of the text.

The dualism of the narrative situation of *Nachdenken über Christa T.* is repeated in other works besides *Auf der Suche nach Gatt*. In Martin Stade's historical novel *Der König und sein Narr* the philosopher Gundling on his death-bed is writing his memoirs, which are dominated by the figure of King Frederick William I of Prussia. Stade is not especially concerned with narrative plausibility. Gundling is still writing as he dies and in places resembles an old-fashioned extradiegetic narrator. What is important here is a subjective focus on events. As we shall see in Chapter 7 there are echoes of Lukács's theory of the historical novel in the technique. Joachim Walther's novel *Bewerbung bei Hofe* confronts the philistine narrator Johann von Besser, diarist and court poet of August the Strong of Saxony, and the brilliant young poet Johann Christian Günther. The chief drawback of the first-person narrative is, as with Stade's novel, the question of insights into events happening elsewhere. Walther solves the problem with an artificial but ingenious device. In order to know what Günther is up to Besser employs a spy, who listens at doors and peers through windows. In this way Walther is also able to convey the atmosphere of suspicion and surveillance in an authoritarian state. On the whole he is successful in implying a dialectic between conformist and nonconformist in a way which goes further than Wolf's novel. For although the reader's sympathies are with Günther, the central figure of the novel remains Besser. Instead of the caricature one expects, he becomes a rather pitiful figure, one who, like Gundling, betrayed his talents for the sake of dubious social status, who was capable of genuine affection in the case of his first wife, who much against his will is fascinated by the young poet, and who is acutely aware of his own mortality. Helga Königsdorf's *Respektloser Umgang* is a further example of the mode, and one to which we shall return later.

By focusing on two poets with opposing views of poetry *Bewerbung bei Hofe* does not only thematise the act of writing, it also thematises literature itself. The contrast between Besser and Günther is partly that between the poetry of the court and the poetry of the people: Günther appreciates folksong, which Besser abhors. In terms of the GDR's cultural policies Günther is respectably on the side of the popular. But he also believes in 'pure poetry' (pp. 170, 297), rejecting that which has a specific aim. In this respect he is hardly being partisan. Besser's poetry upholds the values of the state. Günther's words on the true nature of poetry have their special resonance in the GDR:

> Poetry has an inner morality . . . it must not fall silent out of opportunism, it must take a stand, even when this is not advisable. . . . Poetry . . . does not paint the transfigured picture of the present such as many would like to see. It paints the true picture of the world as it is – in its beauty and with all its faults, imperfections and failings, and counsels the reader with his innate common sense to take up sensible residence in it.[19] (pp. 175–7)

Literature and its role is a theme of many other works. All of Wolf's own novels have been highly self-conscious in this way. *Kindheitsmuster* has three narrative layers: the story of Nelly's childhood in the Third Reich, the description of a journey to Poland in July 1971 and the account of the writing of the book which is to link the first two. *Kein Ort. Nirgends* begins with the voice of a narrator addressing Heinrich von Kleist and Karoline von Günderrode, the protagonists of the story, as her 'predecessors'. *Kassandra*, at least in its GDR form, consists of a version of the Greek myth of Cassandra preceded by four essays in which Wolf outlines her researches on the subject and its topicality, and elaborates a feminine aesthetic. The Kleist and Günderrode of *Kein Ort. Nirgends* were themselves early nineteenth-century writers and writers are the central figures of the novels *Irreführung der Behörden* by Jurek Becker, *Preisverleihung* by Günter de Bruyn and *Tod am Meer* by Werner Heiduczek, each of whom criticises and rejects his opportunistic past. Even the narrator-protagonist of Hermann Kant's *Der Aufenthalt* may be viewed as an artist figure: some Polish women mistake him for an 'artiste' when he is first taken prisoner and his fertile imagination enables him to entertain his fellow-prisoners. The various mishaps which he suffers, some comic, some less so, suggest he is a clown, and clowns have been frequent surrogates of the artist in postwar fiction. In this context, as Helmut John has pointed out, it is interesting to note the number of GDR writers, among them Christa Wolf, Günter de Bruyn and Irmtraud Morgner, who have dismissed their own early work and the even greater number who have felt impelled to publish accounts of their own literary theory (Pestalozzi, ed., 1986, pp. 212–15).

In view of Wolf's insistence that literature should be unfilmable it is ironic that film is frequently used as a metaphor for literature, possibly because the constraints on the East German film-maker are especially obvious. *Irreführung der Behörden* by Jurek Becker, whose early career involved writing for the cinema, is the story of a young man who compromises his integrity in order to become a successful writer of filmscripts. Himself a writer for the cinema, Hitchcock-like Plenzdorf puts in a brief appearance in his own *Die neuen Leiden* as the angry scriptwriter interviewed by the schoolboys on a visit to the film studios. His script for the pre-Honecker, socialist realist film *Kennen Sie Urban?* of 1969 is subjected to the scorn of his youthful protagonist. *Die neuen Leiden* is a work in which the nonconformist is *not* brought back into line by a friendly party worker. Karl-Heinz Jakobs's *Die Interviewer* takes its title from the documentary film Kritzki is making on a light-bulb factory. Kritzki, who has a preconceived notion of reality as Marxism-Leninism would have it be, is looking for positive heroes. At the end of the novel he proclaims that his film is 'realistic', 'synchronous with reality' (p. 262), because it has harmonised and explained away the apparent contradictions he encountered in its making. When shortly afterwards he learns that the heroine of his film, Liane Radek, has a son who has just been sent to borstal he is at first bewildered: 'There's no meaning in that.'[20] He resolves to ignore it, declaring with comic pomposity: 'Art is the art of omission. One might also say the art of thinking away. I shall think all these inferior, disturbing details away and present you in your clear, simple beauty'[21] (pp. 265–6). Similar ironies lie at the basis of Schütz's *Julia*. Gabriel Tischer is a film cameraman. His current project is the documentation of a paradigmatic case, a woman who has grown up in the GDR, with working-class parents; someone who was enabled to go to university by the socialist institution of the Workers' and Peasants' Faculty, who is a member of the Party, is a professional singer and a mother with children. Julia appears to fit the bill. But various events defeat the project: she leaves the choir and her husband Ulrich. Gabriel himself has an accident, loses his camera and the roll of film remains undeveloped.

Films are also influential, in GDR writing as elsewhere, in relation to narrative technique. Since the emergence of film as an art form in the 1920s it has been credited with influencing the development of montage in the novel. Again there are peculiar resonances for the GDR's writers. The concept of montage was central to the debates on the avant-garde in the 1930s. As early as 1917 Alfred Döblin had declared programmatically: 'If a novel cannot be cut into ten pieces like an earthworm and every piece moves on its own, then it is worthless'[22] (1963, p. 21). Brecht alluded to Döblin's words in defence of his own epic, i.e. narrative, theatre in an essay of the 1930s, in which he proceeded to assert that whereas the conventional theatre was characterised by 'organic growth', epic theatre was characterised by 'montage' (1957, pp. 62, 20). For Brecht the dramatic plot which developed organically was part of the bourgeois tradition which he rejected as incapable of activating the spectator. But organic growth was the essential quality of the 'novel of education' which Georg Lukács favoured for socialist writers. Montage represented for Lukács all that was decadent in the modern novel. Although superficially exciting, he regarded it as no more than a fashionable gimmick (1971, p. 328).

Here, too, the 1970s and beyond have seen the influence of Lukács comprehensively demolished. Heiner Müller, for example, has gone far beyond Brecht in what has been described as a 'post-modernist' attack on the conventional notions of the 'unity' of a work of literature (Teraoka 1985). Despite his insistence that the plot of the well-made play numbed the spectator's consciousness Brecht's plays all contain a recognisable story attached to a stable set of recognisable characters. Müller's early plays were written in the didactic Brechtian tradition. From the 1970s onwards, however, Müller began to transcend his master. Although *Zement*, based on a novel by

Gladkov, retains the 'epic' qualities of Brecht's theatre, presenting episodes from the early years of the Soviet revolution and focusing on a fixed set of characters, in three places the action is interrupted by a kind of 'tableau vivant', a narrative passage based on Greek mythology, wholly divorced from the contemporary events. These narrative passages subsequently gain increasing importance in Müller's plays, until with *Bildbeschreibung* they have taken over the whole. The montage element is at its most obvious in works such as *Leben Gundlings Friedrich von Preußen Lessings Schlaf Traum Schrei*, whose very title, lacking all punctuation, reflects a technique in which disparate scenes are juxtaposed, ranging from historical figures of the eighteenth century into a future dominated by robots. Müller's most radical plays have not yet been performed in the GDR. However, even the structure of a relatively conventional play like *Der Auftrag*, which has had several productions there, is exploded by a scene in which a mysterious 'man in a lift' appears. Not only is it divorced in time and space from the late eighteenth-century events of the play – the speaker is transported to South America after some nuclear catastrophe has occurred – but it is not even clear to whom the lines spoken are to be allotted.

Montage techniques of a kind can be found in the GDR's novel as early as 1963 in Wolf's *Der geteilte Himmel* and again in 1966 in Hermann Kant's *Die Aula*. In both these works the narrative is broken into alternating blocks set in the past and in the present. *Nachdenken über Christa T.* is incomparably more complex in this respect. The introduction of 'documents' by another hand – Christa T.'s own writings – further explodes the unity of narration. Helga Schütz's novel *Julia* switches from first- to third-person narration and between various time levels in a manner which is so confusing that one reviewer placed events in the early 1970s (Schachtsiek-Freitag 1982) while another was equally convinced that they took place at the end of the decade (Böck 1982). In fact the death of 'popes' referred to towards the end of the novel (p. 235) occurred in 1978 and the hysteria described earlier in West Germany over the Baader-Meinhof murders must relate to the year 1977. When the title of Marcel Proust's novel is quoted it implies that *Julia*, too, is a 'search for time lost' (p. 207).

The relation between film and narrative technique is obvious in Jakobs's *Die Interviewer*, which even contains a hidden reference to Resnais's avant-garde film *L'année dernière à Marienbad*, when the ominous Kritzki plays the matchstick game associated with the ominous husband in Resnais's film (p. 45). The montage effect here is produced largely through the arbitrary breaks between chapters, so that sometimes a chapter ends and the next one begins in the middle of the same scene. But it is to Irmtraud Morgner that we must look for the most radical employment of the technique. Her *Hochzeit in Konstantinopel* of 1968 is still relatively straightforward, a contemporary *Arabian Nights*, whose Scheherazade on a premarital holiday in Yugoslavia attempts to convert her rationalist fiancé, an atomic physicist, to a new appreciation of the world of the imagination with her nightly stories, twenty-one in all. *Leben und Abenteuer der Trobadora Beatriz* and its sequel *Amanda* not only embody the montage technique, but also supply their own theory. All three are further examples of novels in which literature itself is thematic, discussed moreover in an altogether different manner from that of Wolf, namely fantastic, ironic, humorous.

That *Trobadora Beatriz* is an artist novel is indicated by the title itself, although the life and adventures of Beatriz, a medieval poet from southern France, are only part of the text. Indignant at the way she is treated by men both as poet and as woman, she drinks a potion which enables her to sleep for 810 years, by which time she imagines the world will have created circumstances more favourable for women. That this is not altogether true, even in the GDR, which has been described to her as the 'promised land', is just one of the discoveries she makes on awakening. It is an outstanding feminist novel and we shall examine this aspect elsewhere. But one of its aims is to explore the function of poetry in the contemporary world and in the GDR in particular. Initially the effects tend to be comic, as the expectations of a medieval lady clash with the reality of the twentieth century. In Provence Beatriz is regarded as a busker, at best as an official tourist attraction. In the GDR, where public recitals by poets are popular and a major feature of literary life, she finds it easier to adapt. She opens a 'poetry-smith's shop', supplying mechanically-produced poems to order. A sample of them is included. At first sight they appear entirely non-representational, as in the 'Voices of the steel foundrymen' (Figure 1). These apparent scansion markings, can, however, be deciphered as morse code, beaten out, as it were, on the 'anvil'. The steelworkers are actually singing 'Bier her' (Bring us beer) three times over. The satire is at the expense both of the purely pragmatic functionalist approach to literature associated with socialist countries and of the modishly avant-garde 'concrete poetry' of the West which Franz Fühmann had jokingly dabbled in a year previously in his Hungarian diary *Zweiundzwanzig Tage* (pp. 73 4). There are other satirical references to aspects of the GDR's literary scene, to the requirement of a 'positive ending', for example, and to the Bitterfeld movement. But

Beyond Formalism

–◡◡ ◡◡ ◡ ◡–◡

◡◡◡ ◡ ◡–◡

–◡◡ ◡◡ ◡ ◡–◡

◡◡◡ ◡ ◡–◡

–◡◡ ◡◡ ◡ ◡–◡

◡◡◡ ◡ ◡–◡

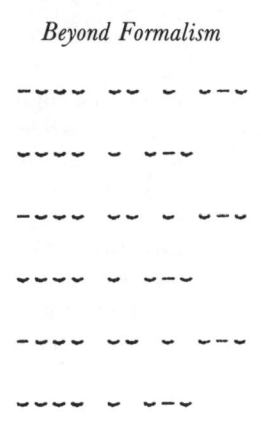

Figure 1. 'Voices of the steel foundrymen'

Beatriz writes highly erotic poetry as well, which tends to shock her male listeners.

Near the beginning of the novel she makes a pact with her sister-in-law, the fairy-cum-sphinx Melusine. The latter is to focus on capitalist society, composing protest songs, making propaganda on behalf of socialism which alone can guarantee women's emancipation. Beatriz will concentrate on countries which have already become socialist. The function of her poetry will be to change attitudes rather than institutions, the attitudes which persist in regarding women as inferior beings. One important area in this respect is the celebration of sexuality, traditionally the province of men. But Beatriz also inspires others to write, notably Laura Salman, a tram-driver and a mother, who is first engaged as her assistant – all troubadours had their minstrels – and gradually becomes more and more independent. Many of the episodes of *Trobadora Beatriz* are told by Laura, relating various facets of male-female relationships in the contemporary GDR. Morgner's novel itself therefore performs the function allotted to Beatriz's poetry in the pact with Melusine.

The novel's structure also runs diametrically counter to the socialist realist model. To begin with it is difficult to distil from the novel any coherent, organic plot such as Lukács regarded as essential. Beatriz is one of three main female personages of the novel, each of whom represents a different social grouping: Laura Salman, the daughter of an engine driver, belongs to the traditional proletariat; Beatriz is aristocratic and represents the artist; Valeska Kantus is a scientist and represents the intelligentsia. There are therefore three largely separate stories based on each of these individuals, who interlock mainly through their menfolk (Laura passes her lover Lutz on to Beatriz, while Valeska is married to Laura's former husband). But although the characters develop in consciousness, even these 'stories' remain sketchy. Far more important as a structural principle is the collage of disparate texts. As well as the more conventional narrative relating to the three main protagonists we find poems, some original, others by Paul Wiens and Volker Braun, independent stories, often with a fantastic, fairy-tale atmosphere, extracts from newspapers, from a sex manual, from a parliamentary debate, from the memoirs of the Soviet feminist Alexandra Kollontai and of Lenin's widow Nadeshda Krupskaya, and from scientific papers. There are even seven 'intermezzi' taken from Morgner's unpublished novel of 1964, 'Rumba auf einen Herbst', which relate in a fragmentary manner the background to some of the male characters encountered in the rest of the novel.

The rationale for this technique is contained in the novel itself. Ostensibly on behalf of Beatriz Laura Salman conducts negotiations with the Aufbau Verlag (which actually published the novel) over her literary project, a 'montage novel'. The dialogue with the publisher's reader is reproduced. Some of the arguments are satirical: the montage novel ought to be the ideal form for the publishers, since it can survive the most extreme mutilations required by the censor at any stage. Others are more serious. From the point of view of the producer, the montage novel is ideal for the woman writer: traditional novels require exclusive concentration over a long period of time, something which the working mother cannot find. Brecht's claim that montage aids the spectator's critical awareness is repeated when Laura describes the form as 'interventionist'; a mosaic is more than the sum of its parts and it is up to the reader to create the overall meaning. Lukács had rejected the naturalistic preoccupation with detail; a merely additive approach was no guarantee of the epic totality which he demanded. Laura, by contrast, declares that this epic monumentality must today of necessity be effete; it is the exact detail that is important (p. 171).

Paradoxically there *is* something approaching totality in *Trobadora Beatriz*, but it is closer to the German Romantic theorist Friedrich Schlegel's concept of a 'progressive universal poetry' than to Weimar Goethe. Morgner's universe is one in which poetry, politics and science are linked by the imagination. For example, the physicists' discovery of 'antimatter' is described as 'archpoetical' (p. 198). The notion of a 'model', taken from cybernetics, is applied to Luther's theology and Marx's philosophy, neither of which corresponds to anything which really exists but both of which have proved extraordinarily fruitful in influencing people's behaviour. Morgner's Beatriz is a comparable 'model'. The Romantic association is compounded by the introduction of 'real' people such as Sarah Kirsch and Volker Braun as well as Morgner herself, who not only introduces herself in the preface, where she is accosted by Laura Salman offering to sell her account of the life of Beatriz, but is also to be witnessed later interviewing Laura. In the sequel, *Amanda*, Morgner is accused by the narrator Beatriz, now a 'siren', of having been her own censor. Later she has to justify herself to Laura Salman, who complains that she had told only half the truth in the earlier work. Ironies of this kind link Morgner's novels to the German Romantic tradition of Clemens Brentano and E.T.A. Hoffmann.

Morgner's novels are almost unique in East German fiction. Gerhard Dahne attempted a comparable coup with his novel *Die ganz merkwürdigen Sichten und Gesichte des Hans Greifer*. In the midst of a tenuous plot utopian visions alternate with historical anecdotes and fairy-tales. The narrator finds himself involved in his own narrative and in four 'letters to the publisher' argues against censorship and in favour of the creative imagination. Eberhard Hilscher's *Die Weltzeituhr*, discussed in Chapter 1, is altogether weightier. As we have seen, a montage effect is created visually by the use of three different type-faces, indicating three different kinds of text. If the scientific avant-garde is embodied in Einstein, then the artistic avant-garde is represented in the novel by his counterparts Picasso and Brecht. In an address of 1952 Guido Möglich outlines his (and no doubt the author's) ideal of a 'universal poetry which is entertainingly didactic, rich in allusions, full of imagination',[23] one which would unite the experimental prose of a Joyce, Gide and Döblin with the contemporary world of work demanded by the cultural authorities of the day (pp. 264–5), and one which is largely fulfilled in the novel itself.

Morgner's Romantic irony, whereby the author's reality intrudes on the narrator's fiction is, however, also to be found in Braun's *Hinze-Kunze-Roman*, at least in the East German edition, at the beginning of which the reader is directed to a 'belletristical aid to reading by Dieter Schlenstedt as an appendix',[24] omitted in the West German edition. The pomposity of the words 'belletristical aid to reading' suggests that we are not to take it too seriously, and the tone corresponds to some of the ironies we have already seen in the main text. However, the appendix turns out to consist of the publisher's correspondence with Schlenstedt, who had been asked to comment on the work's suitability for publication, as well as a personal letter from Schlenstedt to the author and a further letter to the chairman of the critics' section in the Writers' Union suggesting an open discussion of the novel. As we have seen, Braun's text posed problems for the censorship. The appendices are intended to forestall the accusation that it should never have been published. But there is more to them than that. For when Schlenstedt writes that Braun's earlier works, *Das ungezwungene Leben Kasts* and *Unvollendete Geschichte* have been popular with many readers, he and his readers know very well that *Unvollendete Geschichte* was accessible only very briefly when it was printed in *Sinn und Form* in 1975 and at the time of writing had not been reprinted in the GDR. Furthermore the appendices themselves have an appendix written by the narrator of the novel itself, who returns to the scene of his story to tell his characters of his success, and finds that in the four years between the writing and printing of the novel the slums it describes have been renovated. Braun's narrative technique compounds irony upon irony in Romantic fashion and Schlenstedt's contribution becomes part of the fiction, as indeed his misleading allusion to *Unvollendete Geschichte* itself implies.

Christa Wolf's formula 'subjective authenticity' is often taken as the key to the GDR's literary developments in the Honecker years. Although the undertones and implications are always different in the authoritarian society of the GDR, the term applies equally to much West German literature of the same time. Helmut Kreuzer, for example, suggests that the autobiographical mode of the 1970s satisfies both the desire for authenticity and the concern for the self (1978, p. 11). On the face of it, two trends in current East German literature threaten to split the formula into its component parts once more. The one is the fantastic mode, potentially an extreme form of subjectivity, the other is documentarism, where authenticity rules and the writer's self is largely suppressed. In fact they may be regarded as two sides of the same coin.

Wolf's 'Juninachmittag' already rejected the cosy certainties contained in the socialist realist 'jug' in favour of a 'vision' which her readers might or might not understand. Since 1968, however, prosaic reality 'reflected' in the GDR's prose has been pierced again and again by unreal, fantastic events. The *Märchen* (folk-tale or fairy-tale) has enjoyed a remarkable renaissance. Hanne Castein speaks of a veritable 'wave' breaking in the 1970s (1988, p. 195), in which both traditional stories are reinterpreted and new motifs developed. Shorter prose fiction has been especially affected by the fashion. In many of Günter Kunert's stories everyday reality is suddenly undermined by a grotesque, supernatural or fantastic occurrence: a fanatical swimmer develops the scales of a fish ('Schwimmer'); overcrowding in the cemeteries leads to the dead being unloaded in the homes of those responsible for their deaths ('Lieferung frei Haus'); and a man encounters one 'doppelgänger' after another ('Ich und ich'). In stories by Rainer Kirsch we encounter a man who buys a helmet of invisibility ('Erste Niederschrift') or who is offered a 'free day' by a little lilac cloud ('Der geschenkte Tag'). Fritz Rudolf Fries describes Albrecht van der Wahl's encounter with a naked woman in the street, whom only he can see; eventually he himself disappears ('Das nackte Mädchen auf der Straße'). Edith Anderson edited an anthology in 1975 devoted to stories dealing with a sudden change of sex (*Blitz aus heiterem Himmel*). In Heiner Müller's *Bildbeschreibung* an initially serene landscape becomes filled with menace, turning into a landscape 'on the other side of death'.

The novel proper has tended to remain more firmly grounded in traditional, if not socialist, realism. Irmtraud Morgner, however, has produced exceptions to this rule. The twenty-one stories told by Bele to her prosaic, unimaginative boyfriend in *Hochzeit in Konstantinopel* include such fantasy narratives as 'Himmelbett', in which nightly the narrator flies through the air in her bed, 'Für die Katz', in which she turns into a cat and gobbles up the man who claims that 'nonsense' is a waste of time, and 'Faungesicht', in which a faun turns to stone in the cold. These are still short stories, but Morgner's next novels, *Gustav der Weltfahrer*, *Trobadora Beatriz* and *Amanda* make a more protracted use of the fantastic mode. Morgner has been a prime influence on GDR writers, the explicit inspiration of, for example, Helga Königsdorf's story 'Meine ungehörigen Träume'.

Early GDR fiction tended to avoid these motifs. Not only did they conflict with the rationality of 'scientific socialism', interpreted in a particularly narrow way, but, as Horst Heidtmann points out, irrationality itself had been a major tool of National Socialism in leading the German nation astray (cit. Hohendahl and Herminghouse, eds., 1983, pp. 196–7). Romanticism had exploited the 'dark side of life', but in the Lukácsian 1950s and 1960s it was out of favour. The 1970s witnessed a rehabilitation of Romanticism. This entailed not only a reassessment of writers associated with the movement but also the acceptability of their techniques (Hardy 1988). Dreams, fairy-tales, the 'doppelgänger' motif used by Kunert, the grotesque mingling of the human and the mechanical found in Müller, these are all part of the Romantic tradition. Anna Seghers is often considered to have pointed the way for these developments. The three stories collected under the title *Sonderbare Begegnungen*, which appeared in 1973, use motifs of the fantastic, including science fiction. The third describes an imaginary meeting between three historical writers who have been associated with the genre, E.T.A. Hoffmann, Nicolai Gogol and Franz Kafka. While Seghers may well have contributed to making this kind of writing respectable, it has to be pointed out that Morgner preceded her by a number of years.

Although the GDR has no monopoly on fantasy, within the context of bureaucratic socialism it does have its peculiar flavour. As in the West, it is related to a widespread revulsion against the mechanisation of contemporary life. Science is no longer regarded as the unquestioned guarantor of progress, and the distrust of science implied in some of these works provides grounds for suspicion among some of the GDR's critics (Kaufmann 1980, p. 113). Jurij Brězan's *Krabat* mingles motifs from traditional legend with contemporary, comparably 'fantastic' developments in biogenetics in his visionary journey through the centuries. Helga Königsdorf's *Respektloser Umgang* takes up the relation between science and society by confronting a contemporary scientist with a ghost from the past, the physicist Lise Meitner. In Müller's *Leben Gundlings* the enlightenment vision of La Mettrie's 'L'homme machine', a humanity which can be totally explained in rational terms, is projected into a future in which the 'last president of the United States' is found in a car dump presided over by a robot on an electric chair. In the case of Morgner's works, however, the fantastic is more of an alienation device designed to startle her readers into questioning their assumptions about social roles: flying through the air on a broomstick in *Amanda* enables women to attend to their 'household duties' *and* to find intellectual and emotional fulfilment. What is often overlooked, however, is that fantasy is the supreme indication of the literary imagination, a metaphor for literature itself. In this sense the fantastic aspects of the GDR's recent literature are yet another indication of the importance of the aesthetic dimension.

The complement to the fantastic mode is the documentary. It is ironic that in 1978 Jean Villain bemoaned the poverty of literary journalism in the GDR (cit. Kaufmann 1986), for the 1980s have seen a flood of 'non-fictional' works on topics traditionally the concern of novelists. Some of these are conventional autobiographies: Karl Mundstock's *Meine tausend Jahre Jugend*, Valerie Radtke's *Ich suche Liebe*, Gerhard Holtz-Baumert's *Die pucklige Verwandtschaft*, for example. Using letters, diaries, drawings, Sibylle Muthesius's *Flucht in die Wolken* attempts to reconstruct the life of a daughter who has committed suicide. Ingrid Johannis's *Das siebente Brennesselhemd* is the edited diary of a woman alcoholic. The earliest form of the current wave of literary journalism is the taped interview, first used by Sarah Kirsch in 1973 for *Die Pantherfrau*, and followed by Maxie

Wander's *Guten Morgen, du Schöne* in 1977, which had a spectacular success. Both Kirsch's and Wander's anthologies furnished important material for the GDR's unofficial feminist movement, authentic texts which help their readers to understand themselves better in relation to the experiences of others. Christine Müller's *Männerprotokolle* is a conscious attempt to do for men what Wander had done for women, that is to allow them to articulate freely their feelings about life, work and the opposite sex, and was followed by a similar collection edited by Christine Lambrecht, *Männerbekanntschaften*. Irina Liebmann interviewed the numerous inhabitants of a Berlin tenement block for her *Berliner Mietshaus*.

As with the fantastic mode, it must be said that this interest in documentary literature is not peculiar to the GDR. In the later 1960s the Federal Republic's literary scene was dominated by the documentary. Peter Weiss's play *Die Ermittlung*, premiered simultaneously in East and West, used the transcripts of the Auschwitz trial in Frankfurt, Erika Runge interviewed workers for her *Bottroper Protokolle* and Günter Wallraff was beginning the peculiar form of literary investigative journalism which he has pursued to the present day. As we have already seen, the 'death of literature' proclaimed in 1968 was to have as corollary the requirement to document the struggle of the workers against exploitation and of the Vietnamese against imperialism. In the GDR, however, the literary context is a quite different one. Literary reportage has a socialist tradition which goes back to the work of the 'worker correspondents' of the 1920s, itself taken up in the GDR in the immediate postwar years by writers such as Willi Bredel and later revived in the Bitterfeld movement. It was yet another form of literature which Georg Lukács opposed. The works listed above differ considerably, however, both from the West German works of the later 1960s and from the earlier GDR trends in that they are considerably more individualistic. Inasmuch as interviews and personal histories are both subjective and authentic, Eva Kaufmann (1986) can relate them to the general literary concern for 'subjective authenticity' which characterises the 1970s and 1980s. Their popularity with readers undoubtedly has its roots in a widespread wish to know what other people 'really' think, a wish which is left unsatisfied by the GDR media. Suicide and alcoholism are genuine problems of GDR society, but ones usually ignored by the press. Criticism takes second place to reports of successes, and where criticism goes too far in these documentary works it risks being suppressed too. Looked at from the point of view of their subjects, however, these 'documents' may be regarded as evidence of a widespread yearning for self-expression. Hans Kaufmann views this yearning as positive and natural (1981, pp. 36–7), but it must also be linked to the lack of genuine freedom of expression in the political sphere.

The developments outlined in this chapter represent important innovations within the context of the GDR's traditional literature. Within the context of European literature they are unremarkable; however impressive the quality of the individual writing, they do not break new ground for literature. The two possible exceptions are the texts by Morgner and Müller, whose plays are among the most challenging of texts produced anywhere in the European world. The decline of the European avant-garde is frequently lamented by Western critics; post-modernist eclecticism has so far not been especially innovative. As we saw in the previous chapter, one feature of the GDR's cultural climate in recent years has been an officially respected reception of the historical avant-garde in the shape of, for example, Kafka and Beckett. Other, less well-known East German writers have been experimenting with literary techniques too.

The existence of an alternative GDR culture, loosely based on a group of writers and artists living in the Prenzlauer Berg district of East Berlin, first became generally known outside the GDR in 1985 with the publication in the Federal Republic of the anthology *Berührung ist nur eine Randerscheinung*, originally to have been published simultaneously in the GDR but withdrawn, not because of its content but because a number of the contributors had in the meantime emigrated to West Germany. A further anthology, *Sprache und Antwort*, appeared in the West in 1988. These young authors are 'dropouts' in that they reject the traditional media, preferring to use their own hand-presses, frequently collaborating with graphic artists, reading from their works in churches and private houses. Most of them earn their living by non-literary, often unconventional means: Thomas Günther, for example, is a graveyard attendant, while Leonhard Lorek simply describes himself as 'antisocial'. They are hardly 'dissidents', since they reject political commitment of any kind. Fritz-Hendrick Melle, for example, has given up trying to sustain a dialogue with the established order: in the words which gave the first anthology its title: 'Contact is purely marginal' (p. 145). For these writers literature is not making statements, but experimenting with language. And here their efforts take up some of the devices explored by the avant-garde of the early part of the twentieth century. There are echoes of Joyce in Volker Palma's torrent of untranslatable encyclopaedic alliterations: 'lianenhaft, libellistisch, liberal, libertinisch, libidinös, lichenoid, limpid, lingual, lipophob, so liquet und liquid, lirico, lithogenesisch lithophen, lithophil, litoral, litotistisch. . . .' (p. 197). Thomas Günther experiments with aleatory poetry in the manner of Dada: he printed out a short poem sixteen times, pasted the sixteen versions together in the shape of a circle, and the only meaningful phrases which remained turned out to be 'I came once' on the circumference and 'fed up'[25] in the centre (p. 30). Here, if anywhere, the 'monological literature' diagnosed by Wolfgang Emmerich is to be found.

Perhaps the most intriguing longer publication of recent years is Brigitte Burmeister's novel *Anders oder Vom Aufenthalt in der Fremde*. As we have seen, in her essay 'Lesen und Schreiben' Wolf tried to trace a path between the Scylla of socialist realism and the Charybdis of the *nouveau roman* as practised by Alain Robbe-Grillet in particular. Burmeister is a literary scholar, whose main field of research is postwar French literature. Her major publication prior to *Anders* was a study on the *nouveau roman*, with a subtitle which anticipates her novel: 'a different literature and its readers'.[26] *Anders* takes its name from its narrator and principal character David Anders; 'Anders', however, means 'different' and *Anders* is indeed very different. Its fifty-three chapters correspond to the weeks of the year. The first and last chapters are identical almost to a word, as a new year begins. As the days grow longer, so do the chapters, until in Chapter 27, midway between 1 and 53 and set on 2 July, they reach a climax from which they begin to grow shorter once more. Their descent is rather less regular than their ascent had been, as Figure 2 shows, a diagram reminiscent of the skyline of a modern city, possibly East Berlin, which is one of the themes of the novel. It is hard to imagine a novel more 'formalist' than this.

The story-line in *Anders* is minimal. Anders takes up his new job in the city at the beginning of January. He visits an exhibition, goes for walks in parks, takes part in the office outing and party. Of the few friends he makes, D. and his wife disappear halfway through the year. Otherwise he appears to spend his spare time writing the text which forms the novel, ostensibly 'letters' to his family at home, but it is more reminiscent of a diary. He meets an author, who gives him some encouragement in his writing, and at the end of the year he moves on to a new post elsewhere. But even this account of the story makes certain assumptions which cannot be verified. Burmeister has introduced what André Gide called a 'mise en abyme' (Rimmon-Kenan 1983, p. 93), calling in question any attempt to reconstruct a story from the text. In Chapter 25 Anders writes a story for D.'s wife in which he imagines D., a 'worker who writes', visiting an Author, 'one who writes about workers' – the ironic reference is to the Bitterfeld movement. Ten chapters later Anders finds himself, en-

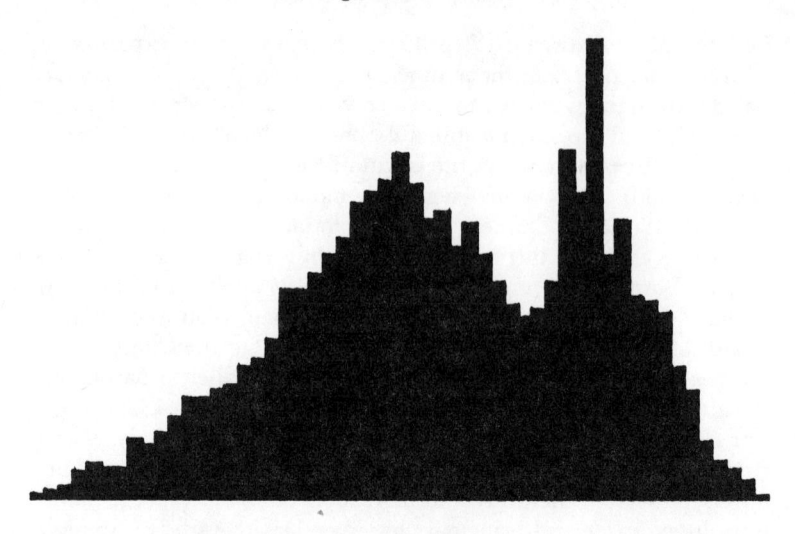

Figure 2. The structure of Burmeister's *Anders*

tirely by chance it seems, meeting just this Author in precisely the surroundings he had earlier described. When in the course of their conversation the Author alludes to an earlier incident at which only D. and Anders were present, Anders can only turn pale and the reader wonder who is telling whom. The Author writes novels in the socialist realist tradition. His present project is a trilogy, a 'novel of education', whose first volume deals with the 'difficult phase of reconstruction', an allusion to Eduard Claudius's early story *Vom schweren Anfang*, and whose subsequent volumes will describe the 'current transitional phase' and the triumphant ascent of the socialist peak (p. 93). Anders, filled with admiration at the Author's ability to create rounded characters, laments that he could never be a character in such a novel; he is instead a 'person in search of an author' (p. 240), an allusion this time to Pirandello's modernist play.

There is yet another writer in Burmeister's novel, D.'s wife. Her 'feminine writing' – 'obsessive scribbling', D. calls it – is interrupted by 'monthly breaks' (p. 21). After one of his visits she gives Anders some of the paper she has written on, encouraging him to write in the spaces between her texts or even on top of what she has written. Deconstructionists like to *read* between the lines, Anders is to *write* between the lines. The text may therefore be regarded as a kind of 'palimpsest', like one of the paintings which Anders encounters at an exhibition (p. 31). Doubts are raised as to whether D.

exists at all, when Anders realises that the letter D occurs three times in his own name. But at the end of the novel when Anders breaks into D.'s flat he finds that the roles are reversed: it is his own writings which are furnished with glosses by the woman and comments by D. As he reads them he becomes impatient to find out how it will all end. D.'s wife claims to have invented Anders – and of course it is the woman Brigitte Burmeister who is ultimately responsible for all of them.

Anders is therefore a text quite different from all the others so far explored. However much they diverge from the socialist realist model they remain mimetic in essence, mirroring and illuminating a reality external to themselves. *Anders* operates with reality as a child might operate with building blocks. It has some splendid satirical scenes, such as the office outing at which Anders initially feels a wonderful sense of community with his colleagues only to lose touch with them almost immediately and end up at the wrong inn, or the Author's public reading, which rehearses all the old literary clichés. It is very much an 'East German novel': the setting is unmistakably East Berlin; the literary persiflage is at the expense of GDR forms. But there is no overriding context. It is not a novel which can be used as a source of information on GDR society, only on the GDR's literature. In *Anders* the text is simply text: the attempt to reconstruct a reality, whether story-based or character-based, which it might be reproducing is doomed to failure. Although it is closest perhaps to Braun's *Hinze-Kunze-Roman*, where Braun remains self-evidently a socialist, tirelessly endeavouring to inspire the reader into socialist activity, Burmeister's *Anders* lacks this element. This really is literature on literature, the self-reflecting novel. The games played with the reader have various functions. When the literary figure of the Author turns up as a 'real' figure, the joke is at the expense of the traditional notion embodied in the works of this same man, whereby a character 'takes on a life of his own' (p. 186). But there is more to it than a joke. A through-going theme is that of the subjectivity of perceptions: the camel passing Anders's window turns out to be the loaded trailer of a car; viewed from a distance the patterns of car lights on the streets give rise to fantastic accounts of cause and effect; and the signs of what he takes to be a failed revolution turn out to be merely those of vandalism by drunken teenagers. One of the effects of the text is therefore to sharpen the reader's perceptions, to undermine assumptions on the nature of reality itself. This may even have political connotations. When Anders reflects that people have learned to recognise the primacy of the real world over their idea of it, whether they like it or not, and gives as an example the 'actually existing house' which they buy or intend to build (p. 26), he is echoing the phrase 'actually existing socialism', which people have learned to put up with rather than yearn for as some ideal.

The true significance of the 'formalism' of *Anders* goes deeper, however. For Theodor W. Adorno the 'function' of the avant-garde work of art was to have no function at all; it thereby distinguished itself from all other aspects of rationalised, late bourgeois society, and by its negation of what is implied the possibility of something else, something 'different'. In the authoritarian, thoroughly organised and rationalised society of the GDR this perception finds its true fulfilment. Paradoxically, however, the very publishing of the text must tend to undermine it. Avant-garde literature such as *Anders* depends for its existence on friction with the social circumstances under which it is produced. The new liberalism in the artistic sphere reduces the potential for friction. This conclusion is borne out by the current treatment of some of the 'dropouts' who featured in the West German anthology *Berührung ist nur eine Randerscheinung*. With a new series entitled 'Außer der Reihe' ('out of turn'), edited by Gerhard Wolf, the Aufbau Verlag has begun to attempt to integrate these writers by bringing out 'respectable' editions of their works. To what extent they will succeed remains to be seen.

Notes

1. Eine Geschichte? Etwas Festes, Greifbares, wie ein Topf mit zwei Henkeln, zum Anfassen und zum Daraus-Trinken?
Eine Vision vielleicht, falls Sie verstehen, was ich meine.
2. nicht als dem Verstummen nahendes Vor-sich-hin-Sprechen, sondern als Aussprache, die des Gegenübers bedarf.
3. Angebot, dessen Wert sich erst in der Mitwirkung der Leser entscheidet.
4. Spiel mit offenen Möglichkeiten.
5. subjektive Authentizität.
6. Das Bedürfnis, auf eine neue Art zu schreiben, folgt, wenn auch mit Abstand, einer neuen Art, in der Welt zu sein.
7. ein Mittel durch das das Bewußtsein des einzelnen nicht *weiter* aber *genauer* wird, als ein Mittel zum Empfindlichmachen: zum Reizbarmachen: zum Reagieren: als ein Mittel, auf die Welt zu kommen.
8. Was ist das: Dieses Zu-sich-selber-Kommen des Menschen?
9. dies ist der Weg zu uns selber.
10. Wann, wenn nicht jetzt?
11. Nicht mehr lange wird an dieser Krankheit gestorben werden.

12. Daß ich nur schreibend über die Dinge komme!

13. Wir nämlich waren vollauf damit beschäftigt, uns unantastbar zu machen ... Nicht nur nichts Fremdes in uns aufnehmen – und was alles erklärten wir für fremd! – , auch im eigenen Innern nichts Fremdes aufkommen lassen, und wenn es schon aufkam – ein Zweifel, ein Verdacht, Beobachtungen, Fragen – , dann doch nichts davon anmerken zu lassen.

14. Einmal im Leben, zur rechten Zeit, sollte man an Unmögliches geglaubt haben.

15. Wieso nur einmal? Unsere Generation zeichnet die Ungeduld aus. Wir wollen mehr, wir wollen immer wieder mehr.

16. Die Bewegung mehr lieben als das Ziel.

17. Von gewissen festen Positionen aus gibt es keine Tabus.

18. zahlreich, unkontrolliert und nicht durchweg zuständig.

19. Die Poesie hat eine innere Moral ... sie darf nicht schweigen aus Bequemlichkeit, muß sich bekennen, auch wenn es nicht sehr ratsam ist.... Die Poesie ... malt nicht das verklärte Bild der Gegenwart, so wie sie mancher sehen möchte. Sie malt das wahre Bild der Welt, so wie sie ist – in ihrer Schönheit und mit allen ihren Fehlern, Unvollkommenheiten und Gebrechen, und rät dem Leser, sich mit seiner angeborenen Vernunft darin vernünftig einzurichten.

20. Das ergibt keinen Sinn.

21. Kunst, das ist die Kunst des Weglassens. Man kann auch sagen, die Kunst des Wegdenkens. Ich denke mir alle diese minderwertigen und störenden Einzelheiten weg und stelle euch dar in eurer klaren, schlichten Schönheit.

22. Wenn ein Roman nicht wie ein Regenwurm in zehn Stücke geschnitten werden kann und jeder Teil bewegt sich selbst, dann taugt er nichts.

23. heiter-didaktische, beziehungsreiche, phantasievolle Universalpoesie.

24. Mit einer schöngeistigen Lesehilfe von Dieter Schlenstedt im Anhang.

25. Ich kam einmal ... Schnauze voll.

26. Eine andere Literatur und ihre Leser.

–4–

Difficulties Crossing the Plain

> But the plain is a mountain once more, at
>   least it has chasms.
> Leap with your brains you must, dialectics
>   on your backs.[1]
> >   (Volker Braun, 'Berlinische Epigramme': *Langsamer
> >   knirschender Morgen*)

At the close of Günter de Bruyn's novel *Preisverleihung* there is a party attended mainly by writers and academics. One of the older guests expresses his surprise at how seldom the word 'socialism' is used in these circles. Professor Liebscher replies that people only talk about bread when they have none. That is the easy answer; in the context of the novel it can only be ironic. 'Socialism is as follows', says the 1963 programme of the SED:

> Relationships between people are characterised by comradely cooperation and mutual aid. With socialism there begins to be realised a community of free people, who are connected through common, free and creative work. The ideals of socialist morality – socialist patriotism and internationalism, responsibility towards society, love of work and of working people, a socialist discipline at work – enable the community and the individual to act for the welfare of the nation and peace in the world.[2] (Weber 1986, p. 268)

Preisverleihung shows a society of opportunists, careerists and seducers. Liebscher's own motto could have come from the mouth of Andrew Carnegie or Henry Ford: 'It is everyone's duty to be successful'[3] (*Im Querschnitt*, p. 62). Now not even the most uncritical supporters of the GDR's establishment would wish to argue that the GDR's socialism was perfect. When Hermann Kant claimed in 1973 at the Seventh Writers' Congress that as far as literature was concerned the conflicts in the GDR's society were no longer antagonistic in nature (1981, p. 189), he was contradicting Jürgen Kuczynski (1979), who pointed out that, for example, the security of employment which socialism had bestowed on its workers had led to a relaxation of work discipline: socialist progress continued to conflict with 'petty bourgeois' attitudes. If socialism is a dynamic system, as the politicians never tire of explaining, then one of the duties of socialist literature must be to point out the imperfections of the present in the name of a better future. This might be the function of the 'critical socialist realism' propagated by Schlenstedt (Haase et al 1984, p. 1605). Unfortunately the parameters within which this criticism in the name of socialism may be voiced are fairly circumscribed.

In this chapter we shall examine the way in which contemporary topics have been handled by the GDR's writers. Such topics have always been problematical. As a member of the delegation of writers which met Walter Ulbricht in 1971 Erik Neutsch complained that the author of an adventure story or detective story had an easier passage than the writer who attempted to depict the new problems of socialism (Rüß, ed., 1976, p. 43). As Christoph Hein has pointed out, even Friedrich Wolf's play *Cyankali* of 1929, which attacks the oppressive abortion legislation of the Weimar Republic, was not performed in the GDR until *after* the GDR's own abortion laws had been liberalised (1987, p. 105).

It would be an exaggeration to claim that the term 'socialism' had dropped out of the GDR's literature. Writers such as Erik Neutsch, Helmut Sakowski and Hedda Zinner ensure that committed socialists are present in their works, even where they are critical of certain aspects of contemporary society. Nevertheless, much of the literature published since 1970 appears non-political when compared with that of the previous twenty years. In Wolf's *Der geteilte Himmel* the heroine had to choose between the capitalist West and the socialist East, while Kant's *Die Aula* described the construction of a socialist university and Neutsch's *Spur der Steine* the construction of a socialist industry. By 1970 these battles had been won. Brecht's early postwar poem 'Wahrnehmung' is often quoted to characterise the situation:

> The difficulties of the mountains lie behind us
> Before us lie the difficulties of the plain.[4] (1967, vol. 10, p. 960)

Brecht had been referring to the defeat of fascism and the problems of creating socialism. But while achieving socialism was itself like climbing a mountain, at the top there was still an exhausting plain to be traversed before communism could be reached. The lines form the entirely serious motto for Neutsch's *Spur der Steine* of 1964. By 1978 they provided only an ironic subtitle for Erich Loest's novel *Es geht seinen Gang*. When quoted in Burmeister's *Anders* (p. 93), furthermore, they are merely a comic cliché. Socialism itself is not called in question; indeed it is taken for granted. Writers tend to focus on the often banal problems of everyday life. More ambitiously, they treat the relationship between the individual and society.

One consequence of the timidity of the GDR's press is, as already suggested, that literature takes over some of the functions that investigative journalism holds in a Western democracy. This applies not only to 'documentary' literature. A substantial amount of the GDR's fiction takes up social 'problems' which developed socialism has not managed to solve. For example, Erik Neutsch has on a number of occasions been critical of certain aspects of the education system, especially the unsocialist competitiveness which it encourages. *Zwei leere Stühle* contrasts the careers of two contemporaries: the one had been a brilliant success at school, the other was a trouble-maker, asking, for example, awkward questions on the invasion of Czechoslovakia by the Warsaw Pact countries. Today, however, the former is in the West, while the latter lost his life in the service of his comrades in the army. Neutsch questions an education system which fails to detect mere opportunism on the one hand and genuine idealism on the other. In Hans Weber's novel *Alter Schwede*, which deals with the problem of unwanted children, the central character Sven was unfortunate enough to be one of twins whose parents had budgeted for only one child and insisted on sending him to an orphanage. As mentioned earlier, de Bruyn's *Neue Herrlichkeit* portrays the horrendous conditions which prevail in homes for the elderly. Hermann Kant's most recent works have been satires on various aspects of contemporary life. The best of them, 'Der dritte Nagel', is a hilarious account of the need for the right contacts which the GDR's shortage of commodities and services imposes on its people. In the better examples of this kind of literature one is sometimes reminded of Charles Dickens, who was similarly involved with specific social problems.

Broadly speaking, this literature falls into two types. The one concerns itself with social issues, the outstanding problems faced by a socialist society. Here it may well be individualistic ambitions which are hampering socialist development. Where the authority of the ruling Party is felt to be infringed, difficulties with the censor inevitably emerge. The second type is more common and less problematical in political terms. It turns to the individual, his or her existential aspirations and fears. Clearly it would be foolish to try to separate these two forms exactly. Criticism of social institutions may well be formulated in terms of the existential aspirations of the individual, and in an authoritarian, monolithic state *all* manifestations of individuality, especially those which stress the right to privacy, inevitably have political undertones at least. *Nachdenken über Christa T.*, for example, provoked the authorities because of its insistence on the individual's right to self-realisation and its claim that certain aspects of real existing socialism were stifling this right.

The traditional social novel in the GDR was the *Betriebsroman*, a novel which described the activities of a work collective in a factory or other industrial enterprise. From Eduard Claudius's *Menschen an unsrer Seite* to Wolf's *Der geteilte Himmel* and Neutsch's *Spur der Steine*, writers presented the struggle of the forces of progress against opportunism, idleness or downright sabotage, and the heroic efforts of the workers headed by a committed Party secretary inevitably led to developments which would further both the political and the economic success of the GDR. In the literary landscape of the 1970s and 1980s Dieter Noll's *Kippenberg* stands out like an erratic block left over from an earlier era. Although the narrative standpoint is 1977, the novel looks back to 1967, when the GDR was in the throes of the scientific-technical revolution and computers were believed to be the solution to all problems. Earlier industrial novels were set in factories or on building sites; *Kippenberg* is set in a pharmaceutical research institute in Berlin, a late example of the 'managerial literature' demanded by the Second Bitterfeld Conference. The 'Institute for Biologically Active Substances' finds itself at a crossroads. Originally devoted to pure research, it is now faced with demands from the state that it cooperate more closely with industry and orientate its activities towards more practical applications, and the advent of the new technology is calling in question the working methods of the older members of the institute. The conflict is illustrated by the physical division of the institute into an 'old building' and a 'new building', the former the seat of the institute's director Lankwitz, the latter that of the 'Kippenberg group', who have just taken charge of a new computer. In *Menschen an unsrer Seite* the story revolved on the heroic innovatory activities of Hans Aehre, who rebuilds a foundry furnace without letting it cool down, thereby saving considerable losses in output. The Kippenberg group have evolved a method of producing a synthetic version of a vital and scarce substance which will save the country millions in foreign currency and may become an important export commodity. Because of Lankwitz's distrust of new technology and indifference to the needs of industry the new process has been taken no further. The matter comes to a head when Kippenberg discovers that the state is about to buy an expensive Japanese factory to produce this substance by a much less efficient method and he has just a fortnight to have the decision reversed. These two weeks are filled with dramatic events, cross-country journeys, feverish nights spent at the computer, commands and counter-commands as Lankwitz and his henchmen attempt to sabotage the project, as internal office rivalries erupt. In the end the reactionaries are put to flight and the forces of reason triumph. Although such an account of the story makes it seem unacceptably schematic, it is impossible while reading it not to feel drawn into the action. Moreover, the issues with which the novel deals are topical not only in a socialist state.

Kippenberg is a socialist realist novel and suffers from many of the weaknesses of the genre: a predictable plot and characters who tend to move like clockwork. It is filled with the heroic archetypes of socialist realist fiction. Bosskow, the Party secretary who spent ten years in Buchenwald is the one unquestionably positive figure in the novel, while Lankwitz is the bourgeois survivor from a bygone age and Kortner the opportunistic placeman. There is above all the nostalgia for the early pioneering years of the GDR, when the problems were more concrete and the optimism more immediate. Kortner's nineteen-year-old daughter Eva is a crucial figure. One of the teenagers interviewed by Maxie Wander envied her predecessors, who had something they could fight for, namely socialism, which she and her contemporaries had simply been given (*Guten Morgen, du Schöne*, p. 83). Eva is a comparable character. At a time when Beatlemania is rife and other decadent Western-oriented fashions such as miniskirts and long hair are prevalent among the young, she has decided to abandon the conventional career which her father has mapped out for her, giving up her university place and her comfortable life in Berlin in order to 'go into the wilds', to engage herself for socialism on the fringes of the GDR. This contrast between Berlin and the rest of the GDR is noted by Kippenberg himself, when he visits the industrial concern which is most directly involved in the use of the new process. Out in Thuringia he encounters an archaic sense of community absent from Berlin, and, as Dennis Tate (1984) has shown, a search for community is central to the GDR's early fiction. Just how mythical this community is is implicitly admitted by Noll himself, when his characters refer throughout to the outlying regions as being 'behind the seven mountains', where in the folk-tale Snow White and the seven dwarfs live. However, it is in the context of such myths that figures such as Plenzdorf's Edgar Wibeau and Christa Wolf's Lenka have to be viewed.

Even *Kippenberg*, however, makes concessions to the new subjectivity of the 1970s. Unlike the great industrial novels of earlier years it is, at least nominally, narrated in the first person by the central character, Joachim Kippenberg himself. This at once implies the importance of the individual, a fact which is borne out when we realise that Kippenberg is frequently reporting what he cannot possibly know, not only events which took place in his absence but also the thought processes of other people. At one point the implausibility is stated in the space of a few lines, when Kippenberg states that he did not know what was going on in the minds of Bosskow and Charlotte, his wife, only to tell us immediately afterwards what Bosskow *was* thinking (pp. 601-2). Noll must have been aware of the contradiction; clearly he had decided that the advantages of the first-person narrative outweighed the disadvantages. For the conflicts of contemporary GDR society are crystallised in the personality of Kippenberg himself, who is not a little reminiscent of Joe Lampton in John Braine's *Room at the Top*. Of impeccable proletarian origin, he learned from his father to distrust political parties and to look after Number One. He married Lankwitz's daughter not out of love, but, at least unconsciously, in the knowledge that it would benefit his career. His early revolutionary fervour has given way to opportunism; he is running with the wolves while still attempting to hunt with the hounds. His have become the petty bourgeois values referred to by Kuczynski: individualism, egoism, being content with the possession of a motor car and a weekend cottage in the country. These values collide with the dynamic socialism of a Bosskow. In the course of the novel we discover that the real impediment to progress over the new project is Kippenberg's own guilty conscience, his awareness that it was his cooperation with his father-in-law which prevented the development of the synthetic process in the first place. It is Eva who rekindles in him his earlier dynamism, enables him to fight for the project and to own up to his responsibility to his colleagues and the Party. In one of the many coincidences of the novel he encounters her in a bar one evening and becomes aware that there is a 'life' beyond the routine which he has allowed himself to fall into. *Kippenberg* is a novel of self-criticism, a form which we encounter again and again in the literature of the GDR; in this invocation of 'life', even one defined in terms of socialism, there are also existentialist undertones, reminiscent of the Hesse of *Steppenwolf* or the Böll of *Das Brot der frühen Jahre*.

None the less it remains a novel which *mutatis mutandis* might have been written at almost any point in the GDR's history. This is not the case with Karl-Heinz Jakobs's novel *Die Interviewer*, which appeared a few years earlier. Set in an ancient mining town in the Erzgebirge, it describes both the production difficulties of a factory which produces light bulbs and the private problems of Herrmann Radek and his family. As in *Kippenberg*, we encounter the conflict between technological innovation and tradition, but in this case the traditional values are those of a humane socialism. Radek is the leader of a team of operations researchers who are studying the causes of the factory's difficulties. All their studies lead to the personality of Alfred Baumann, a sexagenarian and former activist who did sterling service for socialism in the early years of the GDR, expropriating capitalists and landowners, but who has been unable to keep pace with technological developments. The factory manager was similarly conservative. While he was in hospital after a heart attack his deputy had introduced a time and motion study. When he returned there was a violent argument in which he accused his deputy of reinstating capitalist methods, had a further heart attack and died. Baumann, meanwhile, is to be demoted.

What makes the novel different from the socialist realist model is that none of the conflicts is resolved unambiguously. Radek resigns after his recommendations have been effected. Baumann is popular and humane; although all his subordinates agree that he is incompetent and does nothing to improve production, none is willing to see him go. Having him demoted means that efficiency has taken precedence over humanity. In this case it is not remnants of a pre-revolutionary bourgeois ideology which are the brake on progress. Radek himself, a trained psychologist, is unable to control his sixteen-year-old son Ernst, who eventually runs away and is temporarily placed in a borstal. Radek is a rationalist, rather like Joachim Kippenberg, who believes that everything can be calculated in mathematical terms. But he is jealous of Kritzki, who appears to be trying to seduce his wife Liane, and he himself is having an affair with Baumann's sixteen-year-old daughter Lore, who is determined to lose her virginity to an older man and persuades him to sleep with her.

Die Interviewer begins with the manager's funeral. In the 1950s and 1960s death was generally a taboo area: the deaths of Strittmatter's Ole Bienkopp and Wolf's Christa T. were regarded as unnecessarily pessimistic, calling in question socialism's ability to triumph over all foes. Since 1970, however, this is no longer the case. Edgar Wibeau dies at the end of *Die neuen Leiden*, as does Beatriz de Dia in *Trobadora Beatriz*, in neither case of old age. Perhaps the most moving scene of Uwe Saeger's *Nöhr* is the protagonist's account of his father's dying hours. Hedda Zinner's *Katja* consists of the reflections of a mother during the funeral of her daughter, who has committed suicide. Christoph Hein's *Der fremde Freund* also begins with a funeral, and as with *Die Interviewer* the circumstances are macabre. There the problem is that Claudia is not sure whether she is at the right funeral, since she does not know any of Henry's relatives, and is embarrassed by having to encounter Henry's wife. Here the proceedings are disturbed by the film crew making preparations to interview some of the top people at the works where the deceased was manager. Death is something which cannot be planned, and the novel is largely about the attempt to introduce exact methods of planning into the factory. The social aspects of *Die Interviewer* thereby become subordinated to such of more existential significance.

Brigitte Reimann's novel *Franziska Linkerhand* is another work which takes issue with the archetypes so uncritically handled in *Kippenberg*. One of these is the heroic myth of socialist construction confronting the untamed wilds, embodied by Noll in the story of Eva Kortner. The bulk of Reimann's novel is an account of Franziska's actual experiences as an architect working in Neustadt, literally a 'new town', which is being built in the South East fringes of the GDR. Franziska is filled with idealism; her models are Le Corbusier and Oscar Niemeyer, the designer of Brasilia. But the reality of Neustadt is very different from the myth. It is one which is perhaps more familiar to British than to West German readers, remembering the appalling new satellite towns which were thrown up around such cities as London and Glasgow after the Second World War. The architects and civil engineers on site have constantly to battle with their masters in Berlin over materials, equipment and priorities. Franziska's training has remained faithful to the old-fashioned view of architecture as an art; in Neustadt she finds art has been replaced with technology, architecture subjected to the dictates of economy. The anonymous blocks of flats are 'accommodation silos' (p. 152), 'TV caves' (p. 351), behind whose thin walls domestic life is carried on practically in public, replacing picturesque peasant cottages which for all their lack of amenities at least guaranteed a form of community which the new town lacks. Vandalism, drunkenness and violence reign nightly in Neustadt. Some of the scenes are as harsh as those of Werner Bräunig's 'Rummelplatz', which caused offence in 1965. Neustadt has no cinema, roads and dwellings holding a higher priority. The suicide rate is a closely guarded secret. There is an interminable conflict between the petty bourgeois ambition to own a plot of land and surround it with a fence, and the desire of the planners to create communal areas. Socialist commitment is conspicuously absent: there is good money to be earned by architects prepared in their spare time to design weekend cottages for the nouveaux riches. The one character in the novel who wears the badge of the SED is Franziska's immediate superior, Schafheutlin.

He himself lives a few miles away in petty bourgeois comfort, with his own house and garden in a village which has remained relatively intact.

This clash between petty bourgeois and socialist values is not resolved. Franziska herself comes from a wealthy middle-class family and grew up in a provincial town in a large house with a garden. With the arrival of the Red Army comes a new word for the seven-year-old Franziska: 'capitaleest'. Her father is a publisher and her mother so incorrigibly 'respectable' that Franziska revolts and embarks on a disastrous marriage with working-class Wolfgang Exß. Her attempt to break the barriers of class ends in divorce, whereupon Wolfgang's family ransack the couple's flat, triumphantly bearing away some of Franziska's most cherished personal possessions. In a supposedly socialist society class differences appear insurmountable. In Neustadt she is given a room in what can best be described as a civilian barracks for women, with a former circus strongman as caretaker to watch over their morality. Living on her own sets her apart from the other women, who have to share, four to a room. She is regarded as being of the intelligentsia and initially shunned by her fellows. It is therefore at least paradoxical that it should be Franziska who is so anxious to eradicate remnants of bourgeois individualism, dismissing the peasant cottages, for example, as 'romanticism without drains' (p. 208). The reader is left with the feeling that Franziska is the romantic idealist. None of the major characters of *Franziska Linkerhand* is predictable in the way that the characters of *Kippenberg* are. Schafheutlin appears at first to be the typical unimaginative, dogmatic functionary; but Franziska and the reader gradually learn to appreciate his vulnerability and sensitivity. He, too, suffers from a disastrous marriage to someone who is the epitome of petty bourgeois womanhood, devoted to keeping the house spick and span, and suspicious of anything out of the ordinary.

Franziska Linkerhand was left unfinished by its author, who died of cancer in 1973, and was published posthumously. As a torso of some six hundred pages it is none the less a substantial achievement. Reimann employs a flexible and sophisticated narrative technique. What begins as a first-person narrative, told by Franziska herself, after just over a page abruptly becomes a third-person narrative, told by an anonymous narrator, and throughout the novel there is a regular oscillation between the two points of view. In the course of the novel it emerges that Franziska is writing in 1967, some years after the events described, most of which take place in 1961 and 1962, but is dissatisfied with her manuscript. Although this is never made clear, it is possible that the anonymous narrator is Franziska too, attempting to objectify her own experiences. Whether this is the case or not, the insights into the thought processes of others, such as Schafheutlin, which are to be found in the third-person narrative, need not be viewed as inconsistencies (Tate 1984, pp. 141–2), but imply rather that this layer of the novel is qualitatively different from the other. For *Franziska Linkerhand* is only partly the social novel described up to now. It is also, and perhaps essentially, the story of a passionate and hopeless love affair. The first-person narrative is addressed to 'Ben', invoked in the opening sentence of the novel. It gradually emerges that this is the name Franziska has given Wolfgang Trojanowicz, one of the drivers of the building site, to whom she was attracted at first sight. Trojanowicz had been a victim of the purges which followed the uprising in Budapest in 1956. An assistant lecturer in contemporary affairs, he had had a brilliant career before him, until a friend deserted to the West and he failed to condemn him in sufficiently explicit terms. Franziska does not discover these details until very late in the affair. It is a stormy relationship, reminiscent of the love dramas in the novels of Stendhal, who is invoked from time to time. Both Franziska and Trojanowicz are too proud to give any part of themselves away. He is bound by feelings of loyalty to a woman who had remained loyal to him during his years of disgrace and is too weak to break this tie. Accordingly their passion ebbs and flows, and even having sex together does not dispense them from using the formal mode of address.

Franziska Linkerhand appeared in 1974, a remarkable year for women writers in the GDR, which also saw the publication of Irmtraud Morgner's *Leben und Abenteuer der Trobadora Beatriz*, Gerti Tetzner's *Karen W.* and Christa Wolf's *Unter den Linden*. Even before the 1970s women had held an important place in the GDR's literary spectrum. Since the deaths of Brecht and Becher Anna Seghers had been the most respected and influential author of the older generation, and writers such as Margarete Neumann and Elfriede Brüning had been prominent even before the new generation of Wolf and Reimann appeared. From the mid-1960s onwards, however, the list has grown: Sarah Kirsch, Irmtraud Morgner, Helga Königsdorf, Helga Schubert, Helga Schütz, Angela Stachowa and Waldtraut Lewin have ensured that women are as at least as well represented as men in GDR literature. Moreover a new quality has developed in women's writing, one in which strong elements of a specifically feminist consciousness are being expressed. In *Franziska Linkerhand*, for example, this is to be seen less in the fact that Franziska is a woman working in a traditionally male occupation, for such topics were the stuff of many early GDR novels. Rather the feminism of Reimann's novel consists, firstly, in the theme of female sexuality. Franziska finds men's bodies erotic. Sexual arousal was not a common theme anywhere in the GDR's literature prior to 1970, but as seen from a woman's point of view it was unheard of. Secondly, the one moment of social community that Franziska experiences in Neustadt is when the women of the barracks gather round one night to comfort and support one of their number who is giving birth to an illegitimate child. This element of feminine solidarity in a situation which is peculiarly that of a woman underlines sexual difference rather than socialist class consciousness.

Such themes are developed by many of the other women writers of the GDR in the 1970s. Morgner's Beatriz, for example, is a sensual woman, who writes erotic poetry. Her medieval husband's disregard of her sexual needs contributed to her decision to sleep for over eight hundred years and to her great disappointment she finds on awakening that men are as sexually selfish as ever. Laura, her assistant in the novel, hopes that the GDR's liberalisation of the abortion laws will unleash the 'productive force of sexuality' (p. 336) by placing men and women on an equal footing, removing the fear of unwanted children. Literature of this kind can be related to the feminist literature which developed in Western Europe and the United States in the course of the 1960s, of which East German women writers are well aware. Since the issue of women's rights does not directly conflict with the SED's social policies it is an acceptable topic for literature. On the whole the literary achievements of the GDR's women authors have been more considerable in this respect than those of their West German counterparts. This in turn must be related to the context of the GDR's own social achievements in the area of women's rights.

Two main factors have determined the position of women in GDR society. The first is ideological, the Marxist tenet that the dependent status of women is a function of the relation between capital and labour, that women can therefore be emancipated only in socialism. Since emancipation is viewed primarily in economic terms, its main feature must be the woman's economic independence, which can be achieved only when women, like men, find fulfilment in unalienated labour. The second factor is pragmatism: since the disastrous outflow of *man*power to the West in the 1950s, the acute shortage of labour has necessitated the employment of every available human being. Consequently the GDR has systematically realised what in theory are the ideal conditions to enable men and women to coexist in complete equality. The constitution guarantees this equality in all areas of public life. The Family Laws of 1965, for example, declare it the duty of both marital partners to see to the education and welfare of their children and to enable each other to improve their professional qualifications. Arrangements for pregnant women and mothers with young children are most generous. As a result the GDR has the highest percentage of women in paid employment in the whole of Europe: in 1982 the figure was 82.6% of those between the ages of 15 and 60, and 49.6% of the working population was female (Zimmermann, ed., 1985, pp. 443–9).

On the face of it therefore, women's economic independence from men has been realised. That this is not after all sufficient to create genuine emancipation or genuine equality is something which the GDR's writers, but also the GDR's social scientists, have been stressing ever more urgently in recent years. Three main aspects are problematical. The first is the uneven distribution of women in the career structure: as in the West, the greater the responsibility held, whether in politics, industry or the professions, the less likely it is that the occupant of the post will be a woman. In Irmtraud Morgner's novel *Amanda* we encounter, for example, Hilde Ferber, who holds a relatively high office in the Council of Ministers; but she is a caricature and has regularly to be sent to a health farm to recuperate from her superwoman exertions. The second is more insidious, for the many measures taken to enable women to be working mothers, both housewives and employees, imply that they are somehow handicapped by being women and that special allowances have to be made, thereby consolidating rather than overcoming the problems. The assumption remains that it is the female rather than the male partner who is responsible for the children and the housework and that by the provision of such facilities as laundries and shops at her place of work she can be helped to cope with her 'two shifts'. One of the stories of Morgner's *Trobadora Beatriz* relates how Vera Hill, who works in a physics laboratory, can combine her job with her duties to her child only by means of a tightrope stretching between her home and her place of employment. Eventually she loses her balance and falls to her death. In *Amanda* Heinrich Fakal's wife knows that she will always remain undisturbed in the kitchen, where her husband never sets foot, preferring instead to watch five television sets tuned to different channels simultaneously. He used to have a secretary who claimed at a trade union meeting that unlike West Germany the GDR had no need of foreign workers to create its Economic Miracle, as they had women to do the Turks' work on their second and third shift. She was sacked at the earliest opportunity. The third problematical area is that of family relationships. The GDR has a very high divorce rate, itself a sign of women's independence, as most divorces are initiated by women who are unhappy at being expected to work a 'second shift', but also a possible factor in the relatively high rate of teenage criminality. Broken homes, long periods in institutions such as creches from a very early age do not always contribute to mature personalities. This, too, is a topic which crops up in contemporary GDR literature.

Patricia Herminghouse distinguishes three phases in the development of women's writing in the GDR (Hohendahl and Herminghouse, eds., 1976, pp. 281–334). The first is linked to the propaganda effort to encourage women to enter traditional male occupations. To Adorno's 'boy-meets-tractor literature' there corresponds what might be called a 'girl-meets-crane literature' (the frequency of the choice of crane driver which Herminghouse detects must surely be Freudian, the phallic symbolism underlining the tenor of these texts in which women are, as it were, turned into men and gender-specific qualities blurred). The second phase is more sophisticated, focusing on the psychological tensions to which women, like men, may be subjected, once they have made the correct choice of contributing to socialist productivity. Thus Rita Seidel in Wolf's *Der geteilte Himmel* has no difficulty in integrating with the male labour force in the carriage works; she breaks down, however, after having to choose between the socialist community and her lover, who has defected to the West. In keeping with the more private nature of the literature which has been written since the late 1960s, in the third phase of women's writing the emphasis has shifted yet again. Now it is the distinctively female experience that is at issue. The claim that the GDR has resolved the social problem of male–female relationships is tested *ad feminam*, and the assumption that male-oriented occupations, behaviour and values are the norm is called in question. Anna Seghers's reaction to Annemarie Auer's enthusiastic account of Morgner's *Trobadora Beatriz* is an indication of the difference between the generations: for Seghers the novel appeared merely to incorporate the 'United Nations resolutions on women' (Auer 1977, p. 302). Others, too, have been unhappy about the ideological implications of this literature. Wilhelm Girnus (1983a) accused Christa Wolf of substituting the sex war for the class war, a complaint which she promptly rebutted (1983) with a quotation from Engels's *Origin of the Family*: 'The first class antagonism to appear in history coincides with the development of the antagonism between man and woman in marriage, and the first oppression based on class coincides with that of

Difficulties Crossing the Plain

the female sex by the male'[5] (Marx/Engels 1956ff, vol. 21, p. 68).

Although not overtly 'feminist', once again Wolf's *Nachdenken über Christa T.* set the pace. The experiences and voices of Christa T. and the narrator are authentically female. To claim, as Alexander Stephan does (1979/80, p. 25), that the fact that Christa T. is a woman rather than a man is of little importance is to miss the point. For centuries literature was dominated by the male voice. Female authors of subjective literature lack, as Renate Möhrmann points out, role models such as Goethe's Werther (1981, p. 342). Christa T., who actually invokes Werther in one of her letters, writes of 'the difficulty of saying "I"'[6] (p. 164).

Gerti Tetzner's *Karen W.* owes much to Wolf's encouragement. Another first-person, present-tense narrative, it is Karen Waldau's account of the nine months subsequent to her decision to leave her friend Peters and, taking their seven-year-old daughter with her, return to her roots in the country. A brief week of reconciliation over Christmas is followed by further estrangement, while a new relationship ends when her lover asks her to marry him. Although at the end Karen returns to Leipzig, it is not to her old life with Peters. Traces of the earlier model of women's writing can be detected in *Karen W.* There the breakup of a partnership was often caused by the man's ideological backwardness, his refusal to recognise the woman's desire for a career or even his lack of the woman's orthodox political commitment. Karen's friend Linda, now a lawyer, has triumphed over just such circumstances. Tetzner provocatively reverses the terms of the equation. Although Karen herself trained to be a lawyer and subsequently abandoned her career in order to live with Peters, her commitment to the law was not especially strong in any case. One reason for her disillusionment with Peters is the discovery that he has opportunistically abandoned the early revolutionary fervour which led him to call in question Party orthodoxy. Peters is a historian, who for years has been working to modify the official view that history is determined by class conflict and that the personality of outstanding individuals has no part to play. Having failed to make any academic headway he is now prepared to capitulate to the official line. Karen by contrast earlier believed that changing social conditions was sufficient to change the relationships between people; now she does so no longer. *Karen W.* is a novel which firmly believes in individuality. Peters's betrayal of his own beliefs is just one example of the motif which is central to the novel, an existentialist search for authenticity. Karen's life has been inauthentic up to now. She studied law in reaction against what she falsely supposed to be the Nazi past of her father. However, the paragraphs and sections and sub-sections of the law turned out to be the opposite of 'life itself' (p. 261). At the same time the initial passion of her love for Peters turned into routine, so that she eventually felt stifled by their relationship. During the nine months covered by the novel she is looking for her 'own pattern' (p. 264), rather than one governed by external forces. Whether she will find one is left open.

The authentic female voice is to be heard in Morgner's *Trobadora Beatriz*. One of Laura Salman's stories ends with the words: 'That is our part. Mine. That much is certain when I say: I. When I say: I am a woman'[7] (p. 197). Morgner's novel was described by a West German reviewer as 'something like a bible of contemporary women's liberation' (Markgraf 1975), and it has been at least as popular in the West as in the East. Nevertheless it is a work which could have been written nowhere other than the GDR. Morgner leaves the reader in no doubt as to her orthodox stand on socialism. The numerous scenes set in the capitalist West describe a merciless jungle of mutual exploitation, while the Vietnam war is documented in all its American-inspired horrors. When Beatriz is disillusioned with 1968 France it is to the GDR that she turns, enthused by the glowing account provided by Uwe Parnitzke in Paris in words which must have been taken straight from an official GDR publication. And although she is disappointed with what she finds in the GDR, it is unambiguously clear that if socialism does not guarantee the equality of men and women it is the precondition for that equality. One of the important documents of the novel is the extract from the debate in the People's Chamber over the liberalisation of the GDR's abortion laws, giving women at last, as Laura puts it, full rights over their own bodies. A visit to Rome convinces Beatriz that there are no prospects for genuine emancipation in the capitalist West: 'Moral conditions can be revolutionised only after economic conditions have been revolutionised. The second step cannot be taken before the first. In the GDR the first step has long since been taken. Now we are occupied with the second, selah'[8] (p. 385).

In keeping with these assumptions Morgner adopts a humanist attitude to feminism. Both in *Trobadora Beatriz* and in its sequel *Amanda* we encounter figures who represent those women's groups which demand not merely the overthrow of patriarchy but the restoration of matriarchy. They are invariably ridiculed. In *Trobadora Beatriz* they are represented by Persephone and Demeter, who appear in a concrete bunker singing 'the same old incantations' (p. 19); in *Amanda* by the comic witch Isebel with her paper crown and broomstick. Morgner's outlook can be summed up in the words of one of the characters of *Amanda*, parodying the eleventh of Marx's theses on Feuerbach: 'Hitherto philosophers have merely interpreted the world in a male way. But it is up to us to interpret it also in a female way, in order to change it in a human way'[9] (p. 312).

In *Trobadora Beatriz* the 'male' view of reality is associated both with Stalinism and with the fanatical pursuit of knowledge for its own sake. Thus the death of 'Papa Stalin' left Uwe with the feeling of being fatherless, while the Soviet grandmaster Solovjev declares that women will never be able to compete with men at chess, because they lack fanaticism. What is only hinted at in *Trobadora Beatriz* becomes explicit in *Amanda*: the division of labour, which made capitalism and technological progress possible, also resulted in a splitting of the human personality into the rational and the intuitive, the destructive and the creative, the warring and the caring. These in turn have become associated with the male and the female principles respectively. A socialism whose goal is to overcome the division of labour must also seek to overcome the division of the sexes. In *Trobadora Beatriz* Morgner is relatively optimistic: Benno Pakulat is a male who is both manly and tender. In *Amanda* the optimism is less obvious. Indeed Margy Gerber (1986/87) has found signs in recent East German women's writing to suggest that the revolutionary elan of the early 1970s has given way to introspection and retreat. The scarring effects of abortions are stressed, as are the negative results of a lack of tender loving care in early childhood when the working mother leaves her child in a creche.

Trobadora Beatriz is a social novel. In choosing three separate protagonists, Beatriz the artist, Laura the working-class mother and Valeska the physicist, together with their men-folk, it presents a cross-section of GDR society. The reform of the abortion laws is one measure which society can and does take to help right the imbalance between the sexes; further steps, now that socialism has been established, will depend on the behaviour of individuals. This is the message of the remarkable collection of satires *Blitz aus heiterm Himmel*, which appeared a year later in 1975, seven texts by men and women writers, whose point of departure was a sudden change of sex on the part of the protagonist. One of the stories of *Trobadora Beatriz* had been written for the anthology but rejected. In it Valeska discovers the ability to change her sex at will, thereby achieving utopian wholeness, a synthesis of male and female qualities in one body. Sarah Kirsch's contribution, which gave the anthology its title, describes how Katharina, on her transformation into a man, finds that all of a sudden her partner helps with the housework and allows her to accompany him on his journeys as a long-distance lorry-driver. At one stroke she has achieved 'emancipation'. By implication the story parodies the notion that by, as it were, waving a magic wand society can create equality. The most challenging of the stories is by Christa Wolf, whose 'Selbstversuch', already published in *Unter den Linden*, uses the science fiction format. The narrator, herself a research chemist, is the guinea-pig for a substance developed by her professor to turn women into men (there would be no market for one which performed the opposite service). The experiment is successful. Numerous satirical details describe her discovery of the different treatment which she receives in her male form. But the sting is in the tail. Just before the effects of the drug have become permanent she breaks off the experiment. She has seen into the world of men and she did not like what she saw. However favourable the social position of men may be it cannot compensate for the stunting of the emotional life which it entails. Like Morgner, Wolf looks forward to a future society in which androgyny rules, where neither man nor woman is the yardstick but 'man and woman' (1987, p. 800).

The sex change theme of these stories belongs to the world of fantasy. But it opens a question which has taken on some considerable importance in the GDR's literature, that of sexual identity itself. The earlier theme of class has, as it were, given way to the theme of gender. While there is still no East German Hubert Fichte, no overtly 'gay' literature, at least the theme of homosexuality is one which is broached from time to time. The interviews published by Maxie Wander and by Christine Lambrecht include open references to unorthodox sexual proclivities. In *Kippenberg* Harra has been secretly living with another man for the past twenty years, afraid of gossip and ridicule. Kippenberg admits that while homosexuality is no longer a crime, it still entails social discrimination and even the risk of falling into the hands of old-fashioned doctors who regard it as a disease to be cured. Harra is not part of the 'gay' scene, however, which Kippenberg regards as a function of discrimination on the one hand and sexual marketing on the other. The crisis of identity described in Uwe Saeger's *Nöhr* partly involves the narrator-protagonist's sexual insecurity. Nöhr's wife suspects him of being a latent homosexual. Although the episode remains unclear, it seems that during a stay in a neurological clinic he was found in the bed of his room-mate Bols. Nöhr is probably a bisexual, hence the significance of the numerous references to the myth of Teiresias, which was also used in Wolf's 'Selbstversuch'. Waldtraud Lewin's historical Federico is explicitly presented as bisexual, as happy with his male as with his female sexual partners. Saeger's *Sinon* introduces a further variant. It begins when the narrator has just returned to his wife after an affair with one Lucie, who has died. Only gradually does it emerge that 'Lucie' was a transsexual. When in *Trobadora Beatriz* Valeska is able to change sex at will and carries on a relationship with both her husband and a woman lover the implication is that lesbianism, or even bisexuality, is normal. It is unexpectedly regressive to find that in Christa Wolf's *Kassandra* to all the other negative characteristics of the brutish Achilles is added his homosexuality.

The early GDR novel was exceedingly prudish. Eroticism was regarded as characteristic of decadent, bourgeois literature. Since the end of the 1960s this has changed. In Günter de Bruyn's *Preisverleihung* Overbeck's seminar springs into life when one of the students suggests that the GDR's literature deals with love as if they were still living in the Middle Ages. She is not, however, primarily concerned with explicit descriptions of the physical act, but with the motives and causes of falling in love. People's political development has been frequently described, never their emotional development. The discussion that follows runs on for an hour over the normal time. It includes questions such as whether private emotions are a luxury in view of the American presence in Vietnam, whether socialist morality is no more than that of the Protestant petty bourgeoisie, and whether there should be a socialist 'sex wave' like the one currently enveloping the Federal Republic. In the years that followed the publication of *Preisverleihung* something approaching a sex wave has indeed broken. We have already seen the provocation of female sexuality in *Franziska Linkerhand* and *Trobadora Beatriz*. In the title story of Bernd Ulbrich's *Abends im Park* there is an explicit account of an old man's encounter with a young prostitute in a public park. In the same collection, 'Fang die Sonne auf' describes the masturbatory fantasies of a teenager. Part of the popularity of Maxie Wander's interviews *Guten Morgen, du Schöne* must have been due to the insights afforded into the sexual habits of some of those interviewed. The change in climate is most striking if we compare de Bruyn's *Buridans Esel*, which appeared in 1968, with Saeger's *Warten auf Schnee*, written just over a decade later. While both are novels which describe a man's inability to choose between two women, his wife and his lover, where de Bruyn's text is ironic and discreet, Saeger's is openly erotic.

Sexuality might be one of the 'new themes' encouraged by Honecker in his 1971 address. But it is more than a mere thematic widening of frontiers. In *Die Interviewer* sexuality, like death, is an aspect of humanity which cannot be controlled mathematically. This is the true significance of the theme. Authoritarian societies tend to be prudish out of fear, fear of what they cannot control. Uwe Saeger's novel *Nöhr* is especially interesting in this respect. Nöhr's sexual insecurity is related to his social and political insecurity. As the illegitimate son of a Russian soldier and a German woman he experienced social discrimination in childhood. Whereas his wife is a doctor, he is a simple mechanic who has worked his way up to the position of engineer but still feels inferior and under pressure. In his job he is aware of the cheating which occurs to enable the firm to claim that it has over-fulfilled its production targets, but he cannot make up his mind what to do about it. At the beginning of the novel he returns, almost literally, from the dead: he had driven his car into a river, partly by accident, partly in a suicide bid, had managed to extricate himself but instead of going to the police had gone into hiding, and was assumed to have drowned. The novel is largely his own review of his past as he waits to be found.

One of the characters of Werner Bräunig's short story of 1969 'Der schöne Monat August' reflects, only half-ironically: 'Progress is when the working man can afford to have marital problems'[10] (*Ein Kranich*, p. 276). It is only when the struggle for survival under the conditions of capitalism has ended with the victory of socialism that the working-class individual has time for a private life. That might be one explanation. The material security afforded to women under the GDR's equal rights legislation is clearly another factor in the break-up of marriages which earlier would have held together out of sheer economic necessity. What is certain is that the theme of marital crisis broached by de Bruyn and by Saeger is an important one in the contemporary literary spectrum. It is partly related to a new interest in individual psychology, expressed in the incompatibility of the two partners. It may, however, also indicate a wider sense of dissatisfaction with the development of society. As we have seen, Tetzner's Karen Waldau feels not only that her marriage has gone stale, but that her partner has abandoned his earlier ideals and given in to the demands of the Establishment. Helga Schütz's Julia, too, leaves her husband at the same time as she ceases to 'sing in chorus'. The 'mid-life crisis' is a crisis of the GDR itself. In this sense 'breaking out' from a stale marriage is comparable to the more or less existentialist revolt of Eva Kortner in *Kippenberg* or of Edgar Wibeau in *Die neuen Leiden des jungen W*. It is a revolt against opportunism and inauthenticity, against the 'lie'.

Klaus Schlesinger's short novel *Alte Filme* is a further illustration of this underlying crisis. Günter Kotte's life follows a predetermined pattern, divided between work, do-it-yourself carpentry and watching old films on television. He has lost interest in sex and fears his wife Karla's advances. One evening he discovers that Frau Jeske, the old asthmatic woman who shares their flat, is a former dancer and that as a young actor she played a part in the film he is watching. Confronted with the reality of time and aging, Kotte is physically affected by the awareness of his own mortality to the extent that he is for the first time in his life unable to go to work. He turns down an opportunity to improve his qualifications and instead of devoting his evenings to decorating the flat he spends them at the pub. When Karla departs for the weekend on a training course Kotte goes on a drinking spree, during which he is drawn into the bohemian world of artists and their lovers and has a sexual adventure with one of them. The ending is deeply ironic. On his arrival home he finds that Frau Jeske has collapsed and has to be taken away in an ambulance. Now the Kottes will have more room in their flat, more room to breathe. The departure of the person who initiated Kotte's desire to break free means that he can settle down again. He has had his adventure. The unremitting friendliness of those he has met, even of the policemen who arrest him for climbing up the fountains on the Alexanderplatz, suggest it was as unreal as the 'old films' of the novel's title. Karla meantime, it seems, has had her own adventure. Whether their relationship has changed for the better remains to be seen.

Kotte's experience of the bureaucracy which administers the GDR's living accommodation adds to his feeling of suffocation. It is one which is shared by others, his colleague Harry, who expresses his sense of having 'missed the train' (p. 38), the painter Jakob, who rejects marriage and a steady job. But this existentialist critique has its peculiarly socialist dimension as well. Kotte started out as a fitter, but was encouraged to graduate to a managerial position. There is a degree of nostalgia when he briefly returns to his former place of work. His alienation is at least partly due to his loss of contact with his working-class origins. This in turn is related to the central paradox of the GDR's socialism. In ideological terms the working class is the progressive class; but the workers are constantly being urged to 'improve themselves', to acquire better qualifications, consequently to lose their working-class attributes. In *Alte Filme* we learn that when Jakob was at art school he stepped out of line and was punished by being sent to do factory work. It is a motif which recurs again and again in the GDR's literature. We have already encountered it in the figure of Reimann's Trojanowicz. Karen Waldau experienced a similar punishment, as does the protagonist of Volker Braun's *Unvollendete Geschichte*. Braun's comment is biting: 'To factory work ON TRIAL. But what kind of thinking is it that regards that as a punishment?'[11] (p. 92). If unalienated labour is the expression of man's humanity, how can it be a *punishment* to be sent to work in a socialist factory?

In Tetzner's *Karen W.* Peters is a rationalist, unable to comprehend the attachment Karen has rediscovered to her village roots, afraid to show his feelings. In Wolf's 'Selbstversuch', as in other works by women authors, rationality is the province of the male, warmth and the emotions belong to the female. It is not surprising that this over-schematic contrast of 'male' and 'female' qualities provoked alternative accounts. Indeed in *Trobadora Beatriz* it is Benno Pakulat's first wife who is cold and ambitious, nagging at her husband to get promotion so that they can afford a car and a new three-piece suite. This is the pattern of Erich Loest's novel *Es geht seinen Gang*. Like Schlesinger's Kotte in *Alte Filme*, the narrator, Wolfgang Wülff, is of working-class origins and has worked his way up in the world to the position of engineer; he, too, regrets having lost contact with the workbench in the process. Wülff's wife Jutta, however, is the daughter of a former factory owner, and his mother is neither surprised nor sorry when the marriage eventually fails. Two quarrels lead to the break. The first is Wülff's refusal to study for an engineering diploma in spite of all the promptings of Jutta. The second and most serious is their disagreement over the upbringing of their daughter Bianca. Wülff is devoted to Bianca, going for walks with her, telling her stories. Jutta is more of a disciplinarian and the decisive clash occurs over Bianca's swimming lessons: when Wülff accompanies them one day he is horrified to find the terrified children being forced into the water and Bianca in tears. Eventually he calls one particularly arrogant father a 'fascist'. When Jutta insists he apologise Wülff refuses, the matter goes to court and Wülff is fined 250 marks. The incident, moreover, is the final blow to the Wülffs' marriage. Loest subverts two literary models in *Es geht seinen Gang*. Here it is the man who is caring and tender, the woman who is cold and ambitious. Moreover, since it is the GDR's international successes in competitive sports, especially swimming, which have contributed in no small measure to what sense of national identity it has, it is possible to regard Jutta as the ideologically sound partner, comparable to the heroines of earlier women's writing. Here, however, the narrative focus ensures that it is with the 'reactionary' husband that we sympathise.

There is a further provocation in that the representative of the working classes is the passive element in the novel. Unlike David Groth in Kant's *Das Impressum*, who in spite of his opening words 'But I don't want to become a minister!'[12] in the course of the day described in the novel does accept ministerial office, Loest's Wülff refuses to accept the historical mission of the working class mapped out for him by the GDR's Establishment. In *Es geht seinen Gang* the working classes are largely uninterested in politics. Wülff's mother is sceptical of the new rulers. Wülff knows that in the pubs in his area of Leipzig the conversation seldom touches political affairs. But what exactly is the 'working class' in the new GDR, which is supposed to be moving towards a classless society? This question, too, is posed by the novel. Wülff's friend, the blind historian Wilfried, is working on a committee set up to redefine it, but even the existence of this committee is supposed to be secret, let alone its findings. Clearly it is an achievement-oriented society, as the swimming lessons indicate, and one which takes its toll on those who compete. Wülff's boss Grosser, for instance, survives on pills and eventually suffers a heart attack at his desk. Although the strains on the GDR's functionaries are stressed in *Das Impressum* too, Groth heroically accepts his responsibilities in spite of them, whereas Wülff refuses.

This rejection of competitiveness and performance was a common enough motif in West German literature a few years previously to elicit a furious polemic from Helmut Schelsky (1975). In Wülff's case, however, there is one personal reason for standing back, and since his author has made him almost exactly as old as the German Democratic Republic itself (Loest 1984, p. 7) we must regard him as a representative figure. The year 1965, as we have seen, was a repressive turning-point in the GDR's cultural policies; it was also a turning-point in Wülff's life. Everyone was talking of the Beatles, listening to their music, growing their hair long. Wülff and his friends played their own version of English rock music in the cellar of a friend's house. After initially approving of the Beatles' working-class origins and the social criticism of some of their lyrics, the authorities became alarmed and proscribed the most prominent of the local groups which they had inspired. When a public demonstration in their support was planned, pupils were warned against attending it. The few hundred who turned up, partly out of curiosity, found it all rather desultory until the authorities intervened with police-dogs and water-cannon. Wülff was bitten by a police-dog as he attempted to escape:

> Before the battle on Leuschner Square the world was clearly divided for me. The enemy was in the West; the Americans were bombing Vietnam, Kiesinger was a fascist. Now I was bitten by one of our dogs which really ought to have been biting an American unloading his bombs on Vietnam.

I was not throwing napalm, no GDR dog had any right to snap at me. Vengeance therefore. How?[13] (p. 23)

The scars of the police-dog's bite are long-lasting. It is a basic disappointment with his own society that is the cause of Wülff's refusal to conform. This disillusionment, the sense of betrayal, is a motif which can be traced through so many of the GDR's novels: *Nachdenken über Christa T.*, *Karen W.*, *Unvollendete Geschichte*, *Der fremde Freund*, *Kassandra*.

Western-style rock music is the inspiration of Plenzdorf's teenager Edgar Wibeau, but by 1971, when *Die neuen Leiden* is set, it was no longer regarded as subversive. One oblique way of levelling criticism at contemporary political circumstances in the GDR is through the constellation of generations represented in the text. There is little argument that the original impetus which created the GDR was an admirable one. At least since Hermann Kant's *Die Aula* participation in the International Brigades during the Spanish Civil War has been a literary indication of impeccable socialist commitment. The men and women who endangered their own lives by resisting fascism were also those who established the GDR. In *Kippenberg* the older generation of socialists, represented by Bosskow, who have directly experienced the repressions of the Third Reich, has greater moral stature than their younger colleagues, and the third generation, represented by Eva Kortner, yearns after the challenges with which the first was faced. In *Die Interviewer*, too, all three generations are represented, but the accents are different. Although Baumann is of the generation which created the GDR, had to overcome the remnants of fascism and establish socialism, he is out of touch with the contemporary Establishment. In prewar days the actor Markus Linck was an important member of the anti-fascist theatre movement; today he is impossibly arrogant and incompetent. Of the middle generation, Radek is a technocrat, taking socialism for granted and not politically motivated at all, which Kritzki, who is making a documentary on the factory, is a womaniser and an opportunist, doctoring reality to make it conform with what his taskmasters want to hear. The third generation, represented by Lore Baumann and Ernst Radek, appears essentially disoriented. It is this generation on which Ulrich Plenzdorf focuses. In *Die neuen Leiden des jungen W.* the first generation is represented by Zaremba, who fought in the Spanish Civil War and helped to establish socialism in the GDR after the war and for whom Edgar has nothing but admiration. The middle generation, as represented by Edgar's mother and the foreman of the labourers with whom Edgar works, is characterised by its petty bourgeois respectability and lack of imagination. Edgar himself is almost entirely defined by his status as teenager, expressed in the jargon he uses, the music he prefers and the jeans that he wears, and Plenzdorf owed his success largely to the authenticity with which he presented the teenager mentality.

In *Die neuen Leiden* Plenzdorf succeeds in subverting most of the clichés of socialist realist literature while at the same time leaving open the extent to which his work criticises actually existing socialism itself. Like Eva Kortner in *Kippenberg*, Edgar breaks out of an existence in which even his future pension is predictable, leaving a mother whose sole concern is that he 'gets on in life' and 'stays respectable'. Here, however, it is the dullness of provincial life that he leaves behind in favour of the bright lights and discos of Berlin, and the 'wilderness' where he settles is an abandoned allotment. As in *Kippenberg* we encounter a 'great invention' which will rescue the GDR's economy, in this case a non-misting paint-spray. The group of workers who are trying to develop it, however, are a motley collection, from a tattooed septuagenarian down to a former dropout, and when they try to demonstrate their invention to the experts, the result is pure slapstick, as they drench everyone in paint. Edgar himself resolves to succeed where the others have failed. In keeping with the literary model he is under pressure of time (his lodging place is about to be bulldozed to make room for new flats and his mother is on her way to fetch him home), and he has to make do with the bits of scrap metal he finds in the allotments (an ironic commentary on the GDR's make-and-mend economy). Finally he goes out with a bang, blowing his summerhouse to pieces. But *Die neuen Leiden* is also a text of self-criticism, whose first-person narrator from beyond the grave intersperses his account of his activities with numerous terms of disparagement. In this way Plenzdorf is able to leave his text open to interpretation and to satisfy the Beckmessers of the Establishment, for if it can be read as demonstrating the futility of trying to break out of the socialist collective then it is an acceptable part of the literary canon. The self-criticism, however, a cliché of GDR life and literature, is itself ironised, coming as it does from beyond the grave. As Gerhard Kluge has suggested (1978), Wibeau can be regarded as a picaro, telling the Establishment what it wants to hear, while roguishly winking at the reader to cast doubt on the sincerity of his protestations.

Die neuen Leiden is not a directly political text; it does not criticise circumstances in political terms, but in terms of the existentialist values of authenticity and spontaneity. The political framework is taken for granted. By contrast, Joachim Wohlgemuth's paradigmatic

Egon of 1962, still a best-selling novel for teenagers, portrays the integration of a young tearaway with the help of the Communist Youth Movement (FDJ). In *Die neuen Leiden* the FDJ is merely a rubber stamp on an obituary notice and Wibeau refuses to be integrated. It goes without saying that this in itself has its political implications. Plenzdorf's text was enormously influential, sparking off numerous imitators and creating a new wave of 'youth fiction' or 'jeans prose' (Flaker 1975; Watson 1987). In *Egon* those who wear jeans are regarded as infected by Western ideology and dismissed as 'Nieten in Hosen', an untranslatable pun on 'Niethosen' (studded trousers, i.e. jeans) and 'Nieten' (worthless blanks drawn in a lottery). In this context, as so often, Edgar's passion for jeans has associations which the Western reader can easily overlook. Even so, Edgar explicitly associates the wearing of jeans with authenticity of life-style rather than with political attitudes.

The best-known imitation of *Die neuen Leiden* is by Rolf Schneider, who chose a female counterpart to Edgar. In *Die Reise nach Jarosław* Gittie Marczinkowski is the teenager who 'drops out' when she fails to gain the place at sixth-form college she believes herself entitled to, and sets off on a journey to the Polish town where her grandparents originated. Like that of Edgar, her narrative is in the teenage colloquial register, although her reference to her parents as 'ancients' ('Greise') owes more to Thomas Mann's 'Unordnung und frühes Leid' than to contemporary vocabulary. The intertextuality is explicit when she encounters one 'Ed' at the railway station, wearing 'first-class blue jeans', living in a summerhouse in Lichtenberg and raving about 'beat music'. Again the middle generation appears in a poor light: Gittie's parents are fully integrated members of the Establishment and conform to petty bourgeois norms; they own a car, which Gittie despises, and a weekend bungalow in the country; both have responsible jobs and little time for their daughter, whose emotional allegiance is to her grandmother. In the end, however, Schneider blurs the issue of rebellious youth within socialism. Gittie is confronted with the spectre of German wartime guilt and eventually returns to the bosom of society to take a job in a hotel.

The teenage viewpoint, conveyed through the medium of teenage slang, is adopted by other contemporary writers, including Horst Deichfuß (*Windmacher*) and Hans-Georg Lietz (*Das Hexenhaus*). But young people figure prominently in other works, such as Christa Wolf's *Kindheitsmuster* and Hedda Zinner's *Katja*. There are a number of reasons for this flourishing of youth fiction from the 1970s onwards. Influences from abroad were important. The late 1960s saw the emergence of youth as a force to be reckoned with the whole world over. Television and radio do not respect international frontiers, not even the Iron Curtain. Internal factors, however, were at least as significant. By 1970 a generation had come of age which had grown up entirely in the GDR under the conditions of socialism. Their deficiencies could no longer be attributed to the distortions caused by fascism. The state has endeavoured to attend to the needs of young people in such a comprehensive way as to obviate the temptations of the West, increasing both the pressures to conform and at the same time the attractions of an alternative life-style. As Werner Heiduczek has put it, they risk either losing all autonomy or living a double life, conforming in public but rebelling in private (cit. Thomas 1973, pp. 64–5). The choice of teenagers as subject-matter was potentially the most direct way of questioning the achievements of the GDR's social engineering. Thus when Edgar admits to feeling that nobody should live longer that seventeen or eighteen, since thereafter they will have become entirely integrated in the routine of life, although many West European teenagers may share his apprehension, in the context of the GDR's youth policies this is a peculiarly damning criticism. Finally, there is a literary dimension to the phenomenon. In earlier GDR literature young people, rather like the sons of Laocoön in the Vatican group, appeared as scaled-down versions of adults, the FDJ taking the place of the SED. If in the 1970s the accent had moved from the struggle to establish socialism to the problems of life in everyday socialism, it was natural that literature on teenagers should now attempt to see teenagers as they were rather than as they ought to be.

The teenagers in Volker Braun's *Unvollendete Geschichte* are slightly older than Edgar Wibeau. Frank has had, as it were, his 'Wibeau period', when he used Western slang and hung about in bars – he has even served a period in borstal – but now he is a reformed character. Despite her faded jeans Karin has never been 'young' in this sense. Her father is a local politician, both parents are pillars of the Establishment, and it has never occurred to her to question their authority. Two events shake her out of her unthinking complacency: her father tells her to stop seeing her boyfriend Frank, who is suspected of planning some unspecified offence, and when she begins work at a newspaper office, for the first time she encounters the gulf between social reality and the harmonious gloss placed on it by the media. Braun's story presents a society whose rulers mistrust those they rule. Just as the newspaper filters out information it regards as unsuitable for ordinary minds, so nobody will tell Karin or Frank why he is under suspicion. By the time it turns out that he is falsely believed to be planning to defect to the West she has been pressurised into leaving him and he has attempted to commit suicide. The arrogant silence at the top poisons relationships between parents and children, between one individual and another.

Unvollendete Geschichte has frequently been related to Büchner's *Lenz* (Koerner 1979; Tate 1984). It is at least as indebted to Goethe's *Die Leiden des jungen Werthers* – via *Die neuen Leiden*. In a central passage Karin encounters Plenzdorf's text, which her younger brother has furnished with enthusiastic annotations. Karin herself is less impressed. At school she had read *Werther*, which Wibeau is always quoting, and she finds Goethe's work both more profound and closer to her own case. To her Wibeau's conflict with his surroundings remains a superficial one, whereas in *Werther* there is a 'split' not only between the individual and society but within both society and the individual himself. Karin, too, faces the dilemma of divided loyalties, to her parents and to Frank, to the state and to herself. Immediately after this passage she goes to collect her belongings from Frank's flat. Although he has evidently taken an overdose of sleeping tablets, she refuses to believe he is trying to kill himself and leaves. Only later, when a telephone call comes from Frank's father, does she realise the enormity of her actions. The parallel with *Werther* is striking. It is the subsidiary figure Frank who is the Werther in Braun's story; to the book of *Emilia Galotti* found open on Werther's table after his death there even corresponds the edition of Heiner Müller's *Philoktet* which Frank has been reading. Karin is like Lotte, who is torn between love for Werther and loyalty to the conventional domesticity embodied in her marriage to Albert. Lotte provides the pistols with which Werther kills himself, and if Karin does not supply the sleeping pills, her behaviour is psychologically no less complex.

With consummate dialectical skill Braun pursues the theme of the 'splits' which penetrate every level of life. The political division between West and East Germany is evidence of one kind of split. Karin is even alienated from her own body; in her dreams she becomes an object, men probing her every orifice; when she finds herself pregnant by Frank her mother insists she have an abortion. She has been taught to believe that the GDR is divided into two clear groups, those who 'know' and those who have to be 'persuaded'. Frank's mother, however, while being politically active, also watches Western television, evidence for Karin of acute schizophrenia. Frank's father regards the pressure on Karin to leave Frank as evidence that they are regarded as 'not good enough' for Karin's family, that the GDR's society has social divisions as in the West. This in turn is related to the division between the conscious and unconscious mind. The function of a socialist newspaper, as Lenin put it, is to furnish the proletariat, the progressive class, with its revolutionary awareness. In fact Karin finds it repressing what is inconvenient, and the result of the state's mistrust for Frank is that he literally 'loses consciousness'. All these divisions indicate that, as the title implies, the GDR's history is still 'unfinished', that a satisfactory synthesis is still awaited. In another dream Karin finds the answer to her and society's problems: the individual is freed of the web of bureaucratic edicts, people begin to talk to one another freely and openly and on the basis of equality. But this *glasnost'* remains a dream and when she awakes she has forgotten what she unconsciously knows.

Braun is the writer who has been most energetic in propagating political issues concerning the relation between worker and state. Because of this he is singled out for scorn by Fritz-Henrick Melle, for example, one of the young dropouts represented in the anthology *Berührung ist nur eine Randerscheinung*: 'I can only say the lad is torturing himself. All that leaves me cold'[14] (p. 151). For Karin this abandonment of political commitment to which she is tempted would be 'suicide, not of the body but of thought'[15] (p. 74). Braun sees the relation as a dialectical one. The GDR is a 'workers' and peasants' state'; in his poem 'Regierungserlaß' the worker is no longer the object of decrees, but, at least nominally, issues the decrees himself. But in another poem from the same collection, *Wir und nicht sie*, Braun alludes to Brecht's poem 'Fragen eines lesenden Arbeiters'. Brecht's 'reading worker', living under the conditions of capitalism, expresses his surprise that the history books credit only kings and generals for the great events of history, as if, for example, they had built Babylon single-handed. In 'Fragen eines regierenden Arbeiters' Braun's worker, now a 'ruling worker', asks why those in whose name the decrees are promulgated are not consulted more frequently. There still is a gap between rulers and ruled; and this is the fault not only of the rulers but also of the ruled, who 'still keep their mouths hidden / like a private part'[16] (*Gedichte*, p. 42). A genuine socialist democracy demands both that the administration treats its subjects as subjects rather than objects, as adults rather than children, but also that the subjects themselves behave like adults. One of Braun's collections is entitled *Training des aufrechten Gangs* ('learning to walk erect'). It takes its title from the prose piece 'Höhlengleichnis', an adaptation of Plato's 'parable of the cave'. For five thousand years man crouched cramped in a cave, only to discover that the cave was his own creation, its walls his own assumptions and apparatus. When he tries to stand up he continues to bump his head on these same assumptions. The process of learning to stand on his two feet is one which will take further centuries. This is one theme of Braun's *Hinze-Kunze-Roman*.

Hinze and Kunze are the German equivalent of Tom, Dick and Harry, ordinary people therefore. In Braun's novel, however, Kunze is a top official of the 'people's Party', probably of ministerial rank, although that is one of the many secrets which the narrator is not allowed to divulge, and Hinze is his chauffeur. They are thus both 'ordinary' and not so ordinary; at any rate they have representative significance. In some respects *Hinze-Kunze-Roman* is a very private GDR novel, demanding of the reader inside knowledge not only of the GDR's society but even of individuals in it. As we have seen elsewhere, the narration is full of ironies, as the narrator atttempts to conform to the demands of the literary Establishment. At one point he is brought before a committee, presumably of the Writers' Union, where he is taken to task by 'Frau Professor Messerle': why is he not writing a novel like that of 'Author N.', whose 'Dr. Wackelbach' becomes a model individual through the love of a young girl? 'Author N.' is, of course, Dieter Noll and his novel is *Kippenberg* (Kippenberg = 'tilting mountain', Wackelbach = 'wobbling stream'), and although Professor Messerle's name associates her with the Beckmesser of Wagner's *Die Meistersinger*, Braun evidently also had in mind Professor Anneliese Löffler ('Messer' = knife, 'Löffel' = spoon), who promptly gave the novel a poor review (1985; see Kleinschmid 1985b).

Hinze-Kunze-Roman, unlike *Kippenberg*, does not furnish a harmonious view of a socialist community; rather it confirms the image presented in Franz Fühmann's story 'Drei nackte Männer', which Braun quotes extensively, and in which even the nakedness of the sauna cannot disguise the fact that some are in command and others must obey. Kunze lives in a bungalow with a private garden, Hinze in a crumbling tenement flat near the city centre. Kunze, not Hinze, can travel to the West, and it is Kunze who makes the decisions, while Hinze accepts them. There are yet more literary models quoted in *Hinze-Kunze-Roman*. One is Diderot's *Jacques le Fataliste*, Kunze being the master and Hinze his servant, 'riding across the Prussian prairie' (p. 35). The other is indirect but equally obvious to all who know German socialist literature: Brecht's play *Herr Puntila und sein Knecht Matti*, in which Puntila is the rich landowner and Matti his servant. Since the GDR is supposed to have overthrown feudal or capitalist structures of authority, these are the most provocative allusions of all. There are even echoes of the most flagrant feudal abuse of authority, the *droit du seigneur*, most memorably treated in Beaumarchais's *Le mariage de Figaro*. For Kunze is a womaniser and his first encounter with Hinze's wife Lisa arouses immediate lust in him, a lust which he satisfies in the course of the novel.

Hinze, however, no Figaro, merely accepts Kunze's behaviour. And whereas in Brecht's play Matti is the reasonable, progressive force, Braun suggests that in many ways Hinze is responsible for his own exploitation. This 'ruling worker', too, fails to open his mouth, leaving politics to the politicians, just like the pub acquaintances of Wülff in Loest's *Es geht seinen Gang*. At times Kunze appears as the progressive element. When he enjoins, 'Help me to rule, man!' Hinze replies, 'Give over. I've too much on at the moment'[17] (p. 25). When his master asks something outrageous of him he wags his tail like a dog. It is into his mouth that are placed the quotations from the anti-feminist philosophers of the nineteenth century, Hermann Ploß and Rudolf Hermann Lotze. Kunze appears more enlightened – but exploits women all the same. Braun's dialectics may be taken one stage further. In Brecht's play, too, Puntila can be highly enlightened, but only when he is drunk. Matti knows this and keeps his counsel, aware that when his master has sobered up the old relationship will return. Hinze is perhaps being equally cunning when he produces the paternalistic arguments against greater freedoms for the people. Kunze can afford to have a 'uniform outlook', whereas Hinze needs a 'double consciousness' in order to survive (p. 115). Small wonder that Kurt Hager, although he named no names, felt provoked into denying that there was any 'master-servant relationship' in the GDR (1986, p. 20).

For all their probing, Braun's works in many ways belong to the GDR's tradition of socialist writing, upholding the direct link between literature and political praxis. A rather different standpoint is adopted by Christoph Hein, the most exciting new writer to emerge in the GDR in recent years. Although he has been writing plays since the early 1970s, most of them still await performance. Disappointed with this state of affairs, he turned to prose fiction, publishing a first collection of short texts in 1980, *Einladung zum Lever Bourgeois*. Hein is less concerned with political structures than with the psychology and behaviour of individuals within these structures and in this sense his works are more representative of current literary fashions than Braun's are.

His novella *Der fremde Freund*, which appeared in 1982, brought him the breakthrough to critical acclaim. For copyright reasons the West German edition had to be given the title *Drachenblut* when it came out a year later. A linear narrative, covering the narrator's year-long affair with Henry, the 'stranger friend' of the title, is framed within an account of his funeral and of the six months in which the narrator's life subsequently returned to normal. What is unusual about the narrative is Hein's astonishingly convincing adoption of the role of a woman as narrator. The virtuoso way in which the 'alien' narrative point of view is handled, however, is itself a kind of 'alienation effect' in the Brechtian sense, encouraging the reader to study, see through and criticise Claudia, something which was ignored by most of the East German critics of the story. Claudia sees everything in negative terms: her aging parents are a burden, she has no time for her father's political interests, she is divorced and every marriage she encounters seems based on exploitation or sado-masochism. Growing old is a nightmare, but the teenagers she encounters are unfulfilled, violent and alcoholic, and she constantly has the feeling that her neighbours and society at large are spying on her. Her hobby is taking photographs, but only of inanimate objects, as photographing people would, she feels, be an unwarranted intrusion into their lives. She herself has attempted to make herself invulnerable to emotional upheavals by bathing in the 'dragon's blood' of the West German title. By the clever use of narrative focus Hein has left open the question as to what extent Claudia is what she is because GDR reality is as bleak as she says it is, or whether she sees her surroundings in this alienated way because of her own flawed character. There is, for example, a contradiction between her profession, that of doctor, caring for others, and the cynicism which she voices. And if like Siegfried she has bathed in dragon's blood then like Siegfried she must have her vulnerable spot, as we indeed see from time to time whenever she is caught off balance by the unforeseen.

The original East German title focuses on Henry, implying with its oxymoron the traditional pattern in the German novella of the unexpected or unheard-of, here the friend who remained a stranger. But there is a further literary allusion, this time to Albert Camus, the German title of whose *L'Etranger* is *Der Fremde*. Henry is the existentialist of the story. Since life to him is meaningless he attempts to give it meaning for himself by fast, dangerous driving, or by cynically exploiting others, inviting himself into Claudia's bed on their first meeting, for example, and revealing to her only much later that he is already married. His death in a brawl with some teenagers is certainly absurd. Whether it confirms his outlook or is a kind of punishment for his nihilism is once more up to the reader to decide. The debate whether an individualist or a sociological interpretation is more appropriate is further fuelled by Hein's introduction of psychoanalysis into the story. At its very beginning, set off from the rest of the text by its italic typeface, there is the description of a dream, a nightmare, in which the dreamer, presumably Claudia, finds herself on a narrow plank over a chasm while from the opposite side five runners appear, threatening to cause her to lose her balance. The runners are all men, so alike they might be quintuplets, running in the steady rhythm of automata. They have a rune-like symbol on their singlets, possibly like the SS in Nazi times. *Der fremde Freund* appeared in the year in which a first selection of works by Freud was published in the GDR. Claudia explicitly rejects analysis, but the implication here as elsewhere is a refusal to face up to the reality of her own self. The dream may indicate that Claudia is oppressed by the monolithic collective of GDR society, which, like the Third Reich, suppresses individuality, an individuality which in the case of Henry reasserts itself in fast driving, in Claudia's in the vain attempt to insulate herself from the outside world. But the text goes further. In a central scene Claudia travels back to the scenes of her childhood, literally, but with implications of a Freudian analysis. It becomes clear that her personality was seriously distorted in the early 1950s when she was an adolescent. Her mother, disappointed in her own marriage, explained sex to Claudia in wholly negative terms. When at about the same time, in June 1953, a tank appeared in the town, nobody was prepared to discuss it openly. Most seriously of all, the authorities' hostility to religion ended an intimate friendship with Katharina, whom Claudia eventually 'betrayed' in public; thereafter her friend, the only friend she ever had, left with her family for the West. Hein's story implies that just as in the personal sphere Claudia's repression of her past has led to a serious neurosis in the present, so in the public domain the GDR's repression of its Stalinist past has caused the current mood of alienation, cynicism and even inhumanity. In this analysis, as we shall see in a later chapter, he is not alone.

Der fremde Freund sums up many of the themes of this chapter. Claudia can see nothing of the socialist community invoked by *Kippenberg*. When she grows old she will have nothing of the satisfaction of a Bosskow or a David Groth at having 'done her bit' for socialism. The exploitation of women by men is to be found on every other page; here, too, there is no evidence that actually existing socialism has created a new quality of human relationships. The behaviour of the young people, the citizens of the future, does not suggest that things are going to improve. Once more an individual feels personally betrayed by society, as in *Unvollendete Geschichte* and *Es geht seinen Gang*. The darkness of the narrative, however, may be read as a provocation to the reader to engage in dialogue with the text. Hein defended the Soviet film *Repentance* with the words: '... only an artist who in spite of the crimes of the Stalin age did not abandon his hope in communism as the sole humane alternative can work so inexorably exactly and unwaveringly'[18] (Schriftstellerverband, ed., 1988, vol. 2, p. 237). These words may be applied to his own work too.

Notes

1. Aber die Ebne ist wieder ein Berg, jedenfalls hat sie Klüfte. / Springen müßt ihr, mit Witz, die Dialektik am Hals.
2. Der Sozialismus, das ist: Die Beziehungen der Menschen zueinander sind gekennzeichnet durch kameradschaftliche Zusammenarbeit und gegenseitige Hilfe. Mit dem Sozialismus beginnt die Gemeinschaft freier Menschen Wirklichkeit zu werden, die durch gemeinsame, freie und schöpferische Arbeit verbunden sind. Die Ideale der sozialistischen Moral – sozialistischer Patriotismus und Internationalismus, Verantwortungsbewußtsein gegenüber der Gesellschaft, Liebe zur Arbeit und zu den arbeitenden Menschen, sozialistische Arbeitsdisziplin – befähigen die Gemeinschaft und den einzelnen, für das Wohl des Volkes und für den Frieden in der Welt zu handeln.
3. Erfolg haben ist Pflicht für jeden.
4. Die Mühen der Gebirge liegen hinter uns / Vor uns liegen die Mühen der Ebene.
5. Der erste Klassengegensatz, der in der Geschichte auftritt, fällt zusammen mit der Entwicklung des Antagonismus von Mann und Weib in der Einzelehe, und die erste Klassenunterdrückung mit der des weiblichen Geschlechts durch das männliche.
6. die Schwierigkeit, "ich" zu sagen.
7. Das ist unser Teil. Meiner. Soviel ist gewiß, wenn ich sage: ich. Wenn ich sage: ich bin eine Frau.
8. Sittliche Verhältnisse lassen sich nur revolutionieren nach der Revolutionierung der ökonomischen Verhältnisse. Man kann den zweiten Schritt nicht vor dem ersten tun. In der DDR ist der erste Schritt längst getan. Jetzt beschäftigt uns der zweite, sela.
9. Die Philosophen haben die Welt bisher nur männlich interpretiert. Es kommt aber darauf an, sie auch weiblich zu interpretieren, um sie menschlich verändern zu können.
10. Fortschritt ist, wenn der Arbeiter sich Eheprobleme leisten kann.
11. ZUR BEWÄHRUNG in die Produktion. Aber was für ein Denken, dem das als Strafe gilt?
12. Ich will aber nicht Minister werden!
13. Vor der Schlacht auf dem Leuschnerplatz war für mich die Welt sauber eingeteilt. Der Feind stand im Westen; die Amerikaner bombardierten Vietnam, Kiesinger war Faschist. Nun biß mich einer unserer Hunde, der eigentlich einen Ami hätte beißen sollen, der Bomben auf Vietnam ausklinkte. Ich schmiß kein Napalm, nach mir hatte gefälligst kein DDR-Hund zu schnappen. Also Rache. Wie?
14. Da kann ich nur sagen, der Junge quält sich. Dazu habe ich keine Beziehung mehr.

15. Selbstmord, nicht des Körpers sondern des Denkens.
16. Halten noch immer den Mund versteckt / Wie ein Schamteil.
17. Hilf mir regieren, Mensch! – Laß man. Ich steh so im Streß.
18. ... so unerbittlich genau und unbeirrt kann nur ein Künstler arbeiten, der trotz der Verbrechen der Stalinzeit die Hoffnung auf den Kommunismus als einzige humane Alternative nicht aufgab.

–5–

How Did We Become As We Are?

> He who ignores the past will be forced to reenact it.[1]
> (Christoph Hein in conversation with Krzysztof Jachimczak, 1988)

In Hein's *Der fremde Freund*, shortly after Claudia betrays her schoolfriend Katharina her world is shaken by yet another event. Her favourite uncle Gerhard, who has always treated her more like a granddaughter or foster-child, turns out to have betrayed the local members of the Social Democratic and Communist parties to the Nazis. He is found guilty of complicity in the murder of four people and sentenced to five years' imprisonment. Already an elderly man, he dies in prison. At the time Claudia is an idealistic teenager, filled with righteous horror at the crimes of the Nazis, which she has learned about at school. Suddenly she feels contaminated by these crimes herself, believing she has lost any right to condemn the criminals and to feel sympathy with their victims. At home nobody talks about Uncle Gerhard, while in class she is silent, already developing the carapace of 'dragon's blood' against emotional upheavals. Claudia may be viewed as yet another victim of fascism, her present state a product of Germany's past.

Since contemporary issues may be problematical for GDR writers in their relations with the cultural authorities, historical topics are common and in this and the two subsequent chapters we shall investigate the major areas of the past to which writers have turned their attention. It is a preoccupation which also relates to the ideological premises of Marxism itself, which is nothing if not a philosophy of history. Socialist realist writing emphasises the revolutionary dynamic of history within which its stories are anchored. This is nowhere clearer than in such a paradigmatic work as Erik Neutsch's 'Drei Tage unseres Lebens', which appeared in the closing years of the Ulbricht regime. The major strand of the story concerns the reconstruction of the city of Halle. A motorway has to be built to connect the town to the modern communications network of the GDR, which will entail tearing down many old buildings, some of them slums, others, however, valuable parts of the cultural heritage. In the end a sensible compromise is reached: the motorway will indeed be built, but it will take a different route, one which will preserve of the old what is worth preserving, while at the same time enabling the city to look forward to the twenty-first century. At the centre of the discussion there is an extraordinary set-piece lecture by the new Party secretary, in which he outlines the development of human history from the point at which man broke away from the animal kingdom by developing tools, through the emergence of class-based societies, the invention of printing and science, and the Bolshevik Revolution of 1917, down to the present-day GDR, and looks forward to a time fifty years hence when man will have landed on Venus and the whole world will be socialist. These are the historical dimensions in which the debate is to be carried on. Clearly not everyone will share Neutsch's historical confidence and it is more than a little comic to link a debate on town planning with the ascent of man and the conquest of space. Socialist realist writing of this kind is no longer central to the GDR's literature. Nevertheless it continues to be written and remains the implied model for the more conservative critics and cultural politicians. 'Historical pessimism' is one of the supreme heresies of which writers such as Günter Kunert and Heiner Müller are sometimes accused. In his review of Saeger's novel *Nöhr* Klaus Kändler bemoaned the inability of young writers nowadays to tell 'history in story' (1981, p. 157). Fritz J. Raddatz (1988a), by contrast, has found a characteristic historical dimension in the writings even of those writers who have left the GDR and settled in the Federal Republic, and Christoph Hein himself has declared that he could make no statements on the present without knowing his own history and that of his society (Jachimczak 1988, p. 351). In both *Der fremde Freund* and his later novel *Horns Ende* the past is crucial for a proper understanding of the present.

The most crucial question for all Germans, East and West, has been the relationship between postwar society and the National Socialist era. In West Germany in the years immediately following the collapse of the Reich it was fashionable to speak of the 30 April 1945 as 'Zero hour' ('Stunde Null'), the moment when time changed, the slate was washed clean, a new beginning was made. Since the mid-1960s numerous studies have demonstrated how misleading this notion was. Hans Dieter Schäfer (1977), for example, has uncovered numerous strands of continuity between the 1930s and the 1950s in West German culture. In the GDR the concept of a 'zero hour' was never officially held. As Wolfgang Joho put it (1965): 'We did not begin in the year Zero.'[2] As a socialist state the GDR could, with a certain amount of justification, claim to have a quite different relationship to the Nazi past from the Federal Republic. Socialists had resisted fascism and were among the first to be oppressed by the Nazis, incarcerated in concentration camps, tortured and murdered. The GDR was the heir not of Hitler's Germany but of resistance to Hitler. There had been a not inconsiderable underground continuity of socialist resistance to the Nazis throughout the Third Reich by means of handbills and flyposters produced on clandestine printers aimed at counteracting official propaganda, and a number of left-wing groups, notably the Schulze-Boysen-Harnack group, had plotted to assassinate Hitler. In West Germany the 'Day of Resistance' remembered every year is, significantly, the anniversary of the plot by army officers to kill Hitler on 20 July 1944, officers who were motivated as much by alarm over the prospect of military defeat by the Soviet Union as by hatred of fascism. But it was the Soviet Union which suffered most under the Nazis, and it was the Red Army which defeated them, liberated a large part of Germany and was the guarantor of socialism in the GDR. In the West the Germans had merely been defeated, in the East they could regard themselves as the 'victors of history', for in the Marxist view of history socialism was the society of the future. This, as Stephan Hermlin has pointed out, both helped to stabilise East German society and also made it too easy to regard the case as closed, the crimes of the Nazis as something which had been purged by the mere act of inaugurating a socialist state (1983, pp. 399–400). This is the context which explains the enormity of Wolfgang Wülff's accusing a respectable GDR citizen of 'fascism' in Loest's *Es geht seinen Gang*. The GDR prides itself on having brought genuine war criminals to justice and claims that those who had fled westwards were more likely to receive milder treatment. Commenting on the fashionable term used in the West to denote coming to terms with past guilt, 'Bewältigung der Vergangenheit' (overcoming the past), Wilhelm Girnus (1977) suggested sardonically that it would be more appropriate to 'overcome the criminals' and bring them to justice.

Karl-Heinz Hartmann (1977) and Alexander Stephan (1980) distinguish three phases in East German writing on the topic. Early presentations of the Third Reich tended to concentrate on the underground resistance movement, illegal printing presses producing antifascist leaflets, and the sabotaging of the war effort. The theme of resistance was the major difference between East and West German portrayals of the Third Reich in the 1950s. In his war novel *Wo warst du, Adam?* Heinrich Böll, for example, admired and published in the GDR as a 'humanist' writer, presented war as a 'disease', the army as a machine from which there was no escape. A constant criticism of his works by GDR scholars was that they offered no alternative to death (e.g. Baum 1955, p. 141). However, as it was obvious that not every citizen of the GDR had been an active resistance fighter it soon became necessary to develop an alternative pattern, that of the 'conversion novel' (*Wandlungsroman*), in which the misguided fascist, the unfortunate member of the Hitler youth was led to see the error of his ways by a sympathetic communist, often a representative of the Red Army. In fact some of the major early works which deal with the Third Reich do not conform to either of these patterns. Anna Seghers's novel *Die Toten bleiben jung* does include indications that resistance was taking place, but the two protagonists on the side of humanity, Marie and her son Hans, are either unpolitical or, in the case of Hans, helpless when forced to bear arms against the Soviet Union, the country which he has learned to love as the birthplace of socialism. Franz Fühmann's novella *Kameraden* is a masterly demolition of the military ideology of comradeship which helps to cloak the most evil of deeds, but it lacks both the element of resistance and that of conversion. For these reasons both works had their critics when they first appeared. Thirty years after the war's end a generation had come of age whose failings could not be attributed to the Nazis and which was unwilling to accept cosy answers from its elders on the nature of the Third Reich. Moreover the new and more sophisticated narrative techniques which had been developed since the mid-1960s undermined the credibility of the black and white portrayals of earlier years. The favoured pattern of the novel of education with its concept of organic development was latently undermined by the decidedly non-organic nature of conversion (Tate 1984). The third phase therefore treats the phenomenon of fascism in a much more subtle way: not only are the 'villains' harder to distinguish from the ordinary men and women living today, but the patterns of behaviour which enabled Hitler to rule are shown to be still present in contemporary GDR life. After the title of Mikhail Romm's influential Soviet film of 1964, *Obyknovennie Fashizm*, 'ordinary fascism' became the watchword.

Jurek Becker's *Irreführung der Behörden* illustrates the tensions which might arise between those who uphold the conventional presentation of the past and those who have a more differentiated view. In 1967 Gregor Bienek has written the script for a film which deals mainly with a contemporary marriage. In a flashback scene, however, the couple is shown meeting thirty years earlier. She is fifteen, he is sixteen and wearing the uniform of the Hitler Youth movement. As the man is now a prominent communist, Bienek is called to account for this detail, which is liable to undermine the authority of the ruling Party. Bienek had wished to show that not everyone who had survived the Third Reich and gone on to fame and fortune in the GDR had been a resistance fighter: it was precisely the man's mediocrity which was important and which made his relationship to his future wife plausible. In the end, however, he is forced to leave out the Hitler Youth uniform. Becker's novel was published in 1973. The fact that this detail was included implies a critical attitude to the clichés which were expected under Ulbricht. Nevertheless, when Christa Wolf's novel *Kindheitsmuster* appeared a few years later, it still elicited an angry response from Annemarie Auer (1977), who took exception to Wolf's presentation of ordinary unheroic people in the Third Reich: they were not 'representative', not 'typical', as they were not in tune with the driving force of history, namely socialism.

A more drastic criticism of the conventional literature of the resistance is to be found in Jakobs's *Die Interviewer*, when Baumann relates how he used to give talks to school-classes on his experiences of escaping from the Nazis until one day he was stopped in his tracks when a young boy declared: 'I want to be a traitor and escape from the thugs too'[3] (p. 229). Idealising the victims of the Third Reich was not helping to understand the nature of fascism. The problem was most clearly stated by Wolf in an interview of 1974. For those like herself who grew up in the Third Reich the past came back in waves. For a time they had tried to associate fascism only with 'the others', the West, and had claimed the tradition of the antifascists and resistance fighters as their own; but increasingly young people were expressing puzzlement at how their parents had managed to survive unscathed. It was true that the 'process of maturing' which her generation had undergone was a fascinating one. Nevertheless, there was no date at which they could say they had 'overcome' fascism. The topic could no longer be simply the 'socio-economic roots' of fascism, but 'the structure of my generation's relations to the past, that is, overcoming the past in the present'[4] (1987, p. 790).

Wolf's words had in fact been anticipated by a member of a generation younger than her own. Klaus Schlesinger's *Michael*, begun in the 1960s but not published until 1971, is one of the first works to question the easy, conventional assumptions. Six months before the narrative begins, in an international documentation of Nazi crimes he found in a secondhand bookshop, Michael Berger, the 23-year-old narrator, had come across a photograph showing German soldiers shooting Polish hostages; one of the men appeared to be his father, with whom he subsequently broke off relations. On the day of the narrative he has received a letter from Poland stating that the man in question was himself executed for war-crimes in 1947 and therefore cannot be his father. *Michael* consists of the inner monologue of the narrator as he reviews these events which have turned his life upside down, remembering the closing weeks of the war as he experienced them as a child, and through various significant events of his past attempting to find a pattern in his own life.

In style and technique the work is so reminiscent of the early novels of Böll that some conscious influence must be assumed. Its locations, a café, a graveyard, a fairground, are all familiar motifs of Böll's work. Like many of Böll's characters Michael's mind is often obsessed with detail as it wanders through the various stages of his past. But it is above all the treatment of time which owes much to Böll. The relation between past and present, the presence of the past in the present, is conveyed by Michael's inner monologue, in which in the space of three hours a whole lifetime is evoked. It is the technique of *Das Brot der frühen Jahre*, where tensions between father and son play a similar role, and of *Billard um halbzehn*, where the Nazi past is shown to be past only for those opportunists who conveniently forget it. This influence implies an alternative reading of the GDR's relationship with the past.

Michael's school class was once taken to witness the trial of a former SS doctor. During the break the boys express their surprise that he had not chosen to settle in the West, where, it is implied, he would have had a better chance of escaping detection. There are other details in the novel which allude to the conventional treatment of the past rejected by Wolf. Kapinski, one of Michael's older colleagues at work, was an inmate of the Sachsenhausen concentration camp. He explains fascism in terms of 'economic structures' and stresses the role of resistance. Thus the memoirs he is writing include details on the 'Work of the illegal camp committee' or 'The organisation of the resistance struggle in the Pintsch works'. Moreover, he tries to dissuade Michael from pursuing his inquiries on the grounds that it would not be fruitful to pursue 'individual conflicts' (p. 45). The 'conversion pattern' is illustrated by Gessener, the comrade of Michael's father, who had been a fanatical Nazi until shortly before the end of the war, when, influenced by the crimes which the Germans were committing against the Russians, he refused to defend a village which he knew would therefore be destroyed by the Red Army, and was executed by the SS. But the novel is not about Kapinski or Gessener; like so many works of the 1970s it *is* about individual conflicts. Michael's father was not a war criminal, but he was not a hero either. The war was a harrowing experience which he would not wish on anyone; none the less encounters with other former soldiers lead to animated conversation as they recount anecdotes which suggest that the war had after all been a fulfilling time. Nor does he especially identify with the new society of the GDR: when Michael is threatened with expulsion from school for a stupid prank he in turn threatens to leave for the West. *Michael* is a novel which implies that the older generation in the GDR has little more moral authority than its counterparts in the West. Although it is set in 1960, the slogan of the West German 1968 generation, 'Trust nobody over thirty', seems to apply here too.

In fact *Michael* is more conciliatory than this. Martin Watson has shown how Schlesinger modified his original conception to play down the father's guilt (1987, pp. 43–57). Like *Nachdenken über Christa T.* it is the novel of a search, Michael's search for the truth about his father. It is not the story of Michael's father but the story of a relationship. As such it anticipates the flood of West German novels which appeared between 1975 and 1980, novels such as Elisabeth Plessen's *Mitteilung an den Adel*, Bernward Vesper's *Die Reise*, Paul Kersten's *Der alltägliche Tod meines Vaters*, Ruth Rehmann's *Der Mann auf der Kanzel*, Peter Härtling's *Nachgetragene Liebe* and Christoph Meckel's *Suchbild*, which variously treat the relationship between son/daughter and Nazi father. In East German fiction traces of the motif are to be found in Gerti Tetzner's *Karen W.* and Uwe Saeger's *Nöhr*. As Helmut Peitsch (Bullivant and Althof, eds., 1987) has pointed out, one of the dangers of the genre is that as the child comes to understand the father more clearly, he or she simultaneously loses sight of the actual barbarity of the regime under which the father was living.

What is distinctive about Schlesinger's novel is that the emphasis gradually shifts from the father to the son himself, so that the question at the end is no longer 'Who is my father?' but 'Who am I?' (p. 201). Michael is pampered by his landlady because he reminds her of her own son, who had died in the war. When Michael studies his photograph he notices that the insignia of the SS have been carefully touched out from the uniform. Overcoming fascism has to be more than merely tampering with a photograph, but Michael begins to wonder how he himself would have behaved if he had been old enough to be conscripted. Michael's innocence is perhaps, in the words of *Nachdenken über Christa T.*, 'innocence for not having being an adult'[5] (*Nachdenken*, p. 30). This is dangerously close to the comforting notion that to understand everything is to forgive everything. But Michael also begins to review his own behaviour. He has been no more committed to the society he lives in than his father is.

His girl-friend Thea fell out with him because of his lack of involvement. She, by contrast, chose to give up the comforts of a life in Berlin for the new challenges of a provincial practice, anticipating Eva Kortner in *Kippenberg*. *Michael* is not simply critical of the German past; it is a novel of self-criticism too. In this way it fulfils Wolf's demand that the past be overcome in the present. Its central symbol is the fairground Wall of Death whose rotation suspends the forces of gravity operating on the participant. At the beginning of the novel Michael has lost all sense of orientation, as he did initially in the Wall of Death. By the end he has realised that in life, too, one can regain one's balance by focusing on a single object. What this object will be, however, is left open.

When Wolf spoke of the new challenge which the past presented to her generation she was already in the middle of the novel which was to answer the challenge in the most comprehensive and moving way. The central question of *Kindheitsmuster*, repeated three times, is 'How did we become as we are today?'[6] (pp. 276, 418, 477).

Wolf's narrative technique matches the complexity of her subject-matter. Three interlinked time layers can be distiguished. The core of the novel is the portrayal of the childhood and adolescence of Nelly Jordan, who was born in 1929 in the small town of L., then in the East of Germany, now G. and in Poland. There she lived until in January 1945 her family fled westwards from the advancing Red Army. Although the town can easily be identified as Gorzów Wielkopolski, formerly Landsberg, where Wolf was born, the use of abbreviations to denote it is a characteristic feature of the author's deliberate blurring of the boundaries between fiction and biography. When this layer of the novel ends in 1947 in Mecklenburg, now under Soviet occupation, the trauma of the last three years has led to Nelly's breakdown, one which, although officially diagnosed as tuberculosis, is clearly as much spiritual as physical. On leaving hospital she is determined to come to terms with herself and the past. The second layer is the account of two days in July 1971, when the narrator, her husband, her brother and her teenage daughter Lenka visit the town of G., which neither the narrator nor her brother have seen since they left in 1945. Finally there is the present time of the writing of the novel, a period of two and a half years, beginning on 3 November 1972 and ending on 2 May 1975, thirty years after the 'liberation' (p. 512), three days after the fall of Saigon and the end of thirty years of war 'at another point on the globe' (p. 530). One function of this juxtaposition of past and present is to relativise the end of the Second World War. There are frequent references to the war in Vietnam, but also to the conflict between Israel and Egypt and to the fascist dictatorships in Greece and Chile. History, remarks the narrator, has an 'awful tendency to repeat itself', and it is important to arm oneself against this (p. 223). But the technique is also part of the insistence that the past is not over. In *Kindheitsmuster* Christa Wolf, like Proust before her, is searching for lost time, her own childhood; the search is not only for identity but also for morality.

To the three layers of time correspond the three forms of the personal pronoun which the narrator employs. Nelly is referred to in the third person throughout; the narrator is looking at herself as a child, as something in a sense alien to herself. But as narrator, while visiting G. and for most of her account of writing the novel, she does not use the first person either, rather avoiding the pronoun, writing incomplete sentences, employing the impersonal 'one', or, alternatively, addressing herself in the second person. This has two main effects. Its ambiguity draws the reader into the narrative, as at first he or she appears to be the object of the 'you'. But it also suggests a split within the narrator herself. *Nachdenken über Christa T.* had already spoken of 'the difficulty of saying "I"'. There it was a question of the meaning of subjectivity itself. Here it is a more concrete difficulty: that of taking responsibility for one's life, one's memory, one's actions, even the act of writing a book. The novel opens with a comment on the way we tend to 'alienate' the past from ourselves, an (unacknowledged) quotation from William Faulkner (Smith 1987, p. 319): 'The past is not dead; it is not even past. We sever it from ourselves and pretend not to know.'[7] It is not simply the past as such that is 'alienated'. For a year and a half the narrator has been struggling with her book, trying to overcome her doubts about the ability of language to cope with the horrors of the Third Reich. Objectifying herself, referring to herself as a child in the third person, as adult narrator in the second person, is at one and the same time a sign of her alienation and a device to overcome it. Thus it is only at the end of the novel when the narrator can say 'I' that she has come to terms with herself and her own past.

Such an ending might well appear too artificial, too pat. Helga Schütz was to employ a similar device in *Julia*. There is, however, a GDR tradition of playing with pronouns, which illuminates Wolf's method. The collectivist stance of the early years was expressed in the slogan 'From the I to the We'.[8] Günter Kunert, for example, was accused by Alexander Abusch in 1963 of wishing to turn the clock back 'from the We to the I' (Schubbe, ed., 1972, p. 881). The narrator's rediscovery of her 'I' represents an insistence on the responsibility of the individual, who may not hide behind a collective. Moreover the ending of the novel remains open, questioning, not authoritative.

> The child which had hidden in me – has it emerged? Or has it, startled, found a deeper, more inaccessible hiding-place? Has memory done what was required of it? Or has it connived in misleading us to accept that it is impossible to escape the mortal sin of this age, which is not to want to know oneself?
>
> And the past, which could decree rules about language, could split the first person into a second and third one – has its domination been broken? Will the voices die down?
>
> I do not know.[9] (p. 530)

The German title of the novel literally means 'pattern' or 'patterns of childhood'. The Third Reich is portrayed in *Kindheitsmuster* mainly through the childhood experiences of Nelly. Her life was relatively sheltered. L. was sufficiently far to the East not to be affected by British or American bombing raids and her father, Bruno Jordan, was only briefly called up for military service. He had already served in the First World War and was allowed to return to his grocer's shop after the successful campaign in Poland. *Kindheitsmuster* directs its attention to the 'home front' rather than the war, to 'ordinary fascism'. This in itself makes it less easy for readers to regard the past as something which is over and done with. The normality of people's behaviour is something they have in common with their contemporaries. The danger is that the narrative may lapse into nostalgia, as do so many of the accounts of childhood under the Nazis which swept the West German book market in the later 1970s, novels such as Klaus Stiller's *Weihnachten* or, even earlier, Walter Kempowski's *Tadellöser & Wolff*. The narrator is aware that 'tourism to half-sunken childhoods is thriving'[10] (p. 14).

A further function of the third level of narration is to provide the background. The narrator's researches into newspaper archives place Nelly's subjective experiences into a more objective context of antisemitic legislation and physical attacks on Jews. These researches are especially important for Nelly's early years, when memory is notoriously unreliable. How much would she have understood of what was going on around her, when her father joined the stormtroopers, when the domestic servant confided to her that her family had been communists and had wept when the communist flags were ceremonially burned in March 1933, when her father read out terms such as 'racially alien' or 'sterilisation' from the newspapers? Wolf's achievement here is to combine the subjective with the authentic, accounts of harmless childhood games with a documentation of the far from harmless political context. As she grows older Nelly falls more and more into line with the propaganda of the Nazis. Although her parents had been social democrats, there was no question of heroic resistance to Hitler. Charlotte is given to speaking her mind, but usually only in private. She comes across as a sensible, but unpolitical woman. When Nelly reports her schoolteacher's words that Jesus would have hated the Jews if he had been alive today, her sardonic comment is that hating was not one of Jesus's strong points. Her husband by contrast prefers not to intervene. When during the war one of the Ukrainian women who are forced to work for the Germans asks for help for a friend who is about to have a baby, Charlotte sacrifices one of her sheets. But Nelly hears about this only years later. The brutality of the regime is made clear with visits from the SA in 1933 and even from the Gestapo in 1944 when Charlotte lets slip a careless remark in public. It may be regrettable but it is understandable that neither Charlotte nor Bruno is a hero in the tradition of antifascist literature.

At school Nelly is taught to hate Jews and Communists, although as far as she is aware she has seen neither. Spontaneously she learns and recites patriotic poems which blame the Jews for Germany's defeat in the First World War. The outbreak of war instils in her a craving for ecstatic experiences, waving flags, looking up to a leader to impress, hero-worshipping her teacher, Julia Strauch, a woman reminiscent of Muriel Spark's Jean Brodie. She cannot wait to become a member of the Hitler Youth, where she learns the new word 'comradeship'. By the time the family is preparing to flee from their house in L., she has become a group leader herself and is trying to work out how to join the Werewolf guerrilla organisation which the Nazi leadership had called into being to resist the invaders. So complete is Nelly's blindness to the reality around her that the news of Hitler's death sends her into a stupor and it is several months before she is able to come to terms with the thought of a life after the Führer.

Kindheitsmuster is not the novel of a conversion. Nelly does not encounter a friendly communist who puts her on the right path, indeed the lack of guidance after the collapse of the Reich is one reason for her breakdown. One particularly revealing incident shows Nelly picking potatoes in a field alongside Ukrainian women, who are forced labourers, practically slaves. A common motif of East German literature on the Third Reich is the moment of insight when one of the characters, hitherto an unthinking fellow-traveller, encounters just such a forced labourer, and suddenly realises their common humanity. Anna Seghers was a seminal influence on Wolf.

How Did We Become As We Are?

In her novel *Die Toten bleiben jung* Anneliese, the teenage daughter of a Prussian officer, has been taught to believe that the Ukrainian women working on the estate where she is doing agricultural training are subhuman. She is curious about them, manages to get close to one, and there is a moment of startled recognition when each sees the other as a human being. In a later short story 'Vierzig Jahre der Margarete Wolf', Seghers portrays secret acts of solidarity between German women and female Russian factory-workers. Writing much later in a different cultural and political context, Heinrich Böll chose an illicit relationship between a German woman and a Russian prisoner-of-war as the provocative central scene of his novel *Gruppenbild mit Dame* (1971). Leni's spontaneous act of offering Boris a cup of 'real' coffee was both courageous and dangerous. In *Kindheitsmuster*, by contrast, the narrator confesses that far from *daring* to share her food with the Ukrainian women it did not even occur to Nelly that she might do so.

Kindheitsmuster is an impressively honest evocation of daily life under fascism. But if it asks 'How have we *become* as we are today?' it also invites the question, how *are* we today? At a reading from the work in progress the narrator is asked by a member of the audience what the point is of constantly returning to the past. Would it not be better, it is implied, to turn one's attention to the future? Not all East Germans are as self-critical as the narrator. She encounters a taxi driver who is prepared to admit German responsibility for the war, even for the deaths of twenty million Soviet citizens, but not that the Germans committed atrocities against Russians as the Russians had done to Germans. East German tourists in Czechoslovakia are just as forgetful of contexts as West Germans can be, when they sing the anti-Polish songs which were current a historical epoch previously.

The personality of the narrator herself is one feature of the GDR in the present. She is anything but the self-confident, self-satisfied proclaimer of truths who would imply that the past has been digested (see McPherson, in Wallace, ed., 1984a, p. 111). A contrasting 'pattern of childhood' is furnished by the narrator's daughter Lenka, who accompanies her on the visit to G. and plays a crucial role in the relation between past and present. Whereas Nelly was easily carried away by enthusiasms, Lenka is down-to-earth. Politically loaded terms such as 'homeland' (*Heimat*) (p. 160) and 'German' (p. 237) are not part of Lenka's vocabulary. She demands answers to her questions, where Nelly was easily distracted from asking, for example, what had happened to Aunt Jette, a victim of the Nazis' euthanasia programme. In other ways, however, Lenka embodies a youthful innocence which her mother envies: Lenka's parents have never been 'young' in this sense. Lenka has never had to see the ashen face of a father reporting that he has just missed having to execute hostages. In these ways Lenka is the positive contrast to Nelly, 'put there to ask the awkward questions' as Joyce Crick suggests (1983, p. 174). The contrast might imply an over-cosy implication that the GDR has created the conditions in which fascism could never reemerge. During the writing of the novel, however, Lenka loses her innocence. Her teacher commits suicide over political pressures, while at work she finds that in spite of what she has been told, the 'antagonistic conflicts' between socialist labour and egotistical behaviour persist (p. 357), and that the pressures to achieve are barely tolerable. Other teenagers behave less questioningly, less consciously: the star pupil of her class, for example, proposes euthanasia as a solution to world famine, evidently unaware of the Nazi euthanasia programme. Buchenwald has become little more than a tourist attraction. While political education in the abstract is impeccable, what is lacking is the emotional associations which enable the pupil or citizen to realise the connection with their own lives. A function of *Kindheitsmuster* is to make good this deficiency.

There was a certain degree of piquancy in the fact that just one year after *Kindheitsmuster*, Hermann Kant's *Der Aufenthalt* was published. Wolf had been one of the leading dissidents in the Biermann affair, whereas Kant was on the opposite side. Both novels centre on teenagers who are involved with National Socialism but who cannot be held directly responsible for the crimes of their elders. Both are set, at least in part, in what is now Poland. But there the similarities end. Mark Niebuhr, the narrator-protagonist of *Der Aufenthalt* comes from a proletarian family in a remote country district of north-west Germany; Nelly's parents are of the petty bourgeoisie. Mark was a member of the Hitler Youth movement, but unlike Nelly he was unenthusiastic and in any case in his village it was of minor importance. While Mark's father and brother are killed in the war, Nelly's family remains intact. Moreover, as a male eighteen-year-old, Mark is drafted into the war just before Christmas 1944; his experiences thereafter are not those of the home front but of war, captivity and the company of men. His career in the army is shortlived. In January 1945 he is taken prisoner in Poland. Along with a few hundred other German soldiers he moves through various camps until in October, as he is waiting at a suburban goods station in Warsaw a Polish woman claims to recognise him as one of those responsible for the massacre of Polish civilians at Lublin. He spends the next six months in solitary confinement and a further seven months in a cell with a motley collection of men from Auschwitz, officers accused of executing hostages and others accused of the murder of Poles. In November 1946 his innocence is established and he is released to Germany.

Der Aufenthalt is an interesting mixture of older and newer models of antifascist literature. It does not attempt to uncover the 'socio-economic roots of fascism', to show, for example, how it was the capitalist system of exploitation that led to the German invasion of Poland in 1939. Although Kant does stress the existence of the class system both in prewar Germany and in the micro-social groupings that emerge among the German prisoners-of-war, successfully unmasking the Nazi dogma of national community (*Volksgemeinschaft*), the novel is not obviously a Marxist analysis of history. There are no far-sighted socialists in the novel, actively combating fascism or guiding the young hero in the right direction. In fact apart from the 'natural' resistance of the Poles and the Russians to the German invaders, resistance to fascism is remarkable by its absence. In one of his prison camps Mark encounters two members of the 'Free Germany Committee' ('Komitee Freies Deutschland'), the communist organisation set up in 1943 in exile to bring together all those who were opposed to Hitler for whatever reason. But they are frustrated by the mania for crossword puzzles which Mark has initiated and which distracts the men from all serious pursuits. This does indicate a reprehensible lack of political commitment among the Germans; but the two 'agitators' appear to Mark like characters from a film, and it is difficult for the reader to take them seriously either.

Guidance does come – from a Russian woman doctor and from a Polish lieutenant – but it is of a moral rather than a political nature. Mark learns to see Poles, Jews and Russians as individuals, to put himself or his mother, for example, in the position of the foreign workers forced to do labour for the Germans. He realises that although he played only a minor role in the war, without him and others like him it would not have been possible, and the novel implies at the end that such a viewpoint will help to prevent future wars. In the Cold War, whether of the late 1940s or of 1977, the liberal value of 'scepticism' which Mark learns (p. 471) can as easily be turned against the socialist side as against the capitalist one.

In one way *Der Aufenthalt* reverts to older literary models. It is a 'novel of education', as the motto by Brecht, 'Thus does man become educated',[11] leads the reader to expect from the outset. It is a first-person narrative told rather in the manner of *David Copperfield*, the nearest equivalent in English to the German tradition, in which the narrator is looking back on his 'sojourn' in Poland at some unspecified distance, commenting on his experiences from the position of superiority which such a narrative posture endows. This is not to say that the reader is not from time to time hoodwinked – at one point we are led to suppose that Mark may have spent fifteen years in prison – but we do know that he was *not* executed for crimes he did not commit. Within the limitations of the traditional form Kant succeeds on the whole in avoiding both the Scylla that Mark had nothing to learn and the Charybdis that the moral message is thrust on the reader at every turn. However, narration itself is not problematical as it was for Christa Wolf. It is thematised only in the sense that the narrator himself is learning from his own attempts to set down what he experienced. Mark Niebuhr has no difficulty in saying 'I' – on the contrary, he is at times exhaustingly garrulous in his anecdotes about his relatives, his pranks and his own development, but his egocentricity is one of the characteristics he learns to criticise. Mark develops from carefree ignorance to the acceptance of personal responsibility, but *Der Aufenthalt* is not a 'conversion novel' for the simple reason that he was never a fascist. Rather than Goethe's *Wilhelm Meister*, it is the seventeenth-century *Simplicissimus* by Grimmelshausen that is the model, or even the *Parzival* of Wolfram von Eschenbach. Initially Mark is characterised by his fundamental naivety, coupled with a strong dose of native wit. Like Grimmelshausen, Kant is able to use this naivety to point up the absurdities of adult male behaviour, especially those of the military persuasion: one of the games played by the prisoners with whom he shares a cell consists in taking turns to be slapped on the bottom and guess the name of the man who did it. Mark is a clown, but an unselfconscious one: some of his escapades are comic, but they often end in near-disaster, as when he almost suffocates in the comfortable crib of hay which he chooses as a bed, or when he falls off the back of the lorry on which he has taken a nap. In the end naivety is no excuse. He feels comfortable enough in the camouflage jacket of the SS which he is given in prison to keep himself warm. Only gradually does he realise that everyone he meets now assumes he belongs to the SS. Like so many Germans after the war and with more justification than most, Mark can claim that he did not know what had been happening in Poland. Kant suggests that not *asking* was the prime fault. Precisely this was the sin committed by Parzival, and like the 'fool' Parzival Mark has to learn the hard way. He might have been released from prison much earlier. To check his credentials he is led before a battalion of German prisoners who are asked if they can identify him. One of them is a man with whom he had spent hours discussing old films during the first part of his captivity. As their acquaintance had, however, never extended beyond this, neither knows anything of the other, and out of a mistaken sense of comradeship (the pattern of Fühmann's *Kameraden* once more), assuming that recognition might mean incrimination rather than alibi each pretends not to know the other.

This failure in communication is symptomatic of the wider refusal to accept responsibility, the readiness to be distracted by trivia rather than ask the crucial questions. The outstanding scene of the novel describes how after the inconclusive identification parade the military jeep conveying them back to prison breaks down and Mark has to be led through the remains of the Warsaw ghetto by his guard, a Polish lieutenant. Here is when the true horrors of German war crimes strike through to Mark as he is confronted with a flattened city, with wreaths at every corner commemorating civilians shot by Germans, and when he has no answer to the probing questions of his companion. What makes the scene especially moving is that the words of the lieutenant are in halting, broken German; here at last the fluent loquacity of the narrator is silenced. When Mark returns to his cell he is no longer prepared to make common cause with his fellow-prisoners. They continue to deny their guilt, although they are responsible for the most horrific crimes. Mark by contrast is filled with a feeling of responsibility, although he is, in the strictly legal sense, innocent. Like Kafka's Joseph K., he has been arrested although he believes he has done nothing wrong. Unlike Joseph K., as Rulo Melchert points out, he learns to accept his guilt (1977, p. 891).

Although in contrast to *Michael* and *Kindheitsmuster*, *Der Aufenthalt* is not directly concerned with the present day, some of the values it propagates are clearly relevant to current tensions. One aspect is especially important, the relationship between Germans and Poles (see Bulmahn 1984/85). In *Blickwinkel* Helga Schubert quotes a Polish teacher who declares that no German, whatever his date of birth, should doubt his guilt. At least since the medieval colonisation of Eastern Europe by the Teutonic Knights Germany has been regarded by Poland with distrust if not loathing, and Hitler was not the first to portray the Poles as subhuman. Gustav Freytag's immensely popular nineteenth-century novel *Soll und Haben* is not only antisemitic but also propagates a view of the Polish peasantry as slovenly and incompetent where their German equivalents are clean and efficient. In Rolf Schneider's *Die Reise nach Jarosław* Gittie's visit to Poland and her recognition of the German guilt towards the Poles helps to enable her to return to her own country and settle there. Since the end of the Second World War the GDR has been Poland's Western neighbour, and the two countries belong to the same economic and military configurations. This has not automatically meant better human relations; Poland remains economically poorer than the GDR and prejudice against Poles can still be encountered at times of crisis. In this context Kant's novel is an impressively humane statement. That the film which was based on it met with hostility in Poland, where it was regarded as anti-Polish, indicates the extent of the problem.

If the poisoning of Polish–German relations is one legacy of the past, another is responsibility for the attempted extermination of the Jews. After his walk through Warsaw Mark Niebuhr remembers two revealing pieces of popular German usage. A term for chronic disorder is 'Polish housekeeping' and noisy chaos is associated with 'a Jewish school' (p. 433). By concentrating on the role of the socialist resistance movement early GDR anti-fascist literature tended to overlook the persecution of the Jews. Thus in *Kindheitsmuster* Lenka's history book contains one hundred pages on the fascist dictatorship but no mention of Adolf Eichmann, the bureaucrat responsible for carrying out the 'Final Solution' (and, incidentally, the epitome of bourgeois normality). Since the later 1960s the balance has been rectified. In Hermann Kant's *Das Impressum*, for example, it is antisemitism which characterises the Nazis as much as anything, and the theme is repeated in *Der Aufenthalt*. The American *Holocaust* series, which was broadcast on West German television in 1979, provoked lively reactions across the border in the GDR too, where it had evidently been widely viewed. Klaus Schlesinger described the search for an adequate response to the crimes committed by the Nazis in the name of the German people as 'a journey without end' for all Germans, whether in the West or in the East (cit. Kleinschmid 1979a, p. 228), and according to Stephan Hermlin the debate led to the award of the GDR's highest honour to Peter Edel for his autobiography *Wenn es ans Leben geht*, in which he describes his experiences as a young Jew in the Third Reich (1983, p. 400). But ten years earlier Jurek Becker's first novel *Jakob der Lügner* had already deviated from the GDR norm, both in its presentation of resistance to fascism and in its choice of victim. It is a story set in the ghetto of an East European town in 1943, whose Jewish inhabitants are subject to inhuman indignities. From time to time the inhabitants of a whole street are deported to Auschwitz or some other extermination camp, while those who remain have little to eat, are forced to work for the Germans, and must observe a strict curfew. Jakob, the novel's protagonist, has adopted the child Lisa, whose parents were sent to Auschwitz while she was out playing. Half way through the novel the narrator raises the question of heroism, of resistance:

> And the resistance, you will ask, what about the resistance? Are perhaps the heroes assembling in the shoe factory or at the freight station, a few at least? At the southern border, which is the least open to view and therefore the most difficult to guard, have they found dark sewers through which weapons can be smuggled into the ghetto?[12] (p. 92)

Bruno Apitz's *Nackt unter Wölfen* (1957) is the most famous GDR novel of the Nazi concentration camps. Set in Buchenwald in March 1945 it portrays the heroic struggle of a clandestine communist-led organisation against the brutality and cowardice of the SS. Weapons have in fact been smuggled into the camp and concealed in the most unlikely places. Here, too, a Jewish child has been rescued and hidden. Regretfully, the narrator of *Jakob der Lügner* has to admit there was no resistance of the kind described in Apitz's novel at all. At best there was one moment of passive resistance, when Dr Kirschbaum, called out to attend to SS-chief Hardtloff, who has suffered a heart attack, commits suicide rather than help to prolong the life of the individual in charge of their persecution. The narrator presents us with two endings to his story. The first is a happy one, in which the Red Army arrives and liberates them. But reality was much more tedious and unimaginative, prompting the 'absurd' question, 'what was it all for?' (p. 259). The ghetto is emptied by the Germans and the Jews are transported to the extermination camps, which only the narrator has survived. *Jakob der Lügner* thus refuses to conform to the socialist realist model.

Becker's novel, however, is not as gloomy as this might sound. It is full of humorous episodes in which the Germans are briefly outwitted or the warmth of human relationships equally briefly prevails. Although the narrator refuses to offer easy solutions in the shape of happy endings, the story he is telling implies that such stories may in certain circumstances have an important role to play in helping human beings to survive. The eponymous hero is himself a 'storyteller' and in order to prevent his friend Mischa from trying to steal potatoes and be shot he tells him on the spur of the moment he has a radio and that the Russians are only a few hundred miles from the ghetto. The news spreads like wildfire and from this point on Jakob has constantly to invent new stories on the Russian advances. Jakob is a 'storyteller' in the sense that he is a 'liar'. But from the moment at which he begins to tell almost wholly fictitious stories about the imminent end to their troubles the mood in the ghetto is transformed. Suicide becomes a thing of the past and people make plans for the future. Storytelling, 'literature', however fantastic, may itself be a form of resistance. Here, too, literature is a theme of literature.

Becker himself had survived ghetto and concentration camp as a child in Poland and he returned to the topic in two later novels, both set in the postwar years, showing how the wounds of the past will always remain open and suggesting that it is impossible for those who were not involved to establish any natural relationship to those who were. The second of these, *Bronsteins Kinder*, was written while its author was living in the West, and although it has appeared in the GDR it falls outside the parameters of this study. Suffice it to say that it describes on the one hand the unrelenting refusal of the older generation of Jews to accept the past as over, and on the other, through the behaviour of their children, calls in question the notion of a Jewish identity. Bronstein and some friends have discovered a former guard at the concentration camp where they were incarcerated. Instead of handing him over to the authorities, whom they distrust, they keep him prisoner under inhumane conditions in Bronstein's datcha, where Bronstein's son finds him, eventually liberating him. The presentation of Jews as oppressors is intentionally provocative and must remind readers of current events in Israel's occupied territories.

Previously, however, *Der Boxer* had anticipated some of these themes in a less controversial manner. It is especially impressive in the indirect way in which it conveys the horrors of what happened in the camps, restricting itself to the postwar history of Aron Blank, a Jew who survived the concentration camps and returned to live in East Berlin. His baby son Mark had been taken away from him, but miraculously he, too, appears to have survived and in due course father and son are reunited. Mark has never heard the word 'son' before, and as his father cannot recognise him after six years he cannot even be sure that Mark is in fact his son. The authorities could pass on any child of the appropriate age if they so chose. Aron's indelible hatred of anything which might be associated with the system which incarcerated him leads him into extreme behaviour. When he goes to see Mark for the first time he sleeps in the woods rather than associate with those who might have been involved with the camp where Mark was kept. He approves of the atomic destruction of Hiroshima and is impatient with the Russians for observing the legal niceties in their dealings with the Germans. He is reluctant to let Mark go to school where he believes he will meet the children of former Nazis, and when his son is beaten up at school he at once assumes that it was out of antisemitism. His attitude gives an indirect insight into what has made him thus, for if the Russian officer Wasin, whose wife and parents were killed by the Germans, is able to maintain a more reasonable attitude, one assumes that Aron's experiences were that much worse.

The novel's title is taken from the episode when Aron sends Mark to boxing lessons so that he will be able to defend himself if attacked again. Aron himself is the boxer. He is in a state of permanent defensiveness against other people, so scarred by his experiences that he is unable to lead a normal life even in a society which does everything that could be expected of it to enable him to do so. He is given a flat that had belonged to a wealthy Nazi, assistance to find his son Mark, and an identity card to certify that he is a 'victim of fascism' and entitled to special allowances. People are kind to him: when he is not seen for a couple of days the caretaker knocks on the door to make sure he is all right. A succession of women look after him and his son, but they eventually leave when they find it is a one-way relationship. Financially he is comfortably off: in the days of the black market he becomes an accountant for a racketeer; later he is taken on by the Soviet administration as an interpreter only to resign when he inherits money from America. Outwardly he invariably falls on his feet like 'lucky Jack' in the folk-tale. In spite of all this he remains a lonely, bitter man, unable to form relationships with other people, indifferent to the society he lives in. The two people he is most friendly with are similar victims of Hitler: one, a Jew like himself, emigrates to Israel, the other, a former anarchist who spent eleven years in a concentration camp, commits suicide. In neither case does Aron go out of his way to deepen their friendship. He lavishes all his love and care on his son, but Mark, too, eventually leaves the country, first to West Germany, then, after travelling the world, to Israel, where it seems that he is killed during the Six Day War of 1967. Mark writes to his father; Aron never replies.

Again the act of narration is thematised. As mentioned in Chapter 3 *Der Boxer* is the novel of a search, the search for Aron Blank. The narrator has been interviewing Aron over a period of eighteen months in the early 1970s. His story is based on Aron's account; it is also interspersed with comments on their relationship, doubts about the reliability of Aron's testimony, but also Aron's queries on the narrator's reliability. Aron becomes dependent on the narrator for company, but the narrator is equally dependent on Aron for his material and when Aron falls gravely ill he feels guilty about fearing for his novel above all else. Although the narrator is sparing in his comments, he cannot avoid interpreting Aron's behaviour, contextualising, criticising, drawing general conclusions from it. That is precisely what Aron wishes to avoid. At one point he stresses that he is not telling the story of postwar Germany, only what happened to him personally. When it is finally finished he refuses to read what the narrator has written, saying that that is only what the narrator thinks is his biography. As with *Nachdenken über Christa T.* there is the biographer's permanent dilemma, that words must inevitably categorise, thereby detracting from unique individuality.

There is, however, an added dimension to the dilemma, inasmuch as Aron is a Jew and Jews have traditionally suffered from categorisation. Right at the beginning, when Aron has been released and walks down the street emaciated and with shaven head he is recognised as a Jew, rather than a former political prisoner, by his nose. He associates at first with other Jews, who congregate in a back room, a kind of ghetto. Money is important to Aron, at least in the sense that he uses it to solve all his problems, as a bribe or to compensate Irma, the woman he has lived with for many years, for sending her away. The narrator is particularly embarrassed to discover that the racketeers of the immediate postwar years were Jews. It would be possible to retell the story in antisemitic terms. Seeking reasons for Mark's decision to go to Israel, Aron claims that one thing he did not do was 'make a Jew of him' (p. 297); he himself has no more affinity to the state of Israel than to the GDR. Like Max Frisch's play *Andorra* (1961) Becker's novel invites the reader to ponder the mechanisms by which people are placed in categories and become what they are said to be. It may well have been his father's indifference which paradoxically made Mark feel fascinated by his Jewish origins. The Germans' bad conscience with regard to the Jews has made it difficult for them to criticise their behaviour. The narrator at one point suggests that tolerance should not be identified with an uncritical attitude. If Israel has become 'the boxer' of the Middle East, Becker's novel implies some explanations without necessarily inviting our approval.

In 1988 the Western media gave prominence to reports of an upsurge in neo-Nazi activities in the GDR. Between November 1987 and July 1988 at least thirty-nine young skinheads were convicted of crimes of violence coloured with fascist attitudes. It has been estimated that there are some 1,500 young East Germans who call themselves 'neo-Nazis'. During the 1970s isolated instances in which Jewish cemeteries in the GDR were vandalised or sprayed with antisemitic slogans were registered, while in the 1980s members of the unofficial peace movement or environmental groups have been physically attacked by such groups (Ammer 1988). While much of this behaviour must be the copying of similar activities in the West, particularly in West Berlin, clearly it is disturbing for a state which has set such great store by its antifascist antecedents and its socialist education. A novel of 1980, however, anticipated the problem and suggested an alternative reason for it.

Hedda Zinner's *Katja* has no great literary merit. Its characters are largely stereotypes and the story of a young woman who commits suicide when her husband is unfaithful is the stuff of pulp fiction. The narrative technique pretends to be modernist: at the funeral the mother is reconstructing in her mind the events which led up to Katja's death; but where Schlesinger in *Michael* succeeds in conveying the confused thought processes of his narrator, Zinner's narrative is little more than a first-person biography punctuated with interruptions by the funeral oration. This said, the content of the narrative is remarkable. Fini Komarski, Katja's mother, is a communist who was arrested for her activities on behalf of the anti-Nazi resistance and spent eight years in the concentration camp at Ravensbrück. Her husband Stephan had managed to flee to the Soviet Union. Their son was taken to England by Fini's mother, but has subsequently never been traced. Their daughter Katja was born in 1948. At Ravensbrück Fini was heroic in her efforts to help her fellow-captives. An actress by profession, she organised concerts and plays to further solidarity and to enable them to survive. After the war, determined to ensure that the sufferings of the victims of fascism will never be forgotten, she devotes her life to lecture tours and concerts which take her to all corners of the GDR and abroad. Thus far the story is conventional. Katja's development is not. Constantly confronted with the past through her parents and their friends, a gifted, sensitive child, she cannot cope, rebels against her parents' authority, fails to do herself justice at school and goes through a variety of sexual partners. When she marries Uwe, he turns out to be mainly hoping that her well-connected parents can influence the authorities into granting the concessions he needs to start a car-repair business. When they refuse he returns to his former women and Katja takes a fatal overdose of sleeping tablets.

Katja is remarkable for the frankness with which it reports uncomfortable attitudes of the new East German generation to the social system in which it lives. Katja's husband views life purely in terms of the desire to satisfy his own material needs, which for him are confined to sex and consumer goods. He believes that success in the GDR depends on whether one is a member of the Party or has connections to others who are. Although he is balanced by others who are more idealistic, his outlook is not presented as eccentric. Indeed Fini does exploit her own connections to find and make habitable a flat for the newly-weds. As Uwe's father was killed in the war, Uwe too, brought up by a single parent, may be regarded partly as a victim of Hitler. But he as much as Katja is also a child of the GDR. And the central message of the novel is that by overloading their children with the burden of the past Fini and her generation have prevented them from coping with the present. Novels such as *Jakob der Lügner*, *Kindheitsmuster* and *Der Aufenthalt* are among the most outstanding contributions of the GDR's writers to the literatures of the German-speaking peoples. It is, however, perhaps no coincidence that the topic of National Socialism has been less prominent in the GDR's literature in the 1980s.

Notes

1. Wer die Vergangenheit nicht wahrnimmt, ist genötigt, sie zu wiederholen.
2. Wir begannen nicht im Jahre Null.
3. Ich will auch Hochverräter werden und den Häschern entkommen.
4. die Struktur der Vergangenheitsbeziehungen meiner Generation, das heißt: Bewältigung der Vergangenheit in der Gegenwart.
5. Schuldlosigkeit aus Mangel an Erwachsensein.
6. Wie sind wir so geworden, wie wir heute sind?
7. Das Vergangene ist nicht tot; es ist nicht einmal vergangen. Wir trennen es von uns ab und stellen uns fremd.
8. Vom Ich zum Wir.
9. Das Kind, das in mir verkrochen war – ist es hervorgekommen? Oder hat es sich, aufgescheucht, ein tieferes, unzugänglicheres Versteck gesucht? Hat das Gedächtnis seine Schuldigkeit getan? Oder hat es sich dazu hergegeben, durch Irreführung zu beweisen, daß es unmöglich ist, der Todsünde dieser Zeit zu entgehen, die da heißt: sich nicht kennenlernen wollen?

Und die Vergangenheit, die noch Sprachregelungen verfügen, die erste Person in eine zweite und dritte spalten konnte – ist ihre Vormacht gebrochen? Werden die Stimmen sich beruhigen?
Ich weiß es nicht.
10. der Tourismus in halbversunkene Kindheiten blüht.
11. So bildet sich der Mensch.
12. Und der Widerstand, wird man fragen, wo bleibt der Widerstand? Sammeln sich die Helden vielleicht in der Schuhfabrik oder auf dem Güterbahnhof, wenigstens einige? Sind an der Südgrenze, die am unübersichtlichsten ist und darum am schwersten zu bewachen, dunkle Kanäle ausfindig gemacht worden, durch die sich Waffen ins Ghetto schmuggeln lassen?

–6–

Stalinism Past and Present

> Tell me now, who on earth was this Khruschev![1]
> (Christa Wolf, *Kindheitsmuster*)

Kindheitsmuster answers the question 'How did we become as we are?' largely in terms of the experience of 'ordinary fascism', the distortions of consciousness caused by life in the Third Reich. In the same novel, however, the narrator reports the dream she repeatedly has of a solemn funeral procession in which the mourners are bewildered when they come to a gravestone with the name 'Stalin' on it: 'So he is dead already? He is lying there already? And whom are we really burying?' Stalin, it seems, has to be buried again and again. 'When,' she asks, '... will we begin to talk about that too?'[2] (pp. 321–2). Forty years after the end of the Second World War the majority of the population has no direct recollection of National Socialism. The GDR has developed its own history. As Helga Schubert, born in 1940, points out in *Blickwinkel*, hers is the first generation which did not have to begin school lessons with the Nazi salute (p. 9). The formative years of the middle generation are dominated rather by the experience of Stalinism in the 1950s and beyond, and the older generation is coming under greater pressure to discuss this aspect of the GDR's past.

Jürgen Kuczynski, born in 1904, devoted one of the chapters of his *Dialog mit meinem Urenkel* to the question of his own behaviour in the time of Stalin, speaking of his personal shame over one particular episode in which he had defended the arrest of Bukharin and the son of Kuczynski's friend Hermann Duncker. After Kruschev's revelations of the crimes of Stalin at the Twentieth Congress of the Soviet Communist Party in 1956 nobody was allowed to quote Stalin any longer. Kuczynski had to receive a special dispensation for his monumental *Geschichte der Lage der Arbeiter* on which he was working at the time. The prohibition, however, he points out, was itself a 'continuation of Stalinism', whereby anyone who had fallen into disfavour became a non-person. For Kuczynski the most lasting effect of Stalinism has been the stifling of genuine debate (1983, pp. 77–85). Stephan Hermlin, too, a few years younger than Kuczynski, has confessed his 'shame and bitterness' over an article he published in 1949 in which he denied that writers such as Gumilev, Mandelstam, Jessenin and Majakovsky had been victims of Stalinist oppression, admitting that he had been afraid of the truth (1983, pp. 409–10). Hermlin's admission is striking not least because it came just before the publication of his autobiographical *Abendlicht*, in which he reproaches those who profess to have known nothing of the crimes perpetrated by the Nazis of having repressed their consciousness. In the text the one comparable passage on similar repressions under Stalin, when news reaches him of the arrest of Sinoviev, Kamenjev and others accused of the assassination of Kirov, is oddly oblique.

A more striking example of *glasnost'*, however, was the posthumous publication in *Sinn und Form* in 1988 under the title 'Selbstzensur' of seven posthumous pieces by Johannes R. Becher. Originally composed under the impact of the Twentieth Party Congress in Moscow, they had been intended for publication in the fourth volume of his *Bemühungen*. At the proof stage, however, Becher had removed them. In them Becher speaks of his personal guilt at not having spoken out earlier. For him the revelations of Stalin's crimes were nothing new. He had loved and admired Stalin more than any other man; at the same time he had been filled with horror at the crimes which were being committed in his name. He views Stalinism as the greatest tragedy of the age, tragic not only in the awfulness of its results, but also in the feeling of impotence which it provoked in those who witnessed it; it was crucial not to trivialise it, as some had been doing. What is remarkable about the publication of 'Selbstzensur' is not so much its content: although Becher's prominent position as the GDR's first Minister of Culture gives it especial weight, it hardly goes further than Kuczynski's earlier statement, and in any case the GDR is still more hesitant over disclosing Stalin's crimes than the Soviet Union itself. Rather it is the admission that in 1957, when that volume of *Bemühungen* appeared, these passages were censored out, whether voluntarily on Becher's part or under pressure from others, the admission that in the GDR in 1957 Stalinism was still rampant. The term 'self-censorship', moreover, recalls the contemporary situation of the writer. The self is the 'first' of Loest's censors (1984), and 'self-censorship' was one of the words struck out of Wolf's Frankfurt lectures for the GDR version of *Kassandra* (see *Voraussetzungen*, p. 109).

An example of the Stalinist creation of 'non-persons' is to be found in Klaus Schlesinger's *Leben im Winter*. It includes a story in which a boy comes across an old photograph in which Lenin and Trotsky are standing side by side. He remembers seeing the same picture in one of his schoolbooks, compares the two and discovers that there Trotsky has been spotted out. Trotsky was still so problematical that it was almost ten years before Schlesinger's book could appear in the GDR. The Stalinist rewriting of history is reflected in other works. In Loest's *Es geht seinen Gang* the historian Wilfried has a problem in reconciling West and East German figures on the number of Soviet aircraft shot down in the Second World War, the GDR figures suggesting a much stronger Soviet airforce than the West Germans' do, and Wülff is reminded of the official picture book of the GDR in which even the dirty smoke from the factory chimneys in Schwedt has been edited out. Günter de Bruyn's *Märkische Forschungen* is the story of a provincial schoolteacher, Ernst Pötsch, who discovers that the early nineteenth-century poet and historian Max Schwedenow was not the progressive revolutionary that Professor Menzel makes him out to be, but a conservative reactionary. But since Menzel is the doyen of East Germany's early nineteenth-century scholarship Pötsch is unable to publish his findings in the GDR, and the West German journal he contacts rejects it likewise because his paper is written from a socialist standpoint. Near the beginning of Waldtraud Lewin's *Federico* the narrator encounters Clio, the muse of history, a bored, untidy secretary, and her 'minder', an aggressive man with close-cropped hair. She realises that both are in reality rather frightened of her: 'Evidently they had frequently been forced to run off in order to reopen the cases for trial and revise canonisation or curse'[3] (p. 24). The East German historian must always be apprehensive of changes in policy which may require him to revise his findings.

The novel which deals most centrally with Stalinist historiography, however, is Stefan Heym's *Der König David Bericht*, the appearance of which in the GDR in 1973 marked the beginning of an all too brief rehabilitation of its author. Heym, a Jew and a Marxist, had emigrated from Nazi Germany in 1933 and had been an American citizen from 1935 to 1952, when he moved to East Germany in protest against McCarthyism. Ironically, in view of his later experiences, he justified his move with the words: 'I could not and would not work in a country in which writers are muzzled. No. There is no muzzle and no censorship here'[4] (cit. Dorman 1981, p. 146). In *Der König David Bericht* Ethan ben Hoshaia relates how he was called upon by King Solomon of Israel to write the official history of Solomon's father and predecessor David. Heym's novel is another story of an investigation, a novel of the writing of a novel. In the course of his researches Ethan discovers that the facts do not correspond to the legend: David was a tyrant, an arbitrary ruler, at times a renegade, but Ethan can publish only what places the founder of Israel in a favourable light. When he uncovers more than is expected of him his punishment, like that of Heym himself, is to be silenced. There are two kinds of truth, one which corresponds to reality and one which confirms the teachings of the prophets and priests of Jehovah. If they conflict the latter must take precedence. The task of the historian is 'to reflect the grandeur of the age'. Contradictions have to be smoothed away, because Solomon wishes 'the more edifying aspects of life' to be emphasised (p. 37). Writers have the ability to create the legends which people believe; they are the ones who immortalise the rulers. The censoring of writers is therefore at the same time an implicit acknowledgement of their social and political importance.

Heym's novel is entertaining. Its quasi-historical, mythical setting enables him to avoid most of the cheap effects to which the plots of his novels are frequently prone. Its language is an elevated pastiche of that of the Bible, but occasional anachronisms – the chief of police chews gum – subvert the authenticity and invite the reader to draw parallels with the more recent past or indeed present. Heym's later novel *Collin* treats the history of socialism directly and, as already indicated, seems unlikely to be published in the foreseeable future. *Der König David Bericht* uses analogies from a remote historical period to make similar points and, at least temporarily, evaded the censor. Heym is satirising Stalinism. The novel contains numerous parallels with the history both of the Soviet Union and of the GDR: the cult of personality, the forced confessions of guilt which finally become so common that nobody believes them, the purges which turn people into 'unpersons', the subsequent rehabilitations, the grandiose public buildings which the state cannot afford but which contribute to the glorification of the ruler, and, of course, official history-writing itself. David's temporary siding with the Philistines is a hidden allusion to the Hitler–Stalin pact, which has to be explained by the historians in such a way that the readers will not come to dangerous conclusions. Solomon's state is one in which Orwellian double-think prevails. In the restaurant of the Academy of Arts Ethan is entertained by the court chamberlain Amenhoteph, who praises the ability of the mind to divide itself into compartments, 'because this enables man to do what the laws of the real world demand, without thereby having to abandon the pleasant belief in the teachings of the sages and judges and prophets . . .'[5] (p. 103). But the ironic satirical humour does not conceal the bleak terror which governs the totalitarian state. Amenhoteph is a eunuch, and he recommends that Ethan 'castrate' his own thinking. In the early 1950s Brecht had adapted the eighteenth-century play *Der Hofmeister* by J.M.R. Lenz, at the end of which the tutor castrates himself; the intellectual could survive in feudal society only by self-mutilation. On the evidence of Heym's novel Stalinist socialism is in this respect no better than feudalism.

Stalinism had been one of the targets of criticism in some of the texts which established the 'new' GDR literature in the early 1960s. Wolf's *Der geteilte Himmel*, for example, had contrasted the dogmatist Mangold, who refuses to make any allowances for human frailties, with the humane Schwarzenbach, who is concerned that individuals should feel that the Party is there for them and not merely vice versa. *Nachdenken über Christa T.* had greater difficulties when it portrayed the 1950s as years in which initial socialist idealism turned to opportunism, when the newspapers were filled with photographs of 'frightfully beaming heroes', when individuals were hidden behind the 'larger than life cardboard posters they were carrying' and shunned no sacrifice to keep the mechanism of the state well-oiled, even at the expense of 'extinguishing themselves' (p. 57). Heiner Müller's play *Philoktet*, which, significantly, is found at the side of the would-be suicide Frank, falsely suspected of disloyalty to the state in Braun's *Unvollendete Geschichte*, dramatised the Stalinist abuse of individuals by state power in the guise of classical myth, but it had to wait a long time to be performed. Hermann Kant's *Die Aula*, finally, is both an affectionately nostalgic view of the camaraderie which marked the early days of the GDR and a reminder that these years were equally marked by an authoritarian intolerance which threatened to poison these same human relationships.

In *Die Aula* the past is conjured up by the invitation to Robert Iswall to deliver a speech commemorating the closing of the Workers' and Peasants' Faculty where he and his friends had met in the early 1950s. Past and present are mingled in his memory. Kant's second novel *Das Impressum* uses a similar technique, although in this case narration is confined to a single day in 1967 when newspaper editor David Groth finds himself invited to take ministerial office and reflects on the events of his life which have brought him to this stage. On the one hand, the novel is Groth's personal biography; on the other, it is the history and prehistory of the GDR, with which, as a journalist, he has been intimately concerned. As in *Die Aula* the novel's narrative technique with regard to time mirrors its thematic premise that the present can be understood only in relation to the past. In his preparations for a series of articles to commemorate the

GDR's twentieth anniversary, Groth notes: 'Direct involvement of the readers in the question, where do we come from. GDR historical consciousness'[6] (p. 302), and it is the question 'Where have we come from?' that the novel attempts to answer both in personal and in social terms. *Das Impressum* therefore, not surprisingly, takes the form of a novel of education; its final chapter recapitulates all the influences which have helped David Groth to become a fully integrated member of the GDR society.

However, the text is less challenging on the GDR's early years than *Die Aula* had been. Although at one point Groth is accused of 'being inclined to political individualism' (p. 222), the examples given of his stepping out of line are on the whole trivial and in any case, as he himself admits, 'fortunately' they had no further consequences for society. Had they had further consequences the novel might have been more interesting. For example, in 1958 he is furious to discover that his colleague Gabelbach had taken part in the book-burnings organised by the Nazis in March 1933, and declares that he is unwilling to work with him any more. He is eventually calmed down by his Editor, who sympathises with his anger but cannot support it 'because it is not historically correct' (p. 234). At the end of the war the 'historically correct' policy had been that opportunists like Gabelbach, as long as they had committed no real crimes, were to be encouraged to cooperate with the new rulers. In any case in 1958 the local Party leadership had quite enough on its plate: evaluating the Fifth Party Congress, preparing for new elections, combating the confusions and uncertainties left behind over the Schirdewan–Wollweber affair, and many other matters, down to digesting the consequences of the Twentieth Party Congress of the Soviet Union.

The list of the Party's activities covers over twenty lines, mingling what is historically trivial with what had the most far-reaching importance for the GDR's development. The Schirdewan–Wollweber affair, for example, marked for the time being the end of attempts at destalinisation. Karl Schirdewan, who for a time had been groomed to succeed Ulbricht, and Ernst Wollweber, Minister for State Security, had been propagating a greater degree of democracy in the GDR and had favoured détente with the West. In February 1958 they were accused of revisionism and expelled from the Party's Central Committee. A year earlier Wolfgang Harich and a number of other intellectuals had been given long prison sentences for similar sins. All these heretics had felt encouraged by Khruschev's denunciation of Stalin at the Twentieth Party Congress in 1956, but events in Hungary and Poland made the East German leadership extremely wary of any form of liberalisation and forced Khruschev himself to retreat on democratisation in the Soviet Union. None of this plays any more than an oblique part in Kant's account of the GDR's past. Although the Twentieth Party Congress is described as an 'unheard-of event', its actual content – Khruschev's denunciation of Stalin – is not elucidated any more than the reference to Schirdewan and Wollweber. Later in the novel there is a reference to the Hungarian uprising of 1956 and there follows a contorted passage which appears to refer to Khruschev's speech, although chronologically the speech preceded events in Budapest: 'and the time came when reports of most bitter errors, of extreme deception, of most frightful death were broadcast for the sake of the cause which can only live in truth, and yet and because of that were hurled back at the cause as a malicious echo: so it was all a lie, all, all, all!'[7] (p. 280).

If socialism is something which 'can only live in truth', then truth is something with which Kant is more than economical. Two further potentially explosive complexes, the events of 17 June 1953 and the forced collectivisation of farming, which led to a mass exodus from the GDR in the late 1950s and ultimately forced the regime to build the Wall in Berlin, are both glossed over. In the latter case the emphasis is entirely on the chicanery and physical violence to which the socialist hero Rikow, entrusted with carrying out the reforms, is subjected by the farmers. The uprising of 1953 receives similarly perfunctory treatment: one of the bricklayers who is leading the riot is evidently not a bricklayer at all and, as with the collectivisation of agriculture, it is the physical attacks on the good socialists that we see, not the causes for discontent among the workers. Indeed, as far as the novel is concerned the uprising is relevant mainly because it reconciles David and Fran, who had fallen out two years earlier; in this novel the turning from public to private issues which characterises the 1970s is truly escapist. Apart from the more sophisticated narrative technique, in many ways *Das Impressum* reads as a pre-1970s novel: the theme of the good Germany (the GDR) struggling against the bad Germany (the FRG), which dominates literature prior to 1970, recurs here. The socialist here has to fight against saboteurs and agents provocateurs rather than against the dogmatists in his own ranks. There *is* a dogmatist in the novel, Bleck, who edited Groth's paper briefly at the end of the 1950s; but he does not last long, and the most important lesson learned by Groth is never to believe himself 'cleverer than the Party' (p. 234).

Few writers to date have dealt comprehensively with the phenomenon of Stalinism in the GDR. Rather it has been a matter of isolated references, implying for the attentive reader unfinished business. We have already seen how Trojanowicz in Reimann's *Franziska Linkerhand* was demoted in the wake of the turmoil following Khruschev's revelations. In Morgner's *Trobadora Beatriz* patriarchal structures are associated with Stalin, 'Papa Stalin', as he was affectionately called until he was deposed from the socialist pantheon. Franz Kantus fled to the Soviet Union on the advent of the National Socialists only to become there a victim of Stalinism; when Khruschev yields to American threats and withdraws his missiles from Cuba in 1962 the opportunist Katschmann deplores this weakness which he believes Stalin would never have shown. In Zinner's *Katja* Fini's husband has never fully recovered from the experience of Stalinism in exile in the Soviet Union; this is a further factor in their disastrous upbringing of their daughter. While these are mainly details within a greater complex, in view of the importance of historical awareness both in the GDR's literature and its official image, they do add a dimension of historical depth. There is some evidence to suggest that the 1950s have been becoming of ever greater interest to writers in recent years.

The most embarrassing event of the 1950s for the new rulers was the uprising of June 1953. It is a topic which has usually been avoided by writers (see Mohr 1983). Western accounts of events differ radically from the East German version. Two major factors set in motion a series of strikes and demonstrations, first in East Berlin, later in other parts of the Republic on 16 and 17 June. One was the Party's decision to impose new output targets on the workforce, whereby they would be expected to increase productivity by 10 per cent without any equivalent rise in wages. The other was the proclamation of a new policy which acknowledged that the middle classes, the intelligentsia, shopkeepers and smallholders had been poorly treated in previous years and promised to improve their lot. Indignation among the workers broke out, the refusal of the Party leadership to meet their representatives fanned the flames, and in the end the Soviet army had to intervene. Although most recently there have been admissions that mistakes were made, official East German sources continue to blame the riots almost entirely on Western agents and saboteurs, aided by the propaganda disseminated by West Berlin radio, who were able to use the dissatisfaction with the pace of progress felt by some workers to instigate an attempted counterrevolution: 17 June had been designated as 'Day X', the day on which the GDR's system was to be subverted. The major embarrassment for the authorities was caused by the fact that it was an uprising dominated by workers, not by the intelligentsia, and the GDR was supposed to be a workers' state (Baring 1965). This embarrassment is expressed in coded form in one of Brecht's *Buckower Elegien*, where the poet reports a dream in which hands worn and gnarled by work point the finger of blame at him. Conformist writers such as Hermann Kant in *Das Impressum* and Erik Neutsch in *Auf der Suche nach Gatt*, however, concentrate wholly on the brutality of the participants and on the involvement of Western agents.

Stefan Heym's novel *5 Tage im Juni* is a much more balanced account of events, which presents in detail the discussions among the workers, in the trade unions and elsewhere, as well as taking account of the undoubted presence of Western agitators and making extensive quotations from Western broadcasts. Begun in the late 1950s it was substantially revised during the 1960s, and published in West Germany in 1974, but it has still not appeared in the East. The fact that Hermlin has publicly described it as the 'best presentation of the events' (1983, p. 411) suggests that this may be a matter of time. Otherwise it is in short episodes that the theme is treated. Heiner Müller's play *Germania Tod in Berlin*, begun in 1956 and completed in 1971, has not been performed in the GDR. It contains two scenes set during the riots. In one of them a building worker is stoned by young hooligans for refusing to join the strike. In the other a communist in prison is set on by former Nazis encouraged by the uprising to believe that their liberation is at hand; when they hear the sound of the Soviet tanks they kill him. Thus far the play confirms the official interpretation of events. But the building worker is provocatively called Hilse, a literary allusion to the old weaver of Gerhart Hauptmann's play *Die Weber* who refused to join the revolt of 1844 and was shot by a stray bullet from the army sent to put it down. Are the two Hilses simply blacklegs, cooperating with the employers whether these be capitalists or socialists? And why is a communist in prison among former Nazis on 17 June 1953? Did he get into trouble with the authorities for opposing their new policies? Müller's play is an account of the historical shortcomings of a German proletariat which under Frederick the Great, at the end of the First World War, in 1933, in 1953, and even in the times of Tacitus, has been hopelessly divided. Its many grotesque symbols include a Frederick who emerges as vampire during an East German official celebration, scenes of cannibalism at Stalingrad and an enormous puppet which puts its own eyes out. Hilse does not die of the stoning, but of cancer, a disease in which cells of the same body make war on each other. His Party is embodied in a whore, as if to suggest that the SED has sold its original ideals for power.

Becker's *Der Boxer* contains a similarly intriguing episode. Aron encounters one of the groups of demonstrators chanting and demanding the retraction of the new production targets. As he has hitherto taken no interest in politics he is baffled and fears that a new pogrom is about to begin. At once he takes his son from his school classroom, goes home, locks the door and does not leave the house for three days, listening only to the radio reports from both East and West. When Irma tells him she has seen tanks he is relieved: tanks are the only way to deal with such a situation. Aron approves of the measures taken by the government, as any good citizen would; but Aron is not a good citizen inasmuch as he consistently refuses to participate in the new democracy or even to take an interest in it. The reader can understand Aron's response; someone as scarred by his experiences as this must regard with suspicion anything which looks like disturbing the status quo. But conversely, the implication runs, only someone as scarred as Aron could greet with enthusiasm the intervention of the Soviet tanks.

In Werner Heiduczek's *Tod am Meer*, too, there is a description of the events of 17 June in one of the GDR's provincial towns. As in *Auf der Suche nach Gatt* the heroic individual communist who tries to calm the populace is brutally attacked; in this case he is killed by a stone from the crowd. But there the similarity ends. *Tod am Meer* gives a more ambiguous account of events. For the victim Immanuel Feister has already appeared as an intolerant dogmatist, solely concerned with consolidating the power of the Communist Party in his area of responsibility. One scene in particular sets Feister against his namesake Immanuel Kant. The liberal professor of philosophy in Halle, Melzer, who had already resigned once in protest against Hitler's rule, is forced to resign again when his lectures on Kant are disrupted by the novel's protagonist Jablonski, who, prompted by Feister, hurls quotations from Stalin at him. Feister's death, however, has its dignity too; his political commitment is genuine and he pays for it with his life. Unlike many of the characters of the novel, he was no mere opportunist and Jablonski later reflects that subsequent developments both for the GDR and for himself might have been better had Melzer and Feister been able to understand one another. Although Jablonski is not prepared to say whether propaganda from the West or the clumsy tactics over the issue of the production targets was responsible for the uprising, the novel portrays the chaotic circumstances surrounding it. Corruption was rife, there were crass differences in life style between factory management and the workforce, and each day saw the departure of yet another skilled worker to the West. Tensions between church and state similarly came to a head in 1953. The state was victorious, but Heiduczek wins at least part of the reader's sympathies for the Protestant minister who is elected to the school governing body and with Brechtian cunning undermines the political propaganda by, for example, placing a picture of St George killing the dragon opposite a bust of Stalin. Jablonski himself reacts to the unrest by sacking four teachers and expelling the children of churchmen from school, only to fall into disgrace himself shortly afterwards, denounced as an enemy of the state and a 'Titoist' and sent to work on a building site.

Jablonski, who narrates the novel, is the author of successful novels, plays, poems and filmscripts, a member of the Academy of Arts and holder of numerous awards. Born in 1927, he is of the GDR's dominant generation of Hermann Kant, Christa Wolf, Erik Neutsch, Heiner Müller and Heiduczek himself. On a visit to Bulgaria in 1974 he falls ill; there in the last three months of his life he writes his final book, his last testament, trying to liberate himself from his memories and his guilty conscience. His recollections begin with the war years and concentrate especially on the postwar years 1945 to 1953. As with *Nachdenken über Christa T.* it is important that he begins with National Socialism, although he was only a teenager then. There is on the one hand the reminder that for all the shortcomings of the early GDR years what preceded them was worse; on the other there are the implicit parallels. A common thread running through all the episodes is the shameful behaviour of men, first and foremost himself, towards women. Jablonski's memory of the war, for example, is dominated by Wanda, a Polish woman he had fallen in love with, who killed a German officer responsible for her mother's death and was hanged . In the postwar chaos he meets the prostitute Ellen, together with whom he enrols on a course to train as a teacher. When her past is disclosed by an anonymous letter she is expelled and returns to prostitution. Jablonski gets another student on the course pregnant. Whereas she has to submit to a degrading illegal abortion, he gets the university place to which she was equally entitled. At university he cynically embarks on an affair with an older woman, and she is the one who is punished. In these same early postwar years an illicit love affair between a German woman and a Russian officer ends when the officer is sent to Siberia. The woman does not survive the humiliation.

Tod am Meer is intensely personal, modelled explicitly on Tolstoy, Heine, the confessions of Rousseau, and the essays of Montaigne. The criticisms it contains are largely of Jablonski's own shortcomings. But since he is a successful public figure and since his biography intersects the development of the GDR at crucial points, it cannot but criticise this development too. The description of the early years is totally lacking in the heroism and cameraderie one finds for example in *Die Aula*. Instead there is pettiness, exploitation, hypocrisy and personal rivalry. It is a time dominated by angst: some have guilty consciences because they have not told the whole truth about their pasts, others anxiously try to find out what they are expected to do rather than what they ought to do. German–Soviet friendship was largely a fiction; in Jablonski's case it consisted in lending Tscherwuchin and Elisa a bed in return for the former's help in running the school. Political opportunism was rife. The real prostitute was not Ellen but Jablonski, who joined the SPD in 1946 not out of political conviction but because he was paid a hundred marks to do so and wanted to get drunk out of shame over the fate of Ellen. Shortly afterwards the SPD and KPD merged to form the SED, amicably and voluntarily on both sides, according to the official claim, one which Jablonski rebuts. With no sense of vocation he trains to be a teacher, then becomes an educational administrator in order to avoid being a teacher. The figure of Stalin menacingly towers over these years. Jablonski found his writings as simple and straightforward as the Bible. If they then persuaded him to reject the individual in favour of the collective, the subjectivism of his present narrative indicates destalinisation of a kind.

If, as suggested elsewhere, in much East German fiction of the past twenty years overt political commitment has given way to a form of existentialist statement, *Tod am Meer* is a prime example. Here it is partly justified by the postwar setting, when, Jablonski tells us, 'Sartre and existentialism' were 'fashionable' (p. 140). In fact this is at odds with official cultural policies in the GDR at the time, when Sartre was rejected as a formalist (Schubbe, ed., 1972, p. 113) and existentialism's 'lachrymose misery' contrasted with Goethe's positive qualities (Becher 1972, p. 290). He reports discussions with his Russian friend on Sartre and 'existential angst', p. 240). Nietzsche and Schopenhauer were further gurus, rather than Marx and Lenin. The implication is that existentialism provided a more satisfying explanation of people's behaviour then than did political analysis, and that this continues to be the case. Throughout his narrative Jablonski is operating entirely in existential terms, truth against falsehood, innocence against guilt, life against death. His self-criticism is in terms of opportunism, his failure to be authentic, rather than the validity of the political ideals. Indeed he stresses the limitations of politics, viewing it as 'simply ridiculous to believe that communism could be in a position to save every individual being from destruction'[8] (p. 182). He 'longs for simplicity and naivety' (p. 155); death is the moment of truth, coming to terms with death in this his last book turns him into a genuine poet at last (p. 180).

The final stage in Jablonski's career has been that of writer, and *Tod am Meer* implies a dismissal of pre-1970s writing just as much as of Stalinist politics. When he lost his post as educationist in 1954 he was sent to a building site to rehabilitate himself. There he became one of the 'worker-writers' encouraged by the Bitterfeld movement. He had dabbled in poetry and drawing much earlier. Looking back, he regards these early poems and drawings as having been more honest than his later ones, when he had learned distance and control and composition. They were not the conventional pictures of Soviet soldiers feeding the starving Germans or protecting small children, but documents of 'angst . . . scepticism, hatred' (pp. 81–2). Today he spurns the literature on which his reputation is based, literature which was not 'authentic' – again the existentialist terminology appears. His first novel 'Helden', on the heroic efforts of an unconventional labour gang, was televised just at the moment when its leader was being arrested for corruption – and Jablonski had meanwhile managed to be sent to Bulgaria as a German teacher. He has just made a successful television film on a similar labour gang; but the hero of the film is now in prison for having murdered out of jealousy the woman Jablonski seduced.

His present narrative therefore represents a break with everything he has previously written. If, for example, he had been telling the story of Wanda ten years earlier, at the beginning of the 1960s, he would have made himself a hero or a tragic figure. Like *Nachdenken über Christa T.* and *Julia, Tod am Meer* is a complex text which constantly fluctuates between past and present. It is not easy to reconstruct the story from it; rather the reader is left with a series of strong impressions based on important episodes. This is partly due to the 'unfinished' nature of the work; Jablonski refers to his manuscripts as 'sketches' and in a sense the text we have before us is the story less of the writing of the book than of the intention to write the book. His manuscripts have been brought back to the GDR by his former wife and published, framed by comments from an editor and from people who knew him, objectifying and relativising what is otherwise a wholly subjective account. This lack of finish itself, however, is the opposite of the well-made structures of socialist realism. What he has to say is uncompromisingly sombre; here is none of the optimism of socialist realism, but its truthfulness is 'more hopeful' than any line he has previously written (p. 257).

Tod am Meer was not the first GDR novel to take stock of a past which had encouraged opportunism in writers. Indeed in view of the importance of the theme of literature in recent East German fiction it is not surprising that the relationship between writers and the cultural Establishment has been a central topic. The tone of Heiduczek's work is self-flagellatory, full of existentialist pathos. Its theme fits neatly into the conventions of a socialist society where self-criticism is part of the mechanism of integration parodied, for example, in *Die neuen Leiden des jungen W*. By contrast Günter de Bruyn's *Preisverleihung*, which appeared a few years earlier, is told in a tone of gentle irony by an anonymous, external narrator. In this work there are no deaths. As with so many East German works of the past twenty years its narrative material is largely taken from the everyday world of personal relationships, human weaknesses, trivial preoccupations. The narrative time covers just one day. Teo Overbeck is a university lecturer in German literature, preparing the eulogy for an old friend, Paul Schuster, who has just been awarded a prize for his first novel. Overbeck's wife Irene is warding off the attentions of a member of a Polish trade delegation for whom she is acting as interpreter. Their daughter Cornelia learns that her school marks are not good enough to earn a place at university. She is suffering the pangs of first love, and a first rendezvous with the object of her passion is acutely disappointing. Overbeck's paper, meanwhile, is a disaster and will not improve his career prospects. At the party afterwards Schuster learns that he is Cornelia's natural father when Teo at last confides in him. De Bruyn's previous novel *Buridans Esel* had described a marriage under strain, when Karl Erp found himself torn between his wife and another woman. At the beginning of *Preisverleihung* the narrator tells us he has been asked to describe a model marriage and this is what he proposes to do. As one might expect, the Overbecks' marriage is hardly a model; it is nevertheless a stable one, partly because Teo is too preoccupied with literature to have any time for affairs and largely because Irene, like so many of de Bruyn's women, is of limited intellect and, de Bruyn implies ironically, therefore a haven of common sense. She is, the narrator tells us, *not* one of those tragic figures who threaten to break down under the clash of the real and the ideal.

The title of the novel, however, indicates that de Bruyn is concerned with other matters besides marital relations. For the single day of the novel's action is expanded back into the past as the narrator informs us, partly through the characters' own thoughts, how they came to be where they are now. Overbeck's speech is a disaster because he finds himself having to praise a novel which he considers worthless, worthless, moreover, because he himself had ruined it. For if Overbeck's daughter is really Schuster's, Schuster's novel is really Overbeck's. He first encountered the author as a student in the early 1950s helping to bring in the harvest, was impressed by his raw and spontaneous powers of expression and encouraged him to write. Overbeck then acted as Schuster's literary adviser in keeping with the fashions of the day. For example, Schuster's father had gone to settle in the West; for its propaganda value he was turned from being a relatively harmless fellow-traveller into a tyrannical Nazi. The Lukácsian values of grandeur and totality were brought into play; what finally emerged was a work entirely lacking in the individuality which had distinguished Schuster in the first place. By the time the novel was acceptable to the publishers Schuster no longer regarded it as his own, withdrew it and departed, leaving his pregnant girlfriend Irene to Overbeck. Schuster became a journalist. Now, many years later, he has disinterred his autobiographical novel and published it at last. *Preisverleihung* is a novel which satirises the literary opportunism of the 1950s. But since Schuster is awarded a literary prize in the narrative's present, presumably the beginning of the 1970s, it also is satirising the continuation of these cultural policies into the contemporary GDR.

Jurek Becker's *Irreführung der Behörden* appeared just one year after *Preisverleihung* and has a similar topic. It relates the career of Gregor Bienek between the years 1959, when he is a student of law, and 1967, when he is a successful writer, mainly of filmscripts. Becker has very little to say about the public, political issues of the day. Early on Bienek is briefly arrested in West Berlin for illegally distributing leaflets on behalf of the SED; during the same exercise one of his fellow-students simply drops his in a dustbin when he thinks nobody is watching, but Bienek is not especially enthusiastic himself. Although a former fellow-student who is now living in West Berlin is portrayed as a highly unattractive individual, the novel contains no stereotypical denunciation of the West, the Christmas TV programmes from the two German states are indistinguishable and the building of the Wall is reported merely as an event which almost stranded Bienek on the wrong side as that night he had been at a West Berlin cinema. The milieu described is relatively affluent: Gregor's fiancée's parents have a car and a dacha and there is much consumption of alcohol and good food. This is highlighted by one motif in particular, when Gregor persuades a pensioner to lend him some money to pay for an abortion for his girlfriend, forgets to repay it, and eventually has to be reminded of his debt once he is a wealthy man himself. Again *Irreführung der Behörden* concentrates on everyday life, especially on relations between the sexes and marital problems. Throughout Gregor remains attached and on the whole faithful to one woman; but he always has his eye open for other sexual opportunities and by the end of the novel his marriage is in a state of crisis.

The crisis, however, has little to do with his extramarital affairs; his dishonesty in his relationships is symptomatic of a general crumbling of personal integrity which can be traced back to the moment when he began to make concessions to the literary authorities over his stories. Gregor is comparable to Peters in Tetzner's *Karen W.*. His development is foreshadowed by the incident when he receives his first contract from a publisher. He has offered the story of a man whose dentist discovers his teeth are made of a unique and valuable substance and who gradually allows them to be extracted for the good of society. The publisher's reader finds the story promising if unpublishable in its present form, suggesting that it could be interpreted to imply that in the GDR the individual's rights are taken away one by one. Nevertheless she offers him a contract. Afterwards she invites Bienek to her flat. They go to bed together but he is embarrassingly impotent. The symbolism becomes clear by the end of the novel. Gregor, like the man in the story, 'loses his teeth'. His stories are sanitised, become trivial and harmless; there is no place in them for a case like, for example, that of the pensioner who lent him money and now has to ask for it back as he cannot survive on the little the state provides. Like Kafka's Gregor Samsa, Gregor Bienek has become a spineless insect. His social impotence is paralleled by his failures in personal relationships.

Like *Tod am Meer*, *Irreführung der Behörden* is a first-person narrative, but unlike Jablonski, Bienek is not looking back over his life. The present tense is used in this case less as a device to enlist the empathy of the reader than an indication that Gregor is narrating as he experiences in a kind of stream of consciousness style. The advantage of this technique over that of Heiduczek is that the over-insistent self-criticism is absent and the readers freed to make their own judgements. Criticism comes from Gregor's interlocutors, especially from his wife Lola; although he reacts violently against this criticism there are clear indications of his own dissatisfaction with himself. One literary detail is interesting. On holiday in Romania Gregor goes for a walk on his own off the tourist route. He feels utterly alien, unable to speak the language or even to comprehend the local currency. The writer Heinrich Böll comes to his mind, whose early work includes Romanian settings, but whose significance here must be to remind the reader – and Gregor subconsciously – of a writer of genuine integrity. The novel is set in the pre-Honecker era, which might indicate that the shortcomings described in the novel are of the past; that in a novel published in 1973 it should be a West German model that Becker mentions implies that this is not so.

The topics of 17 June 1953 and the role of literature in the pre-Honecker era are brought together in Volker Braun's *Das ungezwungene Leben Kasts*, where a further potentially sensitive political issue is also broached, the invasion of Czechoslovakia by the armies of the Warsaw Pact countries on 21 August 1968. *Kast* consisted originally of three semi-autobiographical pieces written in 1959, 1964 and 1968 respectively and relating stages in the life of the narrator, Hans Kast. First published in 1971, it was expanded in 1979 by the addition of one final episode set in the 1970s. Taken together the four parts form a kind of fragmentary novel of education, modelled, however, as Gisela Shaw (1985) has suggested, on Goethe's *Faust* rather than on his *Wilhelm Meister*. Kast is restlessly searching for the synthesis of individual aspirations and the good of the socialist collective; again and again he comes up against authoritarian pronouncements from above but also uncritical opportunism from below. In 1959 he is working on a building site, having been expelled from school when he was overheard telling a friend that his teachers were turning them into hypocrites and that the newspapers told them only half-truths. In 1964 he is at university where he loses his post as student organiser because the drawings he exhibits fail to measure up to the demands of socialist realism; the worker he portrays is not heroic enough – he has mud on his legs – and it is 'decadent' to depict a girl with her blouse open. In 1968 he has joined the theatre and is helping to rehearse a play he has written on the uprising of 1953 when the news of the invasion of Czechoslovakia reaches them. At once the play has to be altered. All aspects which might have bearing on current events and which might lead to criticism are excised and the play becomes lifeless. In 1974 Kast has become a functionary himself and discovers the temptations of power. The gap between those who command and those who obey is as wide as ever. Unable to reconcile the contradictions of actually existing socialism he dies in a car crash.

Once again criticism of authoritarian behaviour focuses on the role of art. The third episode, 'Die Bretter', later retitled 'Die Bühne', is especially interesting. Like Günter Grass in his play *Die Plebejer proben den Aufstand* Braun confronts the literary representation of political events with comparable events in reality. In Grass's play Brecht is rehearsing his adaptation of Shakespeare's

Coriolanus, shifting the emphasis from the great military leader to the revolutionary masses, when news comes of an actual popular uprising, the strike and demonstrations of the building workers in June 1953. In Braun's work the play which is being rehearsed is his own *Hans Faust* which deals with the events of June 1953; it, too, is interrupted by news from outside. Reiner Kunze's protests over the invasion of Czechoslovakia have already been mentioned. The conformist literary treatment of the affair is Max Walter Schulz's novel *Triptychon mit sieben Brücken*, in which both the characters opposed to the invasion, one of them yet another anti-authoritarian teenager, are brought to see the error of their ways. Braun's text refuses to take sides, using the historical events as material to test the reader's ability to think dialectically. Just as he provides little direct information on the content of the play which is being rehearsed, so, too, we learn little that is concrete about the events in Czechoslovakia. Instead we are confronted with individual reactions to the news of the invasion and, in the case of the play, to reactions from spectators, actors and theatre authorities to what is being discussed there. One of the actors supports the military intervention on the grounds that the Prague leadership had proved incompetent and was blinded with a romantic view of socialism. Another disagrees: the problems faced by the reformers had been created by their predecessors. Kast is not surprised at the invasion; he is scornful of the West's sudden concern for 'true socialism' and dislikes the nationalism expressed by the Czech leadership. But he is at the same time taken aback, and he is particularly annoyed at the failure of his country's media to inform him adequately, so that he has to have recourse to broadcasts from the West, which then have to be properly interpreted. The mistrust of the people on the part of the GDR's leadership reflects both the military intervention in Czechoslovakia and the dictatorial behaviour of the theatre manager over Kast's play. Kast tries to turn events to his own advantage. He realises that Brecht's vision of a critical spectator is not enough; rather the spectator should be encouraged to take an active part in proceedings. He takes over the role of the *provocateur* in his play, asking the actors why they allow themselves to be dictated to in this way; but genuine discussion is suppressed. Instead Kast concludes that revolutionary behaviour can only begin at the lowest level, in relations between individuals, that he must start with his own relationship to his friend Susanne and must give greater emphasis to the role played by women in his plays. Personal relationships and the role of women were, as we have seen, to play a significant part in the subsequent development of the GDR's literature.

The most extended accounts of the early years of the GDR are multi-volumed projects by Erwin Strittmatter and Erik Neutsch, *Der Wundertäter* and *Der Friede im Osten* respectively. The first volume of *Der Wundertäter* appeared as early as 1957 and is an entertaining picaresque account of the early life and adventures of Stanislaus Büdner, whose native wit enables him to survive first feudal landowners and later the Nazis. The second and third volumes, however, introduce Büdner to the new republic and there seems no reason why the series should not continue. Neutsch's work is altogether more solemn and monumental. It begins at the end of the Second World War, when Achim Steinhauer and Frank Lutter, members of the Hitler Youth, are tempted to join the Werewolf organisation in order to continue the struggle but are dissuaded from doing so. Their subsequent careers and those of many others are traced through the founding of the GDR, the turbulent early 1950s, the stabilisation brought about in 1961 by the building of the 'antifascist protective wall' in Berlin and the events of 1968, when socialism in Czechoslovakia had to be 'rescued' by the intervention of the Warsaw Pact armies. Four volumes have so far appeared; others are planned.

Der Friede im Osten conforms entirely to the official line on the GDR's development. Quite what will happen to it if in the wake of *glasnost'* the GDR does revise its interpretation of history is hard to predict. Although Neutsch alludes to the uncertainty in the communist world which followed Khruschev's revelations at the Twentieth Party Congress, he has far more to say about the counter-revolutionary activities of the West, and the building of the Wall, like the uprising of 1953, is presented according to the standard SED interpretation. As a satirist, Strittmatter has perhaps the easier task. The second volume of *Der Wundertäter* had already poked fun at some of the simplistic dogmas of the Party, especially those relating to literature; even the terms 'communism' and 'communists' were replaced (in capitals) by the 'CAUSE' and 'COMMUNARDS' on the explicit grounds that they had been used so often as to become trite. The third volume appeared in the same year as Helga Schütz's *Julia*, which, as already discussed in Chapter 1, takes a less orthodox line on the 1950s. In its course Büdner is even expelled from the Party, not for what he has done, but for what a West German journal claims he has done. In this volume Strittmatter grasps the nettle of Stalinism much more firmly than Neutsch, although interestingly Kuczynski (1980) declared that Strittmatter still did not go far enough. The death of Stalin has – literally – central place. During the mourning solemnities Büdner reflects on the 'generalissimo' and comes to the conclusion that many people took Stalin's words to be wise merely because they were Stalin's. He himself cannot accept Stalin's views on language and art, and much of the novel deals with the petty-mindedness of Party bureaucrats in relation to art and literature – thus a reading of Goethe's *Faust* causes the local secretary for agriculture to complain that the play ignored the problems of the farming community and the secretary for propaganda to accuse Goethe of concentrating on 'the negative figures' at the expense of the positive ones. Throughout the novel authoritarian dogmatism in the early years of the GDR is the target of Strittmatter's satire. When Stalin dies selected Party members are detailed to disturb the Sunday activities of the inhabitants of a block of flats in order to ensure that they are not being taken in by Western propaganda; but the unthinking clumsiness of the 'action' merely irritates those at whom it is directed, whether they are committed socialists or not. The aim of the enterprise had been 'enlightenment' – in the end its participants fail to allow *themselves* to be 'enlightened', namely about the real needs and fears of the people. By contrast, there is no irony or self-criticism in Neutsch's *Der Friede im Osten*, where when members of the Communist Youth Organisation visit a village to confront the leader of a religious sect who is agitating against them, they find he is also an alcoholic. There follows a solemn speech in which religion is described as 'the opium of the people' and the irreversible change in political structures is stressed (vol. 3, pp. 23–4).

We have already seen how the problems of Claudia in Christoph Hein's *Der fremde Freund* may be traced to the climate of repression which prevailed in the GDR in the early 1950s. The same author's novel *Horns Ende* is directly concerned with this period and is the most challenging of all the GDR's literary works on the Stalinism complex. It is a carefully composed work, whose eight chapters are divided into thirty-nine sections related successively and with a degree of symmetry by five different narrators, and are each prefaced by a dialogue between two anonymous voices, possibly Thomas, one of the narrators, and Horn, whose 'end' is the novel's theme and who repeatedly adjures Thomas to 'remember'. The dialogues and the act of narration are set in the early 1980s; the narrators are looking back at events which took place in the summer of 1957. Once again we are confronted with a work which insists that the present can be understood only in relation to the past. Horn had been expelled from the Party in 1953 in circumstances which are never explained: 'subjectively' he had committed no offence, but under the principle of collectivity he had had to be disciplined for making concessions to 'bourgeois ideology' (p. 35). In the small town of Bad Guldenberg, to which he moves from Leipzig to become the curator of the local museum, he incurs renewed suspicion from Party officials through his 'humanist' interpretation of history. Again we are given no details, but it seems that at a time when the GDR was officially encouraging the small Slav community of the Sorbs Horn's lectures pointing out that in the early Middle Ages the Sorbs had driven out various Germanic tribes from their area were inopportune. He is accused of having contacts with the West, and at the end of August 1957 he commits suicide. The man most responsible for the hounding of Horn later oversteps the mark when he unjustifiably has a loyal comrade, Alfred Schneeberger, imprisoned on suspicion of embezzling the property of émigrés, and subsequently defects to the West.

If the political details are vague the moral issues are entirely clear. Guldenberg is chosen by Hein as a microcosm of Germany, both the pre-1945 Reich and the postwar GDR. Its name ('golden mountain' or 'mountain of guilders') implies a materialist disregard for humane values. It is the place where an anonymous telephone call betrayed to the Nazi authorities the existence of the mentally handicapped Marlene Gohl, so that they might take her off to a euthanasia hospital. After the war gypsies encounter a similar hostility to that which led to their decimation during the Third Reich. Those who befriend them are outsiders like Horn, Gohl and his daughter. Horn's fate stands for that of many others: in the year of his death Marlene is raped, Schneeberger imprisoned and ill-treated, and it is the last year in which the gypsies visit the town. Guldenberg is a place in which personal relationships are based exclusively on exploitation – usually of women by men, always of the weak by the strong. Betrayal is the leitmotiv of this novel, as of most of Hein's works. It is most obvious in the fate of Marlene. Elsewhere Dr Spodeck has betrayed Christine, the girl who helps in his practice; he loves her, but is too weak to divorce his wife. Gertrud Fischlinger has been abandoned by her husband. In implying a continuity between the Third Reich and the GDR Hein is not equating the two political systems. Rather he is suggesting that to change a political system is not enough; it is the individual people who count and they are less easily changed.

On the face of it *Horns Ende* is 'monological literature' as diagnosed by Wolfgang Emmerich (Hohendahl and Herminghouse, eds., 1983). The five separate narrators are not discernibly addressing specific narratees, any more than Claudia did in *Der fremde Freund*. The dialogues between the chapters may even be taken to be soliloquies of the author or of an external narrator, as Krzysztof Jachimczak suggests (1988, p. 353). The effect is to underline the lack of community, first of all in 1950s Bad Guldenberg, but also ultimately in the narrative present. In view of its temporal setting it is perhaps appropriate that the narrative technique of *Horns Ende* is reminiscent of that of many West German novels of the 1950s. Heinrich Böll used multiple focalisers in such novels as *Haus ohne Hüter* and *Billard um halbzehn*, as did Alfred Andersch in *Sansibar oder der letzte Grund*. Specifically one is reminded of Gerd Gaiser's *Schlußball*, which not only uses a series of first-person 'voices' but also introduces voices of the dead in its satirical portrait of materialist Neu-Spuhl, and of Max Frisch's play *Andorra*, the portrait of a small community which fails to defend its Jew and none of whose inhabitants later is prepared to take the blame. Towards the end of Hein's novel the narrative technique is thematised in a conversation between Horn and Dr Spodeck. Spodeck has come across a newspaper report of a technical device, Shuftan's mirror, which enables historical film documents to be falsified. Henceforth one will no longer be able to have any confidence in the authenticity of historical evidence. Once again the Stalinist rewriting of history is adumbrated; Horn's humanist assumption that there is one historical truth conflicts with the Party's doctrine of the opportune, while Spodeck cynically stands on the sidelines. Spodeck goes on to describe his realisation that consciousness, too, operates 'with a thousand mirrors, each of which is refracted a thousand-fold'[9] (pp. 279–80). While the novel itself insists on the importance of memory, by refracting the past through the memories of a number of people, Hein is also taking account of how consciousness works. Each individual's memory is unreliable, truth must therefore be a collective effort. Far from indulging in monologue, Hein is appealing to his readers to break out of their narrative isolation, to be more humane, perhaps even to realise genuine socialism.

One of the vignettes in Stephan Hermlin's *Abendlicht* describes his study of the *Communist Manifesto*, which he first read at the age of thirteen, read and re-read dozens of times until he knew it, as he thought, inside out. Around 1965, however, he made the startling discovery that he had misread one of its key sentences. Where Marx had written: 'In place of the old bourgeois society with its classes and class antagonisms there comes an association in which the free development of each is the precondition for the free development of all'[10] (Marx/Engels 1956ff, vol. 4, p. 482), Hermlin had been reading ' . . . in which the free development of all is the precondition for the free development of each'.[11] In this distortion of Marx's words we may perhaps see the essence of Stalinism, the denial of the rights of the individual in the name of collective. The recognition of his mistake, Hermlin reports, filled him with horror, until relief set in: 'Suddenly a message had appeared before my eyes which I had long awaited, for which I had been hoping'[12] (pp. 22–3). The concern for the 'free development of each individual' which we have seen to characterise the GDR's literature of the past two decades is the best indication that Stalinism is being overcome – and overcome in keeping with Marx's own vision.

Notes

1. Nun sagt mir bloß mal, wer war denn eigentlich dieser Chrustschow!
2. So ist er schon tot? Er liegt da schon? Und wen beerdigen wir eigentlich? Wann ... werden wir auch darüber zu reden beginnen?
3. Offenbar hatte man sie schon öfter zum Weglaufen genötigt, um die Prozesse neu aufzurollen und Heiligsprechung oder Fluch zu überprüfen.
4. Ich konnte und wollte nicht in einem Lande arbeiten, in dem den Schriftstellern ein Maulkorb umgehängt wird. Nein. Es gibt keinen Maulkorb und keine Zensur bei uns.
5. denn durch ihn kann der Mensch tun, was die Gesetze der wirklichen Welt erfordern, ohne deshalb den schönen Glauben an die Lehren der Weisen und Richter und Propheten aufgeben zu müssen ...
6. Direkte Einbeziehung der Leser in die Überlegung: Woher kommen wir? DDR-Geschichtsbewußtsein.
7. und die Zeit kam, in der die Berichte vom bittersten Irrtum, von äußerster Täuschung, von fürchterlichstem Tod in die Welt gingen der Sache wegen, die nur in der Wahrheit leben kann, und doch und gerade darum auf die Sache zurückgeschleudert wurden als hämisches Echo: Also war alles Lüge, alles, alles, alles!
8. Es ist einfach lächerlich zu glauben, der Kommunismus wäre in der Lage, jeden Menschen vor der Zerstörung zu retten.
9. mit tausend Spiegeln, von denen jeder tausendfach gebrochen ist.
10. An die Stelle der alten bürgerlichen Gesellschaft mit ihren Klassen und Klassengegensätzen tritt eine Assoziation, worin die freie Entwicklung eines jeden die Bedingung für die freie Entwicklung aller ist.
11. worin die freie Entwicklung aller die Bedingung für die freie Entwicklung eines jeden ist.
12. Plötzlich war eine Schrift vor meinem Auge erschienen, die ich lang erwartet, auf die ich gehofft hatte.

–7–

Prussians, Saxons and Others

> Have they returned him? I'm glad. Old
> Fritz on his horse once again.
> That means that Lessing as well has his
> monument back, at its arse.[1]
> (Volker Braun, 'Berlinische Epigramme': *Langsamer knirschender Morgen*)

The concern of writers to remind their readers of the immediate past, whether the Third Reich or the Stalinist 1950s, is one way in which the present is placed in its historical perspective. But the GDR's recent literature is marked by a lively interest in the more remote past, in a history which is not part of living memory. It is in the theatre that it has perhaps been most marked: Peter Hacks's *Ein Gespräch im Hause Stein* is set in Goethe's Weimar, Heiner Müller's *Der Auftrag* in early nineteenth-century France and Jamaica, Volker Braun's *Großer Frieden* in ancient China, Christoph Hein's *Cromwell* in seventeenth-century England and *Lassalle* in nineteenth-century Germany. Plays set in the historical past have to some extent ousted those with contemporary topics, something which is bemoaned from time to time (e.g. Fischborn 1984). But the historical novel has also become not only a popular but a respectable genre, one which employs all the sophistication which has characterised GDR fiction in recent years.

It is popular for many reasons. Action literature and romance are favourite reading in the GDR as in the rest of the world, and the subtitle 'historical novel' is said to guarantee sales (Langermann 1986, p. 1393). The historical novel has always given scope for the erotic, a significant interest of writers in recent years; Jay Rosellini (Hoogeven and Labroisse, eds., 1981, pp. 61–101) gives examples of erotic scenes in the early GDR historical novel, and recent works such as Walther's *Bewerbung bei Hofe* and Lewin's *Federico* have their fair share of these. The genre also satisfies a craving for facts, for authenticity, and this, too, has been a preoccupation of the GDR's literature for many years now. But there may also be something escapist about it, and from Lion Feuchtwanger in the 1920s onwards the authors of historical novels have had to defend themselves against this accusation. In the authoritarian society of the GDR such 'escapism' may not be purely voluntary: if contemporary topics are inclined to be problematical, leading to difficulties with the censor, the past is safer. After the events of June 1953 the proportion of published novels dealing with the present dropped from 26% to 11% in two years, and in 1955 historical novels made up 24% of total output (ibid., p. 77). The current revival of the genre may imply similar problems; conversely, however, it may be possible to infringe taboos by putting on the mask of history.

In 1976, addressing a historians' conference in Mannheim, the Federal German president Walther Scheel suggested that West Germans were in danger of becoming 'a people without a history' (cit. Weidenfeld, ed., 1983, p. 248), appearing to lack any interest in their past; young people were growing up unaware of the great periods of German history. Since then things have changed in the Federal Republic. Even as Scheel was speaking the 'Hitler-wave' was washing its shores: a flood of memoirs, films and novels on everyday life in the Third Reich appeared on West German television and in bookshops, much of which was regarded by East German commentators as trivialising fascism (Bernhard 1977, pp. 62–3). The important Prussia exhibition which opened in 1981 in West Berlin was popular enough to suggest that West Germans were interested also in their less recent past, while the conservative government of the later 1980s provoked a lively debate among historians and politicians when it announced its intention of building a museum of German history in West Berlin.

In theory the East Germans have always had a much greater awareness of history than their West German counterparts. A minor provocation of Plenzdorf's *Die neuen Leiden des jungen W.* is the vagueness of Wibeau's concept of history – he assumes Goethe's Werther to have been a contemporary of Thomas Müntzer, for example – but even he finds in his Huguenot ancestors historical justification for his determination to be true to himself. Moreover, if, in the Marxist sense, history is moving inexorably, albeit with detours, in the direction of socialism and ultimately communism, then the German Democratic Republic as a socialist state must be the embodiment of all the progressive forces of German history. This is the line taken by Erich Honecker in his preface to the standard East German history, where he declares that the GDR is 'the political embodiment of the best traditions of German history', and continues: 'As a socialist workers' and peasants' power it is the inevitable result and culmination of the century-long struggle of the popular masses for social progress'[2] (cit. Weidenfeld, ed., 1983, pp. 108–9). It is regarded as 'essential' that socialist citizens see themselves as the 'legitimate heirs and legal executors of all the significant humanist and revolutionary historical traditions'[3] (Berger et al. 1978, pp. 237–8). One problem raised by what Wilfried von Bredow calls this 'teleological' view of history (Weidenfeld, ed., 1983, p. 107) is the degree of eclecticism it demands: the GDR is the heir only to the 'best' traditions, the 'humanist' traditions, the 'significant' traditions. What were these? Von Bredow lists the following 'canonical' periods: the Peasant Wars of the sixteenth century, the struggle to liberate Germany from Napoleon at the beginning of the nineteenth century, the 1848 revolution, the workers and soldiers councils of 1918–19, isolated efforts at resistance and revolt during the Weimar Republic and the Third Reich, including involvement in the struggle against Franco during the Spanish Civil War (ibid., p. 113). Excluded from 'significant history' are therefore the whole of the seventeenth and eighteenth centuries, including the Thirty Years' War and the age of Prussian absolutism. Unfortunately, moreover, most of these 'canonical' phenomena were failures, and the success of the rest was shortlived. Germany has produced innumerable progressive theorists of the revolution from Thomas Müntzer to Karl Marx, but no revolution itself. Socialism in the GDR was not created by the German communist party but by the intervention of the Red Army. This unfortunate state of affairs is known as the 'deutsche Misere'. It creates difficulties for socialist writers seeking models with which to inspire their public. Thus Friedrich Wolf's 1930 play *Die Matrosen von Cattaro*, which depicts the failure of a mutiny, has to end with the rousing if ultimately unconvincing appeal: 'Comrades, make a better job of it next time!'[4] (vol 1, p. 258).

In the past decade, however, the monolithic view of history has been giving way to a more differentiated one. Since 1978 the GDR has been revising its official image of Prussia, suggesting it contained 'progressive' traditions as well as reactionary ones (Bartel et al. 1979). A symbolic act was the return in 1980 of Christian Rauch's equestrian statue of Frederick II, whom hitherto only reactionaries might call 'the Great', to its place of prominence on Unter den Linden in Berlin. The GDR's early historical novel, Rosellini has shown, was dominated by Martin Luther's antagonist Thomas Müntzer, presented as the progressive forerunner of Marx and Lenin (Hoogeven and Labroisse 1981, pp. 79ff). Luther was referred to almost exclusively in connection with his support of the princes in the Peasant Wars of the sixteenth century. This image, too, has been revised, his 'progressive' achievements, especially by making the Bible accessible to the masses through his translation, are now emphasised and Erich Honecker himself presided over the committee set up to mark the quincentenary celebration of his birth in 1983 (Brayne 1980; Bartel et al. 1981). Official biographies have reassessed not only Frederick the Great (Mittenzwei 1980), but even Otto von Bismarck (Engelberg 1985). This is a remarkable reversal of the view expressed by W. von Hanstein in 1947: 'From a historical point of view there is a straight line leading from Luther via the Great Elector, via Frederick II and his successors, via Bismarck and the Wilhelminian age to Hitler'[5] (cit. Weidenfeld, ed., 1983, p. 230).

Not all of the GDR's writers and intellectuals are happy about these revisions. The plinth of the statue of Frederick the Great, for example, is surrounded with relief figures of the king's contemporaries, military leaders, scholars, writers, and Volker Braun is not the only person to have remarked scornfully on the position of writers such as Lessing under the horse's tail (see opening epigraph). Helmut Sakowski is usually to be found on the side of the Establishment. In an address to the presiding body of the Writers' Union in 1981 he admitted that the GDR's citizens could not claim only to have inherited the mantle of the Peasant Wars, and suggested further areas for reassessment, including the early Middle Ages (1981, p. 11). He himself, however, is evidently more sceptical of the rehabilitation of Prussia than his words implied: the original version of his novel *Wie ein Vogel im Schwarm* was serialised in *Wochenpost* and contained some critical remarks on the 'renaissance of Prussia' which were excised from the book version (Kleinschmidt 1985a, p. 117). Works such as Günter de Bruyn's *Neue Herrlichkeit* and Volker Braun's *Hinze-Kunze-Roman* imply a continuity of history which is not flattering to the GDR. The former takes place in a villa which was built in 1895, presumably by a rich Prussian landowner or industrialist and endowed with the name which gives the novel its title, one which implies both 'new wonders', the optimism of the rapidly expanding economy of the recently founded German Empire, and 'new masters', the Prussian junkers. Today the villa is a country retreat for high-ranking Party members and their offspring, a further set of 'new masters', and it seems that class privileges are as prevalent now as then. Braun implies the continuity between Prussia and the GDR through his parody of Diderot's eighteenth-century novel *Jacques le Fataliste*. It is a feature of some of the GDR's recent historical novels that they refuse to follow political fashions.

In 1979 the journal *Neue deutsche Literatur* published the responses of a number of writers to a questionnaire on the contemporary historical novel. The orthodox view was represented by Establishment author Wolfgang Joho: 'The most outstanding task of the historical novel I regard as being to awaken historical consciousness particularly in the younger generation, to teach them to understand the socialist present into which they have been born as the logical consequence of earlier events, to make them feel themselves to be both the heirs and the executors of history'[6] (Joho et al. 1979, p. 74). In these words there are strong echoes of the theory of the historical novel expounded by Georg Lukács, whose influential *Der historische Roman* was first published in Moscow in 1937, and reprinted in Berlin in 1955. Lukács regarded the historical novel as a genre in no way different from the contemporary social novel. Categories such as the 'typical', in the sense of what was significant for the development of history, were just as important for the historical novel as for any other work. History was for Lukács the 'destiny of the people'; the historical novel should portray 'the kind of individual destiny that can *directly* and at the same time typically express the problems of an epoch'[7] (1965, p. 347). The historical novel should not consist in hidden references to contemporary events; rather it should present the 'prehistory of the present':

> Without a felt relationship to the present, a portrayal of history is impossible. But this relationship, in the case of really great historical art, does not consist in alluding to contemporary events . . . , but in bringing the past to life as the prehistory of the present, in giving poetic life to those historical, social and human forces which, in the course of a long evolution, have made our present-day life what it is and as we experience it.[8] (p. 64)

Other influential features of Lukács's work include his view of the relation between the fictitious hero and the 'world-historical individual', and his rejection of the biographical novel. The historical novel preferred as its subject-matter transitional ages, the crises of history. Walter Scott's success lay in his ability to find 'mediocre' heroes, 'historical-social types' who could embody the totality of certain transitional stages of history (p. 42). The 'world-historical personage', on the other hand, was best treated as a more subsidiary figure, assisting the writer to relate popular movements to the 'historical' events (p. 254). By concentrating on the world-historical individual, the biographical novel falsely displaced the emphasis from the social to the psychological and neglected 'the great driving forces of history' (p. 393).

Just as writers have been rejecting Lukács's insistence on the omniscient, authoritative narrator, so many of these theses no longer apply to a GDR literature which over the past twenty years has been so concerned with subjective authenticity. From Christa Johannsen's *Leibniz* to Sigrid Damm's *Vögel, die verkünden Land* and Volker Ebersbach's *Caroline*, the biographical novel, for example, has been enjoying increasing favour. And yet the notion that the historical novel presents the 'prehistory of the present' has been extraordinarily fruitful. Lukács believed that the classical type of historical novel could only be renewed if writers faced the question how the Hitler regime in Germany had been possible (1965, p. 421). Christa Wolf's *Kindheitsmuster* is a historical novel in the Lukácsian sense. 'How did we become as we are?', it asks; the prehistory of the present is the Third Reich. And if the Aron of Jurek Becker's *Der Boxer* is permanently scarred by the barbarity of the Nazis, then the Claudia of Christoph Hein's *Der fremde Freund* is perhaps equally scarred by her experiences in the early 1950s; it too, like *Horns Ende*, presents the prehistory of the present in terms of Stalinism.

There is, however, an alternative model to that of Lukács and today it is perhaps more important: that of Lion Feuchtwanger, in whose name an annual prize for historical fiction or biography is awarded. In an essay of 1935, Feuchtwanger admitted that the accusation of escapism was sometimes a valid one, but pointed out that from its earliest beginnings great literature had used historical themes (p. 19). Like the author of contemporary fiction, the writer of historical fiction was expressing his own '(contemporary) feeling for life, his subjective world picture' (p. 20). Feuchtwanger's historical novels had the same subject-matter as his other works: 'I have never thought of portraying history for its own sake, I have always seen in costume, in the historical garb merely a means of stylisation, a means to create the illusions of reality in the simplest way possible'[9] (ibid.). His most famous novel, *Jud Suß*, is, on the author's own account, the presentation of the career of Walter Rathenau transposed into the eighteenth century (p. 21). While recognising Feuchtwanger's impeccable socialist and humanist intentions, Lukács disapproved of this technique, which he regarded as dangerously close to a decadent Nietzscheanism, since the use of historical parallels implied that things did not change (1965, pp. 286, 352–62). But precisely this seems to be the message of many of the GDR's recent historical novels. The setting in the past is a costume. This is one aspect of the historical novel which is perhaps peculiarly of the GDR: the relatively monolithic nature of its society and ideological basis makes the historical mode attractive, enabling the drawing of parallels between earlier social structures and those of the present-day in a way which would not apply to liberal democracies such as West Germany. These novels are not describing the 'prehistory of the present' but the 'present' itself.

Waldtraut Lewin, who was awarded the Feuchtwanger prize in 1978, has described her outlook in similar terms to those of Feuchtwanger: 'My interest in the changing forms of history is, to put it crudely, that of the actor for his costume. Man in his relation to society, the ever renewed continuity of his struggle for dignity, liberty and happiness is the eternal object of my curiosity'[10] (Joho et al. 1979, p. 78). But she also sees the historical mode as one which produces 'alienation'. Unlike most of the authors to be discussed here, Lewin's interest has mainly been with more remote historical epochs, especially Roman times, which can scarcely be regarded as the 'prehistory of the present'. Her *Federico* is an account of the life and times of the controversial figure of Frederick II, King of Sicily, Holy Roman Emperor, King of Jerusalem. Denounced in his time as the Antichrist, glorified by others as the Prince of Peace, he has been described as the first Renaissance man. Under the mask of history Lewin introduces topics of contemporary social interest: the bisexuality of Federico, presented as something entirely natural, the active involvement of women in history, and inasmuch as Federico unites Christians and Moslems among his advisers, one may even detect a contemporary international dimension in the novel. But the most significant connection between *Federico* and some of the texts we have discussed which are set in the present is the theme of disillusionment linked to the failure of a revolution. The novel's two parts correspond to the two phases in Frederick's rule. In the first all is optimistic serenity as the brilliant young monarch embarks on the revolutionary restructuring of his state. In the second everything turns sour, as opposition from without and mistakes within lead the Emperor into ever greater acts of cruelty and inhumanity. It is a pattern which we encounter elsewhere. Braun's play *Großer Frieden* portrays a popular revolt in ancient China in which the Emperor is deposed and replaced by a simple peasant; gradually the traditional structures of power are reintroduced until the peasant is as feared as his predecessor had been. It is the dominant theme of Christoph Hein's plays: the English revolution is betrayed by Cromwell, the German social democrats by their leader Lassalle, and in the absurdist *Die wahre Geschichte des Ah Q* when the revolution does break out it merely replaces a 'merciful sir' with a 'revolutionary sir' (p. 124). But it is also, as we have seen, a theme of such works as *Nachdenken über Christa T.*, *Es geht seinen Gang* and *Der fremde Freund*, which are set in the GDR itself. The Stalinist betrayal of the revolution cannot be far from the reader's mind.

It is the eighteenth century, however, which has provided the material for the most significant group of novels, and it is fascinating to observe how writers appear to be taking up each other's motifs, building on them and developing them. A whole 'family' of novels can be traced to the influence of Martin Stade's *Der König und sein Narr*, the fictitious autobiography of Jacob Paul Gundling, who is most famous for having being buried in a wine butt in reference to his favourite vice. But Gundling was a serious scholar in his day, had visited England and conversed with John Locke and Jonathan Swift, and he was appointed Professor of History and Law at the Berlin Academy in 1705. When Frederick William I succeeded his profligate father in 1713 as King of Prussia one of his first acts was to dissolve the Academy. Although Gundling was given various posts at court, and indeed succeeded Leibniz as president of the Academy of Sciences, he was never taken seriously but subjected to all manner of indignities, from which he unsuccessfully attempted to escape. In Stade's novel he is lying on his deathbed looking back on his past, writing his 'last book'. It is yet another self-critical text.

Der König und sein Narr fulfils some of Lukács's demands of the historical novel, while at the same time going beyond them. As its title suggests, it confronts the 'mediocre hero', the obscure philosopher Gundling, with the 'world-historical individual', Frederick William I, the architect of modern Prussia. It is Gundling's story, however, the King remaining a figure whom we see only from without, just as Lukács demanded. Frederick William is portrayed relatively sympathetically: although he devotes much energy and money into building up his army, his posture in foreign relationships is a defensive one; he weeps over every soldier who dies in his service, although he does not hesitate to have them run the gauntlet if they try to desert; he is determined to establish indigenous industries, and to curtail the power of the feudal nobles he inaugurates his famous 'Tabakskollegium' or 'smoking seminars', a kind of miniature Versailles at which he can keep his eye on potential troublemakers; but he is also deeply religious, convinced of his divine mission and driven at times by what the atheist Gundling regards as superstition.

Heiner Müller's play *Leben Gundlings* was almost certainly influenced by Stade's work. The first part of the triptych portrays some of the more repulsive scenes involving Gundling at Frederick William's court. Müller interprets the development of Frederick the Great in relation to the brutalising education he received from his father. His play is an almost unmitigated attack on Prussianism (see Emmerich, in Klussmann and Mohr 1982, pp. 115–58). Stade's portrayal is a more reasoned one, anticipating to some extent the rehabilitation of Prussia which came officially a few years later. Again in keeping with the Lukácsian model, we see a society in transition, here between feudalism and capitalism, between superstition and enlightenment. Religion is unmasked in materialist terms when the orthodox Lutherans are shown to be hostile towards both the Jews and the Calvinist Huguenots because of their economic successes. The King plays the one minority off against the other; the contradictions in his character relate to the nature of the age. The same might be said of Gundling himself, an enlightened liberal with progressive ideas for the reform of industry and society. His fatal flaw is to overestimate his influence on the King, coupled with his weakness for the bottle. In Lukács's terms he lacks a sufficiently close contact with the masses; indeed in places he is seen as an example of the lonely intellectual in his ivory tower. The King by contrast paints the peasants and has ambitions at being a craftsman, although even he is contrasted with the Czar, who likes to mingle with the crowd. In fact the masses play a minor role in the novel. More striking still is the almost complete absence of women: the two we briefly meet, symmetrically placed at the beginning and end of the novel, a serving girl in an inn and Anne de Larrey, who becomes Gundling's wife, introduce elements of beauty and humanity which contrast with the machismo of the Prussian court. The contrast between Prussianism and femininity corresponds to some aspects of the women's writing we have already analysed.

It is when one tries to see the events of Stade's novel in terms of the 'prehistory of the present' that the Lukácsian model is subverted, however, for the GDR claims to have overcome the contradictions of Frederick William's Prussia. Instead it is the analogies which strike the reader, especially the situation of the intellectual in the contemporary GDR. When we read that Voltaire has been permanently banished from within fifty miles of the French court and is on his way to England, the situation of dissident East German intellectuals must come to mind. Unlike Voltaire, Gundling allows himself to be turned into a clown. When he tries to escape, as he does on two occasions, he is recaptured and subjected to further humiliations. The situation of the intellectual in Germany is a desperate one indeed, caught between his own vanity and the total power of the state. In representing him as a court jester, however, allowed to tell the rulers the truth on condition that he is ignored, Stade is adapting a motif which was common in West Germany a decade earlier (Dahrendorf 1965, pp. 318–24), and received its most extended treatment in Heinrich Böll's *Ansichten eines Clowns*.

The 'deutsche Misere' is, after all, common to both German states. Its other side, as with the later *Federico*, is the theme of disillusionment. Here, too, the idealism of an early revolution, that of Frederick William I, gives way, under the force of external circumstances and subjective weaknesses, to pragmatism, brutality and defeat.

A scene in Müller's *Leben Gundlings* shows Frederick William's son and successor, Frederick the Great, accompanied by Voltaire and strolling through the Prussian fields where his peasants are harvesting their turnips; he forces them to eat them raw and call them 'oranges' (his own palace at Potsdam was famous for its orangerie). Prussia, he says, exemplifies the unity of state and people: 'I am the people', he proclaims (p. 95). Voltaire meanwhile is quietly sick. Voltaire's sojourn at the court of Frederick II from 1750 to 1753 has traditionally been adduced by the apologists of Prussia as evidence of Frederick's enlightened outlook as compared to the tyranny and obscurantism of the French court; at the same time they have favourably contrasted Frederick's straightforward German 'earthiness' with the polished, shifting elegance of the Frenchman. Voltaire in Prussia is the subject of the novel *Kammerherr und König* by Hans-Peter Jaeck, a professional historian, who in a postscript discusses the advantages of 'belles lettres' over conventional history-writing and describes his work as 'a realistic fiction' (p. 323). He quotes extensively from contemporary documents, allowing himself only the freedom of occasional invented conversations. *Kammerherr und König*, however, does bear comparison with Stade's novel, whose title it echoes. Again the theme is the relation between intellectual and state. Voltaire becomes an honoured and highly paid member of the Prussian court. Although he is initially flattered to be taken into the King's confidence and enjoys their learned discussions, gradually he realises that he and the other courtiers are regarded by Frederick as 'fools, dwarfs or monkeys' (p. 207). The focus is largely that of Voltaire; the King, as in *Der König und sein Narr*, is seen only from without. Unlike Gundling, Voltaire was able to free himself from the ignominy of life at a philistine Prussian court. Jaeck's sympathies are entirely with the philosopher. It is Frederick who appears as the intriguer, not Voltaire, although after Voltaire's escape the King tried to make out that the reverse was the case. The public burning of the satire *Akakia* was the final blow which persuaded him that he had been treated by Frederick as an 'orange' to be pressed out to the last drop of juice. It ominously foreshadows the book burnings of the Third Reich; but when Voltaire comes up against the limits to the free expression of opinion in Frederick's

Prussia, the reader is implicitly invited to consider the situation in the present GDR.

The old Prussia is one half of the geographical area of the present-day GDR, the other half is Saxony. The former was notorious for its army, its discipline, its efficient bureaucracy; the latter was famous for its wit, the splendour of its architecture, especially at Dresden, and the brilliance of its cultural life, with Leipzig, the centre of the book trade, regarding itself as a smaller version of Paris, an Athens on the Pleisse. The traditional rivalry between the two kingdoms ended in favour of Prussia, victorious in the Seven Years' War. Lessing's comedy of 1767, *Minna von Barnhelm*, is partly a plea for reconciliation between the two states. Saxony, however, also happened to be the area from which the early political leaders of the GDR came. The strong Saxon accent of Walter Ulbricht in particular was a source of much mockery from West Germans and others. In this context Joachim Walther's novel *Bewerbung bei Hofe*, set in eighteenth-century Saxony, has peculiar resonances for East German readers, as it introduces King August the Strong of Saxony himself speaking with a particularly broad accent. In keeping with its setting it deals not with militarism and bureaucracy but with literature and love and their relation to affairs of state.

Walther's novel takes as its starting-off point the same event as *Der König und sein Narr*: the advent of Frederick William as King of Prussia. As the new King favours the army at the expense of culture, court poet and master of ceremonies Johann von Besser is dismissed. In due course Gundling becomes his successor. *Bewerbung bei Hofe* takes up the subsequent story of Besser, now official poet at the Dresden court of August the Strong, who in Stade's novel attempts to enrol Gundling as a spy. Besser is conscious of his fading powers, afraid of losing his influence at court, and looking out for an assistant and possible successor through whom he will be able to maintain his status. The man he has in mind is the young Johann Christian Günther, another figure whom Gundling briefly encounters in Stade's novel, this time in Leipzig on the second of his attempts to escape the Prussian court. Besser envies Günther his poetic facility, but fears that he may either become an incomparable rival or cause offence at court by his independence of mind. In the event both of these things happen. Günther fluffs his chance to show off during an audience with the King, refusing to engage in trivial competition with his rival, the nonentity Johann Ulrich von König, and fails to obtain the post. While he and Besser both die not long after, Günther in poverty and obscurity, it is the latter whose poetry is remembered today, while Besser's is wholly forgotten.

The novel is skillfully organised around two simultaneous events. The first concerns the fate of Günther; the second is the spectacular wedding of August's son and heir and a Habsburg princess. It begins with the arrival of Günther at Dresden and ends with his departure and the simultaneous arrival of the newly married royal couple. *Bewerbung bei Hofe* is a novel about political and social opportunism. Günther, who refused to say what he did not believe, is sent packing. The triumphal procession, by contrast, is a sham, the marriage is an arranged one, designed to consolidate August's position as a European leader. It is not popular, since the bride is a Catholic in a Lutheran state. In this novel the erotic scenes have an integrated function. Besser has prostituted his art of money and status, his behaviour mirroring that of his master, who became a Catholic in order to mount the throne of Poland. Now Besser is sexually almost impotent, just as he is poetically impotent, and needs the stimulus of pornography and whores. Günther by contrast forms natural sexual relationships, just as his poetry is stimulated by nature.

Although it centres on poets, like *Der König und sein Narr*, *Bewerbung bei Hofe* concerns the wider issue of the relation between the intellectual and the state. Again it is an age of transition, both between feudalism and capitalism and between religious superstition and the new philosophy of Leibniz. Besser foresees a future in which the new bourgeoisie will have taken over, and will be ruling by 'reason', but that this enlightenment will be based solely on money. There are Marxist implications here, as in the debate between Besser and Günther, in which Besser is accused of regarding history as a present from Father Christmas, rather than as something which requires active involvement. But the middle classes in the novel do not give the impression of being interested in change, rather in buying their way into the nobility. Instead it is the masses whose revolutionary potential appears waiting to be tapped. Their hunger is vividly illustrated in an episode in which the mob slaughters and butchers a runaway cow in the street. They are the gaping audience for the royal festivities, but it is not always easy to persuade them to cheer enthusiastically, and an anonymous fly-poster calls for an uprising on the English model. They are individualised in the person of Besser's housekeeper, the embodiment of traditional good sense, who has immediate sympathy for Günther. On all these issues Günther is on the side of history in the Marxist sense. He is an atheist and a believer in reason, who defends the interests of the masses against the snobbery of Besser and whose poetry has revolutionary implications. Günther, however, fails to make his mark in eighteenth-century Saxony; the stage is left to the Bessers and the Königs. In this age-old German dichotomy between 'Geist' and 'Macht' (see Parkes 1986), in this conflict between intellectuals and politicians the former are as much to blame as the latter. As Günther puts it: 'The top brass . . . will always find someone to explain why they have to remain at the top!'[11] (p. 123). It is easy to see Besser simply as a buffoon, interested merely in dress and ceremonial, anxious to know whether he is in twentieth or twenty-first position in the court hierarchy. But it is made clear that he was not always thus. He is aware of progressive intellectual currents and on occasion involuntarily agrees with Günther's polemics. He is evidently another Gundling, who has prostituted his intellect in pursuit of status at court.

The novel therefore goes some way to fulfilling Lukács's demand that the historical novel tell the 'prehistory of the present'; the disastrous development of Germany in the twentieth century is explained by its political backwardness in the eighteenth century and an earlier 'trahison des clercs'. The revolutionary dynamic of the masses meanwhile foreshadows the victory of socialism in the GDR. Like *Der König und sein Narr*, however, *Bewerbung bei Hofe* is more critical than this analysis suggests. Ostensibly the text consists of Besser's diary entries from 7 August to 2 September 1719, preceded by his written wish that his diary should not be published until 250 years after his death (he died in 1729) when, as he believes, Günther will be wholly forgotten, he himself immortal and his readers, 'those living in the 20th century will, as I should like to hope, no longer know from their own experience wars, injustice, famine, lust for power, arrogance, orthodoxy, quibbling, treachery, sycophancy, vaingloriousness, falsehood, hypocrisy, corruption, violence, hatred, mindlessness, envy, stupidity . . . and whatever all the other worldly ills may be called . . .'[12] (p. 7). The irony of these words will not escape the reader, who is invited to seek parallels in his own life and times. The inference is that history does *not* change, precisely what Lukács disapproved of in Feuchtwanger.

Although *Bewerbung bei Hofe,* as Gunnar Müller-Waldeck (1984) stresses in his review, is not a *roman à clef*, it is easy to see parallels between the conditions prevailing in the state of Saxony and in the GDR. Saxony is a place of censorship, surveillance and opportunism, where the court lives in luxury at the expense of ordinary people and where literature is supposed to be written according to certain conventions. Young people are causing problems for the authorities. There is unrest in Poland – when the novel appeared the GDR authorities were concerned that the Polish trade union Solidarity might influence their own citizens. Günther's fate mirrors that of the GDR's writers in 1982, many of whom had been driven into exile. The role of the church as a centre of opposition in the GDR, especially in the unofficial peace movement, is paralleled in the activities of the courageous clergyman Löscher, whose sermons are full of hidden and not-so-hidden references to contemporary politics. Even the public festival which the state can ill afford has its counterpart in the GDR. But these parallels should not be overstated. The GDR is not the only country which spies on its own citizens. When civil servant Grotegut refers to Günther and his like as 'rats, bluebottles, pincher dogs'[13] (p. 350), he is repeating words which were actually used by *West* German politicians, the first two by Franz Joseph Strauss, the last by Ludwig Erhard, to refer to oppositional writers of whom they disapproved.

One final aspect of the novel goes beyond the historical and relates it to the mood of many other East German texts of the past twenty years. This is the existential theme of mortality. The most disastrous event of Besser's life was the early death of his wife, whom he genuinely loved. Throughout the novel he is preoccupied with death; his sleep is filled with nightmares. But the motif is not confined to Besser. Günther has just heard of the death of his best friend. His poetry, best known for its celebration of the senses, has undertones of mortality. He fails at the decisive poetry competition when he suddenly becomes aware of how empty it all is. In the course of the novel he passes through a development, initially refusing to accept that life is a vale of tears, finally resigned to his inability to change the world. It is a motif which tends to cancel out the note of historical optimism found elsewhere in the novel.

But what *is* history? In Hermann Kant's *Die Aula* it is the question posed by Professor Riebenlamm in the new students' first history lesson. He recites to them Brecht's poem 'Fragen eines lesenden Arbeiters'. It begins:

> Who built Thebes of the seven gates?
> In the books are the names of kings.
> Was it the kings who hauled the lumps of rock?
> And Babylon frequently destroyed –
> Who rebuilt it so many times?[14] (vol. 9, p. 656)

They have all been taught to see history through middle-class spectacles: 'the image of the world drawn for us there is largely standing on its head. Here we are going to stand it on its feet again'[15] (p. 80). The Workers' and Peasants' Faculty was founded among other things to counteract false bourgeois conceptions of history. The early East German novel, too, was concerned with 'standing history on its feet again', stressing the role of the masses rather than that of the rulers. It is a conception which underlies the historical parts of Jurij Brězan's novel *Krabat*, where the peasants are seen in perpetual conflict with the landowners, the Reissenbergs, whom they frequently outwit. As we have seen, in Gerti Tetzner's *Karen W.* Karen's friend Peters has been unsuccessfully challenging the official view. More recent works, as was pointed out in Greifswald at a conference on the historical novel, have been seeking a more differentiated, dialectical approach to history (Langermann 1986, p. 1394). The masses have little to say in the novels of Stade and Jaeck. Brecht's poem, however, is referred to in Morgner's *Trobadora Beatriz*. In Yugoslavia Beatriz encounters Bele H., the Scheherezade from *Hochzeit in Konstantinopel*. Brecht had been interested in the views of the 'reading working man'; Bele wants to hear the voice of the 'reading working woman', the 'slave of the slaves'. Beatriz retorts that she will wait in vain if she expects a *man* to report this voice, but adds darkly that the 'poetess is nigh' (p. 194). Morgner has described her central theme as 'the entry of woman into history' (Walther 1973, p. 49). It is the hitherto suppressed voice of a trobadora we hear; the authentic diary of Martha Lehmann, who lost son and husband to the war is reproduced in a further attempt to right the balance. Similarly Christa Wolf has 'rediscovered' female writers of the past such as Karoline von Günderrode and Bettina von Arnim, long overlooked in a male-oriented world. Her *Kassandra*, which we shall examine in the following chapter, questions male-oriented history-writing in the name of the unheard female voice. The historical figure of Cassandra, daughter of Priam of Troy, is, says Wolf, the first female voice to have been recorded in history (1987, p. 903); that it has traditionally been associated with negative features – Cassandra as the eternal pessimist – is entirely due to male malevolence.

Kassandra belongs more to myth than to history. In a more directly historical vein, not only does Renate Feyl's novel *Idylle mit Professor* introduce a largely forgotten woman writer, Luise Adelgunde Victoria Gottsched, but it provides a female perspective on her much more famous husband and at the same time takes issue with Prussian values. Victoria is twenty-two when she marries, Gottsched thirty-five and already a famous scholar and writer, professor at the University of Leipzig and arbiter of German literary taste. Initially she is over-awed by her husband, flattered that she has been chosen to be his companion; as an intelligent, educated woman, however, she soon finds that her household duties do not fulfil her. She, too, has her literary ambitions and writes a successful satirical comedy *Die Pietisterei im Fischbeinrocke*. Although she increasingly becomes aware of her husband's vanity and that their literary tastes diverge, she remains a docile, supportive wife, believing that to be her duty. The turning-point comes when at the cost of her own projects she helps her husband to translate Pierre Bayle's *Dictionnaire* into German only to find that her name is nowhere mentioned when the work appears: she realises that she is no more than Gottsched's wife, existing only in relation to him. Generously he buys her a writing-desk so that she can carry on her translating and other literary activities; he takes especial pleasure in filling its shelf with his own publications. She finds herself more and more openly in conflict with her husband's intolerant literary attitudes. His vanity is hurt when he finds visitors more interested in his wife than himself. By the time she dies, not yet fifty, their relationship has become no more than a formality.

Much of the attraction of Feyl's narrative is its cool and understated style. Where Morgner is often heavily ironic, Wolf self-consciously stylised, Feyl lets events speak almost entirely for themselves. In this novel, too, the Prussian element is important. Gottsched, a native of Königsberg, is a Prussian by birth, who came to Saxon Leipzig in order to escape being drafted into Frederick William's army, for which his great height made him a coveted object, and, like Besser, in order to escape the philistinism of the new King. But he cannot deny his origins. His fanatical determination to lay down 'rules' for literature which exclude individual subjectivity is the pendant to Frederick II's Prussian discipline (it also may be read as a gloss on the dictates of socialist realism). Günther appears in this novel too, at least indirectly – Gottsched's review of his poems contents itself with listing their faults. Unlike Voltaire Gottsched is obsequious towards the Prussian monarch and is rewarded with a poem by the King's own pen. Feyl makes no concessions to the new affection for Frederick II and his Prussians. During the Seven Years' War they invade Saxony, march into Leipzig and cause untold misery to thousands. Gottsched, the Prussian, is delighted; but Victoria, a native of the Free City of Danzig, hates 'everything Prussian, moderate, circumscribed, hates this stubborn, narrow-chested rationality, hates this arrogance and above all the carbines, by means of which power can be placed on show but not one feeling of friendship can be gained'[16] (pp. 231–2).

The other major historical area which has been of interest to the GDR's writers is the age of Goethe, the closing decades of the eighteenth century and the beginning of the nineteenth, the time of Weimar classicism but also of German Romanticism. It is not, however, the 'canonical' wars of liberation which are treated, or if they are then they do not appear in a positive light. We have already seen how writers have been no longer prepared to accept the supreme authority of Goethe. As early as 1938 Anna Seghers had pointed out to Lukács the paradox that the literary judgments of Goethe had been extraordinarily erratic and that his rejection of so many of the younger talents of his age had driven many of them into madness or an early death. She singled out Heinrich von Kleist, Jakob Michael Reinhold Lenz, Friedrich Hölderlin, Gottfried August Bürger and Karoline von Günderrode (Lukács 1971, pp. 345–6). With the exception of Bürger, precisely these authors have been the focus of interest in the 1970s and 1980s. Günter Kunert's polemical 'Pamphlet für K.' was such a scathing attack on Goethe and an official GDR publication of 1972 for echoing the 'Olympian's' condemnation of Kleist as 'morbid' that it was rejected by the editor of the anthology for which it was written. Kleist and Günderrode are the central figures of Christa Wolf's *Kein Ort. Nirgends*, Hölderlin the subject of Stephan Hermlin's radio play *Scardanelli* and the novel *Der arme Hölderlin* by Gerhard Wolf, and the inspiration of a number of poems by Volker Braun, while Lenz, often mediated through Büchner, has permeated many of the more challenging narratives of these years and is the subject of Sigrid Damm's biography *Vögel, die verkünden Land*, which was awarded the Lion Feuchtwanger prize in 1987. Dennis Tate has stressed the importance of Büchner's *Lenz* as a literary model, suggesting that the rediscovery and rehabilitation of these writers implies, contrary to official claims, a continuing 'deutsche Misere', an alienation between progressive writers and conservative political institutions (Wallace, ed., 1984b, p. 177–226). In her comprehensive account of the importance of the non-classical tradition for recent writers Beverley Hardy (1988) has added two further names, those of Jean Paul and E.T.A. Hoffmann, the former the subject of a biography by Günter de Bruyn, the latter embraced by Anna Seghers and by Franz Fühmann. Hardy finds two major impulses for the fascination held by such writers: their biographies and their literary techniques. As outsiders spurned by the literary establishment of their time they provide parallels to the situation of the nonconformist writers of the GDR, while the 'openness' of their aesthetic and the importance allotted to the imagination rather than the rational consciousness gives historical justification to the development of the new literature of the 1970s and 1980s.

The oldest of the writers listed by Seghers was Jakob Lenz, only a little younger than Goethe himself. In his 1981 essay 'Waldbruder Lenz' Christoph Hein draws an indirect parallel between Lenz's fate and the present, when he juxtaposes a general critique of the relation between the writer and society with an account of Lenz's experiences at Goethe's Weimar (1987, pp. 70–96). A few years later Damm's *Vögel, die verkünden Land* appeared, which might be regarded as only marginally relevant here, as Damm is a literary scholar and this work, a biography of Lenz, is the fruit of immensely thorough scholarship pursued across Europe from France to Moscow. But the frontier between biography and literature must always be a doubtful one (Kreuzer 1975). The title of the work, described on the dust-cover as the author's 'first longer prose-work', immediately implies more conventional literary qualities. A present-tense narrative and a narrator who expressly does not 'know everything' are features familiar to readers of recent GDR fiction. Phrases such as 'Perhaps it was like that, perhaps quite different'[17] (p. 140) are leitmotivs of the narrative, and Damm empathetically invents details and scenes as she tries to reconstruct the thought-processes of her protagonist. Lenz's development is set within the backward social and political circumstances of his time: serfdom in Lenz's native Livonia, the sale of men by their German rulers to serve in various armies of Europe, the almost insuperable difficulties faced by anyone who wished to become a professional writer. Lenz refuses to accept the degrading profession of private tutor which he satirises in his best-known play *Der Hofmeister*, nor is he willing to become a lawyer or, hypocritically, a priest. This refusal to prostitute himself is related by Damm to the fate of other writers we have encountered: to Johann Christian Günther, to Friedrich Hölderlin, to Georg Trakl and to Franz Kafka (p. 108) – the list itself implies the disastrous continuity of German history. But the most mysterious and unfortunate episode in Lenz's career was his friendship with Goethe, which ended abruptly when he was expelled from the Weimar where Goethe was by now a member of the Establishment. Damm's albeit tentative interpretation of the affair is less than favourable to Goethe. The disparate social origins of the two men made genuine friendship unlikely. While Lenz's aesthetic, based as it was on dissonance, the grotesque and the tragicomic, was always alien to Goethe, the estrangement was essentially due to their diametrically opposing views of the relation between the writer and society. Goethe may or may not have believed that at Weimar the dichotomy of intellectual and politician could be resolved. His actual writing made little attempt to do so. Lenz believed passionately in the direct involvement of the writer in affairs of state; he – and the phrase echoes Stade, Jaeck and Walther – rejected the 'role of court jester' (p. 214).

Friedrich Hölderlin, unlike Lenz, *was* forced into accepting a post as private tutor for a time. His disastrous love affair with the wife of his employer was one factor in the eventual insanity under which he suffered for the last thirty-seven years of his life. Gerhard Wolf's *Der arme Hölderlin* is more obviously 'literary' than Damm's biography of Lenz. Alternate chapters, set off typographically from each other, describe in the first place a visit to the poet's tower during his last years of derangement in Tübingen, and secondly portray the developments which led to his committal to a mental institution in 1806. The latter, major group of chapters do not proceed chronologically, but rather in retrograde movement, ending, significantly, with the news of Napoleon's coup d'état of 1799. This montage technique juxtaposes directly, as it were, cause and effect. The whole is reminiscent of the radio or television feature. Relatively little of the text is conventional narration; if the one set of chapters paraphrases Wilhelm Waiblinger's account of 1831, the other set is dominated by fragmentary quotations from Hölderlin's own writings. As Wolf does not use quotation marks it is not always obvious which passages are by Hölderlin, which not; as a result past (the years of Napoleonic restoration) and present (the 1970s) are blended together. Dennis Tate has pointed out that Wolf's analysis of the method employed by Johannes Bobrowski in his story 'Boehlendorff' applies to his own *Der arme Hölderlin*: the historical subject-matter is 'really only a pretext, an alienation device' (1984, p. 194).

Hölderlin's is a more complex case than that of Lenz. As Helen Fehervary has shown (1975), the GDR, unlike the West Germans, who up to the late 1960s viewed him mainly as the Romantic dreamer, did not need to be reminded of his revolutionary origins. Both Lukács and Becher had regarded him as the 'poet of the revolution'. They had also claimed his utopian vision of a harmonious future as ammunition in their own struggle to preserve neoclassical cultural values. Gerhard Wolf and other contemporary GDR writers, however, stress rather the contradictions both in the French Revolution itself and in Hölderlin's own character, together with the dissonances and fragmentation in Hölderlin's actual writings so that he becomes both a 'metaphor for the GDR writer' (Fehervary 1975, p. 63) and an opponent of the bourgeois heritage which Lukács was trying to preserve. Thus in *Der arme Hölderlin* the poet is quoted declaring that as soon as art deals with a topic which is at all modern the artist must abandon the old classical forms

(p. 102); in this way the modernist technique of Wolf's own text finds its justification. Once again the failure of the giants Goethe and Schiller to sympathise with the young revolutionary poets is stressed. Even in a relatively short text Wolf finds room to relate Hölderlin's fate to that of others: Boehlendorff, Schmid and Emerich. By juxtaposing the reality of post-revolutionary Europe with the optimistic ideals expressed by a Schelling and a Hölderlin Wolf is also stressing the element of disillusionment with facile slogans. Revolutions do not come about as one century follows the other, or, as Brecht had put it earlier in connection with his play *Leben des Galilei*, 'as the morning follows a good night's sleep' (vol. 17, p. 1106). Hölderlin and his friends greet the imminent arrival of the French invaders in the expectation that they will do away with such rulers as the Duke of Württemberg, who treats his game more humanely than his subjects. Jourdan, however, prohibits revolutionary activities in the occupied provinces, the Swiss revolution is frustrated, and in the Palatinate, where the enthusiasm for democratic ideals was greatest, the peasants are fleeing in droves from the barbarity of the French. In this way *Der arme Hölderlin* relates to such other historical novels as *Der König und sein Narr* and *Federico*, to plays such as Braun's *Großer Frieden* and Hein's *Cromwell*. By implication it relates also to the disillusionment with the revolution imposed on the GDR by Stalin. Gundling becomes a court jester, Günther refuses to do so. Mad Hölderlin in his tower is, literally, the 'fool', obsequious to all who visit him. 'I'm not a Jacobin. I don't want to be a Jacobin. Away with all Jacobins. Vive le roi!'[18] (p. 23).

Christa Wolf's *Kein Ort. Nirgends* is the most fictional of these works. The historical Heinrich von Kleist and Karoline von Günderrode may have met, but it is not certain. Wolf's text relates the few hours of a June afternoon when they find themselves in company with the poet Clemens Brentano, his wife Sophie Mereau, the lawyer Friedrich Carl von Savigny and others at the house of the wealthy merchant Joseph Merten in Winkel on the Rhine. The concentration on a few hours together with an extensive use of flashback and memory creates an atmosphere of utopian timelessness, contrasting all the more brutally with the everyday life into which the protagonists will shortly be plunged once more and in which they will eventually perish, both by suicide. As Colin Smith has suggested (1987, pp. 241–3), the function of the narratorial voice is to make plain the relation between past and present. This is nowhere clearer than at the beginning: Kleist and Günderrode are 'predecessors' of the narrator; 'we', she says, 'still persisting in forgiving those who trespass against us . . . still lustful of the ashen taste of words. Still not, as it behoves us to be, dumb'[19] (p. 5). *Kein Ort. Nirgends* was written under the impact of the Biermann affair and reflects the atmosphere of isolation experienced by writers like Christa Wolf at the time.

The year is 1804. Napoleon has just proclaimed himself Emperor, Napoleon in whose name for Kleist is crystallised the 'world's ills' (p. 55). The revolution has been betrayed, opportunism reigns. Savigny cynically mocks both Kleist and Günderrode for their refusal to accept that the 'realm of thought' must be cleanly separated from the 'realm of deeds' (p. 50). Once again Goethe serves as example of the writer who has accommodated himself to circumstances: to be sure, his play *Tasso* presents the conflict between artist and statesman, but in Kleist's view he fails to understand the artist's standpoint, he is afraid of tragedy. The dimension of *Kein Ort. Nirgends* which is Christa Wolf's own is the portrayal of male-female relationships. It is a work which gives the problem presented in 'Selbstversuch' a historical dimension and points forward to *Kassandra*. Günderrode will never marry; her independence of mind means that the man she loves, Savigny, will not marry her for fear of losing his own authority. Kleist is torn between literature and the army; maleness for him is associated with the Prussian military discipline which he rejects. David Jenkinson has argued persuasively that the text shows not the social but the psychological causes of Kleist's and Günderrode's alienation; these include their uncertainty over their sexual identity (Williams, ed., 1987, pp. 136–42). It is true that Wolf has been increasingly preoccupied with the psychology of individuals to an extent perhaps unique among writers in the GDR; it is also the case that sexual identity has been an important theme of other recent writing. To regard the androgynous qualities of both Günderrode and Kleist merely as contributing to their inability to adapt to society is, however, to underestimate the importance of the motif in Wolf's works as a whole. Elsewhere, as we have seen, Wolf implies androgyny as a utopian possibility. In their final conversation each envies the other the advantages conferred by their sex: as a male the ability to act, as a female the freedom of the mind. The dichotomy of thought and action cannot be resolved, neither in 1804 nor, by implication, in 1979; it remains, however, a utopian ideal.

Most of these works are concerned to a greater or lesser extent with the relation between writers and society. This is connected with the increased degree of self-consciousness in the GDR's writing which was analysed earlier. One recent historical novel of merit departs from this tendency: Martin Stade's *Der närrische Krieg*.

Stade's source is the authentic diary of one Lieutenant Rauch for the year 1747 and the corresponding episode in Gustav Freytag's *Bilder aus der deutschen Vergangenheit*. Freytag had been concerned to show the absurdity and pettiness of the behaviour of some of the German mini-princes prior to the unification of Germany in 1870. Disputes over who should succeed to the title if its present holder has married beneath his station and quarrels over precedence at court such as preoccupied Besser in Walther's novel lead in this case to a war between two of the Saxon states, Meiningen and Gotha. In the end, as Freytag puts it, the issue was settled by Frederick the Great, playing the part of the lion in the fable, who resolved a dispute by taking the major part for himself (1925, p. 563). For Freytag Rauch is important only as the narrator of the immediate incidents. In Stade's novel Frederick plays no role at all, and Rauch is the major figure.

In keeping with its source this novel, too, uses the diary form, here the diary of a professional soldier who is caught up in the conflict. Rauch is an embodiment of the traditional military values of honour and discipline who lives for fighting and whoring. He encounters an army doctor who abhors violence and killing and the militarist ethos. Although against his will Rauch is more and more influenced by the doctor, finding himself beginning to question what is going on around him, becoming aware of the cowardice, incompetence and inhumanity of his superior officers, he nevertheless dies in a senseless duel. Initially, as suggested by the novel's title, the war appears 'foolish' indeed, and the shock is all the greater when hostilities begin and the puppets are knocked over. In his narrative technique Stade is economical, perhaps even, by comparison with some of the other texts we have been examining, unsophisticated. The message, however, is as potentially subversive as any. The doctor publishes Rauch's diary with some brief comments of his own at the end, remarking: 'One thing has to be admitted. He had begun to think. Thinking is the most important thing. Thinking and doubting'[20] (p. 205). Appearing as it did at the height of the rearmament debates, the novel is an impressively anti-militarist statement.

Wilfried von Bredow has suggested that historiography is important for the GDR in order to establish its national legitimacy. Constantly forced to confront the prosperity and democracy of its Western neighbour, it must find alternative sources to justify its existence, hence the search for continuity between the past and the present, the attempt to present the GDR as the crowning achievement of German history (Weidenfeld, ed., 1983, p. 107). The rehabilitation of Prussia thus may relate to a justification of the GDR's own militarist posture or its bureaucratic structures. The historical novel or drama has its part to play here too. The GDR critic Henryk Keisch tries to explain the turning to historical drama with reference to the GDR's development of a national identity and compares the situation with that of Shakespeare in Elizabethan England and Schiller in revolutionary Germany: 'It may have something to do with the emergence of historically new political structures, with the consolidation and deepening of a new state conciousness in the GDR, that here an increasing number of works of literature, especially dramatic works, use historical material (or at least indirectly refer to such)'[21] (1981, p. 93).

It is to the credit of the writers whom we have been discussing that their works do not easily lend themselves to such a function. When Heinz Pepperle pleaded for the reassessment of Nietzsche (1986), he was bitterly attacked by Wolfgang Harich, who expressly associated Pepperle's plea with the rehabilitation of Luther, Frederick the Great and Bismarck, which Harich condemned as an imitation of 'Western fashions' and as 'undermining basic principles of cultural policies' (1987, p. 1054), accusations which led Hermann Kant to accuse him in turn of 'Pol-Potism'. Kant's ironic comment 'Just look at our literature – it does not hold Prussia in excessively high regard . . .'[22] (Schriftstellerverband, ed., 1988, pp. 44–5) is, in the light of our examples, nothing but the truth.

Notes

1. Hat man ihn wieder? Mich freuts. Der alte Fritz hoch zu Rosse. / Hat doch auch Lessing zugleich wieder sein Denkmal, am Arsch.

2. die staatliche Verkörperung der besten Traditionen der deutschen Geschichte . . . Als sozialistische Arbeiter- und Bauernmacht ist sie das gesetzmäßige Ergebnis und die Krönung des jahrhundertelangen Kampfes der Volksmassen für den gesellschaftlichen Fortschritt.

3. rechtmäßige Erben und gesetzmäßige Vollstrecker aller bedeutenden humanistischen und revolutionären geschichtlichen Traditionen.

4. Kameraden, das nächste Mal besser!

5. Historisch betrachtet führt eine gerade Linie von Luther über den Großen Kurfürsten, über Friedrich II. und seine Nachfolger, über Bismarck und die wilhelminische Zeit bis zu Hitler.

6. Als die vornehmste Aufgabe des geschichtlichen Romans sehe ich es an, gerade bei den jüngeren Generationen Geschichtsbewußtsein zu wecken, sie die sozialistische Gegenwart, in die sie geboren sind, als das folgerichtige Ergebnis früherer Geschehnisse begreifen zu lehren, sie sich als Erben der Geschichte wie als ihre Vollstrecker fühlen zu lassen.

Prussians, Saxons and Others

7. solche individuellen Schicksale ..., in denen die Lebensprobleme der Epoche *unmittelbar* und zugleich typisch zum Ausdruck gelangen.

8. Ohne eine erlebbare Beziehung zur Gegenwart ist eine Gestaltung der Geschichte unmöglich. Aber diese Beziehung besteht für die wirklich große historische Kunst nicht in Anspielungen auf zeitgenössische Ereignisse ..., sondern in dem Lebendigmachen der Vergangenheit als Vorgeschichte der Gegenwart, in der dichterischen Verlebendigung jener geschichtlichen, sozialen und menschlichen Kräfte, die im Laufe einer langen Entwicklung unser heutiges Leben zu dem geformt haben, was es ist, als was wir selbst es erleben.

9. Ich habe nie daran gedacht, Geschichte um ihrer selbst willen zu gestalten, ich habe im Kostüm, in der historischen Einkleidung immer nur ein Stilisierungsmittel gesehen, ein Mittel, auf die einfachste Art die Illusionen der Realität zu erzielen.

10. Mein Interesse an den wechselnden Formen der Historie ist, grob gesprochen, das des Schauspielers an seinem Kostüm. Der Mensch in seinem Verhalten zur Gesellschaft, das sich ständig erneuernde Kontinuum seines Kampfes um Würde, Freiheit und Glück ist der ewige Gegenstand meiner Neugier.

11. Die Oberen ... finden immer jemanden, der erklärt, warum sie oben bleiben müssen!

12. die dann im 20. Säculum Lebenden, die Kriege, Ungerechtigkeit, Hunger, Machtgier, Hochmut, Rechtgläubigkeit, Wortklauberei, Verrat, Speichelleckerei, Ruhmredigkeit, Lüge, Heuchelei, Korruption, Gewalt, Hass, Stumpfsinn, Neid, Dummheit ... und wie die restlichen Welt-übel alle heißen mögen, aus eigenem Erleben, wie ich gerne hoffen möchte, nicht mehr kennen werden ...

13. Ratten, Schmeißfliegen, Pinscher.

14. Wer baute das siebentorige Theben? / In den Büchern stehen die Namen von Königen./ Haben die Könige die Felsbrocken herbeigeschleppt? / Und das mehrmals zerstörte Babylon – / Wer baute es so viele Male auf?

15. das Bild von der Welt, so wie man es uns dort gemalt hat, steht zu großen Teilen auf dem Kopf. Hier wollen wir ihm wieder auf die Beine helfen.

16. alles Preußische, Maßvolle, Abgezirkelte, haßt diesen sturen, engbrüstigen Verstand, haßt diesen Dünkel und vor allem die Karabiner, mit denen zwar Macht demonstriert wird, aber doch kein einziges freundschaftliches Gefühl erobert werden kann.

17. Vielleicht war es so, vielleicht ganz anders.

18. Ich bin kein Jakobiner. Ich will kein Jakobiner sein. Fort mit allen Jakobinern. Vive le roi!

19. immer noch vergebend unsern Schuldigern ... immer noch gierig auf den Aschegeschmack der Worte. Immer noch nicht, was uns anstünde, stumm.

20. Eines muß man zugeben: Er hatte angefangen nachzudenken. Das Denken ist das wichtigste. Das Denken und der Zweifel.

21. Es mag mit dem Entstehen historisch neuer staatlicher Strukturen, mit der Festigung und Vertiefung eines neuen Staatsbewußtseins in der DDR zusammenhängen, daß sich hier die Literaturwerke, insbesondere die dramatischen Werke mit historischem Stoff (oder auch mit indirektem Bezug auf einen solchen) mehren.

22. Man sehe in unsere Literatur – die hält von Preußen nicht übermäßig viel.

–8–

En Route to Utopia

> On the run
> from pre-stressed concrete
> it is just
> like in the folk-tale; wherever
> you arrive
> it's waiting for you
> grey and thorough.[1]
>   (Günter Kunert, 'Unterwegs nach Utopia II')

In the preceding chapters we have seen how the GDR's writers have given contemporary reality an historical perspective, using the past to obtain a better understanding of the present. But time has a third dimension, and it is perhaps that of the future which has traditionally given socialist literature its peculiar quality. Walter Ulbricht put it succinctly in 1971 when he urged writers and artists 'to consider the present from the point of view of the future'[2] (Rüß, ed., 1976, p. 40). If socialist realism presents literature 'in its revolutionary development', it implies that the conflicts of today *will* be resolved, if not tomorrow then the day after. This revolutionary optimism has its consequences for historical writing. Writers who describe history as filled with the wreckage of failed revolutions run the risk of being accused of 'historical pessimism'. A major reason for the reluctance of the authorities to sanction the writings of Nietzsche is his view of history as eternal cyclical recurrence. Marxism, by contrast, considers history to be moving inexorably in the direction of a communist utopia. Even in 1979 Stephan Hermlin could claim that the GDR was a progressive society, 'like a bow whose arrow is speeding on ahead'[3] (1983, p. 418). In the light of developments since the later 1970s, partly domestic, partly international, Hermlin's optimism may appear inappropriate: disillusionment over the Biermann affair caused many writers to doubt the Party's good faith, the intensification of the arms race and the growing awareness of the threat to the global environment posed by industrialisation in the developed countries have called in question whether the world has *any* future, let alone a socialist one. Moreover socialist realist literature, in which, as Christoph Hein has put it, the narrator played the part of 'signpost', showing the readers the way ahead, belongs emphatically to the past (Jachimczak 1988, pp. 347–8).

Much of the GDR's early literature was indeed future-oriented. The very term 'Aufbauliteratur' implied it: literature which portrays the construction of a shining new society. Brecht's 'Zukunftslied' of 1948 ends with the lines:

> But one day it will no longer be like that
> And the thousand years' distress are at an end.
> Grief's no more: Above the cornstore high is raised
> A banner wonderful, and it is red.[4] (vol. 10, p. 957)

In Kant's *Das Impressum*, Groth's boss Kutschen-Meyer suggests that the confusions they are experiencing in the 1950s are due to the transitional nature of the times: 'The whole funny thing about our present is that we have just taken leave of a tremendously long past and we're encountering a few bits of future already, all jumbled up, and that way your feeling of time gets jumbled up too'[5] (p. 233). Neutsch's 'Drei Tage unseres Lebens' of 1969 not only places the building of an urban motorway in relation to the history of past human civilisation; it also looks forward fifty years to a time when, as the principal character puts it: 'The world, if it has any sense at all, will be a socialist one. That is the one point. We shall land on Venus. That is the other'[6] (p. 547). That Venus is the least hospitable of Earth's closer neighbours, landing on its surface highly undesirable, evidently does not occur to him; linking its exploration to the triumph of socialism is particularly unfortunate. But the connection between the political and the scientific-technological revolutions is an important motif elsewhere too.

A central event of Wolf's *Der geteilte Himmel* had been the news of the Soviet Union's 1961 success in putting a man in space for the first time; so crucial is this that the author invariably italicises it as *'the news'*. We are shown how the GDR is encountering serious obstacles in its progress to socialism: essential raw materials are lacking, the labour force is demoralised by continual defections to the Federal Republic; individual ambitions are being frustrated; even the brakes on the new railway coaches are not working properly. But just as the socialist Soviet Union is winning the space race, so all these problems will have been resolved once the GDR has completed its development towards socialism. While, as Beverley Hardy has argued, we may, especially in retrospect, detect more ominous details in Wolf's words (1988, p. 291), the novel is on the whole full of confidence in science and technology. Not so *Nachdenken über Christa T.*, which appeared five years later, one year before Neutsch's 'Drei Tage'. The uprising in Budapest in 1956 provokes Western glee over the apparent failure of socialism in Hungary, 'what they called "utopia"' (p. 124); it is a glee which is not shared either by the narrator or by Christa T. A year later, however, the talk is all of 'science' and 'the scientific age'. The Soviet Union has sent the first sputnik into space; as with the later flight of Gagarin, socialism appears to be winning in the technological sphere. The narrator and Christa T. go out on to the balcony of their flat one evening to look for the 'new star' on the horizon; but the night is cloudy, they fail to pick it out and ceremonially pour the remains of their wine into the apple tree. The religious symbolism is clear: technology is *not* the new messiah. The episode was one reason for the effective suppression of Wolf's novel for a number of years. In his review Horst Haase, for example, asserted the need for socialist writers to accept the challenge of science, 'the essential factor in human progress' (1969, p. 181), and not to regard it with suspicion as Wolf was doing. Haase's standpoint is reflected by the scientist Nees von Esenbeck in the later work *Kein Ort. Nirgends*. Speaking in 1804, he ridicules the 'hypochondriac lamentations of the literati' over the progress of science. He for his part would give anything to be able to return to earth 'in a century or two', i.e. circa 1979, in order to experience the 'paradisical conditions' which mankind, thanks to science, will be enjoying (p. 80). The reader of 1979 is invited to reflect how 'paradisical' conditions really have become. The text's title gives von Esenbeck the lie: 'Kein Ort' (literally 'no place', i.e. utopia), 'Nirgends' ('nowhere'). While, as we have seen, there *is* a utopian dimension to the novel, one relating to a new ordering of relations between the sexes, it is far from being fulfilled, either in 1804 or in the present.

Scepticism over the direction which science seems to be taking has become increasingly urgent since the mid-1970s. The critique of the scientific-technical revolution has two main thrusts. The one envisages a future in which humanity has been wiped out by the nuclear holocaust, the other fears a more lingering end through ecological disaster. As early as 1963 Günter Kunert's poem 'Laika' had taken yet another example of the Soviet Union's technological prowess to warn of possible doom for mankind. The dog Laika was the first living being to be sent into orbit around the Earth in a space capsule; it never returned, nor was it planned that it should. Kunert draws the parallel between an actual dead dog circling the earth in a capsule made of metal, 'the best that we possess', and a possible future dead human race circling the sun on its planet Earth, 'the best that we possess' (*Der ungebetene Gast*, p. 49). About the same time Peter Huchel was giving a similar warning in his poem 'Psalm', a vision of the remnants of mankind or possibly their leaders in their atomic bunkers watching the world turn into a desert:

> The desert will become history.
> Termites will write it
> With their pincers
> In the sand.
>
> And there will be no researching
> A race
> Industriously endeavouring
> To destroy itself.[7] (p. 84)

Kunert was attacked, again by Horst Haase (1967), for his pessimistic assessment of man's ability to change the world and himself. Huchel's poem could not appear in the GDR at all; by now he had been relieved of his editorship of *Sinn und Form* and was living in a kind of internal exile. But the threat of annihilation by nuclear war is a theme of two novels which appeared simultaneously twenty years after the warnings of Kunert and Huchel, Christa Wolf's *Kassandra* and Irmtraud Morgner's *Amanda*.

The similarity of themes and ideas in these two works is quite remarkable. It is perhaps fortunate that the two authors were unaware of each other's plans (Löffler 1983), as they might else have found themselves in some embarrassment. The congruity extends to the use of identical newspaper sources. Both quote United Nations figures stating that there are now three tons of TNT per head of the Earth's population. Both quote reports on the defective American computer which on several occasions wrongly announced that a Soviet rocket attack had been launched against the United States. Both quote assertions that the American strategy is to impoverish the Soviet Union by forcing it to increase its arms expenditure. Both quote American statements that a nuclear war in Europe could be won by the West. But the similarities do not end there. Both authors link humanity's present predicament with the specifically patriarchal way in which European society has developed. Male concern with scientific and technological progress for its own sake and at the expense of the wider needs of humanity finds expression not only in the subjugation of women but also in the over-exploitation of the Earth's natural resources and ultimately in preparations for war. Hence both novels explore varieties of feminism as responses to the current crisis. They do so, moreover, with reference to myth, both using and revising traditional myths and creating their own as Utopian models for future behaviour. This in turn leads to a reassessment of the role of the poet and writer. One-sided abstract thought has destroyed the 'images' which early humanity used to understand the world. Writers, not least women writers, who are concerned not merely with the logical but also with the sensual appropriation of reality, have the task of re-creating the wholeness of life.

Kassandra has been published in two different forms, three, if we include the English translation. For almost a quarter of a century the University of Frankfurt in West Germany had been running an annual series in which contemporary writers were invited to expound their views on literary theory and practice in a number of lectures and seminars. Ingeborg Bachmann and Heinrich Böll were both honoured in this way. In 1982 Christa Wolf became the first East German to accept the invitation. She delivered four lectures, with a fifth consisting of a version of the story 'Kassandra'. The lectures introduced the story. In the first two Wolf outlines her first encounters with the mythical figure of Cassandra, daughter of Priam of Troy, and a journey to Greece in search of her. The third is a personal diary kept between May 1980 and August 1981, while the fourth takes the form of a letter, in which Wolf proposes a feminine aesthetic. In West Germany, where, as we have seen, it first appeared, the story was published separately from the lectures – presumably the publishers expected to make more money that way. In the GDR, when the text eventually did appear, it was in a single volume and in the order in which the original lectures and story had been delivered. The English translation, while in one volume, reverses the order: the story comes first, followed by the four lectures. An important question of principle is involved here. It makes a considerable difference to one's reading of the story whether one encounters it in isolation or prefaced by four discursive essays. In her working diary Wolf expresses her unease about the 'closed form' of the Cassandra story, which conflicted, she felt, with the fragmentary nature of the myth (p. 153). On similar grounds some West German reviewers contrasted the story unfavourably with the lectures (Pulver 1983; Baumgart 1983). The feminine aesthetic outlined by Wolf in the fourth lecture explicitly rejects male-oriented aesthetics from Aristotle onwards. Epic poetry, says Wolf, arose during the struggle for the establishment of patriarchy; its structure, the insistence on the hero as model, was an instrument to maintain patriarchy. The selection of one story-line, one hero exactly reflects the analytical process which has dominated Western thought, by definition *male* thought, to this day. Against male analysis she sets female synthesis, a 'narrative network' which corresponds more accurately to the network of the brain (p. 150). Although in Wolf's version Cassandra refuses to join her lover Aeneas in exile, knowing that he will become a 'hero', will found a dynasty and an empire, and will himself become the subject of a heroic epic, nevertheless she herself undoubtedly is a central protagonist with whom we are invited to identify. The story's plot is based on her moral and psychological development. In terms of Wolf's own aesthetics it is more traditional than *Nachdenken über Christa T.* had been. By introducing essayistic elements to precede it, elements which, moreover, as Colin Smith points out, are traditional modes of women's writing, the travelogue, the diary and the letter (1987, p. 283), Wolf to some degree relativises and deconstructs the traditional classical form. *Kassandra* is a kind of 'Nachdenken über Kassandra', a 'quest for Cassandra'.

The figure of Cassandra was already foreshadowed in *Kindheitsmuster* in the person of Charlotte Jordan, Nelly's mother: 'Cassandra behind the counter, Cassandra stacking loaves, Cassandra weighing potatoes'[8] (p. 216). Accused in 1939 as war is approaching of always expecting the worst, she is almost arrested in 1944 for unguardedly foretelling that the war is lost. In the same novel Wolf had touched on the question when 'prewar' times begin, when 'postwar' times end (p. 186). It is a central motif of *Kassandra*. Looking back as a prisoner of Agamemnon waiting at Mycenae to be killed, Cassandra asks herself when exactly the 'pre-war' situation had begun. Long before a single Greek set sail for Troy the Greeks were being referred to as 'the enemy' (p. 265). She feels partly responsible for the disaster. Although as priestess and seer it had been her duty to warn her compatriots of the future they were steering towards, she failed to do so until it was too late. The contemporary relevance is plain, made so both by the diary entries of 1980 and 1981 and by the jarring introduction of such modernisms as 'East–West trade' (p. 249) into an otherwise elevated, rhythmical prose. When the militarists of both sides are described as 'needing each other as one old shoe needs another' (p. 308) the world of the 1980s is being described, where each new weapons system deployed by the one side demands an equivalent deployment on the other. It is not difficult to see in Wolf's portrayal of Trojans and Greeks an allegory of East–West relationships, in which under internal and external pressures a basically humane community gradually adopts the materialist, inhumane attributes of its rival. Drawing on Engels, Bachofen and others Wolf describes a society which has only recently replaced a matriarchal with a patriarchal system. The priestesses have been supplanted by priests, Apollo has taken over the position once held by Cybele. Women in *Kassandra* are almost entirely subordinate to men; as the war continues to its bloody end they are systematically excluded from the debates on military strategy. Polyxena and Briseis are in turn sacrificed to male needs; Helen is not the temptress beauty whose face launched a thousand ships but the object of male vanity who does not even reach Troy but is lost to the King of Egypt. We have seen elsewhere how Irmtraud Morgner rejects feminist attempts to restore matriarchy. In *Kassandra* such factions are represented by Penthesilea, a Valerie Solanas figure, who is prepared to die in the struggle to destroy men, and does die, just like her male counterpart Achilles. Similarly Agamemnon will die at the hands of Clytemnestra, who will perish in her turn. Cassandra foresees all these events; her prophecies all come to pass, either within the text or within the reader's knowledge of subsequent developments. But her gift of prophecy has one flaw: because she refused to submit to the embraces of Apollo she can only foresee the future on condition that nobody believes her. In contemporary terms Cassandra is a poet, a writer; women have been marginalised into belles lettres; their poetic evocations of the future are acceptable as 'fiction' – significantly it was only Wolf's 'factual' diary which was censored by the GDR authorities. Wolf herself is Cassandra, warning of humanity's impending doom. Whether her warning will be heeded remains to be seen.

Some of the feminist aspects of *Amanda* have already been described. Beatriz, the trobadora of Morgner's earlier novel, has been reincarnated as a 'siren', not the temptress female who lures men to their doom, as in the anti-feminist *Odyssey*, however, but more akin to the device which *warns* mariners of dangerous rocks or the civilian population of an impending air raid. In *Amanda* sirens are the reincarnation of 'wise women', singing to warn mankind of possible disasters, 'in order that the future may be preserved for the future'[9] (p. 246). These include the threat to world peace by military developments. But Morgner's fears extend beyond nuclear conflict. Mankind is making war not only on his neighbour but on the planet itself. The winged serpent Arke returns from one expedition to report that the ecosystems on which we depend are all under pressure, organic resources are being used up at an accelerating rate, while the demands on them are simultaneously increasing. She concludes that if man continues to maltreat the soil, in twenty years' time one-third of the earth's present agricultural land will be unusable, and in a phrase which directly contradicts the optimism expressed by Neutsch in his 'Drei Tage unseres Lebens' a decade and a half previously, she declares, 'Mankind has thrown the old myths overboard and been trapped by a new myth, that of eternal exponential economic growth'[10] (p. 357).

The concern for the environment found in *Amanda* is a relatively recent development in the GDR's literature. In novels of the early 1960s such as Karl-Heinz Jakobs's *Beschreibung eines Sommers* and Joachim Wohlgemuth's *Egon*, as in much of the poetry and prose of Volker Braun, for example, the ravages of industrial development on the natural landscape are presented almost entirely in terms of the heroic efforts of humanity (see Shaw 1986/87). While in *Unvollendete Geschichte* there is a scene by a hopelessly polluted river, when a harrassed Party leader admits that competition with the West has forced the GDR to take unacceptable shortcuts, it is clear that the 'pollution' here is essentially metaphorical, referring to the poisoning of relations between the state and the individual. Traditional Marxists have never taken a Romantic view of nature as a value in itself, regarding it rather as something to be controlled, socialised and placed in the service of humanity. By contrast it was National Socialism which extolled the values of 'blood and soil'. The reassessment of Romanticism which we have encountered elsewhere includes a reassessment of the status of the natural world. That ecological movements have been springing up in parts of Western Europe and especially in West Germany is not coincidental. Once again, however, the topic has peculiar resonances in an East German context, as is clear from the irritation which 'green' literature sometimes provokes in official circles.

An example is the harmless-looking little book *Swantow* by the poet Hanns Cibulka. The fictitious diary of one Andreas Flemming, describing a summer and autumn on the Baltic coast, it is stylistically pale and full of clichés, a conventionally elegiac meditation on life and death, nature and man, which uses rather obvious methods to make its points: a wasp's nest, for example, which the narrator leaves undisturbed inside his front door and whose inhabitants reward him by ignoring him. But it contains enough dynamite to elicit a riposte from Klaus Höpcke, the minister responsible for literature, himself (1984b). One of Cibulka's anxieties relates to the development of nuclear power. Brigitte Reimann's *Franziska Linkerhand* had already uttered a warning on the subject, when Franziska's brother, the embodiment of scientific optimism, returns from Moscow with what appears to be radiation sickness. An extract from *Swantow* had appeared in the journal *Neue deutsche Literatur* in 1981, and when the book came out a year later it was apparent that two passages from the extract had been omitted, both relating to this topic. A taboo, it seems, had been infringed (Knabe 1983; Mallinckrodt 1986/87). In his diary Flemming lists the half-life of various fission products, indicating that their disposal will be a problem for many generations to come. One of his poems begins:

> With the fathom of death
> fast breeders survey
> the land

and ends

> In the effluent
> accumulates
> guilt.[11] (pp. 77–8)

Nuclear waste, as the last line indicates, is but one symptom of a wider disease, environmental pollution in general. The poem is followed immediately by the description of a fish which has just been caught in the Baltic with a stunted dorsal fin and a cancer in its belly. A long meditation ensues on the way the advanced nations have been polluting the air with lead and the seas with radioactive substances, heavy metals and chemicals, ending with the vision: 'One day the ocean will present us with a darkened mirror, but then it will be too late. The screams of humanity will echo unheard on its coasts. The sea will be the setting for our future catastrophes'[12] (p. 79). The blame, says Flemming, lies with our search for ever more material comforts in the cause of so-called 'progress'. Here, too, the socialist countries are merely imitating the capitalist ones.

In his review of *Swantow* Höpcke admitted that Cibulka's warnings could not be taken seriously enough. But he rejected the author's sceptical attitude towards technology. In words which bridge the gulf between East and West, uniting the forces of state socialism with the conservative governments of the United Kingdom and the Federal Republic, he declared that the peaceful use of nuclear energy was legitimate and uncontroversial (1984b). Earlier, however, he had claimed that in socialism the approach to environmental questions differed from that of capitalism, in that the wealth which a socialist economy generated was devoted to coping with environmental problems. And yet, not long previously, a novel which focused on the effects of the horrendous atmospheric pollution in the industrial city of Bitterfeld, Monika Maron's *Flugasche*, had been banned. Unlike Cibulka, Maron had made the responsibility of the ruling Party explicit. Similar controversies had taken place in 1979 and 1980. Günter Kunert was taken to task by the editor of *Sinn und Form* for having equated the consequences of socialist industrialisation with those under capitalism (Kunert / Girnus 1979), and Jurij Brězan was accused by the biologist Erhard Geissler of being 'hostile to science' (Geissler / Brězan 1980). In both cases the official line had been that only in the West was there cause for concern.

Brězan's novel *Krabat* had taken up the question of genetic engineering. In some ways it is an East German parallel to Friedrich Dürrenmatt's 1961 play *Die Physiker*. There Möbius has discovered the 'key to the universe'; fearing its misuse by politicians he pretends to be insane and is pursued to his asylum by scientists from West and East. In *Krabat* the biologist Jan Serbin has discovered a formula which will enable him both to eradicate disease and to turn people into peace-loving, law-abiding citizens. Like Möbius he is pursued by other scientists, eager to extort his secrets from him; here, however, they are exclusively agents from the West. In the end he destroys his own formula on the grounds that it could be used not only to benefit humanity but also to control and destroy. It is preferable, Serbin realises, to move gradually in the direction of utopia. *Krabat*, too, contains visions of a planet turned into a lunar landscape by a third world war. Its portrait of unscrupulous capitalists and Western agents draws on many of the clichés of conventional GDR literature. Nevertheless it also attacks a pursuit of prosperity and productivity in the GDR which threatens to destroy the traditional landscape.

When on 26 April 1986 the nuclear power plant at Chernobyl in the Soviet Union went out of control the fears of some of these writers appeared vindicated. In West Germany a few weeks earlier Günter Grass's novel *Die Rättin* had imagined an apocalyptic end to the world through nuclear disaster. Now reality had (almost) caught up with the artistic imagination. Christa Wolf's *Störfall* is an immediate reaction to the Chernobyl catastrophe. Written between June and September of the same year, it is the account of a single day in the week following the accident. The narrator, a writer not unlike Wolf herself, lives in an old farmhouse in the remote Mecklenburg countryside. Two events preoccupy her on this day. The one is the progress of the radioactive cloud from the Ukraine, which she constantly follows on radios transmitting from East and West. The other is the long and complicated operation which is taking place on the same day to remove a tumour from the brain of her brother. Again it is something which she can follow only at a distance, in her imagination, waiting for a telephone call from the hospital to inform her of success or failure. Her brother, ignorant of the nuclear disaster, is the primary addressee of her meditations, which relate to the fields of anthropology, medicine, psychology, feminism and literature in their attempt to grasp the full significance of what has happened. Literature itself is called in question: the clouds of traditional nature poetry are now filled with threatening radioactivity; the enormity of the catastrophe 'has spilled over the edge of fiction' (p. 66), and she is filled with disgust at words themselves. The recognition that there may be no future demolishes at a stroke the assumption on which she has hitherto based her life, namely that there is some distant goal, socialism, the harmonising of individual and collective aspirations, a utopia where everything will come together and make sense. Initially this recognition gives a feeling of nihilistic freedom, but it rapidly gives way to the despairing question: how can one live without a goal? The question whether humanity has any future is embedded in memories of the past: an old peasant remembers the atrocities committed by Germans on Russians during the Second World War; the narrator herself is visited by a family which had briefly lived in her farmhouse at the end of the war and had buried a child there who had died of typhoid; and she recalls her Jewish friend Charlotte Wolff in London, who had escaped the Nazis in the late 1930s. While these allusions to German barbarities act partly as a balance to the present guilt of the Soviet leadership, more importantly they place the accident at Chernobyl in the context not only of dangerous scientific experimenting but also of an arms race which might end in even worse disaster.

The title of Wolf's text is multi-layered. Initially East German accounts of the disaster at Chernobyl played down its significance, presenting it merely as a 'Störfall', an interruption of normal service (Gruhn 1986). On this level the title is heavily ironic. But the tumour in the narrator's brother's brain is also an 'interruption'. The one is a private, individual affair, the other highly public, affecting the whole of humanity. That Wolf should link the two is characteristic of her insistence on the importance of the individual. By juxtaposing the benefits of technological progress with its dangers, she is drawing attention, like Hilscher in *Die Weltzeituhr* before her, to the two faces of science. For the narrator of *Störfall* the new Faust is personified in the scientists involved in the Star Wars project, who have succumbed to the fascination of technological progress for its own sake. There is a covert allusion to the '*news*' of *Der geteilte Himmel* in the capitalisation of 'THE NEWS' of the disaster (p. 11). Technology has by now got out of man's control. But the relation between nuclear science and brain surgery is taken a step further when the narrator considers that 'atom' is in Greek what 'individual' is in Latin: both mean an indivisibility which is called in question by nuclear fission on the one hand and schizophrenia on the other. As for Morgner in *Amanda*, division is original sin. This may be the schizophrenic behaviour of the individual scientists. It may also be the division between the sexes: the narrator mingles almost exclusively with women, while the male scientists, who, she presumes, have never had to change a baby's nappy, wash dishes or tend a sick child, have brought the world to its unhappy state. The suggestion that brain surgery might be used to extirpate the atavistic part of the brain which persists in aggressive, destructive behaviour is put forward only to be rejected, as by Brězan before her, as the 'Brave New World' solution (p. 26). Wolf's solution consists rather in a romantic myth of wholeness related to a non-urban, peasant mode of life. The (imagined) high technology of the brain clinic and the power station contrasts with the rural, tradition-laden setting of the narrative.

After the publication of *Kassandra* Wolf had been criticised in some quarters for being 'against enlightenment', an accusation she repudiates as 'undialectical': 'If I am being polemical then I am doing so against the exclusive rule of abstract thought and the concept of science which developed in the nineteenth century. Positivism and pure rationalism are the basis of certain mistakes which today are leading in the direction of the enormous danger of war we find ourselves in'[13] (1987, p. 906).

In the year that *Störfall* appeared a text was published which bears striking resemblances to Wolf's work, but is by a woman who is both practising scientist and writer, Helga Königsdorf's *Respektloser Umgang*. Here, too, science is related both to the future of the planet and the future of one individual, in this case the narrator herself, a scientist in her mid-forties, who has been stricken with a wasting disease the progress of which can be slowed but not stopped by medicine. What makes Königsdorf's text ultimately more interesting than Wolf's is not merely that the authentic voice of the scientist herself is heard and that, possibly because of this, the arguments are less strident, but that here the narrator is confronted with an alternative voice, albeit that of a woman long since dead, and thereby incorporates the 'dialectics' which Wolf merely assumes. Under the influence of the drugs she is taking the narrator hallucinates the presence of Lise Meitner, one of only a few internationally known female scientists in history, who had worked together with Otto Hahn on experiments which eventually contributed to the splitting of the atom and the nuclear weapons which are presently threatening the survival of the species.

Königsdorf, too, builds her text on coincidence: the narrator was born on the day in 1938 when Meitner, a Jew, had to leave Germany. It is a text rich in thematic associations, touching in just over one hundred pages not only on the responsibility of science to society, but also on the Third Reich, the idealism of the early years of the GDR and the women's question. The narrator's own grandmother was a Jew, who starved herself to death in the hospital where she spent her last days. Her father accommodated himself to the Nazi regime, his response to the Nuremberg race laws being one of naive relief at knowing exactly where one stood. Faced with the degradation of a gradual loss of her faculties the narrator imagines some more humane way of dying organised perhaps by the state, an 'Institute for Human Dignity', for example. She goes on to reject such an institution: to take one's own life is to deprive one's family of the opportunity of making their lives meaningful in caring for another; moreover the euthanasia programme of the Nazis is warning enough. Allusions to the Third Reich are better integrated than in *Störfall*, relating both to the direct experience of the narrator and to the question of resistance, resistance to an unjust system and also to the misuse of science for anti-human ends. Whereas the narrator's father did not resist, Meitner claims to have personally delayed the discovery of atomic energy by German scientists at the expense of her own reputation in order to forestall German military superiority. Her 'visits' to the narrator have the purpose of impressing on her the importance of her 'task', her responsibility to humanity. To claim that Hiroshima and Nagasaki have criminalised physics is no more than 'stupid iconoclasm' (p. 92); in today's world science is more important than ever if mankind is to survive. But it is up to the individual scientist to act responsibly and the narrator's task is to 'mobilise humanity' (p. 94), beginning with her son. That the narrator was a daughter, not a son, was a supreme disappointment to her father, who proceeded to bring her up as if she was a boy. Although Meitner herself refuses to accept that she might have experienced discrimination as a woman, the narrator sees it differently. Nevertheless she explicitly rejects the thesis of Wolf's fourth *Kassandra* lecture, that women have for centuries been the objects, not the subjects of history. This, she says, wounds her feminine pride; the mechanisms of power-relationships are not as inescapable as Wolf suggests. In spite of Wolf's insistence that she is not hostile to science, she has been implying that science remains a male province. What is different and challenging about Königsdorf's text is that she is suggesting that women may have a specific part to play in science itself.

The fears for the future we have been examining contradict the traditional naive optimism of socialist realism. But not all is doom and gloom, even if, as the ending of *Respektloser Umgang* puts it, 'the swallows have become fewer'. One important influence is that of the Marxist philosopher Ernst Bloch, who taught at Leipzig until 1957, when he emigrated to West Germany. More than any others, Bloch's 'philosophy of hope' is oriented towards the future, with utopia as its central concern. The preface to *Das Prinzip Hoffnung*, published in West Germany in 1959, contrasts the modish bourgeois philosophies of despair current in the 1950s with forward-looking Marxism. Nevertheless his work was repudiated at the time by East German ideologists, who accused him of disregarding the class-based nature of socialism in favour of an abstract, timeless conception of human hopes and desires. *Das Prinzip Hoffnung* was especially influential in the student movement in West Germany in the late 1960s. In East Germany its influence has been non-explicit. However, both Wolf and Morgner were students in Leipzig in Bloch's time, and his ideas have been traced in their works (Huyssen 1975; Emmerich 1978, p. 152).

Kassandra and *Amanda* do not merely warn against the facile assumptions of the Establishment. They also contain visions of a utopian life transcending the conditions of today. With some justification Andreas Huyssen has even described *Nachdenken über Christa T.* as a 'novel of the future', an appeal to its readers to construct a society in which imagination and individual fulfilment are reconciled with socialist justice and humanity (Huyssen 1975, p. 112). *Kein Ort. Nirgends*, as we have seen, belies its title when it implies a utopian future, albeit one which is radically different from official views. Utopian elements are even clearer in *Kassandra*. Troy, says Wolf, is a 'model for a kind of Utopia' (p. 108). There are two sides to her vision. The one associates Troy, somewhat fancifully but not impossibly, with Minoan Crete, in whose civilisation 'women were free and equal with men' (p. 80), where labour was meaningful and the individual part of a social community without being reduced to a mere function, where one could live in peace with one's neighbour at home and abroad (p. 77). This appears as myth rather than as history: the defloration rites and references to human sacrifice imply a rather different actuality. The other side, however, the more obviously Blochian vision, is embodied in the novel's cave community, where the victims and the opponents of the war find, albeit temporarily, refuge. It is a predominantly but not exclusively female community, whose members enjoy 'the highest privilege of all, that of projecting a narrow band of future into the dark, all-embracing present', a community which unites in harmony body, mind and soul, making artefacts of clay, touching each other, telling each other their dreams and, in the most Blochian phrase of the novel, learning 'how to dream with both feet on the ground'[14] (p. 339).

Much of Bloch's study is devoted to myth, which he regarded not merely as belonging to the past but as embodying human aspirations for the future. One of the many myths he analyses is that of Pandora. He recounts the version by Hesiod in which Pandora is the demonic temptress who brings evil to mankind, pointing out the incongruousness of including hope among these 'evils'. The later hellenistic version is for Bloch 'the only true one' (1959, p. 389). According to this account Pandora brought all values; when they escaped hope remained, the hope which encourages man to strive after the other, lost ones. The myth of Pandora is taken up by Peter Hacks in *Pandora*, the adaptation of a festival play by Goethe. Hacks is the classicist among GDR writers; his reception of Goethe is more reverent than that of many. In the long essay which he appends to his text Hacks describes Goethe's play as 'the story of the transformation of nostalgia, backward-looking hope, into forward-looking hope and fertile activity'[15] (p. 114), terminology which recalls Bloch's phrase (after Lenin) 'forward-dreaming' (1959, p. 1616). Hack's play uses the rivalry between the Titan brothers Prometheus and Epimetheus to present in allegorical form the conflict between doing and thinking, labour and poetry, the transformation of nature and the celebration of nature. Prometheus creates industry; his motorways destroy the landscape, his factories pollute the air and the waters. Epimetheus's resistance to his brother crumbles in the end when he recognises that the same industry which pollutes will also purify again. In the GDR context this is the conformist view. At the close, however, it is Epimetheus the poet who advances to greet the returning Pandora. Hacks envisages this utopian future as a socialist one, but his vision is essentially aesthetic. Pandora represents hope, the hope in a more humane future; the play ends chiliastically with her return.

The influence of Hacks on Morgner is acknowledged with an extensive quotation from his essay in *Amanda* (p. 301). For Hacks Pandora also represents woman, and the attitudes of the two brothers to her sex are an important element in the play. Prometheus is resolutely anti-feminist, believing that woman was sent to destroy man and that she should be kept subordinate to him. Epimetheus on the other hand has spent his days since Pandora's departure mourning her loss; his ultimate vindication implies a utopian future in which woman is equal with man. This is the primary concern of *Amanda*, where the twin threats of nuclear devastation and ecological collapse are viewed as emanating from the essentially male enterprise associated with the Promethean revolution. *Amanda* is embedded in two alternative but complementary creation myths. The one is an eclectic mixture of Jakob Böhme, E.T.A. Hoffmann and Plato's *Symposium*. It postulates a fall from original wholeness represented in the division between Earth and Air, the concrete and the abstract, motherhood and fatherhood, God and Devil, woman as domestic being and woman as witch. Division is a strategy for domination, whether the hegemony of the abstract over the concrete, the rational over the emotional, or of men over women. Humanity has the choice between seeking to dominate or seeking liberation and wholeness; the novel relates ways in which the latter might be achieved. The other creation myth is Greek, based on the story of Prometheus. The novel begins with a contemporary oracle from Delphi: 'In the box hope Prometheus must fetch Pandora win her return urgently serpentine daughters roam song'[16] (p. 11). In due course the words are deciphered as follows: Prometheus – technological man – has created admirable works up to now but his one-sided concern with domination is now threatening to destroy the world; he must be convinced of the fragmentary nature of his activity and persuade Pandora to return to him; the fourth race of human beings which they will beget will be one that for the first time is 'capable of peace . . ., able to deal bloodlessly with differences of interests and opinion and to develop customs which value compromise more than victory and which place a taboo on war'[17] (p. 159). The Promethean revolution must be followed by the Pandoran revolution. This utopian vision makes *Amanda*, too, a 'novel of the future'.

In the GDR myth was long problematical for a number of reasons: Alfred Rosenberg's proto-fascist *Myth of the Twentieth Century* was fresh in the memory; the National Socialists had employed the Nordic, Wagnerian myths to justify their barbaric behaviour; and myth was irrational and at odds with the Marxist explanation of history. In his early story 'Das Gottesgericht' Franz Fühmann had brilliantly exposed the brutalising influence of Nazi mythical thinking on impressionable young minds. He therefore had the credentials to rehabilitate some aspects of myth in 1974 in a wide-ranging address to students in Berlin on the 'mythical element in literature' (1975, pp. 147–219). For Fühmann myth mediated between individual and general human experience; it answered eternal questions of existence, love, mortality, the meaning of life. This unhistorical, existential approach relates Fühmann's essay to some of the tendencies of

GDR literature in the 1970s and 1980s which we have analysed. In the late 1960s, however, Heiner Müller and Peter Hacks had already begun to rework some of the Greek myths in such plays as *Philoktet* and *Amphitryon* in order to convey their view of the present. It was some time later that novelists followed suit. One of the first was Brězan, who in his novel *Krabat* builds on the Sorb folk tradition of the eponymous magician. Some years before Morgner he, too, had given his novel the framework of a creation myth, this time one based on the biblical story but in which Lucifer protests against the Lord's unjust distribution of wealth. The dimension of the future is explicitly invoked in this novel by Jan Serbin, a contemporary embodiment of Krabat, who regards the 'Seventh Day' created by the Lord as merely provisional, the age of humanity's unfreedom; the 'Eighth Day' will be a time when self-determination is finally achieved. Lucifer is a central figure of Stefan Heym's *Ahasver*, one of whose costumes is that of the Wandering Jew; he represents the humanist belief in the liberation of mankind from material and intellectual oppression. Waltraud Lewin's *Federico* is a further text which begins with an unorthodox interpretation of the myth of *Genesis*. Far from being forbidden by God, eating of the fruit of the Tree of Knowledge was actually encouraged. Three races of humanity proceeded from the act of creation: the first was the children of God, a languid, decadent race, too lazy to eat the fruit; the second was the descendants of Adam and Eve, diligent and inventive; the third, however, was the product of the union of God and Eve and they called it 'the restless tribe . . . or salt of the earth'[18] (p. 11). Irritation, provocation, non-conformism, curiosity, as in *Amanda*, are supreme human virtues down the centuries.

Myth, however, has been an important element in cultural developments in the West too. In 1984 Fritz J. Raddatz announced in sensationalist manner the end of enlightenment and its replacement by myth. He has claimed (1986) to detect signs of a turning away from reason and history in the young writers of the GDR and even in Braun's *Hinze-Kunze-Roman*. Lothar Pikulik (1988) has drawn attention to the rapid spread of irrationalist, anti-enlightenment 'New Age' movements in recent years, all of them directed at some kind of holistic, global renewal of human existence. In the realm of high culture he views the writings of Peter Handke and Botho Strauß as part of this development, as they seek to 're-enchant' the world, replacing historical progression with cyclical myth. It must therefore be asked whether the myth-making of the GDR's writers parallels the irrationalism of the New Age movement in the West. Interestingly enough, recent works by both Handke and Strauß have been published in the GDR. It is perhaps not coincidental that even Nietzsche is currently being discussed there. By stressing the 'eternal' features of human life, it might be argued, Fühmann is implying an undialectical view of history, one in which nothing essential changes. While, as we have seen, the historical dimension in the GDR's literature is important, the use of history to comment on the present was regarded by Lukács as akin to Nietzscheanism. The mythical struggle in *Krabat* between the exploiter Wolf Reissenberg and his antagonist Krabat can similarly suggest – against the author's intentions – the ultimate hopelessness of the latter's cause. Botho Strauß's provocative claim that Hitchcock's film *The Birds*, being mythical, will last longer than Brecht's *Mother Courage*, which is merely educational (1981, p. 118), actually finds an echo in Heiner Müller's *Bildbeschreibung* (p. 1047). The penultimate scene of Müller's *Leben Gundlings* ends with the 'New Age' imagery:

HOUR OF WHITE HEAT DEAD BUFFALOS FROM THE CANYONS SQUADRONS OF SHARKS TEETH OF BLACK LIGHT THE ALLIGATORS MY FRIENDS GRAMMAR OF EARTHQUAKES WEDDING OF FIRE AND WATER MEN OF NEW FLESH LAUTREAMONTMALDOROR PRINCE OF ATLANTIS SON OF THE DEAD[19] (p. 101).

The community of the cave in *Kassandra* has its associations with 'New Age' transactional analysis. Nevertheless, with the possible exception of Müller's, these works are on the whole characterised by a belief in enlightenment which is quite foreign to Handke and Strauß. The GDR's major authors are attempting not to turn reality into something magical but to persuade their readers to behave in a more humane, reasonable manner. Strauß's scorn for the West Berlin demonstrators protesting against the demolition of homes to make way for more profitable office blocks (1981, pp. 94–5) would not be shared by any of them. Bloch rather than Nietzsche remains the dominant influence.

If the GDR's fiction has recently been voicing concern about the possible damaging effects of science on the future of mankind, what about 'science fiction' itself? This is a genre in which the future is presented directly, not merely implied; it is also one which has often been associated with dystopias, projections into the future warning of latent dangers in the present, works such as Aldous Huxley's *Brave New World* and George Orwell's *Nineteen Eighty-Four*. Science fiction, often termed 'utopian literature' in the GDR or, after the Soviet model, the 'literature of scientific fantasy', has experienced a striking growth rate in the past twenty years. As we have seen elsewhere, the element of fantasy is one way in which traditional socialist realism has been undermined. Rainer Nägele points out that science fiction was traditionally the one area in which fantasy was permitted (Hohendahl and Herminghouse, eds., 1983, p. 196). Not only is it popular, but it has been taken ever more seriously by critics and academics. Magazines such as *Das neue Abenteuer* were aimed primarily at younger readers; since 1980, however, the almanach *Das Lichtjahr* has confirmed the recognition that adults, too, find fascination and entertainment in science fiction, and in 1982 the first survey of the genre to be published in the GDR listed no fewer than ten dissertations on the subject which had been accepted by the GDR's universities since 1966 (Simon and Spittel). In one of the stories of Anna Seghers's *Sonderbare Begegnungen*, travellers from a distant planet visit Earth during the Peasant Wars of the sixteenth century, while Christa Wolf's 'Selbstversuch', on the author's own account, 'mimics' motifs from 'utopian literature', for which she confesses to having a weakness (1987, p. 798).

One of the features of science fiction in the GDR is the way in which its development mirrors that of literature in general. Between the end of the war and the beginning of the 1960s topics such as the Cold War and the need to boost the economy are simply transferred into the future: in Ludwig Turek's *Die goldene Kugel* an extraterrestrial spaceship lands in the United States, its crew become involved in the class struggle, siding with the progressive forces and leading them to ultimate victory, while Heinz Vieweg's *Ultrasymet bleibt geheim* concerns the development of a synthetic material out of sand crystals, which solves at a stroke the GDR's shortage of raw materials in a manner not unlike that of Dieter Noll's *Kippenberg*. The limitations of these works are admitted by the GDR's own critics. The breakthrough to literary respectability is invariably ascribed to Herbert Ziergiebel's novel *Die andere Welt* (Entner 1976), a work set in the space age but one whose preoccupations are largely psychological, treating the pressures on two groups of astronauts, one trapped in its crippled spaceship, the other sent to rescue them. Its implied political assumptions are interestingly conciliatory. A world is envisaged which is divided into two main areas of control, Eurasia with its 'Supreme Space Authority' based in Prague, and America with its 'Western Space Authority'. Suspicions and espionage are to be found on both sides. But an important message of the novel is the need for peaceful coexistence and international understanding. The crew of the ill-fated *Charles Darwin* includes representatives from India, the Soviet Union, China, Hungary and Britain. But for them the names of their countries have but geographical significance: 'What is left of countries and continents when you go up in a spaceship? After a few miles they have shrunk to allotment size'[20] (p. 188). More significantly still, the crew of the rescue ship *Johannes Kepler* includes an American, albeit the gum-chewing, joke-telling stereotype. The Americans assist the Eurasian Space Authority in detecting signals from the *Darwin*; the participation of Henry Jephson in the rescue mission will be the first act of real cooperation between the two sides, demonstrating that 'we cannot confront one another with the Bomb for all eternity' – even if, for ideological coexistence must be resisted, 'the social problems are not thereby resolved'[21] (p. 112). The real discovery of the rescue mission is that Earth, too, is a spaceship, ultimately one as fragile as the *Darwin*. A fresh world war would extinguish life altogether: 'If people could see the earth like us, as a little ball flying like a spaceship through the depths of the universe, they would not be so ready to place this unique existence at risk'[22] (p. 311). And this was written some years before Buckminster Fuller's catchphrase 'Spaceship Earth' became current in the Western ecological movement.

One of the uses of fantasy is to convey criticism which would be less acceptable if presented directly. Ziergiebel's novel ultimately affirms the value of science and space exploration as, for example, a means of discovering new energy resources. Increasingly, however, the science fiction mode has been employed to warn against developments which are putting any kind of human future in doubt. In view of his pessimism on this score it is not surprising that Günter Kunert has exploited the genre. In 'Schlaf', for example, the narrator is given the opportunity to take a drug enabling him to sleep for twenty years. 'Twenty years, I thought, would let me reach that happy, pain-free future when all men will be brothers . . .' When he awakens he thinks he has been tricked. But no, a newspaper date proves he is 'in the future': 'Greedily I read the front page: the same war as yesterday, no, as in the past, was still in progress. A tribe had been annihilated with sulphuric acid – I see. Floods threatening Florence. Avalanche disaster in the Alps. The final of the tennis cup . . .'[23] (Redlin, ed., *Der Mann vom Anti*, p. 123). Other stories by Kunert such as 'Die kleinen grünen Männer', 'Androiden', 'Von Pluto her' and 'Nach der Landung' use motifs from science fiction in order to make statements on man's primitive instincts, his barbarity, his cunning, and the depersonalising effects of the scientific mentality. 'Andromeda zur Unzeit' is a particularly disturbing story. It is set in the middle of the thirtieth century, when food and fuel are running out and people have to move as slowly as possible to conserve their energy. Every evening a spaceship loaded with refugees takes off for Uranus or Neptune, where artificial worlds of plenty have been created. On the one hand, therefore, we have a gloomy prognostication, a warning against the over-exploitation of the earth's resources, on the other an apparent optimism, similar to Ziergiebel's, that technology will overcome the difficulty. The nocturnal departures are televised. One night in April the anonymous onlooker realises that the sky on the television picture is a November one. Are the emigrations really taking place? The following nights all is normal again and in due course he, too, receives the Green Card permitting him to join the exodus. The ending is left open, the horror remains. The transports to Auschwitz come to mind, whose victims failed to resist because they were misled as to the true nature of their destination. Technology, it seems, will solve man's problems, but only by decimating the population. Technological progress is not accompanied by moral progress.

Other authors have used the motifs of space travel and time travel to convey their warnings. Frank Töppe's 'Die letzten Bilder des Grafikers Schneider' describes an ecological catastrophe caused by the well-intended introduction of technology to a planet orbiting Castor. In Wolfgang Sämann's 'Das Haus des Dr. Pondabel' an 'excursion' into the future encounters desert, cold and a ruined town of Wittenberg. In his dispute with Wilhelm Girnus over ecological problems one of the claims made by Kunert was that people in the West were better informed than those in the GDR, a claim indignantly repudiated by Girnus. One of the more sinister aspects of these stories by Töppe and Sämann is the way in which news of the respective disasters is suppressed by the authorities.

Fritz Rudolf Fries's novel *Verlegung eines mittleren Reiches* is set in some future time after the catastrophe. It, too, is a warning against the arms race: looking back the narrator reflects how ridiculous had been the inventions and projects, 'how one country hunted down the results of the other's experiments, ever higher the missiles, billions squandered on the same old project, the one bomb, endowed with jolly names from mythology...'[24] (p. 9). Now, he surmises, the governments of the opposing states are circling the globe in the space ships to which they have escaped and are still transmitting the same old slogans. The little community in which the story takes place has been invaded by the 'Empire of the Centre'; but what exactly is going on in the world outside them they do not know as they have no radio, no means of travelling beyond what they believe to be a deadly radioactive barrier. The year that follows the catastrophe is one of deprivations. The climate has been altered, although far from the possible 'nuclear winter', it has become warmer. There is no work, no technology; it is the opportunity for a rethinking of their lives. In the end no such rethinking takes place and a further catastrophe destroys the community entirely.

Although the names we encounter seem Chinese, Remann-Zi, Li-weng, De-zah, the cultural allusions are European, not to say German, and there is even a reference to the Prussian monarch who tried to conjure an empire out of the sands (p. 116), an allusion to Frederick II. This is chinoiserie in the tradition of Bertolt Brecht. Fries evidently has in mind as much the months in Germany immediately after the Second World War as the aftermath of any future nuclear war. The people are opportunistic, distrustful of ideologies, unwilling to commit themselves until they know how long the occupying force is likely to remain in power. The rumour that the land 'across the lake' has quickly recovered and its inhabitants are enjoying comforts and prosperity has an unsettling effect, just as the division of Germany into zones of occupation had. *Verlegung eines mittleren Reichs* thus cleverly combines historical criticism with a warning for the future.

It has a dual future, however. The main story consists of diary entries by an anonymous citizen of the invaded country, which are prefaced by an editorial introduction written 'after the Last War' (p. 7), many generations later, in a time when a new utopian society has been founded, an age when people 'know no fear, use machines only for practical everyday operations and have harmonised thought and action'[25] (p. 8). The editor, Alpha 19–05–35, a descendant of the diarist, is contemptuous of his ancestor, 'who by all appearances belonged to the ideological exploiter class of the intellectuals'[26] (p. 7). The ironic sting comes in the tail, however: he is publishing these documents 'with the permission of the highest authority'. Censorship evidently has still not come to an end; by implication 'thought and action' have not become fully congruous after all. Fries's novel was actually written in the late 1970s (Grambow 1986, p. 1385); the 'highest authority' did not give permission to publish it until 1984.

That year was the 'Orwell year'. Klaus Höpcke (1984a) used the occasion to comment on George Orwell's celebrated dystopian novel *Nineteen Eighty-Four* and its relation to the present. It had appeared shortly after the end of the fascist dictatorship in Germany and in the founding year of the GDR. Since then East Germans had successfully overcome the Nazi past, without the help of Orwell's novel, which had been distorted by Western propaganda into a vision which purported to describe communism but which, as was becoming increasingly clearer, contained numerous parallels to contemporary capitalism. 'Big brother' was embodied in the multinational concerns in alliance with the military-industrial complex of the United States and NATO, the large banks and the political apparatus of the West. Pinochet's Chile was fulfilling Orwell's prophecy. 'Newspeak' was when the minister in charge of preparations for war was called 'Defence Minister', when the office which announced the latest unemployment figures was called 'Federal Employment Office', when 'preventive strike', meant 'aggressive attack' and 'acceptable level of casualties' sixty million dead.

Höpcke's words represent a new departure in East German attitudes to Orwell, whose works have never appeared in the GDR. A lexicon of 1970 writes of his anti-colonial views and his early interest in communism but goes on to claim that he became an embittered enemy of socialism and the Soviet Union, which he slandered in grotesque satirical-utopian novels (Steiner, ed., p. 468), and does not even mention *Nineteen Eighty-Four* by name. In 1950 Alexander Abusch contrasted the positive, optimistic literature of the Soviet Union with the decadent literature of the 'hopeless generation' which was currently invading West Germany and 'atomising' all positive human values, a literature which either reflected the personal sickness of its author or, as in the 'sadistic fantasies of a George Orwell', placed itself in the service of the brutal and imperialistic aims of America (Schubbe, ed., 1972, p. 146). A year later Johannes R. Becher disparagingly pointed out that whereas at its zenith the bourgeoisie had produced utopian novels which anticipated a human paradise, today these same classes were 'wallowing in orgies of horror', and he cited *Nineteen Eighty-Four* together with Aldous Huxley's *Ape and Essence* as evidence (ibid., p. 196). Huxley has been regarded more favourably than Orwell, although it was not until 1978 that a translation of *Brave New World* appeared in the GDR. He is given credit for showing up the 'hollowness and decadence of late bourgeois society'; his basic flaw is his pessimism, his inability to envisage a (socialist) solution to the problems he presents (Steiner, ed., 1970, p. 282).

In recent years dystopian works of fiction have been published which bear comparison with those of Orwell and Huxley. Wolf's *Störfall* alludes to *Brave New World* in the context of a critique of science (p. 26), and the framework narrative of *Verlegung eines mittleren Reichs* implies a future totalitarian state. Karlheinz Steinmüller's story 'Der Traum vom Großen Roten Fleck' takes up Huxley's vision of a totally rationalised human society. The setting is Megalopolis; Earth has become a desert of steel and concrete. Society has been 'atomised', people living in isolation from one another in a totally artificial environment, in which everything they need can be called up by pressing a button. Apartments are interchangeable – one uses whichever happens to be vacant, since they are automatically serviced. There are no names, since personal relationships do not occur. For conversation or for sex an order is passed on by computer and the appropriate contact made; thereafter one does not expect to meet again. However, from time to time the system develops a defect. Occasionally individuals run amok and have to be treated by medical robots. The narrator himself sometimes yearns for change, although he regards this as 'anachronistic', a throwback to the 'pre-informational age'. A fault in the circuitry causes the system to break down in more ways than one. The woman he is with reveals the existence of a secret society planning to leave Earth and emigrate to Ganymede. Momentarily they form a genuine relationship, helping each other to leave the apartment through the ceiling; she bandages his arm when he injures it. But the lights go on again and he returns to normal; disgusted at his atavistic behaviour he ejects the woman. He cannot even be sure that the whole experience was not an illusion created by the system in accordance with his own wish for variety.

Inasmuch as Steinmüller's vision of a totalitarian state is of a purely individualistic, 'atomised' society, his warning can be reconciled with collectivist socialism. Franz Fühmann's *Saiäns-Fiktschen* goes much further in that it presents two alternative and rival systems; while containing numerous Huxleyan details it is the closest approximation to Orwell's *Nineteen Eighty-Four* to have appeared in the GDR. Fühmann had warned against the threat to humanity posed by the struggle of the two super-powers elsewhere. His story 'Anna, genannt die Humpelhexe' describes two giants destroying all around them in their attempt to annihilate each other. The biblical story 'Der Mund des Propheten', which quotes the phrase 'Swords to Ploughshares', the slogan of the unofficial peace movement and a taboo, eventually was published posthumously in 1985. Despite many differences, his *Saiäns-Fiktschen*, which appeared two years before *Kassandra*, has much in common with Wolf's work. Wolf goes back in time to reinterpret myth. Fühmann had done the same on many occasions; here he takes the opposite path, setting his stories in the year 3456.

Saiäns-Fiktschen, as the title implies, is not to be taken altogether seriously as a work of science fiction. It consists of seven sketches written independently between 1974 and 1980. Two nuclear wars have taken place; Berlin has been destroyed, the whale is extinct and German has been completely anglicised. As in Ziergiebel's *Die andere Welt* the world is divided into two states, Libroterr and Uniterr (apart from Andorra, which nobody ever mentions). Uniterr covers the whole of Europe, Asia, Africa and Antarctica; Libroterr must therefore consist of America. Uniterr bears many of the hallmarks of Orwell's Airstrip One: the uniform shabbiness, the shortage of commodities, the tasteless food, the power cuts which put the lifts out of order so that propaganda may be beamed across the sky. Orwell's Thought Police have become Fühmann's 'Gesinnungspolizei', who can detect the feelings of those watching a television programme, for example, by means of 'emotiographs', or who can read the thought processes of a man while he is waiting, so he thinks, for an examination to begin, not knowing that the waiting *is* the examination. The desperate attempt to control one's own thoughts leads inevitably, as in Orwell, to complete apathy and emptiness of mind. Uniterr is a place where everyone is being spied on, listened in on, where windows are made of one-way glass which excludes the inquisitive gaze of all but the police, who have devices to see through it, and where every time one goes out one has to register the purpose and duration of the excursion. Libroterr, by contrast, clearly a caricature of the 'free' West, is a place where people can make a fortune out of fruit machines, where pharmaceutical fashions change seven times in fifteen months, where there are ten thousand televisions stations transmitting a round-the-clock mixture of violence and sex; a place of unbridled advertising, where the only restrictions on individual freedom are the inheritance laws.

Historiography is an important theme in *Saiäns-Fiktschen* too. Libroterr is accused of 'historical pessimism' by Uniterr's ideologues; the story 'Das Duell' shows how the latter manipulate history in accordance with preconceived ideological principles. Karin Hirdina (1982) describes Uniterr's system as 'fascist', while admitting that this is an over-simplification. The black uniforms support her diagnosis. Fühmann's word for 'comrade' is not 'Genosse' but 'Kamerad', a word redolent of Nazi militarism, not least from the pen of one whose most famous story *Kameraden* savages the 'comradeship' fostered by fascist ideology. Uniterr certainly cannot be called 'socialist'; nevertheless, too many details imply potential developments out of 'actually existing socialism'. On the role of science Fühmann, like Königsdorf, is more positive. It is totalitarian Uniterr which has banned scientific research for having led to two nuclear wars. In the story 'Der Haufen' it is the spirit of disinterested scientific enquiry, however absurd its object, which affords Janno a brief moment of spiritual freedom.

Saiäns-Fiktschen is told with considerable narrative sophistication. The narrator, like that of Braun's *Hinze-Kunze-Roman*, is personal, teasing and ironic. He plays with the reader's expectations and with the conventions of 'omniscient' narration: 'That sounds incredible, but that is the way it was, or rather that is the way it will be. For we are telling what will have taken place in the future'[27] (p. 100). Volker Braun, too, begins with the disclaimer: 'I do not understand it, I am describing it.'[28] Just as the continued attachment of Hinze to Kunze and vice versa is 'incomprehensible', so is the unthinking acceptance of contradictions in the ruling ideology of Uniterr by its citizens. But even the narrator who knows what will happen in the future cannot tell exactly what the Supreme Council has deliberated: 'It is not given to us to know exact details: nothing of what goes on in the Supreme Council emerges to the outside world. But we do know what the controllers were thinking...'[29] (p. 108). As in *Hinze-Kunze-Roman* narrator and reader must wait outside. In the story 'Bewußtseinserhebung' Janno has to undergo a thought control test to ascertain his loyalty to the state before he can be admitted to a university course; thereafter one of his first tasks is to spy on his own father – 'But that is really not very interesting',[30] the narrator concludes (p. 160). In *Nineteen Eighty-Four*, too, children are encouraged to divulge to the authorities indiscretions committed by their parents. Parsons, for example, who has been more successfully brainwashed than Winston Smith, is proud of his little daughter for having betrayed him. Orwell, however, is more strident than Fühmann. The ironic style of *Saiäns-Fiktschen* is more akin to that of *Brave New World*: Huxley's 'Oh Ford' and 'Thank Ford' have become, in materialist Uniterr, 'O Matter' (p. 139), 'Thank Matter' (p. 51) and even 'Matter forbid!' (p. 129).

In his preface to the stories Fühmann declared that his method was not a 'thinking something to its logical conclusion' but rather a 'fearing something to its logical conclusion': 'The world of these stories is an unreal end of time, the sum and consequence of all the negative things that developing humanity produces; but all these ends have also had their beginnings, and it ought to be important to nip them in the bud, especially at the point where everything begins, in the personal domain'[31] (p. 6). He, too, is a Cassandra, warning of the 'monsters' which contemporary distortions both in the capitalist and in the socialist worlds may produce. The opening story, 'Die Ohnmacht', implies Cassandra's helplessness. In it a time machine is described which enables the user to see into the future, albeit by a modest ten minutes. Everyone who tests it is convinced that it will be a simple matter to refute it, merely by doing the opposite of what has been predicted; but each of them is confounded, as to contradict the vision would be to contradict one's own character. Cassandra, we remember, was allowed to foretell the future on condition that nobody would believe her. The hope which Fühmann leaves his reader is different from that of Christa Wolf, and belongs more to the mainstream of enlightenment thinking. It is that the individual reader may emancipate himself from the conventional assumptions of his society through literature. The final story in the collection, 'Pavlos Papierbuch', suggests that rather than the Cassandra vision of the future which nobody will believe, it is the open-endedness of works like Kafka's *In der Strafkolonie* which will cause the reader to think, to question, to become free.

Saiäns-Fiktschen forms perhaps a fitting conclusion to this study. While clearly distancing itself from the crasser manifestations of unbridled capitalism it paints a critical picture of tendencies which are at least latent in actually existing socialism and satirises the Stalinist rewriting of history to suit ideological requirements. Its insistence that the way to reform lies with the individual rather than with the collective corresponds to the thrust of many of the most challenging works of the past twenty years from *Nachdenken über Christa T.* to *Horns Ende*. Its sophisticated and ironic narrative is many miles away from the ponderous mannerisms of conventional socialist realism. Lastly and by no means least, its explicit confidence in the value of literature itself as a means of raising and expanding the individual's consciousness in an authoritarian society places it within the context of such disparate works as *Die neuen Leiden des jungen W.*, *Leben und Abenteuer der Trobadora Beatriz*, *Der Aufenthalt*, *Bewerbung bei Hofe* – and even *Anders*.

The future of the GDR's literature cannot easily be predicted, any more than that of the GDR's society. The new leader of East Germany has a similar opportunity in the cultural sphere to that grasped by Erich Honecker in 1971. Whether he will announce a further reduction in taboos must remain speculation. That such a policy, desirable as it must be, would automatically increase the richness of the GDR's literature may equally be open to question. Every society has its taboos; some have more than others. When in 1966 Heinrich Böll stated that art must always 'go too far' in order to test the limits of its freedom, he harvested a storm of protest in his own country. If there were no taboos at all, then art might well lose its function. Many of those GDR writers who have come to the West have found that their freedom of self-expression is paid for by a lack of resonance in society at large. Ploughing in water is a singularly unfruitful activity.

En Route to Utopia

Notes

1. Auf der Flucht / vor dem Beton / geht es zu / wie im Märchen: Wo du / auch ankommst / es erwartet dich / grau und gründlich.
2. die Gegenwart aus der Sicht der Zukunft betrachten.
3. Diese Gesellschaft ist ihrer Natur nach vorwärts gespannt, sie ist wie ein Bogen, von dem der Pfeil nach vorn schnellt.
4. Aber eines Tages ist das nicht mehr so / Und zu Ende sind die tausend Jahre Not. / Aus der Jammer: über der Getreidekammer hebt sich hoh / Eine wunderbare Fahne, die ist rot.
5. Der große Trick von unserer Gegenwart ist, daß der Abschied von eine ungeheuer lange Vergangenheit erst stattgefunden hat, und daß ein paar Stücke Zukunft auch schon anzutreffen sind, alles durcheinander, und da kommt einem auch das Zeitgefühl durcheinander.
6. Die Welt, sofern sie nur die geringste Einsicht mit sich selber hat, wird sozialistisch sein. Das ist das eine. Wir landen auf der Venus. Das ist das andere.
7. Die Öde wird Geschichte. / Termiten schreiben sie / Mit ihren Zangen / In den Sand. // Und nicht erforscht wird werden / Ein Geschlecht, / Eifrig bemüht, / Sich zu vernichten.
8. Kassandra hinterm Ladentisch, Kassandra, Brote schichtend, Kassandra, Kartoffeln abwiegend.
9. so ... daß der Zukunft die Zukunft bewahrt wird.
10. Die Menschen haben die alten Mythen über Bord geworfen und sich in die Falle eines neuen Mythos begeben: das des ewigen exponentiellen Wirtschaftwachstums...
11. Mit der Klafter des Todes / vermessen Schnelle Brüter / das Land. / ... Im Abwasser / staut sich die / Schuld.
12. Eines Tages wird uns das Meer seinen blinden Spiegel entgegenhalten, aber dann wird es zu spät sein. Die Schreie der Menschen werden ungehört an den Küsten verhallen. Das Meer wird der Schauplatz unserer künftigen Katastrophen sein.
13. Wenn ich polemisiere, dann polemisiere ich gegen die ausschließliche Herrschaft des Ratio und des Wissenschaftsbegriffs, wie er sich im neunzehnten Jahrhundert entwickelt hat. Der Positivismus und der reine Rationalismus sind die Grundlage für bestimmte Fehlentwicklungen, die heute bis zur ungeheuren Kriegsgefahr führen, in der wir uns befinden.
14. das höchste Vorrecht, das es gibt, ... in die finstere Gegenwart, die alle Zeit besetzt hält, einen schmalen Streifen Zukunft vorzuschieben ... wie man mit beiden Beinen auf der Erde träumt.
15. die Geschichte von der Verwandlung der Sehnsucht, der Hoffnung nach hinten, in Hoffen nach vorn und trächtiges Handeln.
16. In der Büchse die Hoffnung Prometheus muß holen Pandora gewinnen ihre Wiederkehr dringlich serpentische Töchter ziehen Gesang.
17. friedensfähig..., imstande, seine Interessen- und Meinungsverschiedenheiten unblutig zu bewältigen und Sitten zu entwickeln, die Kompromisse höher schätzen als Siege und den Krieg tabuisieren.
18. Unruhvollen Stamm ... oder Salz der Erde.
19. STUNDE DER WEISSGLUT TOTE BÜFFEL AUS DEN CANYONS GESCHWADER VON HAIEN ZÄHNE AUS SCHWARZEM LICHT DIE ALLIGATOREN MEINE FREUNDE GRAMMATIK DER ERDBEBEN HOCHZEIT VON FEUER UND WASSER MENSCHEN AUS NEUEM FLEISCH LAUTREAMONTMALDOROR FÜRST VON ATLANTIS SOHN DER TOTEN.
20. Was bleibt denn von Ländern und Kontinenten, wenn man mit einem Raumschiff aufsteigt? Schon nach wenigen Flugkilometern schrumpfen sie zu Kleingärten zusammen.
21. daß wir uns bis in alle Ewigkeit mit der Bombe gegenüberstehen können. ... die sozialen Probleme werden dadurch nicht gelöst.

22. Sähen die Menschen die Erde so wie wir als eine kleine Kugel, die wie ein Raumschiff durch die Tiefen des Alls fliegt, dann würden sie diese einmalige Existenz vielleicht nicht so leichtfertig aufs Spiel setzen.

23. Ich las begierig die erste Seite: derselbe Krieg wie vorhin, nein, wie in der Vergangenheit, war noch immer im Gange. Ein Völkerstamm war mittels Schwefelsäure ausgerottet worden – soso. Hochwasser bedrohte Florenz. Lawinenunglück in den Alpen. Das Finale im Tenniscup . . .

24. wie ein Land dem andern die Messergebnisse abjagte, höher hinaus die Raketen, Milliarden verpulvert für immer dasselbe Projekt, die eine Bombe, versehen mit neckischen Namen aus der Mythologie . . .

25. die Angst nicht kennen, Maschinen nur für die praktischen Verrichtungen des Alltags benutzen und unser Denken und Handeln zur übereinstimmung gebracht haben.

26. der allem Anschein nach zur ideologischen Ausbeuterklasse der Gelehrten gehörte.

27. Das klingt unglaublich, allein es war so, oder vielmehr: Es wird so sein. Wir erzählen ja, was in der Zukunft geschehn sein wird.

28. Ich begreife es nicht, ich beschreibe es.

29. Es ist uns nicht gegeben, Genaues zu wissen: vom Geschehen im OK-Rat dringt nichts nach außen. Doch wir wissen, was die Kontrolleure dachten. . . .

30. Aber das ist wirklich nicht sehr interessant.

31. Die Welt dieser Geschichten ist irreale Endzeit, Summe und Konsequenz all des Negativen, das die sich bildende Menschheit entäußert; aber alle diese Ende haben auch ihre Anfänge gehabt, und es sollte gelten, denen zu wehren, vor allem da, wo alles anfängt: im persönlichen Bereich.

Bibliography

Primary sources

Note: Editions listed are in most cases first GDR editions; where two editions are listed an asterisk denotes the one quoted in the text. 'Berlin' refers to East Berlin.

Apitz, Bruno, *Nackt unter Wölfen. Roman*, Halle: Mitteldeutscher Verlag, 1958
Becker, Jurek, *Aller Welt Freund. Roman*, Rostock: Hinstorff, 1984
——, *Bronsteins Kinder. Roman*, Rostock, Hinstorff, 1987
——, *Der Boxer*, Rostock: Hinstorff, 1976
——, *Irreführung der Behörden. Roman*, Rostock: Hinstorff, 1973
——, *Jakob der Lügner*, Berlin: Aufbau Verlag, 1969
——, *Schlaflose Tage. Roman*, Frankfurt a.M.: Suhrkamp, 1978
Bieker, Gerd, *Sternschnuppenwünsche. Roman*, Berlin: Verlag Neues Leben, 1965
Bobrowski, Johannes, *Levins Mühle. 34 Sätze über meinen Großvater*, Berlin: Union Verlag, 1964
Braun, Volker, *Das ungezwungene Leben Kasts*, Berlin: Aufbau Verlag, 1971
——, *Gedichte*, Frankfurt a.M.: Suhrkamp, 1979
——, *Hinze-Kunze-Roman*, Halle: Mitteldeutscher Verlag, 1985
——, *Langsamer knirschender Morgen*, Halle: Mitteldeutscher Verlag, 1987
——, *Stücke. Mit einem Nachwort von Klaus Schuhmann*, Berlin: Henschel, 1983
——, *Training des aufrechten Gangs*, Halle: Mitteldeutscher Verlag, 1979
——, *Unvollendete Geschichte*, in *Sinn und Form* 27 (1975), pp. 941–79; in *Unvollendete Geschichte Arbeit für morgen*, Halle: Mitteldeutscher Verlag, 1988
Bräunig, Werner, *Ein Kranich am Himmel. Unbekanntes und Bekanntes*, ed. by Heinz Sachs, Halle: Mitteldeutscher Verlag, 1981
——, 'Rummelplatz', in *Neue deutsche Literatur* 13 (1965), no. 10, pp. 7–29
Brecht, Bertolt, *Gesammelte Werke in 20 Bänden*, Frankfurt: Suhrkamp 1967
Brězan, Jurij, *Krabat oder Die Verwandlung der Welt*, Berlin: Verlag Neues Leben, 1976
Burmeister, Brigitte, *Anders oder Vom Aufenthalt in der Fremde. Roman*, Berlin: Verlag der Nation, 1987; *Darmstadt: Luchterhand, 1988
Cibulka, Hanns, *Swantow. Die Aufzeichnungen des Andreas Flemming*, Halle:

Bibliography

Mitteldeutscher Verlag, 1982

Claudius, Eduard, *Menschen an unsrer Seite*, Berlin: Verlag Volk und Welt, 1951

——, *Vom schweren Anfang. Erzählungen*, Berlin: Verlag Neues Leben, 1950

Dahne, Gerhard, *Die ganz merkwürdigen Sichten und Gesichte des Hans Greifer. Roman*, Halle: Mitteldeutscher Verlag, 1975

Damm, Sigrid, *Vögel, die verkünden Land. Das Leben des Jakob Michael Reinhold Lenz*, Berlin: Aufbau Verlag, 1985

de Bruyn, Günter, *Buridans Esel. Roman*, Halle: Mitteldeutscher Verlag, 1968

——, *Der Hohlweg. Roman*, Halle: Mitteldeutscher Verlag, 1963

——, *Im Querschnitt. Prosa Essay Biographie*, ed. by Werner Liersch, Halle: Mitteldeutscher Verlag, 1979

——, *Märkische Forschungen. Erzählung für Freunde der Literaturgeschichte*, Halle: Mitteldeutscher Verlag, 1979

——, *Neue Herrlichkeit. Roman*, Halle: Mitteldeutscher Verlag, 1985

——, *Preisverleihung. Roman*, Halle: Mitteldeutscher Verlag, 1972

Deichfuß, Horst, *Windmacher. Roman*, Halle: Mitteldeutscher Verlag, 1983

Ebersbach, Volker, *Caroline. Historischer Roman*, Halle: Mitteldeutscher Verlag, 1987

Eckart, Gabriele, *So sehe ick die Sache. Protokolle aus der DDR. Leben im Havelländischen Obstanbaugebiet*, Cologne: Kiepenheuer & Witsch, 1984

Edel, Peter, *Wenn es ans Leben geht. Meine Geschichte* (2 vols), Berlin: Verlag der Nation, 1979

Feyl, Renate, *Idylle mit Professor. Roman*, Berlin: Verlag Neues Leben, 1986

Fries, Fritz Rudolf, *Verlegung einem mittleren Reiches. Aufgefundene Papiere, herausgegeben von einem Nachfahr in späterer Zeit*, Berlin: Aufbau Verlag, 1984

Fühmann, Franz, 'Anna, genannt die Humpelhexe', in *Reineke Fuchs. Märchen nach Shakespeare*, Rostock: Hinstorff, 1981

——, *Böhmen am Meer. Erzählung*, Rostock: Hinstorff, 1962

——, 'Der Mund des Propheten', in *Das Ohr des Dionysios. Nachgelassene Erzählungen*, Rostock: Hinstorff, 1985

——; 'Drei nackte Männer', in *Erzählungen 1955–1975*, Rostock: Hinstorff, 1977

——, *Kameraden. Novelle*, Berlin: Aufbau Verlag, 1955

——, *Saiäns-Fiktschen. Erzählungen*, Rostock: Hinstorff, 1981

——, *Zweiundzwanzig Tage oder Die Hälfte des Lebens* (1st pubd 1973), Leipzig: Reclam, 1980

Hacks, Peter, *Adam und Eva. Komödie in einem Vorspiel und drei Akten*, in *Sinn und Form* 25 (1973), pp. 7–73

——, *Amphitryon. Komödie in drei Akten*, Berlin: Eulenspiegel Verlag, 1969

——, *Ein Gespräch im Hause Stein über den abwesenden Herrn von Goethe*, in *Ausgewählte Dramen*, vol. 2, Berlin: Aufbau Verlag, 1976, pp. 389–454

——, *Moritz Tassow. Komödie*, in *Sinn und Form* 17 (1965), pp. 835–929

——, *Pandora. Drama nach J.W. von Goethe. Mit einem Essay*, Berlin: Aufbau Verlag, 1981

Bibliography

Hauser, Jochen, *Familie Rechlin. Ein Roman aus Berlin*, Rostock: Hinstorff, 1978
Heiduczek, Werner, *Tod am Meer. Roman*, Halle: Mitteldeutscher Verlag, 1977
Hein, Christoph, *Cromwell und andere Stücke*, Berlin: Aufbau Verlag, 1981 (also includes *Lassalle fragt Herrn Herbert nach Sonja*)
——, *Der fremde Freund. Novelle*, Berlin: Aufbau Verlag, 1982; published in West Germany as *Drachenblut*, Darmstadt: Luchterhand, 1983
——, *Die wahre Geschichte des Ah Q. (Zwischen Hund und Wolf)*, in *Theater der Zeit* 38 (1983), 10, pp. 57–64; in *Die wahre Geschichte des Ah Q. Stücke und Essays*, Darmstadt: Luchterhand, 1984
——. *Einladung zum Lever Bourgeois*, Berlin: Aufbau Verlag, 1980
——, *Horns Ende. Roman*, Berlin: Aufbau Verlag, 1985
Hermlin, Stephan, *Abendlicht*, Leipzig: Reclam, 1979
——, *Scardanelli. Ein Hörspiel*, Leipzig: Insel Verlag, 1971
Heym, Stefan, *Ahasver, Roman*, Berlin: Buchverlag Der Morgen, 1988
——, *Collin. Roman*, Munich: Bertelsmann, 1979
——, *Der König David Bericht. Roman*, Berlin: Buchverlag Der Morgen, 1973; *Frankfurt a.M.: Fischer Taschenbuch Verlag, 1974
——, *5 Tage im Juni. Roman*, Munich: Bertelsmann, 1974
Hilscher, Eberhard, *Die Weltzeituhr. Roman einer Epoche*, Berlin: Buchverlag Der Morgen, 1983; *Munich: Goldmann, 1987
Holtz-Baumert, Gerhard, *Die pucklige Verwandtschaft. Aus Kindheit und Jugend in Berlin 017 und Umgebung*, Berlin: Verlag Neues Leben, 1985
Huchel, Peter, *Chausseen Chausseen. Gedichte*, Frankfurt a.M.: Suhrkamp, 1963
Jaeck, Hans-Peter, *Kammerherr und König. Voltaire in Preußen*, Berlin: Buchverlag Der Morgen, 1987
Jakobs, Karl-Heinz, *Beschreibung eines Sommers. Roman*, Berlin: Verlag Neues Leben, 1961
——, *Die Interviewer. Roman*, Berlin: Verlag Neues Leben, 1973
Johannis, Ingrid, *Das siebente Brennesselhemd. Aus dem Tagebuch einer Alkoholkranken*. Berlin: Verlag Neues Leben, 1986
Johannsen, Christa, *Leibniz. Roman seines Lebens*, Berlin: Union Verlag, 1966
Kant, Hermann, *Das Impressum. Roman*, Berlin: Rütten & Loening, 1972; *Frankfurt a.M.: Fischer Taschenbuch Verlag, 1975
——, *Der Aufenthalt. Roman*, Berlin: Rütten & Loening, 1977
——, *Der dritte Nagel. Erzählungen*, Berlin: Rütten & Loening, 1981
——, *Die Aula. Roman*, Berlin: Rütten & Loening, 1965
Kirsch, Rainer, *Sauna oder Die fernherwirkende Trübung. Erzählungen*, Rostock: Hinstorff, 1985
Kirsch, Sarah, *Die Pantherfrau. Fünf Frauen in der DDR*, Berlin: Aufbau Verlag, 1973
——, *Katzenkopfpflaster. Gedichte*, Munich: DTV, 1978
——, *Zaubersprüche*, Berlin: Aufbau Verlag, 1973
Köhler, Erich, *Der Krott oder Das Ding unterm Hut*, Rostock: Hinstorff, 1976

Bibliography

Königsdorf, Helga, *Meine ungehörigen Träume. Geschichten*, Berlin: Aufbau Verlag, 1978
——, *Respektloser Umgang*, Berlin: Aufbau Verlag, 1987; *Darmstadt: Luchterhand, 1987
Kunert, Günter, *Der ungebetene Gast. Gedichte*, Berlin: Aufbau Verlag, 1965
——, *Unterwegs nach Utopia. Gedichte*, Berlin: Aufbau Verlag, 1980; *Warnung vor Spiegeln. Unterwegs nach Utopia. Abtötungsverfahren. Gedichte*, Munich: DTV, 1982
Kunze, Reiner, *Brief mit blauem Siegel. Gedichte*, Leipzig: Reclam, 1973
——, *Die wunderbaren Jahre*, Frankfurt a.M.: Fischer, 1976
Lambrecht, Christine, *Männerbekanntschaften. Freimütige Protokolle*, Halle: Mitteldeutscher Verlag, 1986
Lewin, Waldtraut, *Federico. Roman*, Berlin: Verlag Neues Leben, 1984
Liebmann, Irina, *Berliner Mietshaus. Begegnungen und Gespräche*, Halle: Mitteldeutscher Verlag, 1982
Lietz, Hans-Georg, *Das Hexenhaus. Roman*, Rostock: Hinstorff, 1984
Loest, Erich, *Es geht seinen Gang oder Mühen in unserer Ebene. Roman*, Halle: Mitteldeutscher Verlag, 1978; *Munich: DTV, 1980
Montag, Andreas, *Karl der Große oder Die Suche nach Julie. Roman*, Halle: Mitteldeutscher Verlag, 1985
Morgner, Irmtraud, *Amanda. Ein Hexenroman*, Berlin: Aufbau Verlag, 1983
——, *Die wundersamen Reisen Gustavs des Weltfahrers. Lügenhafter Roman mit Kommentaren*, Berlin: Aufbau Verlag, 1972
——, *Hochzeit in Konstantinopel. Roman*, Berlin: Aufbau Verlag, 1968
——, *Leben und Abenteuer der Trobadora Beatriz nach Zeugnissen ihrer Spielfrau Laura. Roman in dreizehn Büchern und sieben Intermezzos*, Berlin: Aufbau Verlag, 1974; *Darmstadt: Luchterhand, 1977
Müller, Christine, *Männerprotokolle*, Berlin: Buchverlag Der Morgen, 1985
Müller, Heiner, *Bildbeschreibung*, in *Sinn und Form* 37 (1985), pp. 1042–7
——, *Der Auftrag. Erinnerung an eine Revolution*, in *Sinn und Form* 31 (1979), pp. 1244–63
——, *Der Bau*, in *Sinn und Form* 17 (1965), pp. 169–227
——, *Germania Tod in Berlin*, in *Stücke. Texte über Deutschland (1957–1979)*, Leipzig: Reclam, 1989, pp. 191–236
——, *Die Schlacht / Traktor / Leben Gundlings Friedrich von Preußen Lessings Schlaf Traum Schrei*, Berlin: Henschel, 1981
——, *Macbeth*, in *Theater der Zeit* 27 (1972), no. 4, pp. 51–64
——, *Philoktet*, in *Sinn und Form* 17 (1965), pp. 733–65
——, *Zement*, in *Theater der Zeit* 29 (1974), no. 6, pp. 45–64
Mundstock, Karl, *Meine tausend Jahre Jugend*, Halle: Mitteldeutscher Verlag, 1981
Muthesius, Sibylle, *Flucht in die Wolken*, Berlin: Buchverlag Der Morgen, 1981
Neutsch, Erik, *Auf der Suche nach Gatt. Roman*, Halle: Mitteldeutscher Verlag, 1973

Bibliography

———, *Der Friede im Osten* (4 vols.), Halle: Mitteldeutscher Verlag 1974, 1978, 1985, 1987
———, 'Drei Tage unseres Lebens', in *Manuskripte. Almanach neuer Prosa und Lyrik*, ed. by Joachim Ret, Halle: Mitteldeutscher Verlag, 1969, pp. 526–69
———, *Spur der Steine*. Roman, Halle: Mitteldeutscher Verlag, 1964
———, *Zwei leere Stühle*. Novelle, Halle: Mitteldeutscher Verlag, 1979
Noll, Dieter, *Kippenberg*. Roman, Berlin: Aufbau Verlag, 1979
Panitz, Eberhard, *Die unheilige Sophia*. Roman, Halle: Mitteldeutscher Verlag, 1974
Pieske, Manfred, *Schnauzer*. Roman, Rostock: Hinstorff, 1980
Plenzdorf, Ulrich, *Die neuen Leiden des jungen W.*, Rostock: Hinstorff, 1973
———, *Filme*, Rostock: Hinstorff, 1986
———, 'kein runter kein fern', in *Klagenfurter Texte zum Ingeborg-Bachmann-Preis 1978*, ed. by Marcel Reich-Ranicki and Ernst Willner, Munich: List, 1978, pp. 13–31
———, *Legende vom Glück ohne Ende*, Rostock: Hinstorff, 1979
Radtke, Valerie, *Ich suche Liebe. Roman meines Lebens*, Berlin: Buchverlag Der Morgen, 1984
Reimann, Brigitte, *Franziska Linkerhand*. Roman, Berlin: Verlag Neues Leben, 1974; *Munich: DTV, 1977
Saeger, Uwe, *Nöhr*. Roman, Rostock: Hinstorff, 1980
———, *Sinon oder die gefällige Lüge*. Erzählung, Berlin: Buchverlag Der Morgen, 1983
———, *Warten auf Schnee*. Rostock: Hinstorff, 1981
Sämann, Wolfgang, *Das Haus des Dr. Pondabel. Fünf Erzählungen*, Rostock: Hinstorff, 1979
Sakowski, Helmut, *Wie ein Vogel im Schwarm*. Roman, Berlin: Verlag Neues Leben, 1984
Schädlich, Hans Joachim, *Versuchte Nähe*. Prosa, Reinbek: Rowohlt, 1977
Schlesinger, Klaus, *Alte Filme*, Rostock: Hinstorff, 1975
———, *Leben im Winter*, Rostock: Hinstorff, 1989
———, *Matulla und Busch*, Rostock: Hinstorff, 1985
———, *Michael*, Rostock: Hinstorff, 1971
Schneider, Rolf, *Die Reise nach Jarosław*, Rostock: Hinstorff, 1974
———, *November*. Roman, Hamburg: Knaus, 1979
Schubert, Helga, *Blickwinkel. Geschichten*, Berlin: Aufbau Verlag, 1984
Schulz, Max Walter, *Triptychon mit sieben Brücken*. Roman, Halle: Mitteldeutscher Verlag, 1974
Schütz, Helga, *Julia oder Erziehung zum Chorgesang*. Roman, Berlin: Aufbau Verlag, 1980
Seghers, Anna, *Das siebte Kreuz. Roman aus Hitlerdeutschland*, Berlin: Aufbau Verlag, 1946
———, *Die Entscheidung*. Roman, Berlin: Aufbau Verlag, 1959
———, *Die Toten bleiben jung*. Roman, Berlin: Aufbau Verlag, 1949

——, *Sonderbare Begegnungen*, Berlin: Aufbau Verlag, 1973
——, *Überfahrt. Eine Liebesgeschichte*, Berlin: Aufbau Verlag, 1971
——, 'Vierzig Jahre der Margarete Wolf', in *Brot und Salz. Drei Erzählungen*, Berlin: Aufbau Verlag, 1958
Stade, Martin, *Der König und sein Narr. Roman*, Berlin: Buchverlag Der Morgen, 1975
——, *Der närrische Krieg. Historischer Roman*, Berlin: Buchverlag Der Morgen, 1981
Steinmüller, Karlheinz, *Der letzte Tag auf der Venus. Wissenschaftlich-phantastische Erzählungen*, Berlin: Verlag Neues Leben, 1979
Strittmatter, Erwin, *Der Wundertäter. Roman*, 3 vols., Berlin: Aufbau Verlag, 1957, 1973, 1980
——, *Ole Bienkopp. Roman*, Berlin: Aufbau Verlag, 1963
Tetzner, Gerti, *Karen W. Roman*, Halle: Mitteldeutscher Verlag, 1974; *Darmstadt: Luchterhand, 1975
Thürk, Harry, *Der Gaukler. Roman*, Berlin: Verlag Das Neue Berlin, 1978
Töppe, Frank, *Regen auf Tyche. All-Geschichten, erzählt vom Raumpiloten Roul, unter Verwendung von Texten Irdischer und Ausserirdischer*, Berlin: Verlag Das Neue Berlin, 1978
Turek, Ludwig, *Die goldene Kugel. Phantastischer Kurzroman um Atomkraft und Weltraumschiffe*, Berlin: Dietz, 1949
Ulbrich, Bernd, *Abends im Park und nachts und morgens. Erzählungen*, Halle: Mitteldeutscher Verlag, 1983
Vieweg, Heinz, *Ultrasymet bleibt geheim. Zukunftsroman*, Berlin: Verlag Neues Leben, 1955
Walther, Joachim, *Bewerbung bei Hofe. Historischer Roman*, Berlin: Verlag Neues Leben, 1982
Wander, Maxie, *Guten Morgen, du Schöne. Protokolle nach Tonband*, Berlin: Buchverlag Der Morgen, 1977; *Darmstadt: Luchterhand, 1979
Weber, Hans, *Alter Schwede. Roman*, Berlin: Verlag Neues Leben, 1984
Wohlgemuth, Egon, *Egon und das achte Weltwunder*, Berlin: Verlag Neues Leben, 1962
Wolf, Christa, *Der geteilte Himmel. Roman*, Halle: Mitteldeutscher Verlag, 1963
——, 'Juninachmittag', in *Neue Texte. Almanach für deutsche Literatur*, Berlin: Aufbau Verlag, 1967, pp. 166–84
——, *Kassandra. Vier Vorlesungen Eine Erzählung*, Berlin: Aufbau Verlag, 1983
——, *Kein Ort. Nirgends*, Berlin: Aufbau Verlag, 1979; *Darmstadt: Luchterhand, 1979
——, *Kindheitsmuster*, Berlin: Aufbau Verlag, 1976
——, *Nachdenken über Christa T.*, Halle Mitteldeutscher Verlag, 1968; *Darmstadt: Luchterhand (7th edn), 1976
——, *Störfall. Nachrichten eines Tages*, Berlin: Aufbau Verlag, 1987; *Darmstadt: Luchterhand, 1987
——, *Unter den Linden. Drei unwahrscheinliche Geschichten*, Berlin: Aufbau

Bibliography

Verlag, 1974
——, *Voraussetzungen einer Erzählung: Kassandra. Frankfurter Poetik-Vorlesungen*, Darmstadt: Luchterhand, 1983
Wolf, Friedrich, *Werke in zwei Bänden*, ed. by Walther Pollatschek, Berlin: Aufbau Verlag, 1973
Wolf, Gerhard, *Der arme Hölderlin*, Berlin: Union Verlag, 1972; *Darmstadt: Luchterhand, 1982
Ziergiebel, Herbert, *Die andere Welt. Phantastischer Roman*, Halle: Mitteldeutscher Verlag, 1966
Zinner, Hedda, *Katja. Roman*, Berlin: Buchverlag Der Morgen, 1980

Anthologies

The following anthologies contain most of the shorter pieces mentioned:

Anderson, Edith, ed., *Blitz aus heiterm Himmel*, Rostock: Hinstorff, 1975
Castein, Hanne, ed., *Es wird einmal. Märchen für morgen*, Frankfurt a.M.: Suhrkamp, 1988
Erb, Elke and Sascha Anderson, eds., *Berührung ist nur eine Randerscheinung. Neue Literatur aus der DDR*, Cologne: Kiepenheuer & Witsch, 1985
Heidtmann, Horst, ed., *Im Jenseits. Unheimlich-phantastische Geschichten aus der DDR*, Munich, DTV, 1981
Heidtmann, Horst, ed., *Von einem anderen Stern. Science-Fiction-Geschichten aus der DDR*, Munich: DTV, 1981
Hesse, Egmont, ed., *Sprache & Antwort. Stimmen und Texte einer anderen Literatur aus der DDR*, Frankfurt a.M.: Fischer, 1988
Redlin, Ekkehard, ed., *Der Mann vom Anti. Utopische Erzählungen*, Berlin: Verlag Das Neue Berlin, 1975

GDR Literature in English

Note: this select list relates only to works referred to in the text. Stefan Heym translates his own works.

Apitz, Bruno, *Naked among Wolves*, trans. by Edith Anderson, London: Collet, 1960
Becker, Jurek, *Bronstein's Children*, trans. anon, San Diego: Harcourt Brace Jovanovich, 1988
——, *Jacob the Liar*, trans. by Melvin Kornfeld, New York: Harcourt Brace Jovanovich, 1976
——, *Sleepless Days*, trans. by Leila Vennewitz, London: Secker and Warburg, 1977
Bobrowski, Johannes, *Levin's Mill*, trans. by Janet Cooper, London: Calder & Boyars, 1970

Bibliography

Brecht, Bertolt, *Plays, Poetry and Prose*, ed. by John Willett and Ralph Manheim, London: Methuen, 1970ff (various translators)
Heym, Stefan, *Collin*, London: Hodder & Stoughton, 1980
——, *Five Days in June: a novel*, London: Hodder & Stoughton, 1977
——, *The King David Report: A Novel*, London: Hodder & Stoughton, 1973
——, *The Wandering Jew*, New York: Holt, Rinehart, Winston, 1984
Huchel, Peter, *The Garden of Theophrastus and Other Poems*, trans. by Michael Hamburger, Manchester: Carcanet New Press, 1983
——, *Selected Poems*, trans. by Michael Hamburger, Cheadle: Carcanet Press, 1974
Kunze, Reiner, *With the Volume Turned Down, and Other Poems*, trans. by Ewald Osers, London: London Magazine Editions, 1973
Müller, Heiner, *Cement*, trans. by Helen Fehervary, Sue-Ellen Case and Marc D. Silberman, Milwaukee: New German Critique, 1979
——, *The Hamlet Machine*, trans. by Carl Weber, in *Performing Arts Journal*, 12 (1980), pp. 141–6
——, *The Mission*, trans. by Stuart Hood, in *Gambit. International Theatre Review*, vol. 39/40, London: Calder, 1982
Plenzdorf, Ulrich, *The New Sufferings of Young W.: A Novel*, trans. by Kenneth P. Wilcox, New York: Ungar, 1979
Schneider, Rolf, *November: A Novel*, trans. by Michael Bullock, London: Hamilton, 1981
Seghers, Anna, *The Dead Stay Young*, London: Eyre & Spottiswoode, 1950 (translator anon)
——, *The Seventh Cross*, trans. by James A. Galston, Boston: Little, 1942
Wolf, Christa, *Accident*, trans. by Heike Schwarzbauer, London: Virago Press, 1989
——, *A Model Childhood*, trans. by Ursula Molinaro and Hedwig Rappold, London: Virago Press, 1983
——, *Cassandra. A Novel and Four Essays*, trans. by Jan van Heurck, London: Virago Press, 1984
——, *Divided Heaven*, trans. by Joan Becker, Berlin: Seven Seas Books, 1965
——, *The Fourth Dimension: Interviews with Christa Wolf*, trans. by Hilary Pilkington, with an introduction by Karin McPherson, London: Verso, 1988
——, *The Quest for Christa T.*, trans. by Christopher Middleton, New York: Farrar, Straus and Giroux, 1970; repr. London: Virago Press, 1982
——, *The Reader and Writer, Essays, Sketches, Memories*, trans. by Joan Becker, Berlin: Seven Seas Books, 1977
Wolf, Friedrich, *The Sailors of Cattaro*, trans. by Keene Wallis, New York and London: French, 1935

Bibliography

Secondary Literature

Note: this list is not intended to be complete; it does, however, identify all works referred to in the text.

Adorno, Theodor W., 1961, 'Erpreßte Versöhnung. Zu Georg Lukács: "Wider den mißverstandenen Realismus"', in *Noten zur Literatur II*, Frankfurt a.M.: Suhrkamp, pp. 152–87

Akademie der Künste, ed., 1982, *Berliner Begegnung zur Friedensförderung. Protokolle des Schriftstellertreffens am 13./14. Dezember 1981*, Darmstadt: Luchterhand

Ammer, Thomas, 1988, 'Prozesse gegen Skinheads in der DDR', in *Deutschland Archiv*, 21, pp. 804–7

anon., 1955, 'Unsere Meinung', in *Neue deutsche Literatur*, 3, no. 8, pp. 3–7

Auer, Annemarie, 1977a, *Erleben – erfahren – schreiben, Werkprozeß und Kunstverstand*, Halle: Mitteldeutscher Verlag

——, 1977b, 'Gegenerinnerung', in *Sinn und Form*, 29, pp. 847–78

Baring, Arnulf, 1965, *Der 17. Juni 1953*, Cologne: Kiepenheuer & Witsch, 1965

Bartel, Horst et al, 1979, 'Preußen und die deutsche Geschichte', in *Einheit*, 34, pp. 637–46

——, 1981, 'Thesen über Martin Luther. Zum 500. Geburtstag', in *Einheit*, 36, pp. 890–903

Barthélémy-Toraille, Françoise, 1987, 'La Littérature de RDA jugée par neuf écrivains', in *Connaissance de la RDA*, no. 25, pp. 7–16

Bartram, Graham and Anthony Waine, eds., 1984, *Culture and Society in the GDR*, Dundee: GDR Monitor

Batt, Kurt, 1974, *Die Exekution des Erzählers. Westdeutsche Romane zwischen 1968 und 1972*, Leipzig: Reclam

——. 1980, *Schriftsteller. Poetisches und wirkliches Blau. Aufsätze zur Literatur*, Hamburg: Hoffman und Campe

Baum, Werner, 1955, 'Heinrich Böll – Fragen und Antworten', in *Neue deutsche Literatur*, 3, no. 3, pp. 139–46

Baumgart, Reinhard, 1983, 'Ein Marmorengel ohne Schmerz', in *Der Spiegel*, 4.4.1983, pp. 208–10

Becher, Johannes R., 1972, *Bemühungen I*, Berlin: Aufbau Verlag

——, 1988, 'Selbstzensur', in *Sinn und Form*, 40, pp. 543–51

Becker, Jurek, 1988, 'Gedächtnis verloren – Verstand verloren', in *Die Zeit*, 18.11.1988, p. 61

Berger, Manfred et al., 1978, *Kulturpolitisches Wörterbuch*, 2nd edn, Berlin: Dietz

Berger, Christel, 1981, 'Helga Schütz: Julia oder Erziehung zum Chorgesang', in *Weimarer Beiträge*, 27, no. 10, pp. 144–51

Bernhard, Hans Joachim, 1977, 'Positionen und Tendenzen in der Literatur der BRD Mitte der siebziger Jahre', in *Weimarer Beiträge*, 23, no. 12, pp. 53–84

–235–

Bibliography

Bernhardt, Rüdiger, 1986, 'Die Hoffnung der Erzähler. Beobachtungen zur Rolle des Erzählers in Prosa-Neuerscheinungen', in *Weimarer Beiträge*, 32, pp. 675–83

——, et al., 1983, 'Für und Wider: "Der fremde Freund" von Christoph Hein', in *Weimarer Beiträge*, 29, pp. 1635–55

Berschin, Helmut, 1980, 'Wie heißt das Land der Deutschen? Zur sprachpolitischen Bewertung des Namens "Deutschland" und der Namen der beiden deutschen Staaten', in *Deutschland Archiv*, 13, pp. 61–77

Bloch, Ernst, 1959, *Das Prinzip Hoffnung*, Frankfurt a.M.: Suhrkamp

Bloss, Monika, 1986, 'Kolloqium "Massenkultur-populäre Künste-Unterhaltung"', in *Weimarer Beiträge*, 32, pp. 1540–4

Böck, Dorothea, 1982, 'Ein janusköpfiger Epilog', in *Neue deutsche Literatur*, 30, no. 3, pp. 146–52

Böll, Heinrich, 1979, *Essayistische Schriften und Reden I 1952–1963*, ed. by Bernd Balzer, Cologne: Kiepenheuer & Witsch

Brayne, Mark, 1980, 'Luther: "One of the Greatest Sons of the German people"', in *GDR Monitor*, no. 3, pp. 35–43

Brecht, Bertolt, 1957, *Schriften zum Theater. Über eine nicht-aristotelische Dramatik*, ed. by Siegfried Unseld, Frankfurt a.M.: Suhrkamp

Bullivant, Keith and Hans-Joachim Althof, eds., 1987, *Subjektivität – Innerlichkeit – Abkehr vom Politischen? Tendenzen der deutschsprachigen Literatur der 70er Jahre*, Bonn: DAAD

Bulmahn, Heinz, 1984/85, 'GDR *Reisebilder* of Poland: A matter of guilt, reconciliation and understanding', in *GDR Monitor*, no. 12, pp. 18–28

Burmeister, Brigitte, 1983, *Streit um den Nouveau Roman. Eine andere Literatur und ihre Leser*, Berlin: Akademie-Verlag

Castein, Hanne, 1988, 'Nachwort', *Es wird einmal. Märchen für morgen. Moderne Märchen aus der DDR*, Frankfurt a.M.: Suhrkamp 1988, pp. 195–201

Crick, Joyce, 1983, 'Dichtung und Wahrheit: Aspects of Christa Wolf's *Kindheitsmuster*', in *London German Studies*, 2, ed. by J.P. Stern, London: Institute of Germanic Studies, pp. 168–83

Czechowski, Heinz, 1972, 'Es geht um die Realität des Gedichts!', in *Sinn und Form*, 24, pp. 897–902

Dahrendorf, Ralf, 1965, *Gesellschaft und Demokratie in Deutschland*, Munich: Piper

Deicke, Günther, 1988, 'Über meine Jahre als NDL-Redakteur', in *Sinn und Form*, 40, pp. 330–41

Dennis, Mike, ed., 1987–88, *The GDR Approaches the 1990s: The View from Britain*, Bakersfield: California State University

Döblin, Alfred, 1963, *Aufsätze zur Literatur*, ed. by Walter Muschg, Olten: Walter

Dorman, M., 1979, 'Developments in the GDR's *Kulturpolitik* since 1971', in *Modern Languages*, 60, pp. 33–46

——, 1981, 'The State versus the Writer: Recent Developments in Stefan

Bibliography

Heym's struggle against the GDR's Kulturpolitik', in *Modern Languages*, 62, pp. 144–52

Eifler, Margret, 1988, 'Berlin West – Berlin Ost: Ort politischer, filmischer und literarischer Dialektik', in *GDR Monitor*, no. 19, pp. 27–40

Emmerich, Wolfgang, 1978, 'Identität und Geschlechtertausch. Notizen zur Selbstdarstellung der Frau in der neueren DDR-Literatur', in *Basis*, 8, pp. 127–54

Endler, Adolf, 1971, 'Im Zeichen der Inkonsequenz. Über Hans Richters Aufsatzsammlung "Verse Dichter Wirklichkeiten"', in *Sinn und Form*, 23, pp. 1358–66

Engelberg, Ernst, 1985, *Bismarck: Urpreuße und Reichsgründer*, vol. 1, Berlin: Verlag der Wissenschaften

Entner, Heinz, 1976, 'Mauserung einer Gattung. Utopische Literatur eines Jahrzehnts', in *Neue deutsche Literatur*, 24, no. 12, pp. 137–53

Enzensberger, Hans Magnus, 1968, 'Gemeinplätze, die Neueste Literatur betreffend', in *Kursbuch*, no. 15, pp. 187–97

Fehervary, Helen, 1975, 'Hölderlin und Marx in der DDR', in *Basis*, 5, pp. 55–64

Feuchtwanger, Lion, 1935, 'Vom Sinn und Unsinn des historischen Romans', in *Internationale Literatur*, 5, no. 9, pp. 19–23

Fischbeck, Helmut, ed., 1979, *Literaturpolitik und Literaturkritik in der DDR. Eine Dokumentation*, 2nd edn, Frankfurt: Diesterweg

Fischborn, Gottfried, 1984, 'Umgehen mit Geschichte', in *Neue deutsche Literatur*, 32, no. 11, pp. 64–77

Flakar, Aleksandar, 1975, *Modelle der Jeans Prosa: Zur literarischen Opposition bei Plenzdorf im europäischen Romankontext*, Kronberg: Scriptor

Freytag, Gustav, 1925, *Bilder aus der deutschen Vergangenheit*, 2 vols., Berlin: Th. Knaur Nachf.

Fühmann, Franz, 1975, *Erfahrungen und Widersprüche. Versuche über Literatur*, Rostock: Hinstorff

Gaus, Günter, 1981, *Texte zur deutschen Frage*, Darmstadt: Luchterhand

Geissler, Erhard and Jurij Brězan, 1980, 'Briefwechsel zwischen Erhard Geissler und Jurij Brězan', in *Sinn und Form*, 32, pp. 1110–13

Gerber, Margy, 1986/87, '"Wie hoch ist eigentlich der Preis der Emanzipation?" Social issues in recent GDR women's writing', in *GDR Monitor*, no. 16, pp. 55–83

Girnus, Wilhelm, ed., 1973, 'Diskussion um Plenzdorf Die neuen Leiden des jungen W.', in *Sinn und Form*, 25, pp. 219–52

——, 1977, 'Vorbemerkung: Briefe an Annemarie Auer', in *Sinn und Form*, 29, pp. 1311–13

——, 1983a, 'Wer baute das siebentorige Theben? Kritische Bemerkungen zu Christa Wolfs Beitrag in Sinn und Form 1/83', in *Sinn und Form*, 35, pp. 439–47

——, 1983b, '... Kein "Wenn und Aber" und das poetische Licht Sapphos. Noch einmal zu Christa Wolf', in *Sinn und Form*, 35, pp. 1096–1105

Bibliography

Good, Colin H., 1974, 'The Linguistic Division of Germany – Myth or Reality?', in *New German Studies*, 2, pp. 96–115

Grambow, Jürgen, 1986, 'Fritz Rudolf Fries: Verlegung eines mittleren Reiches', in *Weimarer Beiträge*, 32, pp. 1385–92

Grass, Günter, 1980, 'Kulturelle Arbeit im Ausland. Nationbegriff aus der Kultur', in *Politik und Kultur*, 7, no. 4, pp. 3–12 (Diskussion, pp. 13–43)

Graves, Peter J., 1986, 'Christa Wolf's *Kassandra*: The Censoring of the GDR edition', in *The Modern Language Review*, 81, pp. 944–56

Gruhn, Werner, 1986, 'Reaktionen der DDR auf Tschernobyl. Strahlenschutzmaßnahmen und Sicherheit der DDR-Atomkraftwerke', in *Deutschland Archiv*, 19, pp. 676–8

Grunenberg, Antonia, 1986, 'Nichts ist mehr gültig. Der sozialistische Realismus ist out – alles ist erlaubt', in *Die Zeit*, 4.4.1986, p. 48

Haase, Horst, 1967, 'Was kann Lyrik leisten? Aktuelle Probleme der Lyrik in der DDR', in *Neue deutsche Literatur*, 15, no. 5, pp. 25–39

——, 1969, 'Nachdenken über ein Buch', in *Neue deutsche Literatur*, 17, no. 4, pp. 174–85

——, 1986, 'Zur Spezifik der Literatur der Deutschen Demokratischen Republik', in *Weimarer Beiträge*, 32, pp. 671–5

——, et al., 1984, 'DDR-Literaturentwicklung in der Diskussion', in *Weimarer Beiträge*, 30, pp. 1589–616

Hager, Kurt, 1985, 'Tradition und Fortschritt', in *Sinn und Form*, 37, pp. 437–56

——, 1986, 'Probleme der Kulturpolitik vor dem XI. Parteitag der SED', in *Neue deutsche Literatur*, 34, no. 1, pp. 5–27

——, 1987, 'Kurt Hager beantwortete Fragen der Illustrierten "stern"', in *Deutschland Archiv*, 20, pp. 655–60

Hamburger, Käte, 1951, 'Zum Strukturproblem der epischen und dramatischen Dichtung', in *Deutsche Vierteljahreschrift zur Literaturwissenschaft und Geistesgeschichte*, 25, pp. 1–26

Handke, Peter, 1969, *Prosa Gedichte Theaterstücke Hörspiel Aufsätze*, Frankfurt a.M.: Suhrkamp

Hardy, Beverley Grace, 1988, 'Appropriation and Affinity. The Legacy of the Romantic and Non-Classical Writers of the Period around 1800 in GDR Literature with particular reference to Christa Wolf', unpublished thesis, University of Lancaster

Harich, Wolfgang, 1973, 'Der entlaufene Dingo, das vergessene Floß. Aus Anlaß der "Macbeth"-Bearbeitung von Heiner Müller', in *Sinn und Form*, 25, pp. 189–218

——, 1987, '"Revision der marxistischen Nietzsche-Bildes?"', in *Sinn und Form*, 39, pp. 1018–53

Hartmann, Karl-Heinz, 1977, 'Das dritte Reich in der DDR-Literatur. Stationen erzählter Vergangenheit', in *Gegenwartsliteratur und Drittes Reich. Deutsche Autoren in der Auseinandersetzung mit der Vergangenheit*, ed. by Hans Wagener, Stuttgart: Reclam, pp. 307–28

Heidtmann, Horst, 1981, 'Nachwort. Science Fiction in der DDR', in *Von*

Bibliography

einem anderen Stern. Science-Fiction-Geschichten aus der DDR, ed. by Horst Heidtmann, Munich: DTV
Hein, Christoph, 1987, *Öffentlich arbeiten. Essais und Gespräche*, Berlin: Aufbau Verlag
Hermlin, Stephan, 1983, *Äußerungen 1944–1982*, Berlin: Aufbau Verlag
Heym, Stefan, 1983, 'Die Wunde der Teilung eitert weiter', in *Der Spiegel*, 7.11.1983, pp. 58–72
Hinck, Walter, 1981, *Haben wir heute vier deutsche Literaturen oder eine? Plädoyer in einer Streitfrage*, Opladen: Westdeutscher Verlag
Hirdina, Karin, 1982, 'Parodien ohne Komik', in *Sinn und Form*, 34, pp. 907–10
Hohendahl, Peter Uwe and Patricia Herminghouse, eds., 1976, *Literatur und Literaturtheorie in der DDR*, Frankfurt a.M.: Suhrkamp
——, 1983, *Literatur der DDR in den siebziger Jahren*, Frankfurt a.M: Suhrkamp
Holtzhauer, Helmut, 1973, 'Von Sieben, die auszogen, die Klassik zu erlegen', in *Sinn und Form*, 25, pp. 169–88
Hoogeven, Jos and Gerd Labroisse, eds., 1981, *DDR-Roman und Literaturgesellschaft*, Amsterdam: Rodopi
Höpcke, Klaus, 1984a, '"1984"? – 1984!', in *Einheit*, 39, pp. 102–4
——, 1984b, 'Sicht auf Swantow – Überzeugendes und Bezweifelbares', in *Sinn und Form*, 36, pp. 165–77
——, 1984c, 'Tatkräftiges Handeln für den Sozialismus bewirken', in *Neues Deutschland*, 13.6.1984, p. 4
Hutchinson, Peter, 1977, *Literary Presentations of Divided Germany. The development of a central theme in East German fiction 1945–1970*, Cambridge: CUP
Huyssen, Andreas, 1975, 'Auf den Spuren Ernst Blochs. Nachdenken über Christa Wolf', in *Basis*, 5, pp. 100–17
Jachimczak, Krzysztof, 1988, 'Gespräch mit Christoph Hein', in *Sinn und Form*, 40, pp. 342–59
Jäger, Manfred, 1984, 'Wieder gefragt: Der positive Held. Höpckes Griff in die Mottenkiste der 50er Jahre', in *Deutschland Archiv*, 17, pp. 794–6
Joho, Wolfgang, 1965, 'Wir begannen nicht im Jahre Null', in *Neue deutsche Literatur*, 13, no. 5, pp. 5–11
—— et al., 1979, 'Möglichkeiten des Historischen', in *Neue deutsche Literatur*, 27, no. 11, pp. 73–80
Kändler, Klaus, 1981, 'Uwe Saeger: Nöhr', in *Weimarer Beiträge*, 27, no. 9, pp. 155–65
——, 1984, 'Vom Schreiben und dem Schreibenden. Der Schriftsteller als literarische Gestalt in Prosawerken der DDR-Literatur der siebziger Jahre', in *Weimarer Beiträge*, 30, pp. 575–92
Kant, Hermann, 1981, *Zu den Unterlagen. Publizistik 1957–1980*, Berlin: Aufbau Verlag
Kaufmann, Eva, 1986, 'Für und wider das Dokumentarische in der DDR-Literatur', in *Weimarer Beiträge*, 32, pp. 684–9

Bibliography

Kaufmann, Eva and Hans, 1976, *Erwartung und Angebot*. *Studien zum gegenwärtigen Verhältnis von Literatur und Gesellschaft*, Berlin: Akademie-Verlag

Kaufmann, Hans, 1973, 'Zehn Anmerkungen über das Erbe, die Kunst und die Kunst des Erbens', in *Weimarer Beiträge*, 19, pp. 34–53

——, 1980, *Versuch über das Erbe*, Leipzig: Reclam

——, 1981, 'Veränderte Literaturlandschaft', in *Weimarer Beiträge*, 27, no. 3, pp. 27–53

Keisch, Henryk, 1981, 'Geschichte auf dem Theater', in *Neue deutsche Literatur*, 29, no. 6, pp. 93–4

Kersten, Heinz, 1981, 'Nackedeis in "wilden Betten". Das Filmjahr 1981 in der DDR', in *Deutschland Archiv*, 15, pp. 232–4

Klein, Eduard, et al., 1973, 'Der neue Werther. Ein Gespräch', in *Neue deutsche Literatur*, 21, no. 3, pp. 139–49

Kleinschmid, Herald, 1978, 'Zweierlei Realität. Zur Absetzung des Stücks "Die Flüsterparty" in der DDR', in *Deutschland Archiv*, 11, pp. 1245–7

——, 1979a, '"Ein Weg ohne Ende". Zur Reaktion der DDR auf "Holocaust"', in *Deutschland Archiv*, 12, pp. 225–8

——, 1979b, '"Die Rache des kleinen Mannes". Zur kulturpolitischen Situation in der DDR im ersten Halbjahr 1979', in *Deutschland Archiv*, 12, pp. 673–83

——, 1979c, '"Das große Schweigen". Zur kulturpolitischen Situation in der DDR nach dem Ausschluß von neuen Schriftstellern', in *Deutschland Archiv*, 12, pp. 899–905

——, 1985a, 'Tapferkeit und Vorsicht. Unklarheiten in der Kulturpolitik der DDR', in *Deutschland Archiv*, 18, pp. 117–19

——, 1985b, '"Das Privileg ist asozial". Zu Volker Brauns Hinze-Kunze-Roman', in *Deutschland Archiv*, 18, pp. 1258–62

Kluge, Gerhard, 1978, 'Plenzdorfs neuer Werther – Ein Schelm?', in *Amsterdamer Beiträge zur neueren Germanistik*, 7, pp. 165–206

Klussmann, Paul Gerhard and Heinrich Mohr (eds.), 1982, *Deutsche Misere einst und jetzt. Die deutsche Misere als Thema der Gegenwartsliteratur. Das Preußentum in der Literatur der DDR*, Bonn: Bouvier

Knabe, Hubertus, 1983, '"Der Mensch mordet sich selbst". Ökologiekritik in der erzählenden DDR-Literatur', in *Deutschland Archiv*, 16, pp. 954–73

Koerner, Charlotte W., 1979, 'Volker Brauns Unvollendete Geschichte. Erinnerung an Büchners "Lenz"', in *Basis*, 9, pp. 149–168

Krenzlin, Norbert, 1984, '"Die Ästhetik des Widerstands" von Peter Weiss – eine Herausforderung der marxistischen Kritik', in *Weimarer Beiträge*, 30, no. 3, pp. 424–37

Kreuzer, Helmut, 1975, *Veränderungen des Literaturbegriffs. Fünf Beiträge zu aktuellen Problemen der Literaturwissenschaft*, Göttingen: Vandenhoeck & Ruprecht

——, 1978, 'Zur Literatur der siebziger Jahre in der Bundesrepublik', in *Basis*, 8, pp. 7–32

Kuczynski, Jürgen, 1979, 'Replik auf eine Kritik', in *Weimarer Beiträge*, 25,

Bibliography

no. 10, pp. 182–3
——, 1980, 'Jürgen Kuczynski an Hermann Kant', in *Neue deutsche Literatur*, 28, no. 10, pp. 156–65
——, 1983, *Dialog mit meinem Urenkel. Neunzehn Briefe und ein Tagebuch*, Berlin: Aufbau Verlag
Kunert, Günter, 1972, 'Manche, einige, gewisse und sogenannte', in *Sinn und Form*, 24, pp. 1099–104
——, 1975, 'Pamphlet für K.', in *Sinn und Form*, 27, pp. 1091–7
Kunert, Günter and Wilhelm Girnus, 1979, 'Anläßlich Ritsos. Ein Briefwechsel zwischen Günter Kunert und Wilhelm Girnus', in *Sinn und Form*, 31, pp. 850–64
Labroisse, Gerd, 1975, 'Überlegungen zur Interpretationsproblematik von DDR-Literatur an Hand von Plenzdorfs *Die neuen Leiden des jungen W.*', in *Amsterdamer Beiträge zur neueren Germanistik*, 4, pp. 157–81
Langermann, Martina and Detlef, 1986, 'Greifswalder Kolloquium zur historischen Belletristik', in *Weimarer Beiträge*, 32, pp. 1393–6
Lerchner, Gottfried, 1974, 'Zur Spezifik der Gebrauchsweise der deutschen Sprache in der DDR und ihrer gesellschaftlichen Determinanten', in *Deutsch als Fremdsprache*, 11, pp. 259–65
Linzer, Martin, 1980, 'Spur zwischen gestern und morgen. "Der Bau" von Heiner Müller an der Volksbühne uraufgeführt', in *Theater der Zeit*, 34, no. 11, pp. 9–12
Loest, Erich, 1984, *Der vierte Zensor. Vom Entstehen und Sterben eines Romans in der DDR*, Cologne: Verlag Wissenschaft und Politik
Löffler, Anneliese, 1985, 'Wenn Inhalt und Form zur Farce gerinnen. Zu Volker Brauns "Hinze-Kunze-Roman"', in *Neues Deutschland*, 9.10.1985, p. 4
Löffler, Sigrid, 1983, 'Eine anmutige Spinnerin', in *Die Zeit*, 10.6.1983, p. 59
Lukács, Georg, 1971, *Probleme des Realismus I* (Werke, vol. 4), Neuwied: Luchterhand
——, 1965, *Probleme des Realismus III* (Werke, vol. 6), Neuwied: Luchterhand
Mallinckrodt, Anita, 1986/87, 'Environmental dialogue in the GDR. The literary challenge to the sanctity of "progress"', in *GDR Monitor*, no. 16, pp. 1–26
Markgraf, Nikolaus, 1975, 'Die Feministin der DDR', in *Frankfurter Rundschau*, 24.5.1975
Marx, Karl and Friedrich Engels, 1956ff, *Werke*, ed. by Institut für Marxismus-Leninismus beim ZK der SED, Berlin: Dietz
Melchert, Rulo, 1977, 'Ein deutscher Bildungsroman', in *Sinn und Form*, 29, pp. 880–92
Mertz, Peter, 1985, *Und das wurde nicht ihr Staat. Erfahrungen emigrierter Schriftsteller mit Westdeutschland*, Munich: Beck
Michel, Karl Markus, 1968, 'Ein Kranz für die Literatur. Fünf Variationen über eine These', in *Kursbuch*, no. 15, pp. 169–86

Bibliography

Mittenzwei, Ingrid, 1980, *Friedrich II. von Preußen, Eine Biographie*, Berlin: Verlag der Wissenschaften

Mittenzwei, Werner, 1973, 'Brecht und die Probleme der deutschen Klassik', in *Sinn und Form*, 25, pp. 135–68

Mohr, Heinrich, 1983, 'Der Aufstand vom 17. Juni 1953 als Thema belletristischer Literatur aus dem letzten Jahrzehnt', in *Deutschland Archiv*, 16, pp. 478–97

Möhrmann, Renate, 1981, 'Feministische Trends in der deutschen Gegenwartsliteratur', in *Deutsche Gegenwartsliteratur. Ausgangspunkte und aktuelle Entwicklungen*, ed. by Manfred Durzak, Stuttgart: Reclam, pp. 336–58

Müller, Peter, 1969, *Zeitkritik und Utopie in Goethes 'Werther'*, Berlin: Rütten & Loening

Müller-Waldeck, Gunnar, 1984, 'Joachim Walther: Bewerbung bei Hofe', in *Weimarer Beiträge*, 30, no. 2, pp. 319–24

Münz-Koenen, Inge, ed., 1987, *Werke und Wirkungen. DDR-Literatur in der Diskussion*, Leipzig: Reclam

Parkes, K. Stuart, 1986, *Writers and Politics in West Germany*, London: Croom Helm

Pepperle, Heinz, 1986, 'Revision des marxistischen Nietzsche-Bildes', in *Sinn und Form*, 38, pp. 934–69

Pestalozzi, Karl, ed., 1986, *Vier deutsche Literaturen? Literatur seit 1945 – nur die alten Modelle? Medium Film – das Ende der Literatur?*, Tübingen: Niemeyer

Pikulik, Lothar, 1988, 'Mythos und "New Age" bei Peter Handke und Botho Strauß', in *Wirkendes Wort*, 38, pp. 235–52

Pracht, Erwin, ed., 1975, *Einführung in den sozialistischen Realismus*, Berlin: Dietz

Pulver, Elsbeth, 1983, 'Der Zorn gegen Achill. Zu Christa Wolfs "Kassandra" und den Frankfurter Vorlesungen "Voraussetzungen einer Erzählung"', in *Schweizer Monatshefte*, 63, pp. 750–5

Raddatz, Fritz J., 1972, *Traditionen und Tendenzen. Materialien zur Literatur der DDR*, Frankfurt a.M.: Suhrkamp

——, 1979, 'Der gesellschaftliche und politische Rahmen deutscher Literatur heute', in *Politik und Kultur*, 6, no. 1, pp. 3–28

——, 1980a, 'Neue Möglichkeiten, "sich zu leben"', in *Die Zeit*, 15.8.1980, p. 33

——, 1980b, 'Gedanken zur Nationalliteratur', in *Politik und Kultur*, 7, no. 5, pp. 48–53

——, 1984, 'Die Aufklärung entläßt ihre Kinder', in *Die Zeit*, 29.6.1984 and 6.7.1984

——, 1986, 'Abschied von der Ratio – Stigma der jüngsten literarischen Entwicklung in Ost und West', in *Politik und Kultur*, 13, no. 2, pp. 3–19

——, 1988a, 'Die Dritte deutsche Literatur', in *Politik und Kultur*, 15, no. 2, pp. 3–18

——, 1988b, 'Ein Ball des falschen Glücks', in *Die Zeit*, 12.8.1988, p. 35

Bibliography

Reich-Ranicki, Marcel, 1979, *Entgegnung. Zur deutschen Literatur der siebziger Jahre*, Stuttgart: DVA

Reid, J.H., 1983/84, 'Gerd Bieker's *Sternschnuppenwünsche* – A forerunner of *Die neuen Leiden des jungen W.*?', in *German Life and Letters*, 37, pp. 135–49

——, 1984a, 'Dürrenmatt in the GDR. The Dramatist's reception up to 1980', in *The Modern Language Review*, 79, pp. 356–71

——, 1984b, 'En route to Utopia: some visions of the future in East German literature', in *Renaissance and Modern Studies*, 28, pp. 114–28

——, 1985a, 'Another turn in the road: Kafka in the GDR', in *GDR Monitor*, no. 13, pp. 21–38

——, 1985b, 'Woman, Myth and Magic: On Christa Wolf's *Kassandra* and Irmtraud Morgner's *Amanda*', in *Honecker's Germany*, ed. by David Childs, London: Allen & Unwin, pp. 97–117

——, 1990, 'The Recent Historical Novel in the GDR', in *Literature on the Threshold: The German Novel in the 1980s*, ed. by Arthur Williams, Stuart Parkes and Roland Smith, Oxford: Berg, pp. 61–75

Reinhold, Ursula, 1982, *Tendenzen und Autoren. Zur Literatur der siebziger Jahre in der BRD*, Berlin: Dietz

Rimmon-Kenan, Shlomith, 1983, *Narrative Fiction. Contemporary Poetics*, London: Methuen

Ross, Werner, 1982, 'Ernst und Ethos. Zur Sonderstellung der DDR-Literatur im deutschen Sprach- und Kulturraum', in *Die politische Meinung*, 26, no. 204, pp. 64–75

Roßmann, Andreas, 1986, 'Kein leichtes Spiel: DDR-Dramatik im Westen', in *Deutschland Archiv*, 19, pp. 1255–9

Rüß, Gisela, ed., 1976, *Dokumente zur Kunst-, Literatur- und Kulturpolitik der SED 1971–1974*, Stuttgart: Seewald

Sakowski, Helmut, 1981, 'Von Sachsenkaisern, Robotern und dem Sinn für Realitäten', in *Neue deutsche Literatur*, 29, no. 7, pp. 5–15

Sandford, John, 1984/85, 'Alternative Approaches to the German Question', in *German Life and Letters*, 38, pp. 427–41

Schachtsiek-Freitag, Norbert, 1982, 'Fortsetzung der Jette-Geschichten: Julia, Aussteigerin', in *Deutschland Archiv*, 15, pp. 188–9

Schäfer, Hans Dieter, 1977, 'Zur Periodisierung der deutschen Literatur seit 1930', in *Literaturmagazin*, 7, pp. 95–115

Schelsky, Helmut, 1975, *Die Arbeit tun die anderen. Klassenkampf und Priesterherrschaft der Intellektuellen*, Opladen: Westdeutscher Verlag

Schlenstedt, Dieter, 1979, *Wirkungsästhetische Analysen. Poetologie und Prosa in der neueren DDR-Literatur*, Berlin: Akademie-Verlag

Schmitt, Hans-Jürgen, ed., 1973, *Die Expressionismusdebatte. Materialien zu einer marxistischen Realismuskonzeption*, Frankfurt a.M.: Suhrkamp

Schmitt, Hans-Jürgen and Godehard Schramm, eds., 1974, *Sozialistische Realismuskonzeptionen. Dokumente zum 1. Allunionskongreß der Sowjetschriftsteller*, Frankfurt a.M.: Suhrkamp

Schneider, Peter, 1984, *Der Mauerspringer. Erzählung*, Darmstadt: Luchter-

hand
Schriftstellerverband, ed., 1988, *X. Schriftstellerkongreß der Deutschen Demokratischen Republik: 24.–26. November 1987*, 2 vols., Berlin: Aufbau Verlag
Schubbe, Elimar, ed., 1972, *Dokumente zur Kunst-, Literatur- und Kulturpolitik der SED*, Stuttgart: Seewald
Schuhmann, Klaus, 1980, 'Weite und Vielfalt der Wirklichkeitsdarstellung in der DDR-Literatur. Zu einigen Aspekten des Wirklichkeitsverhältnisses von DDR-Schriftstellern', in *Weimarer Beiträge*, 26, no. 7, pp. 5–23
Seufert, Heinrich, ed., 1955, *Abriß der deutschen Literaturgeschichte in Tabellen*, Bonn: Athenäum Verlag
Shaw, Gisela, 1985, 'The Striving of Man: Observations on Volker Braun's *Das ungezwungene Leben Kasts* in the light of Goethe's *Faust*', in *GDR Monitor*, no. 13, pp. 5–20
——, 1986/87, 'Die Landschaftsmetapher bei Volker Braun', in *GDR Monitor*, no. 16, pp. 105–40
Simon, Erik and Olaf R. Spittel, 1982, *Science-fiction. Personalia zu einem Genre in der DDR*, Berlin: Verlag Das neue Berlin
Smith, Colin E., 1987, *Tradition Art and Society. Christa Wolf's Prose*, Essen: Verlag Die Blaue Eule
Sontheimer, Kurt and Wilhelm Bleek, 1972, *Die DDR. Politik, Gesellschaft, Wirtschaft*, Hamburg: Hoffmann und Campe
Staadt, Jochen, 1977, *Konfliktbewußtsein und sozialistischer Anspruch in der DDR-Literatur. Zur Darstellung gesellschaftlicher Widersprüche nach dem VIII. Parteitag der SED 1971*, West Berlin: Spiess
Steiner, Gerhard, ed., 1970, *Fremdsprachige Schriftsteller*, Leipzig: Bibliographisches Institut
Stephan, Alexander, 1979/80, 'The Emancipation of Man. Christa Wolf as a Woman Writer', in *GDR Monitor*, no. 2, pp. 23–31
——, 1980, '"How Did We Become As We Are?" The Treatment of Fascism in GDR Literature', in *GDR Monitor*, no. 3, pp. 5–16
Strauß, Botho, 1981, *Paare, Passanten*, Munich: Hanser
Tate, Dennis, 1984, *The East German Novel. Identity, Community, Continuity*, Bath University Press
Teraoka, Arlene Akiko, 1985, *The Silence of Entropy or Universal Discourse. The Postmodernist Poetics of Heiner Müller*, Berne: Lang
Thomas, Rüdiger, 1973, *Modell DDR. Die kalkulierte Emanzipation*, 3rd edn, Munich: Hanser
Twisk, Russell, 1988, 'Circus of Many Tongues', in *The Guardian*, 5.9.1988, p. 21
Volkmer, Werner, 1984, 'Political Culture and the Nation in the GDR', in *GDR Monitor*, no. 11, pp. 12–23
Wagenbach, Klaus, ed., 1979a, *Vaterland, Muttersprache. Deutsche Schriftsteller und ihr Staat von 1945 bis heute*, West Berlin: Wagenbach
Wagenbach, Klaus, 1979b, 'Wo sind wir zuhause? Gespräch mit Stephan Hermlin', in *Freibeuter*, no. 1, pp. 47–55

Bibliography

Wallace, Ian, ed., 1984a, *The Writer and Society in the GDR*, Tayport: Hutton Press
——, ed., 1984b, *The GDR in the 1980s*, Dundee: GDR Monitor
Walser, Martin, 1979, *Wer ist ein Schriftsteller? Aufsätze und Reden*, Frankfurt a.M.: Suhrkamp
——, 1988, 'Über Deutschland reden', in *Die Zeit*, 4.11.1988, pp. 65–7
Walther, Joachim, 1973, *Meinetwegen Schmetterlinge. Gespräche mit Schriftstellern*, Berlin: Buchverlag Der Morgen
Watson, Martin Norman, 1987, *The Literary Presentation of 'Youth' in GDR Fiction: 1971–1980*, Stuttgart: Heinz
Watt, Ian, 1957, *The Rise of the Novel. Studies in Defoe, Richardson and Fielding*, London: Chatto & Windus
Weber, Hermann, 1985, *Geschichte der DDR*, Munich: DTV
——, ed., 1986, *DDR. Dokumente zur Geschichte der Deutschen Demokratischen Republik 1945–1985*, Munich: DTV
Weidenfeld, Werner, ed., 1983, *Die Identität der Deutschen*, Munich: Hanser
Weigand, Hermann J., 1933, *Thomas Mann's Novel Der Zauberberg. A Study*, New York and London: Appleton-Century
Weisbrod, Peter, 1980, *Literarischer Wandel in der DDR. Untersuchungen zur Entwicklung der Erzählliteratur in den siebziger Jahren*, Heidelberg: Groos
Williams, Ingrid K.J., ed., 1987, *GDR: Individual and Society. Conference Proceedings of the International Conference on the GDR held at Ealing College of Higher Education, September 1987*, London: Ealing College of Higher Education
Winter, Roger, 1974, 'The Study of East and West German', in *New German Studies*, 2, pp. 82–95
Wolf, Christa, 1983, 'Zur Information. Siehe Wilhelm Girnus: Wer baute das siebentorige Theben?', in *Sinn und Form*, 35, pp. 863–6
——, 1987, *Die Dimension des Autors. Essays und Aufsätze Reden und Gespräche 1959–1985*, Darmstadt: Luchterhand
Zimmermann, Hartmut, ed., 1985, *DDR Handbuch*, 3rd edn, Cologne: Verlag Wissenschaft und Politik

Index

abortion, 95, 104, 108, 109
Abs, H., 19
Abuladze, T., *Repentance*, 126
Abusch, A., 136, 220
Ackermann, A., 33
Adenauer, K., 25
Adorno, T.W., 3, 4, 34, 92, 106
Afghanistan, 13, 49
Agence France Presse, 45
Aitmatov, C., 11
Andersch, A., *Sansibar*, 172
Anderson, E., *Blitz aus heiterm Himmel*, 85, 109
androgyny, 110, 194
Apitz, B., *Nackt unter Wölfen*, 3, 145
Arabian Nights, 80
Arendt, E., 45
Aristotle, 202
arms race, 13, 26, 49, 51, 195, 198, 203, 208, 218
Armstrong, N., 25
Arnim, B.v., 188
art for art's sake, 62
artist, 61, 77, 80, 81, 109
Auer, A., 106, 132
Aufbau Verlag, 82, 92
'Aufbauliteratur', 3, 95, 199
August the Strong, 184, 185
Auschwitz, 87, 141, 144, 145, 218
Austria, 7, 8, 9, 10, 12, 13, 15, 50, 55, 75
autobiography, 84, 86
avant-garde, 3, 54, 55, 66, 78, 79, 83, 88, 92
Axen, H., 19

Bachmann, I., 202
Bachofen, J.J., 203
Bahro, R., *Die Alternative*, 47
Baier, L., 15
Balzac, H. de, 65, 66
Bartsch, K., 48, 50
Basic Treaty, 1, 5, 37

Batt, K., 63, 64
Baum, W., 131
Baumgart, R., 202
Bayle, P., 189
Beatles, 98, 115
Beaumarchais, P.A.C. de, *Le mariage de Figaro*, 123
Becher, J.R., 31, 33, 40, 67, 103, 162, 192, 220
Bemühungen, 152
'Selbstzensur', 152
Becker, J., 8, 18, 45, 50, 53, 55
Aller Welt Freund, 18
Bronsteins Kinder, 18, 146
Der Boxer, 72, 146–8, 160, 179
Irreführung der Behörden, 71, 77, 131–2, 165–7
Jakob der Lügner, 144–6, 150
Schlaflose Tage, 46, 47
Beckett, S., 88
Krapps' Last Tape, 54
Waiting for Godot, 54
Behlert, K., 51
Benjamin, W., 3
Benn, G., 3, 54
Bennett, A., 66
Berlin Wall, 9, 19, 20, 22, 24, 36, 75, 157, 165, 169
Berliner Ensemble, 31
Bernhard, H.J., 175
Bernhard, T., 9
Bernhardt, R., 64
Berührung ist nur eine Randerscheinung, 88, 92, 121
Besser, J.v., 75–6, 184–7, 189
'Betriebsroman', 97, 98
Bible, 177, 214
Bieker, G., *Sternschnuppenwünsche*, 42
Bieler, M., 58
Der Bär, 17
Der Mädchenkrieg, 17
Biermann, W., 10, 17, 36, 37, 43–6, 47, 48, 49, 50, 58, 140, 194, 198

Index

biogenetics, 207
biography, 178, 179, 191
Bismarck, O.v., 8, 9, 177, 196
Bitterfeld Conferences, 35, 36, 56, 80, 87, 89, 97, 163
Bloch, E., 34, 211, 212, 215
  Das Prinzip Hoffnung, 211
Bobrowski, J.
  'Boehlendorff', 192
  Levins Mühle, 71
Boehlendorff, C.U., 193
Böhme, J., 213
Böll, H., 1, 66, 133, 166–7, 202, 224
  Ansichten eines Clowns, 182
  Billard um halbzehn, 133, 172
  Das Brot der frühen Jahre, 99, 133
  Gruppenbild mit Dame, 139
  Haus ohne Hüter, 172
  Wo warst du, Adam?, 130–1
Born, N., 12
Bozenhard, M., 51
Braine, J., *Room at the Top*, 99
Brandt, W., 5, 13, 36, 44
Brasch, T., 50, 53
  Mercedes, 55
Braun, V., 9, 10, 11, 37, 38, 45, 50, 53, 82, 83, 121, 177, 190, 205
  'Berlinische Epigramme', 1, 29, 94, 174
  Das ungezwungene Leben Kasts, 42, 84, 167–8
  Die Kipper, 29, 42
  Die Übergangsgesellschaft, 58
  'Fragen eines regierenden Arbeiters', 121
  Großer Frieden, 174, 180, 193
  Hans Faust, 168
  Hinze-Kunze-Roman, 74, 83–4, 91, 122–3, 177, 214, 222–3
  Training des aufrechten Gangs, 121–2
  Unvollendete Geschichte, 21–2, 42–3, 46, 55, 64, 84, 113–14, 116, 119–21, 125, 155, 205
  Wir und nicht sie, 121
Bräunig, W., 'Rummelplatz', 56, 101
'Der schöne Monat August', 112
Brecht, B., 2, 3, 10, 13, 14, 25, 29, 31, 34, 38, 62, 64, 66, 78, 79, 82, 83, 103, 124, 141, 161, 219
  Buckower Elegien, 2, 159
  Coriolan, 167–8
  Der gute Mensch von Sezuan, 64
  Der Hofmeister, 155
  Der kaukasische Kreidekreis, 2

'Fragen eines lesenden Arbeiters', 121, 187, 188
Herr Puntila und sein Knecht Matti, 122–3
Leben des Galilei, 193
Mutter Courage und ihre Kinder, 215
'Wahrnehmung', 95
'Zukunftslied', 199
Bredel, W., 87
Bredow, W.v., 176, 195
Brentano, C., 83
Brentano, H.v., 2
Březan, J., 7, 207
  Krabat, 86, 188, 207, 209, 214, 215
Broch, H., 54
Brüning, E., 103
Buchenwald, 98, 140, 145
Büchner, G., 190
  Lenz, 120, 190
Buckwitz, H., 2
Bukharin, N.I., 151
Bürger, G.A., 190
Burmeister, B., *Anders* 89–92, 95, 224

Camus, A., *L'Etranger*, 124
Carnegie, A., 94
Castein, H., 84
censorship, 17, 32, 41, 42, 48, 49, 51, 52, 56, 58, 75, 82, 83, 84, 96, 117, 152, 153, 154, 166, 175, 183, 184, 186, 201, 218, 219
Chernobyl, 207–8
children's literature, 11
Chile, 136, 220
church, 160–1, 187
Cibulka, H., *Swantow*, 205–6
cinema, 31, 41, 55
class, 104, 110, 120, 122, 141, 177, 211
  conflict, 61, 66, 102, 106, 107, 112, 114, 188, 191, 216
  intelligentsia, 8, 35, 39, 81, 98, 102, 109, 155, 158, 182, 183, 185, 186, 191, 194, 219
  managerial, 36, 97, 113
  middle, 7, 34, 35, 40, 95, 99, 100, 101, 102, 117, 118, 140, 158, 171, 185, 187, 188, 220
  working, 3, 34, 35, 36, 38, 61, 74, 78, 81, 102, 109, 112, 113, 114, 115, 121, 123, 140, 158, 159, 185
classicism, 14, 34, 67, 190, 212
Claudius, E., 3
  Menschen an unsrer Seite, 97
  Vom schweren Anfang, 90

Index

Cold War, 2, 3, 7, 13, 32, 44, 141, 216
collectivisation of agriculture, 32, 157
concrete poetry, 80
Conference on European Security and Cooperation, 44
conflicts, antagonistic, 94, 140
constitution, 6, 7, 44
Crick, J., 140
critical socialist realism, 95
Cuba, 158
cultural heritage, 13, 14, 31, 34, 35, 37, 38, 39, 40, 41, 54, 55, 128, 129
cultural policies, ix, 29–59, 74, 162, 165
Czechoslovakia, 15, 36, 42, 43, 57, 96, 139, 167–8, 169
Czechowski, H., 38

Dada, 89
Dahne, G., *Hans Greifer*, 83
Damm, S., *Vögel, die verkünden Land*, 179, 190, 191–2
Dante Alighieri, 73
de Bruyn, G., 35, 45, 50, 73, 77, 112, 190
 Buridans Essel, 35, 111, 164
 Der Hohlweg, 35
 Märkische Forschungen, 46, 153
 Neue Herrlichkeit, 50, 51, 96, 177
 Preisverleihung, 77, 94, 111, 164–5
death, 100, 101, 113, 163, 187
decadence, 32, 54, 67, 78, 98, 111, 220
deconstruction, 90
DEFA, 31, 41
Defoe, D., *Robinson Crusoe*, 40
Deichfuß, H., *Windmacher*, 118
Deicke, G., 58
Deighton, L., 19
denazification, 31, 32
'deutsche Misere', 176, 183, 190, 191
dialogism, 63, 64, 71, 126
Dickens, C., 96
 David Copperfield, 141
Diderot, D., *Jacques le Fataliste*, 122, 177
division of Germany, 2–26, 44, 63, 95, 120, 157, 165, 203, 219
Döblin, A., 31, 78, 83
documentary literature, 4, 52, 66, 79, 84, 86, 87, 96, 137, 138, 183
Domagk, G., 25
Dorman, M., 44
Dos Passos, J., 34
Duncker, H., 151
Dürrenmatt, F., *Die Physiker*, 57, 207

dystopias, 215, 219, 220

Ebersbach, V., *Caroline*, 179
Eckart, G., 51
 So sehe ick die Sache, 51
Edel, P., *Wenn es ans Leben geht*, 144
Egypt, 136
Eichmann, A., 144
Eifler, M., 22
Einstein, A., 25, 26, 83
Eisler, H., *Johann Faustus*, 55
Emerich, F., 193
emigration, 2, 8, 10, 14, 16, 18, 21, 24, 31, 34, 45, 49, 50, 55, 88, 103, 104, 106, 119, 125, 129, 153, 157, 160, 165, 171, 187, 199, 211
Emmerich, W., 63–4, 71, 89, 171, 181, 211
Endler, A., 37–8, 39, 48
Engelberg, E., 177
Engelmann, B., 52
Engels, F., 34, 203
 Origin of the Family, 106–7
England, 185
enlightenment, 11, 86, 214, 215, 224
environmental issues, 12, 22, 148, 198, 200, 204–10, 212, 213, 217, 218
Enzensberger, H.M., 4, 66
Erhard, L., 187
erotic, 55, 81, 104, 111, 174, 185
eurocommunism, 44
existentialism, 16, 22, 96, 99, 101, 107, 108, 112, 113, 117, 124, 162, 163, 164, 187, 213

fairy-tale, *see* folk-tale
Family Laws, 105
fantasy, 21, 52, 61, 66, 80, 82, 84–6, 110, 215–16, 217
fascism, *see* National Socialism
Faulkner, W., 136
Fehervary, H., 192
feminism, 21, 22, 25, 80, 82, 87, 103–10, 123, 201–4, 208, 213
 see also women
Feuchtwanger, L., 174, 179–80, 186, 190
 Jud Süß, 179
Feyl, R., *Idylle mit Professor*, 188–9
Fichte, H., 110
film, 65, 77–9, 141, 143
Fischborn, G., 174
Flaubert, G., *Madame Bovary*, 65, 70
Fogg, D., 44

–249–

Index

folk-tale, 21, 65, 82, 83, 84, 85, 98, 147, 198
Ford, H., 94
formalism, 32, 33, 35, 54, 59, 62, 89, 92, 162
Forum, 37, 40
France, 14, 89, 108
French Revolution 192
Frank, L., 31
Frederick II, Holy Roman Emperor, 73, 180
Frederick II of Prussia, 174, 176, 177, 181, 183, 189, 195, 196, 219
Frederick William I, 181–3, 184, 189
Free German Youth (FDJ), 40, 118, 119, 170
freedom, 12, 14, 36, 37, 40, 43, 44, 45, 58, 88, 222, 224
Freud, S., 106, 125
Freytag, G.
  Bilder aus der deutschen Vergangenheit, 195
  Soll und Haben, 143
Fried, E., 50
Friedrich, H., 3
Fries, F.R.
  'Das nackte Mädchen auf der Straße', 85
  Verlegung eines mittleren Reiches, 218–9, 220
Frisch, M., 9
  Andorra, 148, 172
Fuchs, J., 45, 50
Fühmann, F., 45, 46, 190, 215
  'Anna, genannt die Humpelhexe', 221
  Böhmen am Meer, 18, 72
  'Das Gottesgericht', 213
  'Der Mund des Propheten', 221
  'Drei nackte Männer', 122
  Kameraden, 3, 131, 143, 222
  Saiäns-Fiktschen, 221–4
  Zweiundzwanzig Tage, 80
Fuller, B., 217
future, 198–224

Gagarin, J., 25, 200
Gaiser, G., *Schlußball*, 172
Gaus, G., 15
GDR Monitor, 2
Geissler, E., 207
generations, 14, 42, 116, 118, 119, 134
Gerber, M., 109
Gide, A., 32, 83, 89

Girnus, W., 33, 40, 52, 106, 130, 207, 218
Gladkov, F.W., 79
glasnost', 58, 121, 152, 169
Goethe, J.W., 16, 33, 34, 38, 67, 82, 162, 174, 189, 190, 191, 193, 194, 212
  Die Leiden des jungen Werthers, 39, 40, 65, 107, 120, 175
  Faust, 73, 167, 170, 208
  Torquato Tasso, 194
  Wilhelm Meisters Lehrjahre, 34, 35, 142, 167
Gogol, N., 86
Good, C., 10
Gorbachev, M., ix, 58
Gorky, M., 67
Gottsched, J.C., 188–9
Gottsched, L.A.V., 188–9
  Die Pietisterei im Fischbeinrocke, 189
Grass, G., 1, 8–9, 52
  Die Blechtrommel, 55
  Die Plebejer proben den Aufstand, 16–17, 167
  Die Rättin, 207
Greece, 136
Greene, G., 32
Grillparzer, F., 8
  Der arme Spielmann, 72
Grimmelshausen, H.J.C.v.,
  Simplicissimus, 142
'Gruppe 61', 3, 35
Guillaume, G., 13
Gumilev, N.S., 152
Günderrode, K.v., 177, 188, 190, 193–4
Gundling, J.P., 181, 184, 186, 193
Günther, J.C., 75–6, 184–7, 189, 191, 193
Günther, T., 88, 89

Haase, H., 11, 12, 67, 200, 201
Hacks, P., 38
  Adam und Eva, 12
  Amphitryon, 214
  Ein Gespräch im Hause Stein, 174
  Moritz Tassow, 36, 55
  Pandora, 212
Hager, K., 40, 53, 54, 58, 123
Hahn, O., 25, 209
Handke, P., 9, 50, 66, 214, 215
Hanstein, W.v., 177
Hardy, B., 190, 199
Harich, W., 38, 156, 196

Index

Härtling, P., *Nachgetragene Liebe*, 134
Hartmann, K.-H., 130
Hašek, F., *The Good Soldier Schwejk*, 35
Hauptmann, G., 31
  Die Weber, 31, 159
Hauser, J., *Familie Rechlin*, 19
Havemann, R., 36, 43, 45, 48
Heidtmann, H., 85
Heiduczek, W., 119
  Tod am Meer, 48, 49, 57, 75, 77, 160–4, 166
Hein, C., 14, 15, 50, 58, 73, 95, 123, 128, 129, 199
  Cromwell, 174, 180, 193
  Der fremde Freund (Drachenblut), 23, 71, 100–1, 116, 123–6, 128, 129, 170, 171, 179, 180
  Die wahre Geschichte des Ah Q, 180
  Einladung zum Lever Bourgeois, 123
  Horns Ende, 129, 170–2, 179, 224
  Lassalle, 174, 180
  'Waldbruder Lenz', 191
Heine, H., 161
Hemingway, E., 32
Herminghouse, P., 106
Hermlin, S., 7, 14, 37, 40, 45, 46, 51, 52, 130, 144, 152, 159, 198
  Abendlicht, 46, 152, 172–3
  Scardanelli, 190
Herzfelde, W., 40
Hesiod, 212
Hesse, H., *Steppenwolf*, 99
Heym, S., 6, 14, 29, 42, 45, 46, 47, 48, 49, 52
  Ahasver, 18, 214
  Collin, 17, 46, 47, 48, 154
  Der König David Bericht, 42, 153–5
  5 Tage im Juni (Der Tag X), 17, 18, 36, 43, 159
  Schwarzenberg, 17
Hildesheimer, W., 14
Hilscher, E., *Die Weltzeituhr*, 24–6, 83, 208
Hinck, W., 8, 13, 16
Hirdina, K., 222
Hiroshima, 146, 210
historical novel, 75, 174–96
historical pessimism, 38, 129, 198, 222
historiography, 25, 42, 58, 107, 121, 153, 154, 169, 172, 183, 188, 195, 222, 224
history, 52, 64, 83, 121, 128, 129, 136, 174–80, 185, 187, 188, 198, 213, 215
Hitchcock, A., 77

The Birds, 215˙
Hitler A., ix, 8, 19, 25, 130, 138, 141, 147, 150, 160, 175, 177, 179
Hitler–Stalin pact, 154
Hitler Youth, 131, 132, 138, 169
Hoffman, E.T.A., 35, 83, 86, 190, 213
Hofmannsthal, H.v., 8
Hölderlin, F., 190, 191, 192–3
Hollis, A., 41
Holocaust, 144
Holtz-Baumert, G., *Die pucklige Verwandtschaft*, 86
Holtzhauer, H., 38
Homer, 65
  Odyssey, 204
homosexuality, 56, 110, 111
Honecker, E., ix, 7, 29, 30, 36, 37, 40, 41, 44, 46, 48, 49, 52, 53, 56, 62, 74, 77, 84, 111, 175, 176, 177, 167, 224
Höpcke, K., 7, 53, 58, 205–6, 219–20
Hörnigk, T., 69
Huchel, P., 14, 50, 55
  'Psalm', 201
Huguenots, 175, 182
humour, 145, 154
Hungary, ix, 35, 57, 58, 103, 156, 157, 200
Hutchinson, P., 18, 20
Huxley, A., 221
  Ape and Essence, 220
  Brave New World, 209, 215, 220, 223
Huyssen, A., 211

In diesem besseren Land, 37
individuality, 11, 16, 38, 40, 41, 42, 61, 63, 66, 68, 72, 74, 96, 107, 112, 123, 133, 136, 141, 148, 156, 168, 173, 213, 224
Intershops, 46
intertextuality, 72, 90, 118, 120, 122, 124, 142–3, 159, 167–8, 181, 183, 208
irony, 61, 73, 74, 78, 80, 83, 84, 94, 113, 117, 164, 219, 222, 224
Israel, 136, 146, 147, 148

Jachimczak, K., 172
Jaeck, H.-P., 192
  Kammerherr und König, 183–4, 188
Jakobs, K.-H., 45, 48, 50
  Beschreibung eines Sommers, 205
  Die Interviewer, 75, 77, 79, 99–101, 111, 116, 132
  Wilhelmsburg, 46

–251–

Index

Jean Paul, 35, 73, 190
Jenkinson, D., 194
Jentzsch, B., 50
Jessenin, S.A., 152
Jews, 8, 24, 73, 137, 138, 141, 143, 144–8, 153, 172, 182, 208, 210, 214
Johannis, I., *Das siebente Brennesselhemd*, 86
Johannsen, C., *Leibniz*, 179
John, H., 77
Johnson, U., 50
  Mutmaßungen über Jakob, 18
  Zwei Ansichten, 18
Joho, W., 129, 178
Joyce, J., 32, 34, 83, 88
  Ulysses, 54
Jünger, E., 3

Kafka, F., 32, 54, 86, 88, 191
  'Beim Bau der chinesischen Mauer', 20
  Der Prozeß, 35, 143
  'Die Verwandlung', 166
  'In der Strafkolonie', 224
Kamenjev, L.B., 152
Kändler, K., 129
Kant, H., 13, 45, 46, 48, 50, 52, 54, 94, 161, 196
  Das Impressum, 5, 19, 42, 57, 114–15, 125, 144, 155–7, 159, 199
  Der Aufenthalt, 77, 140–4, 150, 224
  'Der dritte Nagel', 96
  Die Aula, 18, 21, 22, 23, 36, 79, 95, 116, 155, 156, 162, 187
Kant, I., 8, 160
Kaufmann, E., 87
Kaufmann, H., 11, 38, 40, 61, 86, 88
Kaul, F.K., 40
Kayser, W., 3
Keisch, H., 196
Kelle G., 8
  Der grüne Heinrich, 34
Kempowski, W., *Tadellöser & Wolff*, 137
Kersten, P., *Der alltägliche Tod meines Vaters*, 134
Khruschev, N., 151, 156, 157, 158, 169
Kiesinger, K.G., 2, 115
Kirov, S.M., 152
Kirsch, R.
  'Der geschenkte Tag', 85
  'Erste Niederschrift', 85
Kirsch, S., 37, 45, 50, 58, 83, 103
  'Blitz aus heiterm Himmel', 109–10

'Datum', 19
Die Pantherfrau, 86, 87
Zaubersprüche, 46
Kleist, H.v., 35, 77, 190, 193–4
Kluge, G., 117
Kohl, H., 5
Köhler, E., *Der Krott*, 71
Kollontai, A., 82
'Komitee Freies Deutschland', 141
König, J.U.v., 184, 186
Königsberg, 8, 189
Königsdorf, H., 103, 222
  'Meine ungehörigen Träume', 85
  Respektloser Umgang, 76, 86, 209–11
Korean War, 26
Krenz, Egon, ix
Kreuzer, H., 3, 84, 191
Kroetz, F.X., 14, 15
Krupskaya, N., 82
Kuczynski, J., 15, 57, 94, 99, 152, 169
  Dialog mit meinem Urenkel, 151
  Geschichte der Lage der Arbeiter, 151
Kühn, A., 13
Kunert, G., 10, 38, 45, 46, 50, 55, 58, 84, 85, 129, 136, 207, 218
  'Androiden', 217
  'Andromeda zur Unzeit', 217–18
  'Die kleinen grünen Männer', 217
  'Ich und ich', 85
  'Laika', 200–1
  'Lieferung frei Haus', 85
  'Nach der Landung', 217
  'Pamphlet für K.', 190
  'Schlaf', 217
  'Schwimmer', 84
  'Unterwegs nach Utopia II', 198
  'Von Pluto her', 217
Kunze, R., 16, 36, 43, 44, 50, 168
  Brief mit blauem Siegel, 42
  Die wunderbaren Jahre, 43
  'Kuratorium Unteilbares Deutschland', 13
Kursbuch, 66

La Mettrie, J.O. de, 86
La Roche, S., *Das Fräulein von Sternheim*, 70
Labroisse, G., 41
Lambrecht, C., *Männerbekanntschaften*, 87, 110
Lange-Müller, K., 51
language, 2, 8, 9, 10, 11, 40, 61, 63, 68, 69, 88, 117, 118, 119, 136, 139, 144, 154, 203

–252–

Index

Latin America, 13, 79
Lattmann, D., *Die Brüder*, 19
Le Carré, J., 19
Le Corbusier, 101
Leibniz, G.W.v., 181, 185
Lenin, V.I., 7, 82, 121, 153, 162, 176, 212
Lenz, J.M.R., 35, 190, 191-2
  Der Hofmeister, 155, 191
Lerchner, G., 10
Lessing, G. E., 174, 177
  Emilia Galotti, 120
  Minna von Barnhelm, 184
Lewin, W., 103, 180
  Federico, 73, 110, 153, 174, 180, 183, 193, 214
Lichtjahr, Das, 216
Liebmann, I., *Berliner Mietshaus*, 87
Lietz, H.-G., *Das Hexenhaus*, 118
Linzer, M., 55
Locke, J., 181
Loest, E., 48, 50
  Der vierte Zensor, 48-9, 58, 152
  Es geht seinen Gang, 10, 48-9, 74, 95, 114-16, 123, 125, 130, 153, 180
Löffler, A., 122
Lorek, L., 88
Lotze, R.H., 123
Lukács, G., 4, 34, 35, 38, 61, 65, 66, 75, 78, 81, 82, 85, 87, 165, 178, 179, 181, 182, 186, 190, 192, 215
Luther, M., 82, 176, 177, 196

McCarthy, J. 153
McPherson, K. 139
Majakovsky, V.V., 152
Makarenko, A.S., 67
Mandelstam, O.E., 152
Mann, H., 31
Mann, T., 10, 25, 67
  Doktor Faustus, 69
  Tonio Kröger, 70
  'Unordnung und frühes Leid', 118
Marcuse, H., 4
Maron, M., 51
  Flugasche, 206
Marx, K., 4, 16, 34, 44, 45, 82, 162, 173, 176
  Communist Manifesto, 38, 172
  Theses on Feuerbach, 109
Marxism, 4, 22, 26, 33, 34, 36, 77, 104, 128, 130, 141, 153, 175, 185, 198, 205, 211, 213
Meckel, C., *Suchbild*, 134

Mecklenburg, N., 12
media, 15, 42, 47, 87, 96, 119, 121, 163, 168, 208, 218
Meitner, L., 209-10
Melchert, R., 143
Melle, F.-H., 88, 121
Michalke, R., 46-7
Michel, K.M., 4
Mickel, K., 12, 37
militarism, 203
Mitteldeutscher Verlag, 48, 49
Mittenzwei, W., 38
modernism, 3, 4, 32, 34, 63, 64, 66, 70, 73, 75, 90, 149, 193
Möhrmann, R., 107
monologism, 63, 64, 71, 89, 171, 172
Montag, A., *Karl der Große*, 71
montage, 61, 75, 78-82, 83, 192
Montaigne, M. de, 161
Moog, C., 51
Morgner, I., 50, 77, 86, 88, 103, 110, 189, 204, 211, 214
  Amanda, 22, 80, 83, 85, 86, 105, 108-9, 201-2, 204-5, 209, 211, 212, 213, 214
  Gustav der Weltfahrer, 85
  Hochzeit in Konstantinopel, 80, 85, 188
  Rumba auf einen Herbst, 42, 82
  Trobadora Beatriz, 42, 80-3, 100, 103, 104, 105, 106, 108-9, 111, 114, 158, 188, 204, 224
Müller, C., *Männerprotokolle*, 87
Müller, H., 1, 11, 17, 18, 38, 45, 50, 53, 58, 78, 85, 88, 129, 161
  Bildbeschreibung, 79, 85, 215
  Der Auftrag, 79, 174
  Der Bau, 36, 55
  Die Schlacht, 19
  Germania Tod in Berlin, 19, 159
  Leben Gundlings, 79, 86, 181, 183, 215
  Macbeth, 38
  Philoktet, 55, 120, 155, 214
  Zement, 78-9
Müller-Waldeck, G., 186
Mundstock, K., *Meine tausend Jahre Jugend*, 86
Müntzer, T., 175, 176
music, 115, 116, 117, 118
Musil, R., *Der Mann ohne Eigenschaften*, 54
Muthesius, S., *Flucht in die Wolken*, 86
myth, 11, 52, 77, 79, 98, 101, 110, 154, 155, 188, 202, 204, 205, 211-15

Index

Nagasaki, 210
Nägele, R., 216
Nagy, I., 35
Napoleon, 176, 192, 194
narration, 34, 61–80, 81, 83, 84, 89, 99, 102, 117, 124, 133, 136, 137, 139, 142, 147, 148, 149, 155, 163, 166, 170, 171, 172, 191, 192, 193, 195, 199, 202, 203, 219, 222, 223
National Socialism, 2, 3, 10, 18, 19, 24, 25, 31, 33, 47, 54, 57, 65, 66, 69, 85, 95, 107, 116, 118, 119, 125, 128–50, 151, 152, 153, 156, 158, 159, 161, 165, 169, 171, 179, 203, 205, 208, 210, 213, 219, 222
NATO, 49
nature, 63
neo-nazis, 148
neue Abenteuer, Das, 216
Neue deutsche Literatur, 6, 40, 53, 56, 58, 177, 205
Neues Deutschland, 7, 19, 45
Neumann, M., 103
Neutsch, E., 7, 11, 45, 52, 73, 95, 161
  Auf der Suche nach Gatt, 71–2, 73, 75, 159, 160
  Der Friede im Osten, 19, 169, 170
  'Drei Tage unseres Lebens', 128–9, 199, 200, 205
  Spur der Steine, 36, 95, 97
  'Zwei leere Stühle', 96
New Age, 214–15
New Criticism, 3, 13
Niemeyer, O., 101
Nietzsche, F., 162, 179, 196, 198, 215
Noll, D., 45, 48, 52
  Kippenberg, 97–9, 100, 101, 102, 110, 112, 116, 117, 122, 125, 135, 216
'nouveau roman', 66, 89
'novel of education' ('Entwicklungsroman'), 34, 35, 78, 90, 141, 156, 167
nuclear fission, 6, 12, 23, 49, 79, 200, 201, 204, 205, 206, 207, 209, 210, 213, 217, 219, 221

Ockrent, C., 14
Orwell, G., 154
  Nineteen Eighty-four, 215, 219–20, 221, 222, 223

Palma, V., 51, 88
Panitz, E., *Die unheilige Sophia*, 57
'partisanship' ('Parteilichkeit'), 3, 33–4, 35, 76
peace movement, 5, 11, 18, 52–3, 58, 148, 187, 221
Peasant Wars, 176, 177, 216
Peitsch, H., 134
People's Army, 24, 47, 75, 96
People's Chamber, 41, 108
Pepperle, H., 196
Picasso, P., 25, 83
Piccard, A., 25
Pieske, M., *Schnauzer*, 71
Pikulik, L., 214
Pinochet, A., 220
Pirandello, L., *Six Characters in Search of an Author*, 90
Plato, 121, 213
Plenzdorf, U., 16, 45, 46
  Die neuen Leiden des jungen W., 2, 21, 37, 39–42, 43, 56, 70, 72, 73, 77, 98, 100, 112, 116–19, 120, 164, 175, 224
  'kein runter kein fern', 75
  Kennen Sie Urban?, 77
  Legende vom Glück ohne Ende, 21, 46
Plessen E., *Mitteilung an den Adel*, 134
Ploß, H., 123
Poche, K., 48, 50
  Atemnot, 46
poetry, 37–8
Poland, ix, 15, 31, 58, 132, 135, 137, 139, 140, 141, 142, 143, 144, 146, 156, 161, 164, 185, 186, 187
Politbüro, 49, 56
popular literature, 4, 55
populism ('Volksverbundenheit'), 33, 55, 67, 71, 76
pornography, 33, 38, 55
post-modernism, 78, 88
Pracht, E., 35
Prenzlauer Berg, 88
Proust, M., 32, 34, 54, 79, 136
Prussia, 18, 175, 176, 177, 181, 182, 183, 184, 188, 189, 194, 195, 196, 219
psychology, 125, 208, 216
Pulver, E., 202

Raabe, W., 69
Raddatz, F.J., 2, 12–13, 17, 30, 129, 214
Radtke, V., *Ich suche Liebe*, 86
Rathenau, W., 179
rationalism, 63, 80, 85, 86, 92, 100, 109, 114, 185, 202, 209, 213, 220

–254–

Index

Rauch, C., 176
Ravensbrück, 149
Reformation, 8
Rehmann, R., *Der Mann auf der Kanzel*, 134
Reich-Ranicki, M., 67
Reimann, B., *Franziska Linkerhand*, 101–3, 104, 111, 113, 158, 205
religion, 33, 125, 170, 182, 185
Republican Party, 5
Resnais, A., *L'aanée dernière à Marienbad*, 79
RIAS, 52
Richter, H., 37
Robbe-Grillet, A., 66, 89
Rolling Stones, 75
Rom, M., 51
Romania, 166
Romanticism, 34, 35, 67, 82, 83, 84, 85, 102, 190, 192, 205, 209
Romm, M., *Obyknovennie Fashizm*, 131
Rosellini, J., 174, 176
Rosenberg, A., *Myth of the Twentieth Century*, 213
Ross, W., 14
Rousseau, J.-J., 161
Rovan, J., 8
Rudolph, H., 10, 15
Runge, E., *Bottroper Protokolle*, 87

Sachsenhausen, 133
Saeger, U.
  Nöhr, 71, 74, 100, 110, 112, 129, 134
  Sinon, 111
  Warten auf Schnee, 71, 111
Sakowski, H., 11, 53, 95, 177
  Wie ein Vogel im Schwarm, 177
Sämann, W., 'Das Haus des Dr. Pondabel', 218
Sartre, J.P., 66, 162
satire, 42, 46, 80, 82, 91, 96, 109, 110, 154, 169, 170, 172
Saxony, 184, 186, 189, 195
Schädlich, H.J., 50
  Versuchte Nähe, 46, 47
Schäfer, H.D., 129
Scheel, W., 175
Schelling, F.W., 193
Schelsky, H., 115
Schiller, F., 193, 196
  Kabale und Liebe, 70
Schirdewan, K., 156, 157
Schleef, E., *Gertrud*, 17
Schlegel, F., 82

Schleime, C., 51
Schlenstedt, D., 1, 53–4, 61, 64, 83–4, 95
Schlesinger, K., 16, 18, 30, 43, 45, 46, 48, 50, 55, 144
  Alte Filme, 22, 71, 112–13, 114
  Leben im Winter, 152–3
  Matulla und Busch, 18
  Michael, 132–5, 143, 149
Schmid, S., 193
Schmidt, H., 49
Schneider, P., 8
  Der Mauerspringer, 19
Schneider, R., 45, 46, 48
  Die Reise nach Jarosław, 10, 118, 143–4
  November, 46, 47
Schoene, F., 45
Schönemann, H., 40
Schopenhauer, A., 22, 162
Schubert, D., 48
Schubert, H., 14, 103
  Blickwinkel, 51, 143, 151
  'Das verbotene Zimmer', 20–1
Schuhmann, K., 11, 61
Schulz, M.W., 53
  Triptychon mit sieben Brücken, 168
Schulze-Boysen-Harnack, 130
Schumacher, E., 40
Schütz, H., 45, 50, 103
  Julia, 22–4, 35, 47, 78, 79, 112, 136, 163, 169
Schütz, S., 50
  Medusa, 17
Schweitzer, A., 25
science, 26, 67, 80, 82, 83, 86, 97, 199, 200, 201, 207, 208, 209, 210, 217, 220, 222
  see also technology
science fiction, 11, 55, 85, 110, 215–24
Scott, W., 178
Seghers, A., 3, 11, 13, 31, 34, 45, 46, 66, 103, 106, 138, 190, 191
  Das siebte Kreuz, 31
  Die Entscheidung, 18
  Die Toten bleiben jung, 3, 31, 131, 139
  Sonderbare Begegnungen, 85–6, 216
  Überfahrt, 63
  'Vierzig Jahre der Margarete Wolf', 139
Seidel, I., 3
self-criticism, 99, 117, 135, 161, 164, 181
self-realisation, 38, 66, 67, 72, 97

–255–

Index

Seven Years' War, 184, 189
sexuality, 33, 36, 74, 81, 100, 103, 104, 110, 111, 125, 180, 194
Seyppel, J., 48, 50
Shakespeare, W., 196
 Coriolanus, 167–8
 Hamlet, 35
 Macbeth, 38
 Romeo and Juliet, 20
Shaw, G., 167
Sinn und Form, 37, 38, 39, 40, 42, 43, 50, 51, 52, 55, 84, 152, 201, 207
Sinoviev, G.J., 152
Smith, C., 136, 193, 203
socialist critical realism, 53, 54
socialist realism, 3, 30, 32, 33, 34, 35, 40, 42, 54, 58, 62, 66, 71, 73, 74, 77, 80, 81, 84, 89, 90, 91, 98, 100, 117, 128, 129, 163, 189, 198, 199, 211, 216, 224
Socialist Unity Party (SED, GDR's Communist Party), ix, 6, 7, 14, 15, 25, 29–59, 62, 73, 74, 78, 94, 96, 97, 98, 99, 101, 104, 107, 119, 122, 129, 149, 155, 156, 157, 158, 159, 160, 162, 165, 169, 170, 171, 172, 177, 198, 205, 206
Fifth Party Congress, 156
Eighth Party Congress, 29, 37, 41
Eleventh Party Congress, 53
Solanas, V., 204
Solidarity, 187
Solzhenitsyn, A., 19, 43
Sorbs, 171, 214
Soviet Union, ix, 4, 8, 11, 13, 25, 29, 31, 32, 33, 43, 44, 49, 56–8, 82, 112, 126, 129, 130, 131, 133, 135, 138, 139, 141, 145, 146, 147, 149, 152, 153, 154, 157, 158, 159, 160, 161, 162, 163, 176, 199, 200, 201, 207, 208, 215, 220
Twentieth Congress of the Soviet Communist Party 151, 152, 156, 157, 169
space exploration, 129, 199, 200, 217
Spanish Civil War, 116, 176
Spark, M., *The Prime of Miss Jean Brodie*, 138
sport, 1, 10, 114
Sprache und Antwort, 88
Springer, A.C., 2
Sputnik, ix
Stachowa, A., 103
Stade, M., 48, 192

Der König und sein Narr, 75, 76, 181–3, 184, 185, 186, 188, 193
Der närrische Krieg, 194–5
Staiger, E., 3
Stalin, J., ix, 58, 151, 152, 156, 157, 158, 160, 161, 162, 169, 170, 193
Stalinism, 22, 25, 33, 36, 42, 47, 109, 125, 126, 151–73, 174, 179, 180, 224
Star Wars, 208
Staudte, W., *Die Mörder sind unter uns*, 31
Steinbeck, J., 32
Steinmüller, K., 'Der Traum vom Großen Roten Fleck', 220–1
Stendhal, 103
Stephan, A., 107, 130
Stiller, K., *Weihnachten*, 137
Storm, T., 70
Strahl, R., *Die Flüsterparty*, 46, 47
Strauß, B., 15, 214–15
Strauss, F.J., 187
Strittmatter, E., 73
Der Wundertäter, 57, 169–70
Ole Bienkopp, 71, 100
subjective authenticity, 65, 74, 84, 87, 179
subjectivity, 12, 72, 91, 98, 107, 136, 137, 162
Swift, J., 181
Switzerland, 8, 9, 13, 14, 50, 57

Tacitus, 159
Tate, D., 98, 103, 131, 190, 192
technology, 63, 101, 200, 201, 206, 208, 209, 213, 218
 see also science
Teraoka, A.A., 78
Tetzner, G. *Karen W.*, 74, 78, 103, 107–8, 112, 113, 114, 116, 134, 166, 188
Thatcher, M., 14
Third Reich, 19, 31, 61, 116, 130–2, 136–8, 144, 151, 171, 174, 175, 176, 179, 183, 210
 see also National Socialism
Thirty Years' War, 176
Thürk, H., *Der Gaukler*, 19
Tito, 161
Tolstoy, L., 161
 Anna Karenina, 65
Töppe, F., 'Die letzten Bilder des Grafikers Schneider', 218
tragedy, 33
Trakl, G., 191

–256–

Index

travel restrictions, 21
Trotsky, L., 153
Turek, L., *Die goldene Kugel*, 216
Ulbrich, B.
  Abends im Park, 111
  'Fang die Sonne auf', 75, 111
Ulbricht, W., 25, 26, 29, 36, 37, 95, 128, 132, 156, 184, 198
United Kingdom, 2, 9, 101, 115, 206
United Nations, 37, 106
United States, 1, 2, 3, 9, 10, 24, 86, 104, 108, 111, 115, 147, 153, 158, 201, 216, 220
uprising, 17 June 1953, 36, 67, 72, 125, 157–60, 167, 168, 169, 175
utopia, 83, 109, 193, 194, 198, 200, 202, 207, 208, 211, 212, 213, 215, 216, 219, 220

Vesper, B., *Die Reise*, 134
Vietnam, 87, 108, 111, 115, 135
Vieweg, H., *Ultrasymet bleibt geheim*, 216
Villain, J., 86
Virgil, 73
Volk und Welt, 54
Voltaire, 182, 183, 189

Wagenbach, K., 51
Wagner, R., 213
  Die Meistersinger 122
  Siegfried, 124
Waiblinger, W., 192
Wallace, I., 2
Wallraff, G., 87
Walser, M., 5–6, 8, 14
  Dorle und Wolf, 19
Walther, J., 192
  Bewerbung bei Hofe, 75–6, 174, 184–7, 195, 224
Wander, M., *Guten Morgen, du Schöne*, 87, 98, 110, 111
'Wandlungsroman' (conversion novel), 131, 138, 142
Watson, M.N., 65, 134
Weber, H., *Alter Schwede*, 96
Weimann, R., 40
Weimarer Beiträge, 37, 52, 53
Weisbrod, P., 37, 61
Weiss, P., 50
  Die Ästhetik des Widerstands, 54
  Die Ermittlung, 87
Wells, H.G., 66
Werewolf, 138, 169

'Werkkreis Literatur der Arbeitswelt', 35
Wessel, H., 2
West Germany, 1–26, 31, 32, 35, 36, 37, 38, 41, 43, 44, 45, 47, 48, 49, 50, 51, 54, 55, 58, 63, 64, 66, 83, 84, 87, 88, 92, 101, 104, 105, 106, 108, 111, 119, 120, 123, 125, 129, 130, 133, 134, 137, 139, 144, 146, 147, 149, 153, 157, 158, 159, 160, 165, 167, 168, 169, 170, 171, 172, 175, 180, 182, 184, 187, 199, 202, 205, 206, 207, 211, 214, 220
Baader–Meinhof terrorism, 23, 79
Christian Democratic Union (CDU), 4
Greens Party, 5
Social Democratic Party (SPD) 4
'Ostpolitik', 36
student movement, 4, 38, 211
Wiener, N., 25
Wiens, P., 82
Wismut, 56
Wochenpost, 10, 177
Wohlgemuth, J., *Egon*, 117–18, 205
Wolf, C., 1, 9, 16, 36, 45, 46, 50, 53, 58, 63, 77, 80, 84, 132, 135, 142, 161, 188, 189, 211
  Der geteilte Himmel, 18, 20, 21, 24, 25, 35, 65, 71, 79, 95, 97, 106, 155, 199, 200, 208
  'Juninachmittag' 61, 62–5, 84
  Kassandra, 1, 11, 50, 51–2, 64, 74, 77, 111, 116, 152, 188, 194, 201–4, 209, 210, 211–12, 215, 221, 223, 224
  Kein Ort. Nirgends, 46, 71, 75, 76–7, 190, 193–4, 200, 211
  Kindheitsmuster, 46, 57, 65, 76, 98, 118, 132, 135–40, 143, 144, 150, 151, 179, 203
  'Lesen und Schreiben', 42, 65–7, 68, 72, 89
  Nachdenken über Christa T., 1, 23, 36, 42, 65, 67–71, 72, 73, 75, 76, 79, 97, 100, 107, 116, 134, 136, 148, 155, 161, 163, 180, 200, 203, 211, 224
  'Selbstversuch', 110, 114, 194, 216
  Störfall, 64, 207–9, 210, 220
  Unter den Linden, 103, 110
Wolf, D., 41
Wolf, F., 31
  Cyankali, 95

–257–

Index

Die Matrosen von Cattaro, 176
Wolf, G., 45, 46, 92
Der arme Hölderlin, 190, 192–3
Wolfram von Eschenbach, *Parzival*, 142
Wollweber, E., 156, 157
women, 11, 61, 74, 80–2, 86, 103–7, 109–10, 112, 114, 123, 125, 161, 164, 168, 180, 182, 188–9, 194, 204, 209–10, 212–13
see also feminism
Woolf, V., 32
'Modern Fiction', 66
Workers' and Peasants' Faculty, 22, 78, 155, 187
Writers' Union, 1, 6, 7, 32, 43, 45, 48, 49, 83, 122, 177
Sixth Writers' Congress (1969), 36
Seventh Writers' Congress (1973), 94
Eighth Writers' Congress (1978), 46
Tenth Writers' Congress (1987), 50, 58

Yom Kippur War, 44
youth, 39, 40, 42, 61, 72, 75, 98, 100, 106, 116–19, 124, 125, 140, 168, 186

Zhdanov, A.A., 32
Ziergiebel, H., 218
Die andere Welt, 216–17, 218, 221
Zinner, H., 95
Katja, 100, 118, 149–50, 158
Zuse, K., 25
Zweig, A., 3, 31